JOHN GEORGE NICOLAY

JOHN GEORGE NICOLAY

The Man in Lincoln's Shadow

Allen Carden and Thomas J. Ebert

*To my good buddy
Steve Hall
Good reading
Best wishes
Tom Ebert*

The University of Tennessee Press

Knoxville

Library of Congress Cataloging-in-Publication Data

Names: Carden, Allen, author. | Ebert, Thomas J., author.
Title: John George Nicolay : the man in Lincoln's shadow /
Allen Carden and Thomas J. Ebert.
Description: First edition. | Knoxville : The University of Tennessee
Press, [2019] | Includes bibliographical references and index. |
Identifiers: LCCN 2018042157 (print) | LCCN 2018054694 (ebook) |
ISBN 9781621904984 (pdf) | ISBN 9781621904977 |
ISBN 9781621904977 (hardcover)
Subjects: LCSH: Nicolay, John G. (John George), 1832–1901. |
Presidents—United States—Staff—Biography. | Secretaries—
United States—Biography. | Germans—United States—Biography. |
Immigrants—United States—Biography. | Lincoln, Abraham, 1809–
1865—Friends and associates. | United States—History—Civil War,
1861–1865. | United States—Politics and government—1861–1865.
Classification: LCC E176.47 (ebook) | LCC E176.47 .C37 2019 (print) |
DDC 973.7092 [B] —dc23
LC record available at https://lccn.loc.gov/2018042157

Contents

Illustrations

Preface

Historical biography is too often reserved for notable individuals such as kings, queens, emperors, presidents, popes, politicians, artists, and those historical characters who lived particularly notorious or salacious lives. There are many other people who led quiet lives under the radar of public notice but who nonetheless made significant contributions to the success of their leaders and to the historical record. These individuals often pass into history unnoticed and unappreciated. John George Nicolay was such a person.

When we informed people that we were writing a book about Abraham Lincoln's secretary, the frequent response was, "Oh, that was someone named Kennedy!" The urban myth that Jacqueline Kennedy created lives on. "No," we would reply, "Lincoln didn't have a secretary named Kennedy. His name was John George Nicolay." The purpose of this book is to bring Nicolay's story out into the light, out from the shadow of Lincoln, where the always self-effacing secretary has been hidden for more than a century and a half.

The story of John George Nicolay is the story of an immigrant boy who through hard work, tenaciousness, and a good bit of luck rose to a central position in Abraham Lincoln's administration. Born in the Rhenish Palatinate, John George Nicolay spent most of his life in America. Raised in poverty on the frontier, used to working long hard hours at an early age, and self-educated, he was fortunate in his connections over the years. By a succession of opportune circumstances, John George Nicolay became acquainted with Abraham Lincoln, who came to like and appreciate the young clerk in the Office of the Illinois Secretary of State. He became a trusted intermediary for Lincoln, who subsequently appointed Nicolay his secretary to handle the growing volume of correspondence during the 1860 presidential campaign. Lincoln then appointed him as his private secretary in the White House.

Nicolay served in this position for the entire Lincoln administration. He proved himself to be discreet, self-effacing, trustworthy, efficient, and most important, wholly dedicated to Lincoln. His singular purpose in life evolved into supporting Abraham Lincoln in any way he could. Nicolay became the de facto first White

House chief of staff. His predecessors had not functioned as gatekeepers to the president, but Nicolay did so out of necessity, given the demands on the president brought on by the exigencies of the Civil War. By giving Lincoln his full measure of devotion, he helped make it possible for Lincoln to concentrate his attention on things that mattered, to have the essential time a leader needs to think, away from the pressures of the crowd pressing around him, and to have an organized and efficient White House operation. Nicolay did not make Lincoln great, but he helped make it possible for Lincoln to achieve greatness.

After Lincoln's death, Nicolay, along with his lifelong friend John Hay, dedicated himself to preserving and shaping the Lincoln image for posterity. With the sponsorship and cooperation of Lincoln's son, Robert Todd Lincoln, Nicolay and Hay produced a monumental ten-volume history, *Abraham Lincoln: A History,* for which Nicolay was the primary contributor, researcher, and principal editor. Their efforts came to define Abraham Lincoln and his life's work, eclipsing all other contemporary biographies of Lincoln, even by men who had known him well. Nicolay and Hay had a unique relationship with Lincoln: they not only knew and worked for him but also lived with him under the same roof.

No other contemporary man, no matter how long he had known Lincoln, could claim such intimacy with the sixteenth president. William Herndon, who was Lincoln's last law partner before Lincoln became president, worked tirelessly, albeit unsuccessfully, to temper the image of the all-knowing and all-wise "Father Abraham." Herndon tried to define Lincoln as a man, using interviews of people who knew him. But the public wanted, as did Robert Lincoln, Abraham Lincoln enshrined as a national saint, who like Christ across the sea, was the savior of his people, cruelly slain by his enemies on a Good Friday. To further paraphrase the lyrics of Julia Ward Howe's popular "Battle Hymn of the Republic," "He [Christ] died to make men holy," and Lincoln had died to make men free. Although the truth surrounding Lincoln's life work was far more complicated and conflicted, Robert Lincoln and the American people wanted an uncompromising secular hagiography.

Nicolay and Hay gave the president's son and the American public what they wanted. But they did not base this great work on mere sentimentality or unverified storytelling as so many contemporaries had done; rather, they produced a well-researched, well-documented chronicle of Lincoln and his times based on the president's papers, many of which the two authors had personally prepared. Their work, which is both a Lincoln biography and an account of the Lincoln administration and the Civil War, has therefore become a primary source regularly consulted by Lincoln scholars to this day. Unlike modern memoirs by presidential assistants and cabinet officers that often seek to heighten the author's importance at the center of events while filling the pages with tidbits of gossip and innuendo, *Abraham Lincoln: A History* is notable for scarcely mentioning Nicolay or Hay and for its lack of insider gossip. Nonetheless, these coauthors were not reticent in besmirching the name, motives, or competency of anyone who disappointed, failed, or resisted Lincoln and his greatness; and the list of such persons was formidable. Nicolay and Hay both refused criticism of Lincoln and no doubt took secrets regarding the martyred president to their graves.

As the lead researcher and primary author of the Lincoln history, Nicolay gave future generations an extensive insight into Lincoln and his times. Nicolay can rightly claim the title of the first Lincoln scholar. His meticulous research and his verification of the accuracy of every statement of fact, if not interpretation, has given posterity a truly reliable if biased account of the events of the Lincoln presidency and the man himself. While Nicolay's history of Lincoln and his administration is biased, it continued a trend in the treatment of Lincoln that started the day after his death and has continued almost unchecked to this day. With a few notable exceptions, Abraham Lincoln has until recently been treated uncritically as a national demigod. Yet we know that many of his contemporaries had less than favorable opinions of the sixteenth president, first among them the members of the congressional Joint Committee on the Conduct of the War, as well as the more radical wing of his own Republican Party.

While Nicolay gave us a monumental documentary history of Lincoln, the difficulty in writing a biography of John George Nicolay is the fact that he left relatively little of himself to be researched. His papers in the Library of Congress consist chiefly of his letters to his fiancée, Therena Bates, back in Pittsfield, Illinois, along with scrapbooks, some notes to himself, and business correspondence with the editor of the Century Corporation regarding the publication of the history. There is very limited correspondence between Nicolay and his lifelong friend John Hay in the files. Unlike John Hay, he did not keep a diary. Nicolay's letters to Therena were his way of chronicling events in the Lincoln White House. He apparently burned the letters Therena had written to him at her request. There are some newspaper and magazine articles as well as government reports Nicolay wrote as the result of his travels to Minnesota and Colorado. There are also his consular records in the National Archives, which provide some insight about his time in Paris.

There are some journal articles, references in books about others, or an occasional book chapter on Nicolay, but there has been no comprehensive scholarly biography bringing all the disparate information into a unified focus. Only one biography of Nicolay has been written, a 1949 publication by his then octogenarian daughter, Helen. The Allen County Public Library in Fort Wayne, Indiana, houses the materials Helen used for this work. While the biography gives some insights into her father, it is an uncritical piece which includes some information that cannot be substantiated by the documented facts. Nicolay's daughter provided scant insight into her father's domestic life or his efforts to write and publish the Lincoln history, focusing her attention mainly on his professional responsibilities connected to the Lincoln White House.

Another problem confronting the biographer is that John George Nicolay's life between 1857 and 1865 was so intertwined with his mentor and hero that his story is hard to tell without contextualizing the events of political history and Lincoln's actions and motives for a fuller understanding of the man before April 1865. Nor is it always possible to determine whether Nicolay's opinions on political questions were his own, independently derived, or a reflection of Lincoln's attitudes during the time he worked for Lincoln.

This biography is intended to fill an important gap in the Lincoln literature by examining the life and work of one who knew Lincoln well and was fully devoted to Lincoln's presidency as well as to his place in history. Nicolay's efforts on Lincoln's behalf not only included the application of his organizational skills in running the presidential office, but also in his many trips as emissary and confidant for the president.

Historical biography should reflect the subject as a human being, neither an angel nor a demon. Every human has strengths and faults in different proportions. There were times when we as authors could really admire Nicolay, and there were times when we found him not so admirable, times when we would laugh over some foible, and times when we would shake our heads in disbelief. He was intelligent, a good writer, and a devoted husband and father. He loved parties. He was not very sentimental, and in his lengthy correspondence with his fiancée, Therena, he rarely penned a romantic thought. He did not suffer fools well. He could try to squeeze an extra dollar here and there and use his position to help relatives and friends. In short, he was very much like us.

The portrait that emerges is of an ordinary young man, with few advantages beyond his native intelligence and admirable work ethic. Nicolay used the opportunities that came his way to better himself and to associate with important men while largely keeping in the shadows. He had the gift of recognizing greatness, particularly in a prairie lawyer and gifted politician named Abraham Lincoln. Finding in Lincoln a kindred spirit in many respects, including their political viewpoints, and witnessing the uncanny insights into human nature, political genius, and moral courage that led Lincoln all the way to the White House, Nicolay came to realize his unique responsibility not only to aid in Lincoln's work as president but also to preserve, as a national treasure, the memory of the great man he had come to know and revere. To this end, for the last three and a half decades of his life, John George Nicolay gave the memory of Abraham Lincoln his full measure of devotion while seeking to hide himself in Lincoln's shadow.

Acknowledgments

No book can ever be written without the assistance and support of family, friends, and colleagues.

Special thanks go to the following individuals who took the time to read the original manuscript and provide the authors invaluable feedback, encouragement and suggestions that laid the foundation for the eventual publication of this book. Appreciation also goes to those who assisted us in our research and in the publication process:

Denice Luce Carden, Fresno, California.

Annette Carden-Dale, Los Alamitos, California.

Bob Evans, Pike County Historical Society, Pittsfield, Illinois.

Jane Gastineau, Lincoln Collection, Allen County Public Library, Ft. Wayne, Indiana.

Norma Luce, Lake Forest, California.

Ann Marie Maguire, Helen Nicolay Collection (helennicolay.org)

John Maguire, Helen Nicolay Collection (helennicolay.org)

Staff at the Library of Congress, Manuscript Reading Room, Washington, D.C.

Staff at the National Archives Annex, College Park, Maryland.

Staff at the Huntington Library, San Marino, California.

Staff at the Abraham Lincoln Museum and Library, Springfield, Illinois.

Staff at Oak Hill Cemetery, Washington, D.C.

Staff at the Family History Library, East Fresno Stake, Church of Jesus Christ of Latter-Day Saints, Clovis, California

Mrs. R. John (Cheryl) Ebert, Johnson City, New York.

Paul Lear, director, Fort Ontario State Park, Oswego, New York.

Mrs. George (Paula) Ranous, Oswego, New York.

Teena Shields, Powell Butte, Oregon.

Ken Willis, Gardnerville, Nevada.

Mrs. Ron (Lynne) Willis, Libby, Montana.

We are especially grateful for the efforts of Thomas Wells and Gene Adair at the University of Tennessee Press, whose suggestions and labors have made this volume significantly better than when we first submitted the manuscript.

JOHN GEORGE NICOLAY

CHAPTER ONE

From Essingen to Pittsfield
The Americanization of Johann Georg Nicolai

Essingen is a little village nestled in the Rhenish Palatinate. It was 1832 and Europe was at peace. During the Napoleonic wars, the area had come under French control. After the conclusion of those wars, the region was placed under the jurisdiction of the Kingdom of Bavaria even though it was not linked territorially to Bavaria proper. "Germany," like "Italy" at the time, was a geographical expression that would not achieve political reality until 1871.

It was in Essingen on February 26, 1832, that a child was born to Johann Jacob and Helena Müller Nicolai. They named the boy Johann Georg, after his paternal grandfather, Georg Johann Nicolai, to distinguish him from his older brothers Johann Jacob and Johann. Johann Georg was a late child. His oldest brother, Frederick Lewis, was born in 1817, Johann Jacob in 1818, sister Catherine around 1821, and Johann around 1824, leaving Johann Georg almost eight years younger than his next older sibling. Both parents were in their forties when he was born.

Though the child, unlike his parents, would never experience war in his homeland, he would encounter it in his adopted country during a bloody civil war and on the plains of Minnesota. This child, with few prospects in a land where the right bloodlines meant everything, would rise by the age of twenty-nine through intelligence, tenacity, hard work, self-improvement, and a bit of luck to one of the most influential positions in the rising American republic. While he would never be a leader of men, he would be the right hand of perhaps the most consequential individual in American history, Abraham Lincoln. After Lincoln's death, he would join with his lifelong friend, John Milton Hay, to shape Lincoln's legacy in American history with a massive biography of Lincoln and the publication of Lincoln's papers.

According to Helen Nicolay, whose biography of her father was published in 1949, her father's family lived at a subsistence level. They tilled a *morgenstunde,* a plot of a half acre or so that could be farmed in an hour or not much longer. The primary family business was the cooper's trade—that is, "making the great casks in which the wine of the region was stored."[1] Consequently, the Nicolai men had skills as both carpenters and metal workers, skills that would serve them well on the American frontier. To do this demanding type of work, a man needed to be physically robust. Yet Helen described her father as "physically frail,"[2] a factor that would not only have set the young man apart from his stronger brothers but also from most of his contemporaries on the frontier. Early photos of Nicolay compare favorably to Helen's physical description of his mother, Helena, "as a slight dark-haired woman with regular features and very penetrating dark eyes." Helen also noted that her grandmother reportedly "reverenced religion, loved poetry and music," all attributes, according to Helen, that Helena's son also possessed.[3]

Helen stated that the family decision to immigrate to America was the promise of a better economic future, and, "if we may trust a family legend," a desire to find "liberty" after the eldest son, Frederick Lewis, was forced to stand bareheaded in the pouring rain while a member of the royal house passed by.[4] Most likely, she received this "legend" from her father, who in turn had heard it from his father and brothers. Political repression existed in the German states, but Bavaria, compared to many other German states, especially Prussia and Saxony, was a bastion of moderation. Even after its absorption into the Bavarian kingdom, the Rhenish Palatinate retained the more liberal Napoleonic Code, introduced during the French occupation.

Frederick may have disliked standing in the rain, but it seems highly unlikely that this incident would have sparked migration to the New World. The decision to uproot from the home of generations to cross the Atlantic was never made lightly. It was one thing to divest oneself of a few possessions, a small house, and a small plot of land. It was quite another to leave behind family members and friends who would never be seen again, then travel thousands of miles to a new world with a new language and different customs. It is more likely that the decision to leave was made in 1835 for economic reasons and that Frederick, the oldest son at nineteen, was sent ahead to prepare the way. This allowed the elder Johann Jacob to stay with his wife and younger children. Frederick made the journey in 1836. The rest of the family followed in 1837. For the youngest son, this would be the first of many transitions, some of them quite traumatic, over the ensuing decade.

The Nicolai family packed up their belongings and headed to the French port of Le Havre. From there they endured the Atlantic voyage to New Orleans, arriving on November 20, 1837. The family had not journeyed from the Rhine Valley alone but as part of a larger immigrant group traveling to America from the German states. The passenger list reflects that those on board the ship were almost all German immigrants, all heading for Ohio. Presumably, like the Nicolai family, their destination was Cincinnati.[5] All of this must have been a strange, exhilarating, and at the same time frightening experience for a child. He had vivid memories of New Orleans even though he was only five. Helen wrote that he had "a poignant sensation" upon arrival and found himself "the center of chattering urchins," whose language the five-year old "could not understand." She then related that the language barrier was quickly overcome as her father had "an uncommonly keen ear for differences of sound and was always quick of languages."[6]

Indeed, young George, as he would be called by family and friends, would prove over his lifetime to possess these traits, as a veritable babel of tongues—English, French, Spanish, Portuguese—echoed throughout New Orleans, one of the great American ports of the age. If his ears were full of new aural sensations, his eyes also absorbed alien scenes, unmentioned by his daughter, that would dramatically shape his worldview.

At the dock, he would likely have seen black men for the first time. Some of these men would be dressed in fine clothes driving luxurious carriages; others would be dressed in rags doing heavy work on the wharf; and still others would have their feet, hands, and necks chained. New Orleans was a depot for the internal slave trade. Slaves from the older slave states like Delaware, Maryland, and Virginia would be transported by land or sea to be auctioned off in New Orleans. Slaves disembarked ships to be sold, while at the same time other slaves were boarding steamboats bound for the great plantations in the Mississippi and Missouri valleys, or ships that would carry them west to the new Republic of Texas. This was George's introduction to slavery and the American South.

While the Nicolai family voyaged to Cincinnati, young George must have seen more and more slaves, some of whom were toiling in the cane fields of southern Louisiana. As the steamboat slowly plowed northward against the river's current, the cane fields turned into cotton plantations as far as the eye could see. At each stop along the river—Natchez, Vicksburg, Memphis, Paducah, Louisville, and, finally, Cincinnati—prosperous-looking whites likely came on board or departed with a retinue of blacks. Slaves were taken off at each stop, and others were brought on. Slaves worked the docks. These black men, women, and children were everywhere. When masters or overseers were displeased, they did not hesitate publicly to beat, whip, or otherwise abuse their chattel. It would have been very hard for a five-year-old to comprehend these strange sights.

The United States that the Nicolai family was entering in 1837 was bustling with activity. A Dutchman from the Hudson Valley of New York, Martin Van Buren, had just assumed the presidency after the tumultuous two terms of Andrew Jackson of Tennessee. The country was expanding westward. Although the east bank of the Mississippi River as far north as Illinois and the west bank as far north as Missouri had been organized into states, these regions were still open to settlement and had areas that remained wild both geographically and socially. It had been sixty years since the Declaration of Independence, and individuals who had experienced the Revolution, as well as their children, were still alive. Born in December 1782, Martin Van Buren was the first president to have been born after the Declaration of Independence and was six years old when George Washington was inaugurated for the first time under the Constitution of 1787.

It was the Constitution of 1787 that had established the young republic and had also codified the legitimacy of slavery, which at the time existed throughout the country. By 1837, that legitimacy had become part of a national debate. Pennsylvania enacted a gradual emancipation law in 1780. After that, Northern states had begun to enact similar laws abolishing the institution within their borders. According to the 1840 census, that was the year that all the Northern states except New Jersey reported no slaves within their borders.[7] Meanwhile, a small but determined abolitionist movement began to spread its message in the North. But south of Pennsylvania and the Ohio River, slavery not only survived but was growing every day. These slaveholding regions not only resisted the calls for some form of emancipation but also sought to criminalize even the advocacy of such thoughts. In the year prior to the Nicolai family's arrival in the United States, Southern congressmen had passed a "gag rule" forbidding antislavery petitions to be brought before Congress. Night patrols, censorship of the mails, press censorship, and mob violence were common tools used in the slave states to suppress any discussion of slavery or emancipation that might suggest a change in the Southern social structure or economy.

With the establishment of the Republic of Texas in 1836, the year before young George and his family arrived in America, the issue of slavery once again began to rip through the delicate fabric of national politics. Twice before, territorial compromises had been made to deal with the matter. First, the Continental Congress had passed the Ordinance of 1787, more popularly known as the Northwest Ordinance, banning slavery north of the Ohio River. In 1790, the First Congress reaffirmed the ordinance, including the prohibition of slavery.[8] At the same time, the Congress passed an ordinance for the organization of a territory south of the Ohio that allowed the extension of slavery into that region.[9]

In 1803, the Louisiana Purchase added a vast new territory to the United States, leading eventually, in 1821, to a second territorial divide over slavery while maintaining the political balance between the North and South. The Missouri Compromise divided the lands acquired from France between slave and free. In 1821, this divide made sense as the climate of much of the region north and west of Missouri was inhospitable to plantation agriculture. In fact, both the climate and the soil of the area were viewed as inhospitable to any form of agriculture. The region was then viewed as suitable for Indian reservations, and parts of it were already designated as a future home for Native Americans, who were beginning to be forcibly dispossessed and removed from the eastern portions of the country. However, by the early 1850s, the development of the Deere plow and McCormick reaper would make agriculture on the plains feasible and profitable.

Hence, the proposed annexation of the Republic of Texas posed a real dilemma for the nation. Although the American public had supported the Texas Revolution, especially after the Battle of the Alamo, the idea of annexing the area was rife with problems. Texas, including its sweeping territorial claims, covered an area greater in size than the existing twelve free states combined. The region would not be subject to the territorial divides that had been made in 1790 and 1821. Therefore, the slaveholding states would be adding a vast new territory in which to expand the economic and political power of slavery, to the permanent disadvantage of the North. While the debate over the extension of slavery would deeply affect the future of young George, these issues were quite abstract and foreign to the Nicolai family in 1837. Slavery, and certainly the race-based slavery of African Americans, was unknown to them. Slavery had disappeared from the Rhine Valley centuries before, to be replaced with various forms of serfdom. But in Western Europe, serfdom also had gradually disappeared, with the last vestiges swept away by the French Revolution and the ensuing Napoleonic wars. By the early nineteenth century, only Russia maintained serfdom. In a Western European world deeply affected by the French Revolution, African slavery was becoming a discredited institution. By 1837, slavery was a dying institution in the Western world except for a few of the Spanish colonies, Brazil, the Republic of Texas, and the United States.

The Nicolai family also found a land quite different from their quiet country existence. While the rhythms of life in the old country remained relatively constant over the centuries, their new country was all about constant change. The United States was on the verge of a technological revolution. Already the steamboat had transformed the Ohio and Mississippi Rivers into crowded byways, moving people and produce throughout the inner reaches of Middle America. Within a decade, Samuel Morse's telegraph, John Deere's plow, Cyrus McCormick's reaper, and the expansion of the railroad would transform both the American landscape and agriculture. The North embraced change, constant change, including internal improvements. Good roads, canals, and the Great Lakes were the ever-extending arteries of Northern commerce. Schools and libraries paid for with public funds promoting community education were dotting the landscape. The diversity of languages the Nicolai family first heard in New Orleans could be encountered almost anywhere in the country.

Cincinnati, strategically located on the Ohio River in the heart of a rich agricultural region, was the final destination of the Nicolai family. They, like generations of immigrants before and after them, wanted to settle in a community where they could find their fellow countrymen, and Cincinnati had a well-established German community. Here they reunited with their eldest son, Frederick Lewis. Helen noted that her grandfather purchased a lot and set about building a new home for the family.[10] The 1839 directory for Cincinnati lists "Nicolai Jacob (Ger) cooper res Jackson b 12th and 13th streets."[11]

She then related that "within a week" her father was enrolled in a school that taught German and English "side by side."[12] As she described it, her father had a "keen mind" and quickly adapted to learning the English language.[13] It was around this time that the family adjusted to their new country by anglicizing the spelling of their name from Nicolai to Nicolay. For a boy of five or six, it seemed that the stability he had experienced in his old home in the Palatinate was rediscovered in these new surroundings. Then tragedy struck.

The death of his mother, Helena Nicolay, around 1839, radically changed the world of the seven-year-old boy. His father never remarried.[14] From then on, he would be bereft of the nurturing that only a mother could bring. After Mrs. Nicolay's death, the family left Cincinnati and headed west. For the next two years, George's world was repeatedly uprooted as the older Nicolay men sought work. In the nine-year period from 1837, when the family left Essingen, to 1846, when Nicolay's father died, the family had moved at least five times.

Helen attributed the motivation for the move to her grandfather's grief, but a lack of economic opportunity in Cincinnati may also have been a factor. The family arrived in America just as the country was sinking into the Panic of 1837, in part, the result of Andrew Jackson's war on the Bank of the United States. The effects of this economic crisis lingered into the early 1840s. The young man grew up in the environment of a widowed father's grief and his older brothers' struggles to find a place in their newly adopted country. The family headed westward, first to Indiana, then Missouri, and finally to Illinois.

Missouri was attractive because a German community was already establishing itself in St. Louis. Missouri was a slave state, and though the number of slaves was a relatively small percentage of the population, the institution was concentrated in St. Louis and along the Missouri and Mississippi River valleys. The presence of slavery frequently depressed the already low wages of white laborers. It was during this stay that the young man was immersed in a world where slavery was accepted as a normal way of life.

Throughout all this period, formal schooling was intermittent. Helen recorded that her father's schooling came in Cincinnati and during the family's subsequent migration. She asserted that her father's education amounted to "about as much as Abraham Lincoln had" but noted that, fortunately for her father, "the schools were somewhat better."[15] This comparison to Lincoln does not hold up. If the young Nicolay was enrolled in school "within a week" of the family's 1837 arrival in Cincinnati, he likely remained in school there for about a year and a half to two years before the family pulled up stakes and moved west. And given the likelihood that schools in cities like Cincinnati and St. Louis would be better than a one-room schoolhouse in rural Indiana, where Lincoln spent much of his boyhood, the quality of Nicolay's formal education would indeed have been better than the sixteenth president's. However, Lincoln stated that the sum of his formal education was about one year, a far shorter period of time than that of Nicolay's schooling.

While Lincoln had the encouragement of his stepmother, Sarah Lincoln, despite his father's opposition to his love of reading, the young Nicolay does not appear to have had such a mentor until age fourteen when he moved to White Hall, Illinois, in the fall of 1846 after his father's death. There he met Joel Pennington, the Sunday school teacher in the local church. Until then, he appears to have been alone in his dogged persistence to learn. Helen quoted her father regarding his reading of the biblical histories.[16] It was the Books of Kings, Judges, Ruth, and Esther that fired his imagination. From the Apocrypha, he read from the Books of Maccabees, a history of the Jewish struggle against the Syrian tyrant, Antiochus IV Epiphanes, and his successors. Helen then quoted her father as writing: "The period of Bible reading for relaxation lasted about three years. Afterward, among the few books which fell into my hands, were two of Shakespeare's plays, each bound in a single volume—first, the *Comedy of Errors*, the second the tragedy of *Macbeth*, I must confess that I liked the Dromios better than the ghosts and witches. In both dramas I was deeply absorbed in the movement, but still too young to appreciate their literary beauty and power."[17]

Helen believed that the influence of her father's many hours of reading biblical stories "may be noted time and again in his style of historical narrative."[18] Like Lincoln, Nicolay took advantage of every opportunity to learn and explore. Both men educated themselves through the reading of the Bible, Shakespeare, and Blackstone. Both men were self-educated in the fullest sense of the word; it was a process that requires a great deal of self-motivation to persist. In Nicolay's case especially, this came in the face of familial opposition.

Living in a world of physically strong men, all much older than himself, her father's home life was tactfully described by Helen. The youngest of his family, Nicolay found little companionship at home, and being of a different mental caliber from the other lads at the log schoolhouse, he had few friends of his own age.[19] Boys of this era were expected to be physical, with rowdiness an inherent part of it, since as future men they were going to face an uncompromising, hard environment on what was then America's frontier. Quite likely, he would have been bullied at school for his inability to "measure up" to his world's expectations. He was not only of a "different mental caliber" from his schoolmates but also from his father and brothers. It is not surprising that he would find "little companionship" at home among the physically robust and older men, who as carpenters, metal workers, and later millers had to earn their bread with calluses on their hands. Bereft of a woman's nurturing care, repeatedly uprooted from familiar surroundings and boyhood companionship, and living in a world that put a premium on physical prowess, a "physically frail," intellectual boy was out of place.

He coped with these stresses by creating his own world. His daughter stated that he enjoyed nature, having experienced a sense of community with the world of the forest, noting that while "never a scientific observer, he had throughout his life a sympathetic eye for bird, and beast and place." However, he had a special companion, the family Bible, "printed in crabbed German characters," which the family had carried with them from Essingen.[20] Communing with nature or immersing himself in books may have allowed him to create a comfortable world for himself, but it also hampered the development of necessary social skills when he had to emerge into the rough-and-tumble world of the mid-nineteenth century. Finally, the Nicolay family moved again, this time back across the Mississippi River to Illinois and a short distance north to Pike County.

The county, founded in 1821, is wedged between the Illinois River on the east and the Mississippi River on the west, forming part of Illinois's western bulge. The area was being developed and was still a raw frontier when the Nicolay family arrived, around 1842. Pittsfield, a small town of just over six hundred inhabitants in 1850,[21] had been the county seat since its establishment in 1833. Named for Pittsfield, Massachusetts, the town was home to New England transplants, but the surrounding country was populated by Southerners, with slaveholding Missouri just across the Mississippi River from the western boundary of the county.

Illinois was part of the old Northwest Territory and, according to the Ordinance of 1787, slavery was banned in the region. But the facts on the ground were quite different. Although many French settlers had left Illinois with their slaves to establish St. Louis and other river towns in Spanish Louisiana in the mid-1760s after the French and Indian War, other Frenchmen had remained. Additionally, the three territorial governors, Anthony St. Clair (1787–1801, Northwest Territory), William Henry Harrison (1801–1809, Indiana Territory), and Ninian Edwards (1809–1818, Illinois Territory) were all slaveholders and had brought their slaves into the region. Southerners from Kentucky and other regions of the South had moved openly into the territory with their slaves. When Illinois was admitted as a state in 1818, its constitution did not ban slavery. Instead, "labor contracts," binding individuals for ninety-nine years, was the legal dodge employed to maintain chattel slavery. Slavery was not banned in Illinois until its constitution of 1848, two decades after a state referendum narrowly failed to alter the state constitution to make Illinois a slave state. Illinois was deeply antiblack and had a proslavery population, especially from its central counties southward. At the time the Nicolay family moved to Illinois, the region was very sympathetic to the peculiar institution.

Using their skills as coopers, the Nicolays rented and restored a gristmill in Montezuma Township southeast of Pittsfield. Mills were in demand in the agricultural county. An 1880 history of Pike County describes the need for gristmills and notes their economic importance to local farmers who mostly used them for crushing corn upon which they depended for subsistence.[22] Young George was about ten when he arrived in Pike County. But he had clearly begun to develop the skills that would benefit him throughout his life. With a greater mastery of English than that of his father or siblings and his "clear handwriting," he became the family scribe and interpreter.[23] However, milling grain was not the only moneymaking operation at the gristmill, as the oldest scrap of paper Helen had in her possession in her father's handwriting was a note indicating that the Nicolays owed a customer three gallons of "rectified whiskey."[24]

The move to Pike County was significant in another way for the young lad. In Cincinnati and St. Louis, the family had lived among other German immigrants in an ethnic community, continuing to share the immigrant communal experience. Once removed to Pike County, where there was not an immigrant community to reinforce his ethnic identity, Nicolay's maturing self-identity became more Americanized, though certainly with German antecedents, customs, and attitudes.

The stability of life around the gristmill was short-lived. In 1846, his father died, and the boy of fourteen was dismissed from the family business by his older brother Frederick Lewis, who retained control of the mill until his death.[25] Helen tried to put the best face on this awkward family situation by stating, "Perhaps he [her father] had sought employment even earlier."[26]

Seemingly without any resource, the fourteen-year-old landed employment in Aaron Reno's dry goods store on Main Street in the town of White Hall, Greene County, across the Illinois River.[27] This position lasted for only two years. There Nicolay honed bookkeeping skills for later life,[28] a talent he would bring to the Lincoln White House and numerous arguments with Mary Lincoln over her prodigious spending habits. During this time, he lived in subsistence poverty, a situation in which every penny counted. Helen wrote that though his living costs were minimal, his total savings amounted to two dollars during his first year in White Hall.[29] These experiences, growing up at a subsistence level in his formative years and learning the value of a dollar, would contrast sharply with those of Mary Todd Lincoln, who grew up in a world of financial security and whose attitudes toward spending money were quite different from those of her husband's secretary.

While in White Hall, Nicolay met the first of his many mentors and patrons who would sustain him throughout his life. Joel Pennington supervised the library for the Sunday school at the local Baptist church. George used this library to feed his unquenchable desire for self-improvement. Helen observed that Pennington "was favorably impressed by the diligence of Mr. Reno's clerk in seeking out the best in literature."[30] But this diligence could not compensate for his lack of physical prowess, and he was relieved of his employment at the Reno store after two years. The young man was not particularly interested in the job, especially its physical requirements. He needed to find an occupation that suited his intellectual inquisitiveness while not challenging his physical abilities.[31] Nearly penniless and without prospects, Nicolay went to live with one of his brothers, most likely John Jacob, as it is unlikely that Frederick, who had kicked the young man out two years earlier, would have taken him back in. Then, down on his luck and without prospects, fortune intervened.

Helen related two different stories regarding how her father came to work at the *Pike County Free Press;* the first she claimed to be wholly apocryphal. A fuller version of this story was repeated at the 1926 dedication of a tablet in the local square in Pittsfield honoring Abraham Lincoln, Stephen A. Douglas, John G. Nicolay, and John M. Hay:

> One day in 1848 Z. [Zachariah] N. Garbutt, then editor of the paper, borrowed a horse from Preacher Carter [first minister of Pittsfield's first church, the Congregational] and with a sample of the Free Press in his pocket started out to canvass Pike County for subscribers. While thus canvassing down in the southeast corner of the county he was one day approaching a settler's cabin when a ragged, bare-footed boy dashed around the corner of the cabin and a woman after him with an upraised broom. Garbutt halted at the rail fence in front of the cabin and the boy ran out to him. Garbutt asked the lad what he had done to merit a licking and the boy replied that he hadn't done anything but that "lickin' him was a habit his with step-mother and he reckoned she done it 'cause she liked it, but he didn't." . . . Noting a mill on the bank of a creek not far away where the boy's father was at work, Garbutt took the boy along with him over to the mill where he engaged the father. . . . Garbutt finally persuaded the father to part with the little boy, promising to bring him to Pittsfield and give him an education and teach him the printer's trade.[32]

Among Nicolay's companions in Pittsfield was Thomas W. Shastid. His son, Thomas Hall Shastid, in his memoir, *My Second Life,* stated that the story was true because he heard it retold many times by Mrs. Purkitt, the widow of Z. N. Garbutt. Shastid went on to state that Mrs. Purkitt had been "for years the foster mother of John G. Nicolay" and therefore knew "under what circumstances her boy . . . had come to her."[33] According to Shastid, Mrs. Purkitt described the young Nicolay as "a freckle-faced boy in bedticking trousers and straw hat."[34]

Though poor, Nicolay was not the barefooted Huck Finn rube portrayed in this oft-repeated tale, and the earliest known photograph of Nicolay does not show a "freckle-faced boy." By 1848, both parents were long deceased, and his father had never remarried. Thomas H. Shastid was not born until 1866[35] and therefore was not the beneficiary of Mrs. Purkitt's retelling until at least thirty years after the supposed events. Mrs. Purkitt could not have been "for years the

The earliest known photograph of John George Nicolay, during his Pittsfield residency (date unknown). (From the Lincoln Financial Foundation Collection, courtesy of the Allen County Public Library and Indiana State Museum)

foster mother of John G. Nicolay" since Mr. Garbutt retired from the *Free Press* in 1849, the year after Nicolay arrived in Pittsfield, and went into other businesses before dying in Memphis, Tennessee, in 1855.[36] After coming to Pittsfield, Nicolay lived above the offices of the *Free Press* with another employee, then for a brief time with the Garbutts.[37] However, by 1850, he was a boarder, with another printer named Monroe Benson, in the home of Dr. Thomas Worthington.[38] Nicolay undoubtedly respected and paid great courtesy to the woman whose husband had given him the job that launched his career, but he was not riding on the back of Z. N. Garbutt's horse the day he arrived in Pittsfield.

Likewise, Helen's version also has a bit of a Horatio Alger theme. According to her version, "one of [Joel] Pennington's boys" read an advertisement for a printer's assistant, "thought of John George," and "sent it to him with the message that here is a job after his own heart."[39] Her father then allegedly "trudged" the "long" miles to Pittsfield, spent the night on a sack of wool, and started work the next morning. According to the census records, the oldest of Joel Pennington's sons in 1848 was seven-year-old Goin Pennington, an unlikely candidate to be reading the want ads.[40]

The following is a more likely scenario. Joel Pennington, who had been the custodian of the Sunday school library in White Hall, had moved to Pittsfield to become the manager of the Mansion House, one of two hotels on the courthouse square. According to Helen, Joel Pennington had been "favorably impressed" by the young Nicolay. The offices of the *Free Press* were also on the square, two doors from the Mansion House. When Z. N. Garbutt revealed his interest in hiring "an intelligent boy . . . to learn the Printing Business," it is likely that Joel Pennington recommended the young man he had known in White Hall. Once Garbutt expressed interest in the lad, Pennington immediately sent for him, for why would anyone trudge "long miles" without some prospect of success? Likewise, why would the boy sleep on wool sacks when his friend and sponsor ran a hotel and certainly would have had a spare couch, if not a bed, for his young friend?

However he reached Pittsfield in 1848, the heretofore ugly duckling found a home in the town. While Helen's description of the settlers of Pittsfield as having arrived "as a body" from Massachusetts was not accurate, her description of Pittsfield as a "New England community set down on the Illinois prairie"[41] was closer to the mark. Colonel William Ross, the man who had paid for the original survey of the town, had the privilege of naming it for Pittsfield, Massachusetts, where he had once resided. He had seen service in the War of 1812 but owed his colonel's rank to the fact that he had commanded the Illinois state militia. He had also held office as a state senator and was an active member of the Whig Party. The Reverend William Carter, the Congregational minister, was from Connecticut. Dr. Thomas Worthington, who was not only a physician but another local Whig politician, was from Massachusetts. Dorus Bates, a blacksmith and father of a daughter named Therena, who was three years younger than Nicolay,[42] was also from the Bay State. Z. N. Garbutt had been born in the upstate community of Wheatland, New York. Joel Pennington was also a native of the Empire State. Milton Hay, at that time a local attorney, and son-in-law of Abraham Lincoln's then law partner, Stephen T. Logan, had been born in Kentucky. At one time, Milton Hay had been the law partner of Edward D. Baker, another friend and confidant of Abraham Lincoln, after whom the Lincolns named their second son. John Shastid, father of Nicolay's friend Thomas W. Shastid, was another Kentucky native. While Pittsfield was indeed a "New England town set down on the prairie," its inhabitants were not all New England born and bred. But what all these men held in common was the fact that they were educated and appreciated the value of learning. For these men, brains were valued as much, if not more so, than brawn. Young Nicolay had indeed found a home.

The Congregational Church in Pittsfield, with its minister, the Reverend William Carter, was at the center of the community. The 1880 *History of Pike*

County, Illinois describes the church as "intimately associated with the early days of the town," with the Reverend Carter as its first minister in charge and a congregation that included many influential members of the town, including Colonel Ross, who helped erect the large house of worship known to Nicolay in 1846.[43] William Grimshaw, town historian, described the Reverend Carter as a "ripe scholar and pious man," who had his "peculiarities but no man of truer and better manhood ever lived here."[44]

If the Congregational Church was the spiritual anchor of the town, the local newspapers were its voice and guides. The *Pike County Free Press* was the second Whig newspaper with which Pittsfield had been graced. Begun in 1842 under the name of the *Sucker,* the paper's editor was Michael J. Noyes, a New Hampshire native and "an advocate of freedom." The *Pike County Free Press* succeeded the *Sucker* as the area's Whig newspaper; its first edition was published on April 15, 1846, the same year Nicolay's father died. Z. N. Garbutt was the editor.[45] In competition with the Whig *Free Press* were several papers committed to the cause of the Democratic Party, known then as the Democracy. The *Sentinel,* the first Democratic paper in the county, established in 1845, was succeeded in 1849 by the *Union,* which in turn was succeeded by the *Pike County Democrat* in 1857.[46] Newspapers of the time were intensely partisan. Being an antislavery newspaper in central or southern Illinois had its particular risks. On November 27, 1837, a mob in Alton, Illinois, while trying to destroy his press and shut down his abolitionist newspaper for the fourth time, killed newspaper editor Elijah Lovejoy. Though Pittsfield was farther from the Missouri line than Alton, the feelings surrounding slavery and abolition frequently resulted in mob violence in all sections of the country.

Local news, other than vital statistics and social events, was often scarce except when the county court was in session or when politicians passed through the county seat canvassing for votes. Like many frontier newspapers, the *Free Press* was published weekly on Thursdays, leaving a lot of free time for its editor to pursue other intellectual interests while waiting in the office for news stories.

The telegraph was coming into use across the country, making news from the outside world more available. Speeches and articles from other newspapers were readily copied. Helen observed that her father's predecessors at the *Free Press* did not focus on political news as much as her father later did. "Mr. Garbutt, in his editorial days, had given generous space to religious articles, poetry and fiction," she noted, while "Mr. Parkes's [a co-owner with Garbutt] taste ran to long extracts from the English quarterlies."[47]

During the court sessions or political campaigning, the little county seat of Pittsfield would be full of activity. Lawyers from Springfield and elsewhere in the state would converge on the small town. They would take up residence in the local hotels or with friends in the town during the session of the circuit court. Abraham Lincoln sometimes dined with the Shastid family during his sojourns to Pittsfield.[48] People would come in from around the county to have their cases heard or simply to observe the court proceedings and legal wrangling, listen to speeches and otherwise engage in a variety of social activities. Then the local papers would be full of descriptions of the people, events, and political controversies swirling around the local square immediately outside the offices of the *Free Press*. Town historian William Grimshaw provided a detailed description of Zachariah N. Garbutt, the *Free Press* editor, and his connections to the community: "Zachariah N. Garbutt the original editor of the *Free Press* of this county, was a member of the bar, and for a time Master in Chancery of the county; he was a very merry soul. In the Mormon War, he earned laurels by piling big sweet potatoes for the troops of anti-Mormons. Earnest and somewhat original in his opinions, very independent in the expression of his thoughts, he was an upright man and something of a genius. He died before he reached the median of life."[49]

As a newspaper man, Garbutt would be immersed in conversations while reporting on court proceedings and political activities ranging from speeches in the public square to who was meeting with whom in the local taverns. As a printer's apprentice, Nicolay at first would have been more of an observer than a participant in these events. But as he matured and moved up the ladder from printer's apprentice to reporter, he would also begin to immerse himself in the activities around the square. Thus, concurrent with his education in the printing business, he began an apprenticeship in practical politics in the town square.

Nicolay also continued other aspects of his self-education. At a time when public libraries were scarce almost anywhere in the country, Pittsfield, this New England town on the prairie, had one.[50] Also, being acquainted with men in town who possessed private book collections, such as Mr. Garbutt, Dr. Worthington, and the Reverend Carter, was a godsend to a lad whose desire to acquire learning was insatiable. He also found time to begin to read the law in Milton Hay's law office. First and foremost in any young man's reading of the law would have been William Blackstone's *Commentaries on the Laws of England*.

Not only did little Pittsfield have a public library and men with small private libraries, it also had an academy of learning founded in 1849, the year after

The Pike County Court House in Pittsfield, Illinois. Constructed in 1839 and in use until it was replaced in 1894, it was a very familiar building to attorney Lincoln and journalist Nicolay. The *Free Press* office was across the street on Court House Square. (Pike County Historical Society)

Nicolay arrived in the community. John D. Thomson, an immigrant from Ireland, and his wife had established the Thomson School or Academy, whose primary purpose was to be a preparatory school for young men intending to go on to college or "even greater universities of the East." The Thomson Academy taught a number of languages both ancient and modern. Beyond languages the academy also taught mathematics and "certain other branches" of learning.[51]

Proof of the quality of the school can be found in the fact that in 1851 a young man from nearby Warsaw, Illinois, named John Milton Hay was sent to the home of his uncle Milton in Pittsfield so that he could attend the Thomson School. Six years younger than Nicolay, Hay gravitated toward the intellectual Nicolay and spent long hours in the offices of the *Free Press* with his friend. German was among the subjects the young Hay was studying, and Nicolay, being a native speaker, was a valuable asset to the young scholar. During this year, these young men established a friendship that would last a lifetime; it would only end with Nicolay's death half a century later. The creative, artistic Hay and the matter-of-fact reporter Nicolay formed a complementary team that would serve Abraham Lincoln well in the White House and beyond. After a year in Pittsfield,

The modest building that once housed the *Pike County Free Press* on Court House Square in Pittsfield, Illinois. Nicolay for a time lived in a room on the second floor. The building no longer exists. (Pike County Historical Society)

Hay moved to Springfield to live with his uncle Leonard and attend Illinois State University while making final preparations for his entrance into the prestigious Brown University.[52]

While Hay would later go off to Springfield and Providence, Nicolay continued to hone his writing skills at the *Free Press*. According to his daughter's recollection, he learned "two very useful things . . . patience and the importance of detail."[53] And if he ever had adorned his prose with adjectives, it was, according to Helen, "an indiscretion of early youth, soon over."[54] The Lincoln history, written decades later, would be notable for its lack of adjectives. Yet the first book Nicolay contemplated writing was not a biography of his future hero but a history of the exploration of the Mississippi Valley. For this project he checked out books from the Pittsfield Library, researched records in the State Library in Springfield, and translated manuscripts from the French archives in Paris.[55] Although he would never write a book on this topic, the idea of a historical work of some magnitude had germinated in his mind long before he contemplated the biography of Lincoln.

Nicolay's education was not limited to the printed word. One of those "certain other branches" taught at the Thomson Academy may have been singing, as Helen related that her father "promptly joined it." Though his instruction lasted for only a short time, her father learned "the principles of musical notation" and how to play the organ "with such effect that he was engaged as organist of Mr. Carter's church at a salary of five dollars a year." Playing the organ in the local church also gave him an opportunity to look down on Therena Bates's "olive cheek and a knot of blue-black hair."[56] Therena Bates would become the love of his life.

Being the organ player also meant that he came into contact with the church's most prominent member and town founder, Colonel William Ross, and many other prominent personalities in the community. Colonel Ross and Dr. Worthington were both active in Whig politics, as were other men in the county such as Ozias M. Hatch, the future secretary of state for Illinois. But the county tended to vote Democratic in statewide and national elections. In the mid-1840s, the Fifth Congressional District, which included Pike County, was represented by an ambitious Democratic politician from nearby Quincy, Stephen A. Douglas, who was elected to the U.S. Senate in 1846. By 1848, when Nicolay joined the *Free Press,* the great sectional debate over the extension of slavery, which had been reignited with the debates over the annexation of Texas in 1845 and attempts to ban slavery from the territories acquired at the end of the Mexican War, had now taken an ominous turn in American politics. Congress tried to quiet the slavery issue with the so-called Compromise of 1850, a series of legislative enactments meant to pacify both sections. It turned out to be a fragile peace.

As these events unfolded, Nicolay was finding success and beginning to mature in his political perspectives. As the early 1850s progressed, he assumed more important roles with the *Free Press.* By the time he was twenty-two in 1854, he had become sole proprietor and began to take an active role in Illinois politics in opposition to slavery's expansion into the territories. In January 1854, Senator Douglas proposed the Kansas-Nebraska bill,[57] which would establish territorial governments in those regions. The bill contained a clause to repeal the Missouri Compromise of 1820 and allow for the expansion of slavery not only in the new territories acquired from Mexico, an issue decided by the Compromise of 1850, but also into the areas of the Louisiana Purchase, where slavery had been banned by the Missouri Compromise. The Congress passed the Kansas-Nebraska bill, and President Franklin Pierce signed it on May 30, 1854. These actions unleashed a political firestorm in the North, including Illinois.

In the ensuing elections in 1854, Northern Democrats paid a terrible price at the polls. The party lost seventy-five seats in the House of Representatives, almost all of them in the free states. The American (or Know-Nothing) Party swept New England and the Northeast, while "opposition" candidates, including assorted Whigs and Democrats opposed to the controversial new law, made a strong showing in the western states of Indiana, Michigan, Wisconsin, Iowa, and Illinois. These groups would begin to coalesce around an anti–Nebraska bill platform. Illinois opponents to the expansion of slavery held an organizing convention on October 4–5, 1854, less than five months after President Pierce had signed the Kansas-Nebraska bill. That convention, attended by such luminaries as Lyman Trumbull, Abraham Lincoln, and Owen Lovejoy, was ineffectual and poorly attended.

At this time, Nicolay gradually became involved in the Free Soil movement.[58] As it had been under Zachariah Garbutt, Nicolay's *Pike County Free Press* remained a staunch antislavery Whig paper, if not more so. In late 1855, Paul Selby, editor of the *Morgan Journal,* a Whig paper in Jacksonville, Illinois, which described itself as "independent," called for a state convention of "Anti-Nebraska editors of the state for the purpose of agreeing upon a line of policy to be pursued in the campaign of the year, just opening."[59] This action was endorsed by some Whig papers in the state, including Pittsfield's *Free Press* and its editor.[60] The *Chicago Tribune,* in its editorial of support, not only noted Nicolay's endorsement in the *Pike County Free Press* but quoted from it.[61] The convention met in Decatur, Illinois, starting on February 22, 1856.

In *Abraham Lincoln: A History,* Nicolay and Hay recalled that in the "absence of any existing [antislavery] party machinery, some fifteen editors" who opposed the extension of slavery met on February 22, 1856, in Decatur, Illinois, and called for representatives of an anti-Nebraska coalition to meet at Bloomington, Illinois, on May 29.[62] Among the newspapers represented at the Decatur conference were two influential Chicago papers, the *Chicago Tribune* and George Schneider's German-language *Staats-Zeitung and Journal.* Schneider was an important voice in the German immigrant community, whose support of the Democratic Party was waning in light of the party's support of the expansion of slavery. In the end, there were a dozen editors in attendance, with two or three arriving in the evening because of a snow storm.[63]

Charles Church, in his history of the Illinois Republican Party, provided a list of the twelve editors who participated in the meeting at Decatur. Nicolay was not among them. Nicolay's description of the convention in the Lincoln biography appears to be from proceedings and is rather straightforward. In contrast, his description of the Bloomington Convention, which he is known to have attended, is much more colorful. Another discussion by Nicolay of the Bloomington Convention (included in a paper dated May 19, 1900, which he sent to the McLean County Historical Society) makes no mention of the Decatur meeting.[64] It is possible that he may have been one of the individuals prevented from attending the Decatur meeting by the weather since he was clearly active in the anti-Nebraska cause.

Paul Selby, who did attend the Decatur meeting and reported on it firsthand, believed that its most important work was done in the Committee on Resolutions, which met with Abraham Lincoln during its daylong deliberations. Selby felt that the resulting platform bore the mark of "his [Lincoln's] peculiar intellect."[65] While disavowing interference with slavery in the states where it existed, it opposed the further extension of slavery, called for the reinstatement of the Missouri Compromise (repealed by the Kansas-Nebraska Act), and affirmed the principles contained within the Declaration of Independence.[66] Dr. Selby would later assert in a 1900 speech that the platform contained a "protest" against Know-Nothingism, although the Know Nothings would constitute an important element of Republican politics in its early years. Free Soilers and abolitionists alone could not hope to constitute a successful political movement as demonstrated by the national elections of the previous decade. The immigrant German newspaper editors, including George Schneider, with whom Nicolay, himself an immigrant and still a noncitizen, identified were particularly sensitive to the nativist feelings that had swept the country in the face of the large-scale German and Irish Catholic immigration of the 1840s and 1850s.

The nativists had become especially concerned that many of the recent immigrants were Catholics with their allegiance to a hierarchical clergy and a foreign potentate (the Pope). Anti-Catholicism had deep roots in the English colonies. German immigration during the colonial period had been overwhelmingly Protestant. Now, the large influx of Catholic immigrants from the German states and Ireland, beginning in the 1830s and turning into a flood by the late 1840s, was seen by many Americans as a threat to the democratic ideals of the republic.

Dr. Selby hinted at the split that had to be papered over between the antislavery Germans and the anti-immigrant factions among the editors. In the framing of the platform, Schneider is described as the "faithful representative of the German Anti-Nebraska element" and a spokesman for the rights of the foreign-born to be able to enjoy the rights of American citizenship.[67] The issues surrounding nativism and the new immigrants would continue to boil beneath the surface in

Republican circles for years to come. These issues would also have an important consequence for Nicolay in the future.

As the Decatur meeting concluded, the editors called for an anti-Nebraska state organizing convention to be convened in Bloomington on May 29, 1856. Importantly, and with Lincoln's prompting, the February convention enunciated two principles regarding slavery that would echo in Republican politics in its national platforms of June 1856 and of 1860 and in Lincoln's first inaugural address. The first principle was that slavery, where it existed, would be left unmolested. The second principle was that slavery would not be allowed to expand into the territories, in effect banning the future establishment of any additional slave states. Slavery, if not abolished, was to be contained within its current boundaries.

When the anti-Nebraska organizing convention met in Bloomington on May 29, 1856, slavery was again at the forefront of national divisions. The delegates from Pike County included the venerable Colonel William Ross, Dr. Thomas Worthington, J. Grimshaw, Ozias M. Hatch, and the twenty-four-year-old editor of the *Pike County Free Press,* John G. Nicolay.[68] Nicolay's selection demonstrated his growing importance as a leading man of Pike County.

Two events took place immediately prior to the Bloomington convention that further inflamed the already impassioned feelings of the participants regarding slavery. The first was the raid of Lawrence, Kansas, on May 21, 1856, by proslavery forces. Missouri ruffians burned the local hotel and destroyed the printing press of the local antislavery paper. It reminded the convening delegates of the ongoing war in Kansas over slavery. Second, on the following day, Representatives Preston Brooks and Laurence Keit of South Carolina entered the U.S. Senate chamber. Using a thick gutta-percha cane, Brooks beat the abolitionist senator Charles Sumner of Massachusetts senseless for an unwise and unprovoked speech by Sumner personally attacking Brooks's ailing, elderly relative, Senator Andrew Butler of South Carolina, and his proslavery position.

The Bloomington convention adopted a number of resolutions. In the first resolution, the delegates pledged loyalty to the new party, "foregoing all former differences of opinion." The convention asserted the right of Congress to prohibit slavery in the territories and called the repeal of the Missouri Compromise "unwise, unjust and injurious." The convention further declared that the Pierce administration's attempt "to force slavery into Kansas . . . is an arbitrary and tyrannous violation of the rights of the people to govern themselves." The delegates proclaimed their devotion to the Union and pledged, as many of them would over the coming decade, that they "will to the last extremity, defend it against the efforts now being made by the disunionists of the administration to compass its dissolution." Again, immigration and nativism were topics of discussion, as the convention adopted a mild anti–Know Nothing plank by asserting "the liberty of conscience as well as political freedom" without regard to religious beliefs or national origin.[69] The conclusion of the convention was the occasion for one of Abraham Lincoln's most impassioned speeches, known to history as the "Lost Speech," which so enthralled Lincoln's audience that no one, including the newspapermen present, recorded what he said. Nicolay, too ill to attend the 1900 commemorative meeting, nonetheless wrote briefly about the speech, stating that "never did nobler seed fall upon the minds and hearts of his enthusiastic listeners."[70] On many occasions, Helen Nicolay later remembered, her father "liked to recall the stirring scenes of that convention."[71]

While James Buchanan carried Illinois by a plurality over John C. Frémont, the Republicans did well in the state, capturing the governorship and three additional congressional seats in the northern portion of the state, electing John Farnsworth, Owen Lovejoy (brother of the murdered Elijah), and Elihu Washburne to their first terms. Ozias M. Hatch, Pike County resident and, like Nicolay, a delegate to the May convention, became Illinois secretary of state. Pike County remained firmly Democratic in its voting. After the 1856 election, Nicolay decided to leave the town of Pittsfield and, like his father before him, move on for opportunities elsewhere. He sold the *Free Press* and moved eventually to Springfield, the state capital.

The decision to sell the *Free Press* and leave Pittsfield was the first major milestone in his adult life. In departing Pittsfield, he concluded the formative period of his life. Pittsfield was Nicolay's salvation. Z. N. Garbutt provided him with a job at the center of the community. He had found a frontier town where intellectual prowess was valued as much as raw brawn. Garbutt, Dr. Worthington, Reverend Carter, Milton Hay, Colonel Ross, John Shastid, and John Thomson were all leading men of the community with whom he made connections and who, in turn, fostered his education and promoted his career. This was the home of his beloved Therena, his future wife. This is where he met his lifelong friend and collaborator, John Hay. The convention of May 1856 gave him valuable lessons from, and contacts with, practical politicians. Most of all, these connections provided him with what he yearned for most: access to learning and self-improvement.

Nicolay's experience as a clerk in the family mill and as a bookkeeper in Aaron Reno's mercantile taught him organizational skills. Living a hand-to-mouth existence after being sent out into the cold by his older brother taught him the hard lessons of poverty and self-reliance. He learned that money was a precious commodity, that saving rather than spending was the path to success, and that there was no one more interested in John G. Nicolay than JGN himself. His experience as a newspaperman, editor, and delegate allowed him to be fully conversant with the political issues of the day. It also made him an identifiable and respected man among the newspaper editors of Illinois and Missouri, including the editors of the German-language newspapers of the Midwest, the influential George Schneider of Chicago among them. Through Schneider and his other contacts with German-language editors, he renewed his ties to the German immigrant community.

Nicolay had first seen African American slavery on the docks of New Orleans and on the river trip to Cincinnati. Later, he saw it again close up during the family's brief stay in St. Louis. Even in the free state of Illinois, slavery was just across the Mississippi River, not only downriver in St. Louis but also upriver in Mark Twain's Hannibal. Surrounded by antislavery men like Garbutt and Carter and other leaders of a "New England" town on the Illinois prairie, these associations could only deepen his antislavery opinions. It was at Pittsfield that he became acquainted with Lincoln the political figure and began his lifelong devotion to the man. During this period, he could only know Lincoln from afar. But the rail splitter had an oratorical elegance, a presence that enthralled the young editor as it had done for so many others. Listening to Lincoln had intensified his antislavery views.

In Pittsfield, Nicolay had learned the value of connections, personal and political, that would lead to future opportunities. He realized that a mentor's promotion of his career was important to success. Therefore, despite his somewhat reticent personality, he learned to nurture and profit from these associations. Leaving behind Therena Bates, with whom he would continue to cultivate a close relationship through correspondence and occasional visits, he was ready for the next chapter in his life.

CHAPTER TWO

Springfield
Gateway to Washington

About sixty-four miles east and slightly north of Pittsfield, as the crow flies, lies Springfield, the capital city of Illinois since 1837. That year twenty-eight-year-old Abraham Lincoln joined the twelve hundred or thirteen hundred residents of the young prairie town in calling it home—and it was in Springfield that he was laid to eternal rest twenty-eight years later. John G. Nicolay would move to Springfield in 1857, by now a town approaching ten thousand residents, far larger and more sophisticated than Pittsfield. He arrived in the spring of that year, after spending a few weeks in St. Louis following the sale of his *Pike County Free Press* in Pittsfield. He came to Springfield to work for Ozias M. Hatch, another Pike County resident. Nicolay knew and liked Hatch, newly elected as secretary of state for Illinois, who had enthusiastically embraced the new Republican Party. Nicolay had vigorously supported Hatch's bid for state office both through the pages of the *Free Press* and through several campaign speeches he gave on Hatch's behalf. They had also served together as delegates from Pike County to the Republican state convention in May 1856.

Impressed with the young Nicolay and grateful for his support in the campaign, Hatch offered him the position of chief clerk in the Office of the Illinois Secretary of State. Nicolay eagerly accepted the offer. It was an opportunity for advancement in a stimulating political and intellectual environment, yet not too distant from his connections and interests in Pittsfield, including Therena Bates. Hatch and Nicolay initially rented rooms in the same boarding house, where they rubbed shoulders with other men of influence.

Nicolay's own recollections described his new situation in Springfield and

Ozias M. Hatch was elected Illinois Secretary of State in 1856 and hired his young friend Nicolay to be his clerk in the Capitol in Springfield. It was Hatch who first informed Nicolay that presidential candidate Lincoln wanted to hire him as his secretary.

the important role that the secretary of state's quarters played in Illinois politics. Among those who frequented these precincts was a prominent Springfield attorney by the name of Abraham Lincoln:

> From the spring of 1857 to 1860 I was a clerk in the office of Hon. O.M. Hatch, Secretary of State of the state of Illinois, who in that capacity occupied a large and well-appointed room in the old State House at Springfield. The State Library, of which the Secretary had charge, was in an adjoining room, also large and commodious; which by common usage was used by all political parties when assembled at state conventions, or during sessions of the Legislature as a political caucus-room; the entrance to it being through the Secretary's main office. This office of the Secretary of State was therefore in effect, the State political headquarters, and a common rendezvous for prominent Illinois politicians, more especially the Republicans, to which party Mr. Hatch belonged.
>
> Mr. Lincoln was of course a frequent visitor, and when he came he was always the center of an animated and interested group. It was there during the years mentioned that I made his acquaintance. All election records were kept by the Secretary of State, and I, being Mr. Hatch's principal clerk, had frequent occasion to show Mr. Lincoln, who was an assiduous student of election tables, the latest returns, or the completed record books.[1]

While he claimed to have laid eyes on Lincoln for the first time at a political meeting in Pittsfield, Nicolay made no reference to a claim by Pittsfield resi-

The State Library in the old Illinois Capitol in Springfield
where Nicolay served as clerk for the Secretary of State.
According to Robert Lincoln, it was here that Lincoln
and his future secretary became acquainted, frequently
conversing and playing chess. Lincoln's law office was just
across the street. (Photograph by Allen Carden)

dent Thomas W. Shastid that he (Shastid) was responsible for Nicolay's meeting
Lincoln. According to Shastid, he directed Lincoln to the *Free Press* office when
Lincoln inquired about his need for an honest printer.[2] While he may have been
introduced to Lincoln in Pittsfield, there is little reason to doubt Nicolay's own
words that it was in the secretary of state's office in Springfield where he "made
the acquaintance and close friendship of Abraham Lincoln."[3] Robert Lincoln also
indicated that Springfield was where his father and Nicolay became acquainted.
In a letter to Isaac Markens dated November 4, 1917, Robert recounted what he
believed to be the occasion when Nicolay and his father actually became acquainted. The younger Lincoln noted that the Office of the Secretary Of State had

Springfield's largest library, which his father and Nicolay undoubtedly utilized frequently. The library also served as a meeting room, where the young clerk, described by Robert Lincoln as someone who "played a good game of chess, which my father liked very much," spent hours playing "many games . . . in times of leisure" with the elder Lincoln.[4] While we have no record of the substance of the conversations that occurred between these two men as each contemplated his next move on the chessboard, in all probability the conversations gravitated to both the familiar and the political. It is safe to say that it in these personal conversations, Nicolay's similar views to those of Lincoln on slavery and its extension solidified his admiration of and devotion to the future president.

To this point, Lincoln's political career had seen as much disappointment as success. While living in the town of New Salem on the Sangamon River, Lincoln twice ran for the Illinois Assembly, losing in 1832 but winning a seat in 1834. Lincoln continued to hold a seat in the Assembly until 1842. In 1846 he was elected to the U.S. House of Representatives from the Seventh Congressional District of Illinois, the only Whig seat in the Illinois delegation. In his single term, Lincoln opposed the war with Mexico and strongly supported the Wilmot Proviso, an attempt by Northern congressmen, led by Pennsylvania Democrat David Wilmot, to ban the expansion of slavery into the territories of the Mexican Cession. Lincoln returned to Springfield, abandoning thoughts of future political office in favor of making a good living as an increasingly respected attorney. In this capacity, his most lucrative cases involved his representation of railroad interests, but his most enjoyable times were the cases he took while riding the circuit in central Illinois in the companionship of other circuit-riding lawyers. These cases also offered Lincoln a reprieve from his sometime stormy marital relationship with Mary Lincoln. Yet, Lincoln's interest in politics and his ever-present hatred of the institution of slavery were never far from his mind.

Lincoln returned to the political scene in 1854 after U.S. senator and personal rival Stephen A. Douglas of Chicago had introduced the Kansas-Nebraska bill in Congress. This bill repealed the Missouri Compromise of 1820 and authorized the extension of slavery into all the Western territories, a horrifying prospect to both Lincoln and Nicolay. The bill's eventual passage drove many of Nicolay's fellow German immigrants, particularly the German-language press, away from the Democratic Party. Known as the Forty-Eighters, Germans who had fled the German states after the unsuccessful revolution of 1848 were typically more urban and more liberal than the German immigrants who had preceded them. They had affiliated with the Democratic Party because of the nativism expressed first by the Whigs and then by the American or Know-Nothing Party. But given their more liberal outlook, they came to detest slavery even more than nativism.

In 1855, the term of U.S. senator James Shields of Illinois was expiring, and Lincoln appeared to be the leading candidate to succeed him. United States senators were at that time elected by state legislatures rather than the voters at large, and after several ballots, Lincoln failed to receive the necessary majority, although he led the field of candidates. Lincoln withdrew in favor of Lyman Trumbull, an anti-Nebraska Democrat, rather than allow the pro-Nebraska incumbent Shields to be reelected. Nicolay editorialized in the *Free Press,* without mentioning Lincoln's name, that it would have been preferable to elect "a good Whig to that office," but since that was not possible, "we heartily rejoice at the result as it was"—the election of Trumbull—"an uncompromising anti-Nebraska Democrat."[5]

Both Lincoln and Nicolay had now transitioned from the Whig to the Republican Party by the spring of 1856, and their attendance at the anti-Nebraska organizing convention in Bloomington in May 1856 bore public witness to that fact. According to Nicolay and Hay, among "the brilliant array of eminent names" at the Bloomington gathering, "chief among these, as adviser and actor, was Abraham Lincoln."[6] Lincoln delivered the closing address, to which his law partner, William Herndon, listened so carefully that instead of his usual note taking, he "threw pen and paper away and lived only in the inspiration of the hour." According to Herndon's biography of Lincoln, "His speech was full of fire and energy and force; it was logic; it was pathos; it was enthusiasm; it was justice, equity, truth, and right set ablaze by the divine fires of a soul maddened by the wrong."[7] At the first national Republican convention, held in Philadelphia in June 1856, Lincoln's name was one of fifteen placed in nomination for vice president. On the first ballot, Lincoln came in second place to former New Jersey senator William L. Dayton, who won the nomination on the second ballot. Lincoln expressed the opinion that "I think him a far better man than I for the position he is in."[8]

In *Abraham Lincoln: A History,* Nicolay and Hay looked back on Lincoln's loss of the vice-presidential nomination in 1856 and ruminated on a possible historical twist of fate. They wondered how Lincoln would have fared in the powerless position of vice president while the "impulsive" Frémont wielded the "nation's sword of commander-in-chief."[9]

Although these words were written in retrospect, the election of 1856 had been a close affair. As later events would demonstrate, Frémont could not only be "impulsive" but also imprudent to the point of recklessness. The unexpected electoral strength of the new Republican Party was a dire warning to the South that their hold on the levers of the federal government was weakening. Future electoral success for the Republican Party depended on the candidate the Republicans would choose. Lincoln saw himself as that candidate long before others did and the events of the next four years would propel him into the presidency and Nicolay into a central position in the Lincoln White House.

Thus, it was a man of growing reputation and no little ambition with whom Nicolay bonded in the state library in Springfield in 1857. Though a generation apart in age—Lincoln was forty-eight and Nicolay twenty-five when they became acquainted—the two men discovered they had much in common. Playing chess for hours, they would talk. On a personal level, both men had lost their mothers at an early age; Nicolay was seven, Lincoln nine. Both men had their early lives repeatedly uprooted from their surroundings by their fathers' wanderlust. Both men knew the pain of isolation and ridicule. Lincoln was a tall, gangly, and awkward outsider who had spent much time immersed in books, for which he received criticism from his father and encouragement from his stepmother. Nicolay, the slender, frail outsider, had likewise spent much time reading whatever he could get his hands on, receiving ridicule from his physically robust older brothers while being protected by his father. Lincoln was not close to his father, and Nicolay lost his father while in his early teens. Both men were fascinated by machinery, and both men applied for and received patents. The purpose of Nicolay's initial trip to Washington in 1852 was to file the first of five patents he would obtain in his lifetime. The first patent was for an improved rotary printing press.[10]

Both Lincoln and Nicolay were self-motivated, self-educated, and ambitious men. They had weaned their intellectual prowess on Shakespeare, the Bible, and Blackstone's *Commentaries.* Having access to the state library collection must have been a dream fulfilled for Nicolay as he continued to consume knowledge through the printed page. While neither man realized it at the time, it was their interaction in the secretary of state's office in Springfield that caused them to forge a bond of friendship and mutual respect. It was in the Illinois Capitol that Nicolay's devotion to Lincoln the man, and later Lincoln the icon, took root.

However, it was the issue of slavery and its extension that bound these men closely together. Lincoln had grown up hating slavery. Nicolay had come to despise the peculiar institution through his childhood memories, his associations in Pittsfield, including the sermons of the Reverend Carter, the editorial and personal influence of Z. N. Garbutt, and the books they had given him to read. Politically, he had reached conclusions quite similar to Lincoln's even before his move to Springfield. The chaotic situation in the Kansas Territory had been a catalyst for his developing political perspectives.

During this time period, Nicolay maintained a notebook on the political events of 1856–58. He was convinced that "When Free State men got in [to Kansas], they were mobbed, lynched, tarred & feathered, shot, scalped or driven out, and even sold to niggers by Democrats."[11] He blamed the violence in Kansas on his observation that "Every act of the Dem[ocratic] Party—legislative, executive or judicial has been against the white man & for the Nigger." He agreed with Republican principles that "Free Society" is "right and good" and "Slave Society" is "wrong and evil."[12] Nicolay's use of the pejorative term regarding blacks is best understood as a code word for his negative attitude toward "proslavery" interests and the negative impact of slavery on free white men. While hating slavery in principle, Nicolay had not yet come to focus on individual persons of color and their interests. He used the "n word" not to reference race as much as he used it to define what he perceived to be the Democratic Party's unceasing support of slavery and its spread. Like the pre-presidential Lincoln, he was a conservative when it came to his antislavery sentiments, focusing more on slavery's harmful impact on the white population than on the brutality and injustice experienced by the slaves themselves. Like Lincoln and most of his contemporaries, he did not believe in the equality of the races. As with Lincoln, he would grow in his appreciation for the plight of the slave and in his conviction that slavery and democracy were incompatible.

In Nicolay's political universe, Senator Stephen A. Douglas was the evil puppet master of the Slave Conspiracy. He placed blame for the problems in Kansas at the feet of Douglas, a politician for whom he had little but contempt. He blamed Douglas for the erroneous beliefs that "Slavery [is] equal to Freedom," that "slavery is the rule of Civilization and Christianity," that "uniformity is not possible" [a rationalization for "popular sovereignty"], which is but "an excuse for Slavery which makes it perpetual," and that there "can be no liberty without slavery." Mocking in his notebook the extreme situations he expected Douglas and his belief in popular sovereignty would bring, Nicolay concluded: "Some states must have Slavery—some Polygamy—some Peonage—some Colie [Coolie] Slavery—some Negro Equality. Under this doctrine we must have Abolition in Mass[achusetts]—Nullification in South Carolina—Polygamy in Utah—Peonage in New Mexico—Amalgamation in M[ain]e and Free Love in Ohio."[13] The antidote to this calamity? "Throw overboard our political Jonah [Senator Douglas] before he drags our ship of State to destruction with him."[14]

In contrast, Nicolay and the new Republican Party wanted, to paraphrase the Free Soil campaign slogan from 1848, "Free Soil, Free Labor, Free Men," so long as the labor and men were white. Nicolay and the Republicans also wanted railroads, telegraphs, public schools, and other governmentally supported internal improvements that were anathema to the Southern political philosophy of limited government.[15] His notebook also includes newspaper articles about Lincoln and how much Lincoln and the late Kentucky senator Henry Clay agreed on various aspects of the "Slavery Question." It is clear that both Lincoln and Nicolay held Clay in high esteem.

Events continued to heighten the partisan and sectional divide over slavery in the territories. Nicolay and Hay would devote a chapter in their biography of Lincoln to the *Dred Scott* decision, highlighting its importance in the slavery debate.[16] Dred Scott was a Missouri slave who had been taken by his master to reside in free territory. Scott subsequently sued for his freedom. As Nicolay and Hay noted, the legal case before the Supreme Court revolved around two narrow legal questions: was Dred Scott a citizen entitled to sue, and did his extended residence in Illinois and Minnesota entitle him to claim his freedom?[17] Originally, the court planned to issue a narrow decision prepared by Associate Justice Samuel Nelson of New York. According to Nicolay and Hay, had Nelson's opinion been issued, the court's decision would "have gone to a quiet sleep under the dust of law libraries."[18] Instead, the court's decision became entangled in the swirling issues of the national debate over slavery when Chief Justice Roger Taney, a Maryland slaveholder, decided to rewrite Nelson's opinion in order to settle the political debate over slavery. Commenting on the case over two decades and a civil war later, Nicolay and Hay noted, "In an evil hour they [the Supreme Court] yielded to the demands of 'public interest' and resolved to 'fulfill public expectation.'"[19]

The chief justice's interference made the situation worse. Nicolay and Hay noted the legal babel that became the *Dred Scott* decision, with the court's opinion being read by the chief justice while six associate justices wrote concurring opinions. These separate opinions sometimes agreed, sometimes disagreed, or ignored entirely various elements of the chief justice's logic. The decision denied Dred Scott his freedom; it also denied the right of African Americans to become citizens and thus to bring suit in court, while asserting that slaves were property and therefore Congress had no authority to regulate slavery in the territories. it thus nullified not only the already repealed Missouri Compromise but also the Northwest Ordinance of 1787.[20] In their condemnation of the court's decision, Nicolay and Hay asserted that the "collective utterance of the bench resembled the speeches of a town meeting rather than the decision of a court . . . to order the simple dismissal of a suit."[21]

Even though the court's decision voided Douglas's argument that territorial legislatures could decide on the issue of slavery, the court's declaration that the Missouri Compromise had been unconstitutional all along bolstered the arguments of Douglas justifying the Kansas-Nebraska Act. Douglas, now the heir presumptive for the Democratic presidential nomination in 1860, became a leading member of the Democratic chorus praising the *Dred Scott* decision. However, Northern opinion across party lines was very antagonistic to the broad sweep of the decision. Politicians like Lincoln sensed that Northern opinion was turning against the South and its Northern Democratic allies. Consequently, Lincoln decided to challenge the Little Giant (as Douglas was popularly called) in the 1858 Illinois election for the U.S. Senate.

At this time, Nicolay was able to put his writing skills to use for the cause. When Douglas reluctantly accepted Lincoln's challenge to a series of debates in seven Illinois communities, he knew the stakes were high, for Douglas clearly had presidential ambitions for the 1860 election and he knew Lincoln to be a skilled and popular orator. These debates, which were generally known at the time as the "Douglas-Lincoln Debates" (the incumbent Douglas being the far better known of the two men at the time), were scarcely debates at all in the modern meaning of the term, but as Allen Guelzo has pointed out, "They were sequences of speeches, with only the most meager nod in the direction of interaction between speakers. . . . If there was any clear goal in view with sequential-speech debates, it seemed principally to be getting transcribed and reported in newspapers or published afterward as books. Either way, debate was more often an affirmation of print, rather than a triumph of voice."[22]

Nicolay observed the Douglas-Lincoln race for the U.S. Senate with great interest, writing articles for the *Chicago Tribune* and the *Pike County Free Press* under the name of "Sangamon," in which he elucidated basic Republican principles concerning the evils of slavery and its extension, the betrayal of the Missouri Compromise created by Douglas's Kansas-Nebraska Act, and the dangers of the "Slave Power Conspiracy" of the South. It is not known whether Nicolay was present at any of the seven debates between Douglas and Lincoln. If he was in attendance, no mention of it can be found in his notes or other papers. It is known that he was present to report on a speech given by Douglas in Pittsfield in August 1858, in which Douglas dragged out "his favorite misrepresentations—stating, for instance, that Lincoln was in favor of negro equality—of a war on the South—of abolishing slavery in the States &c." Nicolay reported that the boisterous crowd heckled Douglas at points, with shouts of "That's a lie!" and "We know better!"[23]

Nicolay was also present when Lincoln made a campaign visit to Pittsfield on September 30–October 1, 1858. Lincoln liked to follow up his debates with Douglas by making campaign-tour appearances that shadowed those of his opponent, and Pittsfield offered the prospect of a large crowd since he was well known in the community. As Louis Fischer noted in his article on Lincoln's visit to Pittsfield, "Lincoln liked speaking after Douglas for another reason, for Lincoln was known to have written to a political friend, it 'is the very thing . . . it is in fact, a concluding speech on him.'"[24] After finishing his two-hour speech, Lincoln engaged in the backslapping and joke-swapping camaraderie typical of nineteenth-century politics. When the folksy interchanges were complete, Lincoln joined Nicolay for cider and gingerbread at Heck's Bakery, highlighting once again the close personal affinity each man had for the other.[25] Despite Lincoln's personal popularity in Pittsfield, the election of 1858 found Pike County voting Democrat as usual, thus sending that party's candidates to the state legislature, who would in turn cast votes for Douglas's reelection.[26]

The importance of the Lincoln-Douglas debates and the subsequent publication of those debates during the campaign of 1860, in which Nicolay would have a significant role, should not be underestimated. The *New York Times,* a Republican paper, stated that in 1858 Illinois was "the most interesting political battle-ground in the Union,"[27] and the *Richmond Enquirer* observed that "the great battle of the next Presidential election is being fought in Illinois."[28] Republican politics on the national level and Lincoln's campaign had been complicated in 1858 by Douglas's break with his own party over the ill-fated proslavery Lecompton Constitution of Kansas, which President Buchanan favored and Douglas opposed. Major Eastern newspapers that generally favored Republican positions and candidates came out in praise of Douglas over this issue. Even the stalwart Republican senator William H. Seward praised Douglas. Illinois senator Lyman Trumbull wrote to Lincoln on January 3, 1858, that he approved of the actions being pursued by Senator Douglas, and Horace Greeley's praise of Douglas over the Lecompton issue was loud and clear in the *New York Tribune* (a newspaper read by thousands of Illinois subscribers). From December 1857 through June 1858, Greeley urged Republicans to work with Douglas, supported his reelection to the Senate, and as late as June 1858 expressed regret at Lincoln's bid to oppose him in the U.S. Senate race. Even more problematic for Lincoln and anti-Douglas

Illinois Republicans was "the real delight of eastern politicos and editors that he [Douglas] might be[come] a Republican recruit."[29]

Despite Lincoln's overall strong showing in the campaign against Douglas, enough Democrats were elected to the Illinois legislature on November 2, 1858, to assure that this body, rather than the voters of Illinois themselves, would again send Douglas to the Senate when the new General Assembly began its session in January 1859.[30] In this contest with Douglas, Lincoln had succeeded, however, in making a national name for himself as an antislavery, Republican voice of reason, with potential as a possible contender for the party's 1860 presidential nomination. Nicolay, the clerk in the capitol building in Springfield, "had the satisfaction of believing he played a small part in making Mr. Lincoln's views better known" through his writings.[31] Six days after the 1858 election in Illinois made it clear that Lincoln was not going to the U.S. Senate, he did Nicolay the favor of writing a letter of introduction to Horace Greeley, who had not been helpful in Lincoln's campaign against Douglas, indicating that Nicolay would like to be a correspondent for Greeley's newspaper.[32] Apparently, Greeley was disinclined to consider a request from the defeated senatorial candidate as there is no record of Nicolay ever writing for the *New York Tribune* despite his background as a newspaper publisher and a correspondent for several Midwestern newspapers. Fortunately for Nicolay, he would remain an obscure figure to an East Coast political elite, their disinterest in him making it possible for Nicolay to become Lincoln's private secretary and a significant contributor to the president's success during the Civil War.

While carrying out the duties of chief clerk to the Illinois secretary of state in 1859, Nicolay took advantage of some opportunities that came his way, while declining others. He pursued a course of reading in the law, mentored by his friend and boss Ozias Hatch, which resulted in his licensure as "Attorney and Counselor at Law" by the Illinois Supreme Court on January 7, 1859.[33] He joined a Zouave militia known as the Springfield Grays, in which he held the rank of second lieutenant. He frequented the home of wealthy banker Nicholas Ridgely along with other Springfield young adults, where "music and gaity [*sic*] reigned, and foreign languages were the fashion."[34] His facility with languages would have made him a popular participant in these festivities. He was sent a letter in July 1859 asking him to consider involvement in the startup of a new daily newspaper in Springfield, for which he would be "a most proper Editor" and "undoubtedly qualified."[35] Despite this flattery, he declined the offer, apparently wanting enough time to pursue his career in the secretary of state's office along with his other interests, including Therena back home in Pittsfield.

By this time, the relationship between George and Therena (called "Maggie" by George) had developed into something approaching, if not yet officially, an engagement. It is clear that George and Maggie cared for each other; Nicolay returned to Pittsfield as often as he could, and Therena also traveled to Springfield to visit him. It would be several years, however, before the serious, careful, and sometimes painfully reticent Nicolay was ready to commit himself to matrimony, although the ever-patient Therena appears to have always been his only serious romantic interest.

In May 1859, Nicolay's life in Springfield was further enlivened by the arrival in town of his younger friend from his Pittsfield days, John Milton Hay. Having completed his education at Brown University, where he was named class poet, Hay returned to Illinois and after a few months somewhat reluctantly determined to study law under the tutelage of his uncle, Milton Hay, whose Springfield law office was adjacent to Lincoln's. Finding Springfield a place of "dreary wastes" after his time in New England, the then twenty-one-year-old Hay nonetheless developed a lively social life that included participation in the soirees at the Ridgely household that Nicolay had discovered some time before. Nicolay and Hay, both now in their twenties, rekindled their boyhood friendship, although Nicolay's interest in politics was not initially shared by Hay. Only two weeks before the Republican presidential nominating convention in Chicago in May 1860, Hay wrote to a female friend from his university days of his political apathy: "I occupy myself very pleasantly in thoroughly hating both sides, and abusing the particular tenets of the company I happen to be in.... This position of dignified neutrality I expect to hold for a very long time unless Lincoln is nominated at Chicago."[36] Lincoln's nomination and election would dramatically change the worlds of both Nicolay and Hay.

A few months earlier and completely unknown to him in early 1860, Nicolay's future was about to bring forth amazing opportunities and changes he could never have dreamed possible, thanks to the growing political aspirations of Abraham Lincoln. The state's Republican leadership met with Lincoln in Springfield, urging him to allow his name to be placed in nomination for the presidency. However, the leadership saw Lincoln more as a favorite-son candidate with the idea of making him the vice presidential nominee.[37] Lincoln accepted the proposal because he had another, larger plan in mind.

As the 1860 political nominating season approached, William Henry Seward, the abolitionist senator from Auburn, New York, was the presumptive Republican presidential nominee. But many viewed Seward as too radical. In a speech delivered in Rochester, New York, on October 25, 1858, he had done great harm to his candidacy when he described, in apocalyptic terms, the political struggle between the free and slave systems as an "irresistible conflict" that was leading the nation toward disaster. His speech had enraged the South and frightened the North. Seward had also made enemies in the North because of his principled opposition to the nativist attacks on immigrants. With the Know-Nothings now merging into the Republican ranks, this resulted in more Seward opponents within the senator's own party. On the other hand, Seward had strong support among the German American immigrant community within the party. Consequently, while Seward may have been the presumptive Republican standard-bearer, he did not have the nomination locked up. If Seward faltered, there would be other candidates waiting in the wings.

Lincoln was one of those prospective rivals. He had begun to gather support for his own nomination—and becoming vice president was not what he had in mind. With the Lincoln-Douglas debates having generated considerable interest not only in Illinois but across the country, Lincoln began to lay the groundwork for his dark-horse presidential campaign by actively supporting the Republican gubernatorial candidate in Ohio, William Dennison. After the campaign, some Republican leaders in Ohio who were not backing the favorite-son presidential candidacy of Salmon P. Chase decided that the debates between Douglas and Lincoln should be published.[38] Lincoln agreed. Nicolay was entrusted to deliver a scrapbook of the debates to the publishing firm of Follett, Foster and Company in Columbus, Ohio, rather than "risk their loss by any public conveyance." Lincoln wrote a private letter of introduction for Nicolay to the publisher, Samuel Galloway. Lincoln introduced Nicolay as a "printer, I believe and certainly has conducted a newspaper," and informed Galloway that Nicolay "can give you something of my views a little more in detail than I could write them." Further elucidating on Nicolay's standing, Lincoln told Galloway in a postscript that "Mr. Nicolay is a good Republican . . . a good man and worthy of any confidence that may be bestowed upon him."[39] After successfully completing his mission, Nicolay reported that in Columbus he received a kind reception, with folks being "very ardent" in their expressions of support for Lincoln.[40] In all of this, he was again proving to be a useful, competent, and trustworthy assistant.

Lincoln's letter to Galloway reveals a great deal about Nicolay's relationship to Lincoln. The statement that Lincoln "believe[d]" that Nicolay had been a printer demonstrated Lincoln's unfamiliarity with what Nicolay had done in the offices of the *Free Press*. Thomas W. Shastid's story of directing Lincoln to Nicolay to have some handbills printed indicates that Nicolay, as well as most small newspapers of the time, supplemented his income with small printing jobs. Yet, Lincoln's conditional statement indicates clearly that he did not remember hiring Nicolay's services as a printer while he was in Pittsfield. But through their many conversations over chess and also through his friend and Pike County resident Ozias Hatch, Lincoln would have learned quite a few details about Nicolay's activities as editor of the *Pike County Free Press*. Given his past experiences, Nicolay was the perfect messenger to deal with the publishers, Follett, Foster and Company. The level of trust that Lincoln held in Nicolay is also clearly documented in the letter. Nicolay was dispatched to deliver these sensitive documents in person lest they be lost in the mails or intercepted by Lincoln's political opponents. Lincoln stated clearly that Nicolay could also give Samuel Galloway "something of my views a little more in detail than I could write them." That is, Nicolay was trusted to provide the editor with more in-depth information about Lincoln's plans and wishes than Lincoln dared to put in writing. The missive also conveys the suggestion that Nicolay, as Lincoln's emissary, would follow his instructions to the letter. But the postscript was Lincoln's unequivocal endorsement of Nicolay's trustworthiness. It is a powerful testimonial to the confidence and trust Lincoln had developed in the young man.

As the publication of the Lincoln-Douglas debates moved forward, Nicolay decided that he would take steps to move the candidacy of his idol forward into the public limelight. Aware that Lincoln was contemplating a presidential run and knowing that Lincoln was traveling to New York to give a major speech at the Cooper Union, Nicolay wrote the following editorial for the *Pike County Journal* (the successor to the *Free Press*), which appeared on February 9, 1860. His enthusiastic portrayal of Lincoln as a desirable presidential candidate was well intentioned, premature, and seriously flawed:

FOR PRESIDENT ABRAHAM LINCOLN—Subject to the decision of the National Republican Convention

We are very confident that we express the almost unanimous sentiment of the Republican Party of Pike County in the announcement we make at the head of this article—a sentiment founded not only on the personal attachment to and admiration for Mr. Lincoln, but prompted also by a careful estimate of his qualifications both as to his fitness and availability to be chosen as the candidate in the upcoming campaign. It is conceded that the states of Pennsylvania, New Jersey, Indiana and Illinois will be the decisive battleground in the approaching contest, and of them Pennsylvania and Illinois are most hopeful of Republican success. While Mr. Lincoln would be as acceptable to the Republican voters of Pennsylvania as any man whose name has yet been mentioned, we know he is beyond comparison the strongest man for the state of Illinois. We do not state this on mere speculation. The fact is susceptible of demonstration by figures. Give us Lincoln as the candidate and we can promise the electoral vote of Illinois for the Republicans as a sure result. It is due to the growing interest and power of the West that the next Republican convention shall give her a candidate on the Republican ticket, and to no man in the West does the honor more preeminently belong than to Lincoln. From the introduction of the Nebraska bill to the present time he has fought the extension of slavery as the champion chosen and pitted against the apostle of popular sovereignty, and has wrested triumph after triumph from the Little Giant for Republicanism in the West.

We will have yet one more battle with the delusion of Douglasism in the state of Illinois, and with no man's weapons can we arm ourselves as securely or fight as successfully as with the arguments offensive and defensive with which Abe Lincoln has furnished us. Whatever may be the choice of the politicians, the people of Illinois are undoubtedly for Lincoln. They know him honest and capable, a man of simple habits and plain manners, but possessing a true heart and one of the noblest intellects in the land. He maintains the faith of the fathers of the Republic, he believes in the Declaration of Independence, he yields obedience to the Constitution and laws of his country. He has the radicalism of Jefferson and of Clay, and the conservatism of Washington and Jackson. In his hands the Union would be safe.[41]

Fortunately for Lincoln, this editorial hagiography received little attention, partly because the author was essentially unknown outside of Pike County, Springfield, and a small circle of Illinois Republican activists. One thing Lincoln did not want was to be associated with any form of radicalism. Lincoln's strategy to unseat Seward as the frontrunner for the presidential nomination was based on the premise that his moderate conservative persona was far more appealing to Northern voters than Seward's perceived radicalism on slavery and his outspoken opposition to nativism. For Nicolay to associate Lincoln with "radicalism" was to undermine him as the best alternative to Seward. Nicolay further demonstrated his political and historical tone-deafness in this case by referring to Henry Clay, a demigod in the pantheon of Whig-turned-Republican politicians, as a "radical." Lincoln admired and patterned himself after the Great Compromiser, whom he had come to know personally. Clay, himself a Kentucky slaveholder and defender of the status quo, fought his whole political life for moderation, compromise, and union against the sectional extremism of both North and South. The work of Clay, the architect of the Missouri Compromise and the Compromise of 1850, was undone two years after his death by Douglas's Kansas-Nebraska bill, which had aroused Lincoln out of his self-imposed political retirement. Not only did Nicolay's editorial mislabel Clay and Lincoln as "radical," but it also described the iconoclastic Andrew Jackson, the "great Satan" of Whig politics, as a "conservative" on par with Washington. Furthermore, his editorial clearly identified Lincoln as a regional Western candidate, at a time when Lincoln was trying to develop his stature as a national political figure. While Nicolay was well intentioned in February 1860, had this editorial seen wide circulation and been linked in any way to Lincoln, it could have been detrimental to Lincoln's chances to win the Republican presidential nomination. Young Nicolay was on this occasion afflicted with an ailment described by St. Paul: he had "zeal . . . but not according to knowledge."[42] At times one must be wary of one's friends, and Lincoln, no doubt, took note of his good friend's political naiveté as well as his devotion.

Two weeks after Nicolay's editorial, Lincoln spoke before an audience at the Cooper Union in New York City, hoping to dispel his image as an uncouth western man of the frontier and converting himself into the national and moderate figure he needed to be if his presidential aspirations were to succeed. In the speech, Lincoln contrasted himself not only with Seward's perceived radicalism but that of many Southern politicians. He laid out a moderately conservative agenda: the protection of slavery where it existed, enforcement of the unpopular but lawful Fugitive Slave Act, commitment to the maintenance of the Union, and prohibition of slavery's expansion to new territories. These were the political tenets first laid out at the editor's conference in Decatur, Illinois, in February 1856, very possibly ghostwritten by Lincoln himself. The Cooper Union speech was a rousing success, despite a widely shared view that when he rose to speak, "Lincoln made a picture which did not fit in with New York's conception of a finished statesman."[43] Matthew Brady's photo of Lincoln taken earlier in the day of his speech made him look strikingly presidential; Lincoln is reported to have later remarked, "Brady and the Cooper Institute made me President."[44] Nicolay, as it turned out, would also have a role to play, not only in making Lincoln president but also in crafting a verbal image of Lincoln for posterity.

Lincoln's success at the Cooper Union made him a viable candidate in the eyes of enough eastern Republicans that he became a genuine contender for the Republican presidential nomination to be decided in Chicago in May 1860. He was certainly not the frontrunner, and his experience and name recognition lagged well behind the likes of William Seward and Salmon P. Chase, senator from Ohio. But the Republican convention was scheduled in the up-and-coming city of Chicago, and this gave Lincoln some home-state advantage. What made the Republican convention even more interesting was that a couple of weeks before the Republicans met, the Democrats had unraveled at their Charleston convention and failed to unite behind a single candidate or even a platform on which the delegates could agree. The Democratic Party effectively split into two factions: a new Baltimore convention nominated Illinois senator Stephen A. Douglas in June, while disaffected Southerners selected Vice President John C.

The Wigwam in Chicago, site of the 1860 Republican national convention attended by Nicolay on Lincoln's behalf. It was here that Lincoln received the Republican Party's presidential nomination on the third ballot. The building, built by Chicago business-men to attract the Republican convention in 1860, was later used as an early urban shopping mall containing seventeen stores. It succumbed to a fire in 1869.

Breckinridge, a Kentucky slaveholder, to represent their interests. To make the Republicans even more gleeful, a third party of pro-Union Southerners on May 10 selected John Bell of Tennessee to run on the Constitutional Union ticket.

The Democrats' failed Charleston convention and a Southern third-party movement was enough to put the scent of Republican victory in the air at the Wigwam, the temporary structure built for the Republican gathering. Of course, it all depended on selecting the right candidate. Nicolay believed that candidate to be Lincoln, and off he went to Chicago, as a Lincoln supporter but officially as a correspondent for the *Missouri Democrat*.[45] He still had journalism in his blood, and he was in his element as he reported the events in Chicago. His later recollection of the 1860 Republican convention, captured in the narrative of the Nicolay-Hay history, contains rare rhetorical flourishes that Nicolay could conjure up when he wanted to depart from his otherwise matter-of-fact reporting style. His narrative describes the "rolling cheers" for the favorite-son candidates as they entered the hall, a "solemn hush" during the opening prayer, and "the low wave-like roar of its ordinary conversation." He also recorded that the New York delegation had "deceived itself" when it expected the wholehearted support of the New England delegations, which failed to materialize. Yet he did not explain or seem to care why the New England delegates failed to support Seward. Apparently, he did not care; all he knew was that the delegates' betrayal would assist his hero in achieving his destiny amid the "wildest hurrahs."[46]

Nicolay's description of the events at the Wigwam again reveals a serious political naiveté first exhibited in his editorial endorsement of Lincoln for the presidency. In this description, written years later, he presented his hero as the only, preordained alternative to Seward. There is nothing about the behind-the-scenes deal-making and political maneuvers that made Lincoln the alternative to Seward and propelled him to the nomination. Yet, unknown to Nicolay, these machinations would help make him Lincoln's choice as his private secretary. Nicolay could take satisfaction in his contribution to the publication of the Lincoln-Douglas Debates, copies of which were made available at the Chicago convention. Distribution of these debate transcripts helped further Lincoln's reputation as a moderate, which the *Chicago Press and Tribune* used to endorse Lincoln as just the right compromise candidate between the conservative Edward Bates and the more controversial William Seward.[47]

While Nicolay was present to savor the moment of victory in Chicago, Abraham Lincoln was not. As custom dictated, Lincoln stayed away from the convention, remaining at home in Springfield. He spent May 18, 1860, first playing an early form of handball in a vacant lot next to the *Illinois Journal,* then going to his law office, where he later received a telegram delivered by a messenger from the *Journal,* informing him of the results of the first ballot. Lincoln left the office of Lincoln and Herndon and waited out the second- and third-ballot results in the *Illinois Journal* building. He then headed the few blocks to his home, saying to gathering well-wishers, "Well Gentlemen there is a little woman at our house who is probably more interested in this dispatch than I am."[48]

A jubilant Nicolay returned to Springfield with one ambition—to write the campaign biography of Abraham Lincoln. George would be severely disappointed that the biography went to another individual, the young William Dean Howells. He admitted that Howells "performed the task much more worthily than I could have done." However, while bitterly expressing his disappointment to O. M. Hatch, he was informed that he would become Lincoln's campaign secretary. It was, according to Helen, "the proudest moment of my father's life."[49] Nicolay later wrote, naïvely as ever, that since he had not solicited the position, Lincoln had appointed him "simply on account of the acquaintanceship" formed over a chessboard in Mr. Hatch's office.[50]

Nicolay's letter to Therena, informing her of his appointment, is in his typically restrained style. He wrote her that "Mr. Lincoln has engaged me to act as his private secretary, during the campaign, and pays me at the rate of $75 per month. . . . He has a room here in the State House, and so I go right along without any change of quarters."[51] Despite having been appointed private secretary and acknowledging that Howells had "performed the task more worthily" than he could, he never forgave Howells for being chosen by his hero, Lincoln, over him for the honor of authoring the campaign biography. Over eighty years later, Helen gave a more detailed and poignant account of her father's disappointment, which she heard in the privacy of the Nicolay home. "With no strangers present," he told his daughter that he was "shaken out of his usual reticence" and that he had "chokingly expressed to Mr. Hatch his disappointment," even though he would "not have exchanged the memory of the moment [when he learned from Hatch that he was to be Lincoln's secretary] for the greatest gift an emperor could bestow."[52] Yet, even with this more significant appointment, Nicolay would never forget his disappointment and chagrin that the twenty-three-year-old Howells had been selected for the important task of writing the campaign biography.

Howells, by that time a published poet, was working as a proofreader for Follett, Foster, and Company, which had published the Lincoln-Douglas debates.[53] With the assistance of noted agriculturalist and author John L. Hayes, he wrote a book entitled *Lives and Speeches of Abraham Lincoln and Hannibal Hamlin*.[54] Howells wrote the Lincoln biography, Hayes the biography of Hamlin, the Republicans' vice-presidential nominee. In the preface, Howells admitted that the work was "hurried" but yet was based on the "remembrance of Mr. Lincoln's old friends," suggesting that extensive interviews had taken place.[55] Since the book deadline was a month after Lincoln's nomination, Howells had no opportunity to interview Lincoln or anyone else. The material for the book came from published articles and materials gathered by an assistant named James Q. Howard.[56] According to Howells biographer Susan Goodman, the biography was completed in just over a week.[57] The biography was an example of an instant campaign biography like the ones written today for popular consumption. Howells, who would write such American classics as *The Rise of Silas Lapham*, was later rewarded by Lincoln with a consulship in Venice.

Although Lincoln liked Nicolay, Lincoln could not trust him with the campaign biography. His February 1860 editorial had revealed him as a political novice. His enthusiasm for Lincoln could also get the best of him. There could be no allusions to the "radical" Clay or the "conservative" Jackson in this biography. The biography would be read by a national audience, not merely the readers of the *Free Press*. There would be no time to correct any errors. A misstep could cost Lincoln the presidency. Furthermore, it would have been difficult, if not impossible, for the fastidious Nicolay, the journalist and editorial wordsmith, to have produced such an instantaneous work on his idol.

As he saw it, Nicolay had been denied an opportunity, indeed the critical first opportunity before the nation, to define the Lincoln image. He overlooked the fact it had been his idol Lincoln, not Howells, who had denied him. Throughout the Springfield years, he had repeatedly proven himself to be a reliable, hardworking advocate on Lincoln's behalf. Beyond Lincoln's affinity for him, Nicolay had proven that he could be trusted with tasks large and small but that there were things such as the campaign biography that were best left to others. Lincoln, always the principled pragmatist, knew that Nicolay would not be the appropriate choice for this task, even with his journalistic credentials. What he did possess was a set of organizational and personal skills that Lincoln found essential in his new role as a presidential candidate.

Nicolay's duties included greeting visitors, arranging appointments, and handling correspondence. He was a bit overwhelmed by the surge of correspondence that came in daily. Initially, the volume was around fifty letters a day, but that increased significantly over the course of the campaign when it became clearer that Lincoln was likely to be the next president. After the election, when the correspondence grew even more, George brought in John Hay, presumably with Lincoln's permission, to assist him.[58] To help his overburdened secretary and perhaps to keep himself from saying too much before the November election, Lincoln composed a form letter for Nicolay to use in response to those asking Lincoln to make statements on various political issues:

Dear Sir:

Your letter to Mr. Lincoln of _____ by which you seek to obtain his opinions on certain political points has been received by him. He has received others of a similar character; but he also has a greater number of the exactly opposite character. The latter class beseech him to write nothing whatever upon any point of political doctrine. They say his positions were well known when he was nominated, and that he must not now embarrass the canvass by undertaking to shift or modify them. He regrets that he cannot oblige all, but you perceive it is impossible for him to do so.

Yours &c

J. G. Nicolay[59]

The Governor's Room in the State Capitol, a chamber of about fifteen by twenty-five feet, was loaned to Lincoln for use as a reception and work room during the presidential campaign. According to eyewitness journalist Henry Villard (like Nicolay a German immigrant and later to become the son-in-law of famed abolitionist William Lloyd Garrison), the room was "altogether inadequate for the accommodation of Mr. Lincoln's visitors. Twenty persons will not find standing room in it, and the simultaneous presence of a dozen only will cause inconvenience. The room is furnished with a sofa, half-a-dozen armchairs, a table and a desk, the latter being assigned to the private secretary [Mr. Nicolay], who is always present during visiting hours." Villard also noted the presence of "countless letters and files of newspapers, and quite an assortment of odd presents."[60] Nicolay was also responsible for accepting, inventorying, and handling the numerous gifts sent to candidate Lincoln. The Governor's Room "took on the aspect of a museum, so many axes and wedges and log-chains were sent to the candidate." While in actuality embarrassed by this outpouring of mementos because of his poverty-ridden frontier background, Lincoln made the best of these gifts that flooded in from well-intentioned well-wishers who apparently saw the Railsplitter's humble origins as a great virtue. According to Helen, "He [Lincoln] used them [his "pioneer" gifts] in his explanations and anecdotes of pioneer days, making them serve the double purpose of amusing his visitors and keeping the conversation away from dangerous political reefs."[61]

Meanwhile, Nicolay was also charged with preparing a compilation of Stephen A. Douglas's often contradictory positions on the slavery question. Entitled *The Political Record of Stephen A. Douglas on the Slavery Question*, it was to be published under the auspices of the Illinois Republican Central Committee.[62] The sixteen-page political pamphlet covered Douglas's service in Congress from 1845 to 1860. Divided into three parts, "Antislavery," "Pro-Slavery," and "Miscellaneous," the pamphlet reproduced selective quotes from speeches given in Congress, reports from congressional committees, the Lincoln-Douglas debates, and other speeches crafted to demonstrate Douglas's shifting views on slavery. The pamphlet was well received and went through three printings during the campaign of 1860. As a political document, it presented a scathing indictment of Douglas's unprincipled and vacillating stances on slavery. The nature of the publication did not give Nicolay an opportunity to editorialize on Douglas's candidacy beyond brief asides. He completed his assignment with distinction, his journalistic background again serving his friend and boss well.

Nicolay, being candidate Lincoln's only paid staff member, was kept quite busy during the summer and fall of 1860. Not only did mail flood into the Illinois State Capitol, but each morning at about ten o'clock, when Lincoln came into the Governor's Room, he would bring to Nicolay's desk the piles of letters he had received at his home address, a few blocks away. Following the tradition that the candidate did not campaign, Lincoln remained secluded from the public view beyond Springfield, making no campaign speeches and saying little in response to correspondence he received. This was felt by party operators to be the safest course of action for candidate Lincoln to take, although it must have been difficult for a man with the political ambition of Lincoln to remain on the sidelines during an exciting and crucial campaign season. The situation was exacerbated by the whirlwind campaigning of Stephen A. Douglas, who cast aside tradition and was, it seemed, everywhere in the country actively seeking votes. When Lincoln's law partner Herndon visited him in the Capitol, he described Lincoln as "bored—bored badly. I would not have his place and be bored as he is."[63]

Nicolay, on the other hand, was too busy to be bored. His letters to Therena in Pittsfield indicate his desire and intention to write to her daily, but he generally failed at this, stating often, as he did in a letter of July 16, 1860, "as usual my other work today has occupied me so that I have had no time." On August 9, he wrote her that "I was up until two or three o'clock both last night, and the night

before and as a consequence am most too tired and sleepy to write a letter. . . .
Good night! Your George."[64] It was not until October that he informed her that
"a great many letters have been written to Mr. Lincoln on the subject . . . [of]
being killed off by the cares of the presidency—or as is sometimes hinted by
foul means. It is astonishing how the popular sympathy for Mr. Lincoln draws
fearful forebodings."[65] The intensity and volume of death threats upon Lincoln
must have increased as the election approached for Nicolay to make special note
of this, since such menacing messages were unfortunately common in political
campaigns. Today, of course, unlike in Lincoln's time, threats against public
officials are quickly investigated and can result in severe consequences.

The election of Abraham Lincoln as the sixteenth president of the United
States on November 6, 1860, sent shock waves through the South and jubilation
through the North. Lacking our current ability to call election results often even
before the polls are closed, it took days to know for a certainty who had won. On
Thursday, November 8, Nicolay wrote to Therena, "I intended writing you a few
words last night, but in the excitement and hurry of watching and receiving the
news [of Lincoln's election] did not find time to do so." And then, in understated
Nicolay fashion, he continued, "We have heard enough to make it certain that Mr.
Lincoln is elected President, and we of course all feel happy over it."[66] It would
not be until November 18 that he was able to write to Therena, "A dispatch has
just come in from San Francisco indicating that the Republicans have carried
California. . . . I have no promise of an early chance to visit Pittsfield. From appearances I shall continue to be right busy for some time to come. Just think of
my probably having to read 80 and perhaps 100 letters a day for the next three
months!"[67]

Nicolay now switched roles from being Lincoln's entire campaign staff to being
his one-man transition team. President-elect Lincoln was now sporting a new
look—he had begun his transition into the presidency with the beginnings of
a beard, suggested by an eleven-year-old New York girl who had told him in a
letter that his face was too thin and that the ladies would like him in a beard and
get their husbands to vote for him. Perhaps, too, Lincoln thought the thin-faced
Nicolay's chin whiskers made him more distinguished looking. Historian Ronald
White has described how the two bearded men had their work cut out for them
as they worked together at a corner table. White has drawn a busy picture of
daily life in the office: the clamor for political appointments for themselves or
others "cascaded in from Republican leaders," along with hate mail from the slave
states "comparing Lincoln to the devil," as well as letters threatening the life of the

president-elect by a myriad of means and frequently signed by pseudonyms.[68] All this and more required Nicolay's attention.

While many of Nicolay's letters to Therena are extant, sadly, precious few of her letters to him survive. It is known that in a letter dated December 2, 1860, he responded to her inquiry, "What about secession?" Describing Southern "excitement and anger" as "very foolish" and "very unreasonable," he downplayed the threat of secession, stating that "there is not a single reason why they should secede now." He went on to reiterate that the Republican Party would not have control of Congress and would not have the authority "for two years at least" to effectuate their platform. However, Nicolay then did some thoughtful reflecting and a little back-pedaling. Hedging his bets, he suggested that if secession did come and the "grand American experiment of free government is to be a failure," it would be better that "we should know it now."[69]

Perhaps he was trying to reassure Therena, since her father, Dorus Bates, was a Democrat and Southern sympathizer. But again, his political naiveté shows through. He seems not to have understood that the South felt hemmed in. While there would be no prohibition of slavery in the territories, there would be no new slave states, no attempts to annex Cuba or seize other potential new slave territory. There would not be any more filibustering operations. A Republican president would be nominating several new justices to the Supreme Court, including, quite possibly, a replacement for the octogenarian chief justice, Roger B. Taney.[70] A Republican president would have the power to appoint judges, postmasters, tax collectors at the ports, and a host of lesser officials in the Southern states. These individuals, beholden to the antislavery party in Washington for their benefices, could form the nucleus of an antislavery party in the South. Furthermore, the electoral alliance between the South and the Northern Democratic Party had been shattered. The prospect of the free states electing a succession of antislavery presidents was now very real. The South had lost the levers of national power, but Nicolay did not seem to have grasped this, nor that dissolution of the Union would inevitably result in civil war.

A week later in a lengthy letter dated December 13, 1860, he wrote Therena one of the more interesting letters of their correspondence, in part apparently triggered by Therena's annoyance at the brevity of some of his notes to her. George, who appeared to be a little frustrated himself, replied: "If . . . I had the power to write as rapidly as I could think, there is no doubt but that you would be annoyed with the prolixity rather than the brevity of my epistles. . . . What a melange it would be if the fragmentary and disjointed ideas that flit through one's brain for ten minutes even could be fixed on paper by some subtle system of mental photography!" He then went on to hint for the first time that there were some things he could not share with her, teasingly confiding, "I have no news of importance . . . which I am at liberty to communicate." In this same letter, he suggested that he had "evidence" he deemed "a sufficient guaranty that my present confidential relation to him [Lincoln] will be continued." However, he failed to comment on how the continuation of his "present confidential relation" might impact his relationship with Therena.

In this unusually long letter, Nicolay then turned to his observations about secession and Lincoln's reaction to the threat of disunion. After noting that "the secessionists are still rampant," he stated that Lincoln, "while he is not unmindful of the troubles" and "wishes that they were not existing," was not in the least intimidated or frightened by them Then, George changed direction again and ended on an uncharacteristically romantic note: "I sit here, and shutting my eyes at the murkiness of the clouds, and my ears to the patter of the noise, vainly imagine how pleasant it would be to sit beside you for the evening. I would be willing to give you a dozen warm kisses to have the vision made real." He signed the letter, "Your George."[71]

On this same day he wrote to Therena, Nicolay put together a brief written summary of what he perceived to be Lincoln's views on secession. One could raise a suspicion that he already had conceived in the back of his mind the idea that someday he would write the biography of Lincoln that had been denied him during the campaign of 1860 and that it was not too early to start making notes. Written in the form of a legal brief, his observations about Lincoln and secession reflected Lincoln's ability as a practicing attorney to distill the issues to their essential points. It provides posterity with an important summary of the thinking of the president-elect at this critical moment in time.

Springfield Dec 13th 1860

From conversations and expressions at different times during the last three weeks I think the following are substantially his [Lincoln's] opinions about secession:

The very existence and organization of a general and national government, implies both the legal power, right and duty of maintaining its own integrity. This if not expressed it is at least implied in the Constitution.

The right of a state to secede is not an open or debateable [sic] question. It was fully discussed in Jackson's time, and denied not only by him, but also by a vote . . . in Congress.

It is the duty of a President to execute the laws, and maintain the existing Government. He cannot entertain any proposition for dissolution or dismemberment. He was not elected for any such purpose.

As a matter of theoretical speculation it is probably true that if the people, (with whom the whole question rests) should become tired of the present government they may change it in the manner prescribed by the Constitution.[72]

On December 20, a week after this internal memorandum was written, South Carolina issued a declaration of secession, putting these ideas to the test.

During the postelection period, Lincoln arranged for Nicolay to be present at a table in the back of the room to take notes whenever he met with the influential politicians who traveled to Springfield to proffer their advice, wanted or not, to the president-elect. Nicolay also took notes of interview meetings Lincoln had with prospective cabinet members during this time. When Edward Bates, the powerful Missouri leader who was being considered for attorney general, arrived early at the president-elect's Capitol office in Springfield, it was Nicolay's job to welcome him and make him feel at home until Lincoln's arrival. Being a keen observer of men from his newspaper days, the secretary observed in his conversation with Bates that the Missourian was "very genial and easy—seeming at first to verge on extreme politeness, but soon becoming very attractive." His opinion of the mild-mannered Bates improved when he observed that the man spoke with Lincoln in "clear, concise language . . . indicating a very comprehensive and definite intellectual grasp of ideas." By the time the interview was over, Lincoln had offered Edward Bates the position of attorney general. Nicolay, present throughout the interview, observed that Bates "expressed himself highly gratified at the confidence which Mr. L. manifested in him by the offer just made. He alluded to the fact that years ago he had declined a similar offer made by Mr. Fillmore" but that now the national situation had changed and in Bates's view, "The country was in trouble and danger, and he felt it his duty to sacrifice his personal inclinations, and if he could, to contribute his labor and influence to the restoration of peace in, and the preservation of his country."[73]

Nicolay's role as Lincoln's trusted confidant continued to grow. While Lincoln adopted a self-imposed public silence in the period between his election and his inauguration, the president-elect would confide his sentiments to his private secretary. Nicolay recorded a particular incident in a note dated December 22, 1860. President Buchanan had again demonstrated his unwillingness to assert federal authority even in the face of South Carolina's declaration of secession two days before.

When Mr. Lincoln came to the office this morning, after the usual salutations he asked me what the news was. I asked him if he had seen the morning dispatches. He replied "no." "Then," said I, "there is an important rumor you have not seen. The Times correspondent telegraphs that Buchanan has sent instructions to Maj. Anderson to surrender Fort Moultrie [in Charleston Harbor]if it is attacked."

"If that is true they ought to hang him," said he with warmth.

After some further conversations he remarked—"Among the letters you saw me mail yesterday was one to [Congressman Elihu] Washburne [of Illinois] who had written me that he had just had a long conversation with Gen. [Winfield] Scott, and that the General felt considerably outraged that the President [Buchanan] would not act as he wished him in reinforcing the forts &c. I wrote to Washburne to tell Gen. Scott confidentially, that I wished him to be prepared, immediately after my inauguration to make arrangements at once to hold the forts, or if they have been taken, to take them back again."[74]

Lincoln could entrust these thoughts and sentiments to Nicolay, but no others, because of his confidence that his comments would not go any further than his secretary.

As the year 1860 came to a close, Nicolay wrote to Therena on December 30 that the president-elect's office had moved out of the State Capitol building and Lincoln would now be spending more time at home greeting visitors and preparing for the move to Washington. Nicolay had moved to the Johnson Building, where he would occupy a room sufficiently large to serve both as bedroom and an office, to which "Mr. Lincoln will come . . . occasionally, when I need his advice or he my immediate attention."[75] After being alone in his new quarters for about a week, the stress of the job and isolation was apparently working on his nerves. He wrote to Therena on January 6, 1861, denying that "I have got the blues," but it is clear that he was lonely and really missed her. He indicated that he needed a break from the stress, describing it as a "vague desire to get away from everything and everybody." He told her that he wished her by his side, "you with whom I share my thoughts and feelings and confidence, as with no one else living," adding that she was "nearer to me than any other human being."[76] Nearer perhaps than any human being except Abraham Lincoln, for whom he would put off marrying the then twenty-five-year-old Therena for almost another five years.

Knowing that he would be leaving for Washington in the near future, Nicolay wrote another letter to Therena on January 20 assuring her that his inability to see her the past few months had "wrought up a feeling of no little strength. . . longing for the quietness and the love which I always expect to find by your side."[77] Fearful that he might be too busy to come see her in Pittsfield before leaving with

Lincoln for Washington, he was relieved to be able to write Therena on January 27 that "Mr. Lincoln determined definitely to start from here [Springfield] on the 11th of February. . . . This gives me a few days more time than I expected when I wrote you last. . . . I have determined to try and come over to see you next Saturday—leaving here Friday night and returning on Monday—perhaps Sunday night, as I may be able to find time."[78]

On a rainy February 11, 1861, Lincoln and his party, including Nicolay, boarded a train at the small, unimposing Springfield station a short distance from the Lincoln home and headed east on a circuitous route toward the nation's capital. This would be one of the most significant railroad tours in American history. The specter of civil war hung over the nation. Seven Southern states had already seceded from the Union, and more were threatening to do so. The very existence of the United States was hanging in the balance, as was the future of Abraham Lincoln. Inexorably tied to Lincoln's success or failure was the future of John George Nicolay, the unpretentious German immigrant whom many viewed as an inexplicable choice as presidential secretary.

CHAPTER THREE

A Slow, Strategic Train to Washington

The campaign was over, the voters had made their decision, and the long period between the election and the inauguration was finally drawing to a close. It was time for the president-elect and family, his secretary, and others in the entourage to leave Springfield and head east to the nation's capital. Lincoln set February 11, 1861, the day before his fifty-second birthday, as the date for the departure from Springfield.

The national atmosphere was tense. Fantastic rumors of all sorts were openly discussed and debated, including the possibility of Lincoln being prevented from arriving in Washington for the inauguration by assassination or kidnapping, seizure of the national capital by Southern sympathizers, and disruption of the proceedings of the Electoral College. The newspapers helped spread these and other rumors. At this time, there was no government agency responsible for the safety of the president or available to sort through the daily din of purported plots. Nicolay had been reading such threats almost daily since Lincoln's nomination, and his level of concern for Lincoln's safety had been growing steadily—intensified, no doubt, by what he was reading in the papers. He had even mentioned his concern in a letter to Therena, written shortly before the election, in which he told her that many letters to candidate Lincoln expressed "fearful forebodings" concerning his future.[1] Such was the state of rumors in the country that a Mr. A. W. Flanders of Burlington, Iowa, offered the president-elect a shirt of chain mail for his protection. Flanders was quite persistent in his offers. It fell upon Nicolay to respond to this offer, like so many others, on Lincoln's behalf. Despite

Flanders's persistent entreaties, Nicolay was successful in putting him off until Lincoln's departure from Springfield.[2]

Concerns for Lincoln's safety were valid. Violence was deeply embedded in antebellum culture, in which dueling, mob violence, and other armed altercations were still common. In 1860, there was no practical way to determine which threats were expressions of harmless bravado or matters of genuine concern. Presidential security was left to a few personal bodyguards. This concern for Lincoln's safety was a consideration in selecting the rail route that would be taken to Washington. There were a number of possible routes, the most direct being a train trip from Springfield to St. Louis and then east through Cincinnati to Wheeling, Virginia (now West Virginia). There the Lincoln entourage could have boarded the Baltimore & Ohio Railroad with a direct route to Baltimore and from there to Washington. However, the lines of the B&O Railroad were all below the Mason-Dixon line.[3]

Instead, a more circuitous route across the free states was chosen. As later described by Nicolay, the president-elect had received numerous invitations to speak to Northern audiences, including several state legislatures, "without party distinctions." Similarly, invitations to stop and speak were also tendered by many cities and towns along the route, while "railroads tendered him [Lincoln] special trains for the use of himself and his family."[4] Since railroads did not share their tracks at the time, the more circuitous route would necessitate numerous changes of trains and many more days of travel. The trip would take twelve days, cover nineteen hundred miles, eight states, and seventy different whistle stops, and require the use of eighteen separate railroads.[5] Because of time constraints, Lincoln would stop and speak before all the legislatures that had extended an invitation except that of Massachusetts, which was viewed as too far out of the way. He would also make a stop in Philadelphia at Independence Hall to raise the new thirty-four-star national flag on Washington's Birthday. For Nicolay, it constituted a new adventure. Although he had last visited Washington in 1858, this was the first time he would travel to many of the Northern states.

While there had been journeys to the capital for each new president-elect, the country had not seen anything of this magnitude since the inaugural trip of George Washington from Mount Vernon to New York in 1789. At that time, the country was uniting under a new constitution and beginning the great experiment of launching a federal republic. Americans were also honoring the greatest hero of their Revolution. In the spring of 1861, Lincoln was journeying across the North to unite the free states for the great struggle that many feared was coming and that Lincoln still hoped could somehow be avoided. It was an opportunity for Lincoln to rally the North to the cause of Union. It was also an opportunity for the Northern public to see their new president in person.

For Nicolay, it was an equally momentous journey. The immigrant boy who had arrived in New Orleans almost a quarter century before was going to Washington as the personal secretary to the president of the United States. When his family had arrived in 1837, the main issue related to slavery was whether the newly created Republic of Texas should be admitted to the Union, but now the issue was the very survival of the Union itself. Now he found himself, as Lincoln's secretary, at the center of the maelstrom. Yet, the exhilaration of the crowds certainly enlivened the spirit of the young secretary while lifting the spirits of the entire Lincoln party.

By this time, Lincoln's election had precipitated the secession of seven Southern states, followed by a series of foreboding events that cast a shadow over the nation as the president-elect and his party made their grand tour. On February 4, while the final preparations were being made for Lincoln's inaugural trip, delegations from the first six secessionist states convened in Montgomery, Alabama, to formulate a constitution for the Confederate States of America. Four days later on February 8, the convention adopted a constitution based on the United States Constitution. However, instead of a document to "form a more perfect union," the Confederate Constitution sought merely to "form a permanent federal government." It was a constitution that enshrined perpetual slavery as state policy. There would be no more pretense, as has often been made by Southerners over the decades in the halls of Congress and elsewhere, that the South wanted to find a way to end slavery. The next day, the Confederate Convention elected Jefferson Davis of Mississippi as provisional president and Lincoln's congressional colleague and friend, Alexander Hamilton Stephens of Georgia, as vice president. By taking these actions in rapid succession, the Confederate Convention sought to take advantage of the paralysis of the Buchanan administration and present the president-elect and the Northern people with a fait accompli.

Two decades later, while addressing the secession of South Carolina, Nicolay made a salient point in his 1880 book, *The Outbreak of Rebellion*, about the slaveholder's political philosophy, which in his opinion was their motivation for secession:

Nor can the final and persistent, but false assumption of the South, be admitted that, she was justified by prescriptive privilege; that, because slavery was tolerated at the formation of the government, it must needs be protected in perpetuity. The Constitution makes few features of our system perpetually obligatory. Almost everything is subject to amendment of three-fourths of the States. The New World Republic was formed for reform—not for mere blind conservatism, certainly not for despotic reaction. The slavery question, especially, was ever since 1808 broadly under the control of the people. On one hand the Congress had the power to tolerate the African slave trade; on the other, three-fourths of the States might lawfully abolish slavery, as was done near the close of the Rebellion [i.e., the Civil War]. To effect necessary and salutatory political changes, in the fullness of time, by lawful and peaceful election through constitutional majorities, as a prudent alternative to the violence and horror of revolution [i.e., civil war], is one of the many signal blessings which republican representative government confers on an intelligent nation.[6]

Nicolay had hoped to be in charge of the planning for the trip to Washington, but Thurlow Weed, the New York Republican political boss and a close friend of William H. Seward, had dispatched William S. Wood, a former hotel owner turned travel agent, to fulfill this role, and Lincoln accepted his services. Wood developed a detailed itinerary for the journey, poring over railroad timetables, contacting the affected railroads, making hotel reservations, and dealing with the bizarre fact that each locality determined its own time, thus creating a maze of balkanized time zones throughout the trip. Standard time zones as known today would not be introduced until the 1880s. Wood also prepared detailed instructions to the hotels. The instructions stated that Nicolay and Hay were to have rooms "contingent to the President."[7] Other members of the party were to have rooms as close to Lincoln's as convenient. Given the importance of many members of the party, the location of the secretaries' room must have been dictated by Lincoln himself.

As usual, every politician of note, and many of lesser note, wanted to be on the train with Lincoln. They all believed that being seen with the president-elect would enhance the perception of their power and standing within the new administration. While Nicolay assisted Lincoln in his daily business, he also had to fend off these requests. Thus, when he had asked the president-elect whether John Hay could accompany him to Washington and be his assistant, an exasperated Lincoln initially responded, "We can't take all Illinois with us down to Washington."[8] Nonetheless, Lincoln approved the request, and the White House team of Nicolay and Hay was formed. There is no documentation as to why Lincoln agreed to add Hay to the secretarial staff. Lincoln knew Hay, not only as the friend of his secretary but also as the nephew of his longtime friend

Milton Hay, who had studied law in the Lincoln-Stuart law office and was still a close associate. At some point, Milton Hay had even offered to pay his nephew's salary for six months, but Lincoln declined the offer.[9] The appointment would provide his friend's nephew with a job and, as it turned out, an important start to his successful career. Perhaps during the period after the election, Lincoln had come to realize the magnitude of the correspondence and the variety of tasks that Nicolay would have to face as the presidential secretary. Also, Lincoln thought it a good idea to provide Nicolay with a companion in the White House. It proved to be decision much to Lincoln's liking; once John Hay was part of the team, Lincoln was rarely seen in public without one or the other of his secretaries nearby.

When the train left Springfield on February 11, 1861, there was a formidable presidential party on board. William Turner Coggeshall, a man who would serve as a guard to Lincoln on the train to Washington and, four years later, would accompany Lincoln's body from Washington back to Springfield, left a list of the passengers who accompanied Lincoln on the train after Mary Lincoln and the younger children, Willie and Tad, joined the train at Indianapolis. Robert had

The original Great Western Railroad Depot, a few minutes' walk from the Lincoln home in Springfield. It was from this depot that Lincoln, Nicolay, and other members of the inaugural party boarded a train on a rainy February 11, 1861 at the start of a very indirect trip to Washington, D.C., making stops in many northern cities. Just prior to departure, Lincoln gave a brief farewell address to the assembled crowd. The depot survives, significantly modified with an added second story. (Sangamon County Historical Society)

been a member of the party starting in Springfield. In addition to Lincoln's family, there was a coterie of Lincoln's friends: N. P. Judd, O. H. Browning, David Davis, Ward Hill Lamon, George C. Latham, and J. M. Burgess. By now all of these men would have been known to Nicolay, since they were not only Lincoln's friends but also among his closest advisors, conferring with him on a regular basis.

Along with these politicians were a number of military men, who with one exception were probably unknown to Nicolay before the trip. These were Colonel Edwin V. Sumner, Major David Hunter, Captain John Pope, and everybody's friend, the young Colonel Elmer E. Ellsworth—men with whom Nicolay would correspond on the president's behalf. Rounding out the party was Lincoln's physician, Dr. W. M. Wallace, a nurse, and Nicolay and Hay.[10] Based on her father's notes, Helen's biography added two additional passengers, Lockwood Todd and John Pope, the former a cousin of Mary Todd Lincoln and the latter another, more distant relative by marriage.[11]

Apparently, being on the inaugural train had its career benefits. Each of the military men accompanying Lincoln would play an important role in the Civil War. Colonel Sumner would be promoted to the rank of brigadier general to replace the treasonous General David Twiggs. The appointment came on March 16, 1861, within a fortnight of Lincoln's inauguration. John Pope was a Kentucky native and son of a prominent Illinois judge who was a friend of Lincoln's. Pope would be promoted to brigadier general on May 17, 1861, and for a short time in the summer of 1862 would serve as commander of the Army of the Potomac. After the disaster of Second Bull Run, Pope was sent to Minnesota, where he and Nicolay were destined to interact with each other during the aftermath of the Sioux uprising. Major David Hunter was a career army officer who was serving as an army paymaster stationed at Fort Leavenworth when he wrote the president-elect an impassioned letter in support of Lincoln and the Union. Sufficiently impressed, Lincoln extended a personal invitation to Hunter to join the presidential train. Like the others, Hunter received quick promotions, becoming a brigadier general on May 17, the same day as John Pope. However, Hunter would prove to be an embarrassment, since he, like John C. Frémont, his predecessor in Missouri, would issue a premature and unwelcomed emancipation proclamation; otherwise, however, he had a noteworthy record in the Civil War. Nicolay and Hunter would interact throughout the war. After the war, Hunter presided over the military tribunal that tried the Lincoln assassination conspirators.

The final military man on board was Colonel Elmer E. Ellsworth, the charismatic young leader of a group of Zouaves from Chicago. Henry Villard, then a correspondent for the *New York Herald* who was on the train, referred to Ellsworth as "a sort of pet of Mr. Lincoln."[12] But Ellsworth, born in 1837, fitted in perfectly as a companion to the twenty-nine-year-old Nicolay and the twenty-two-year-old Hay. They had formed a bond during Ellsworth's stay in Springfield. Nicolay, who himself had been a member of a militia unit in Springfield called the Springfield Grays, found a common interest in military matters with Ellsworth. Ellsworth's biographer quoted Nicolay as stating, "I felt almost a direct personal pride and interest in his success." Nicolay, who had been mentored since his meeting with Joel Pennington over a decade before, was assuming the role of the mentor.[13]

Nicolay's duties during the inaugural journey varied with the circumstances. As Lincoln prepared to leave Springfield, he gave what many thought was an extemporaneous speech from the back of the last rail car. While the jaded Villard referred in his memoirs to the speech as "a pathetic formal farewell," he nonetheless claimed credit for the preservation of the speech. Since the speech was "entirely extemporized," he asked Lincoln to write it down "on a pad."[14]

However, there is another claimant to the original document, J. G. Nicolay. Villard's sons, in their work *Lincoln on the Eve of '61*, had a slightly different version of events than their father's. They asserted that the elder Villard had told Lincoln that it was a wonderful address that must be "preserved for posterity." Villard then asked Lincoln to have a copy written out to be telegraphed from the next station for newspapers around the country. Lincoln complied, apparently not knowing that there had been a stenographer present and that John Hay had also taken notes of the event. Nonetheless, "Mr. Lincoln at once complied, wrote the speech out in his own hand and gave the speech to Mr. Villard."[15]

However, according to Nicolay, Villard did not have the original manuscript as he claimed but must have had a copy. Nicolay reserved that honor for himself. He asserted that the address was correctly printed for the first time in the December 1887 issue of the *Century Magazine* "from the original manuscript . . . written down immediately after the train started." Nicolay further claimed that the manuscript was "partly in Mr. Lincoln's own hand, and partly by that of his private secretary [Nicolay] from his [Lincoln's] dictation."[16] In the Lincoln history, where Nicolay's account appears as a footnote, no explanation is given as to why, in the midst of writing out the speech, Lincoln decided to dictate rather than continue writing out the address. Helen Nicolay's account of the event provides some interesting detail that helps sort out the truth. She noted that after the train departed from the Springfield depot, Lincoln "was reminded

that the press would want to print his farewell words." Her account substantiated Villard's claim that Lincoln was told "that the press would want to print his
farewell words." Helen then described Lincoln sitting down "resignedly" to write
out the speech. However, at some point Lincoln handed the pencil to Nicolay
to take dictation.[17]

This is likely because Lincoln was not only tired but the jostling of the train
would have made writing difficult. The original possessed by Nicolay and reproduced in the *Century Magazine* was both in Lincoln's handwriting and his
own; Villard's sons mentioned that the copy they possessed was in Lincoln's
"own hand," to the exclusion of other handwriting. However, the handwriting
in the Villard manuscript was probably Nicolay's, not Lincoln's, for after taking
dictation, Nicolay would likely have prepared a clean copy for Villard.

Nicolay's account is suspiciously silent about who first thought to ask Lincoln
to write down the speech. As he recounted the event, the secretary may later
have had a pique of jealousy that it was Villard, not he, who thought about
memorializing the speech. However, he must have described the event more
fully to Helen, thus leading to the statement by her that Lincoln was reminded
that "the press" would want a copy. Nonetheless, the ever-present secretary was
on hand to relieve the tired president-elect of yet another onerous duty as the
train jostled along the tracks to the party's first stop, Indianapolis. By doing so,
Nicolay came to preserve a very memorable speech that has been reenacted for
over a century and a half on stage and screen.

Nicolay and Hay summarized the journey in their biography of Lincoln: "A
proper description of the Presidential tour which followed would fill a volume.
It embraced two weeks of official receptions by committees, mayors, governors,
and legislatures; of crowded evening receptions and interminable handshakings;
of impromptu or formal addresses at every ceremony; of cheers, salutes, bonfires,
military parades, and imposing processions, amid miles of spectators."[18] Nicolay
and Hay went on to note that for the crowds of well-wishers, "political dissension
was for the moment hushed to the general curiosity to see and hear the man . . .
who had been called to exercise the duties of the Presidential office."[19]

Crowds swarmed everywhere, desiring to see or shake hands with the
president-elect. Security was a real issue. The threats to Lincoln's life, which
had been penned or rumored since almost immediately after his nomination,
prompting Nicolay to express his concerns to Therena the previous October, had
reached a crescendo just prior to the beginning of the trip. The formal proclamation of the Confederate States of America had engendered a renewed sense

of impending danger as its stalwarts North and South focused on preventing the inauguration of Lincoln.

Nicolay wrote Therena from Indianapolis, the first stop on the tour, that the railroad trip had been "rather pleasant." He described the action of the crowds— numbering "50,000 at least," by his estimate, with the Bates House "perfectly jammed full of people." He lamented to her that privacy was nonexistent as "three or four ladies and as many gentlemen have even invaded the room assigned to Mr. Lincoln." And if that were not enough, he reported, he could "hear the crowd pushing and grumbling and shouting" to have access to Lincoln. He told her that "it is a severe ordeal for us, and increased ten-fold for him [Lincoln]."[20] The grand tour was about to turn into the grand nightmare.

An incident occurred at Indianapolis in relation to Lincoln's inaugural address that was long remembered by Nicolay, who later drafted an essay about the trip. The essay was not published in his lifetime. Lincoln had drafted his address in Springfield prior to his departure. He had a single copy made and placed it in a black carpetbag. Lincoln entrusted the bag to the care of his eldest son, Robert. For Lincoln, it was important that the text and tenor of the speech not fall into the hands of the press or his political enemies before its delivery. Nicolay set the stage by describing Robert Lincoln in less than flattering terms, even using the press's uncomplimentary title for him, "The Prince of Rails." According to Nicolay, Robert was "a school boy, not yet eighteen . . . full of the exuberance and carelessness peculiar to that age." In particular, Robert's carelessness was the theme of this tale. When the train arrived in Indianapolis, Lincoln asked for his son. When Robert was found and brought before his father, he was asked about the whereabouts of the carpetbag his father had entrusted to his care. Robert, a bit confused, nonchalantly confessed that he "knew nothing better to do than to hand the carpetbag to the clerk of the hotel—after the usual manner of travelers." Unbeknownst to Robert, the bag contained the draft of Lincoln's inaugural address. The panicked father rushed to the clerk's counter "behind which a small mountain of carpetbags of all colors had accumulated." After searching through the private belongings of others, "fortune favored the President-elect, for after the first half dozen trials, he found his treasure."[21]

Lincoln had found his carpetbag, with its precious contents undisturbed. Judge Davis, Lincoln's old friend, and Nicolay knew the contents of the speech, having been approached by Lincoln for suggestions and comments. The only other person known to have seen the speech prior to Lincoln's reaching Washington was the German American leader Carl Schurz.[22] Showing it to Schurz reinforced

Lincoln's links to the politically important German American community. As Nicolay noted, had the speech fallen into the wrong hands, it could have been catastrophic.[23]

Nicolay must have found a great deal of humor in recalling this incident. The essay was written around 1893, for it refers to Robert Lincoln as the "late minister to England." But he must have also decided that Robert, then a leading member of the Republican Party, would probably not appreciate his younger self being characterized as having "the exuberance of and carelessness peculiar to that age," or of being reminded of yet another awkward moment in his often difficult relationship with his father, or his sobriquet, the "Prince of Rails." So Nicolay drafted the essay, titled "Some Incidents on Lincoln's Journey from Springfield to Washington," and then tucked it away so as not to offend Robert Lincoln, whose goodwill had proven essential to Nicolay's access to sources while writing the Lincoln biography. Helen recounted the incident without referencing her father's characterizations of the late president's eldest son.

After Indianapolis, the journey to Washington was quickly turning into a logistical nightmare as Woods's well-intentioned schedule broke down with the press of crowds and with politicians leaving and joining the entourage as the train passed from one state to another. Crowds at every stop expected a speech from Lincoln, but speeches had been prepared only for specific occasions.[24] Crowds attempted to compel Lincoln to give extemporaneous speeches everywhere. The folly of this was evident when he spoke spontaneously to a crowd from his hotel in Indianapolis. Exhausted from a day of travel, speeches, and receiving politicians, Lincoln gave an uncharacteristically rambling, legalistic speech seeking to differentiate between "coercion" and "invasion" with regard to asserting the government's authority over federal property in the seceded states. These remarks only served to send off alarm bells in the South and undermine his theme of reconciliation and union, which he had sought to convey. Lincoln would spend the next few days backtracking from that ill-advised speech.

Ceremonial parades often took the president-elect and his party through a gauntlet of adoring crowds. William Coggeshall described the parade in Cincinnati as an example of what Lincoln and his party met at each of his major stops. After describing the display of the local military might of infantry and artillery, Coggeshall mentioned that among them was a unit called the German Yagers, who professed their loyalty to the Union while highlighting their growing influence in the Midwest. Lincoln rode in an open carriage drawn by six white horses, surrounded by a police escort and behind them a unit of dragoons. Pulling up the rear were "carriages with the suite of the President-Elect."[25] Helen Nicolay made no mention of her father's thoughts as he rode down the thoroughfares of the city where his family had first arrived in 1837 or whether he thought of the mother he hardly knew, who was buried in a local cemetery.

As private secretary, he had the responsibility to assist the president-elect in reception lines, reading off the little cards of introduction for each person who approached to shake Lincoln's hand. Describing the chaos, Nicolay noted that there was "some sort" of committee everywhere the party turned. The committees were not just the politicians fighting for their moment in the limelight but also came "from the bodies of Wide Awakes . . . bodies of working men" and "from organizations of various sorts," civic, fraternal, and religious. While these expressions of support were made "in perfect sincerity, in genuine hospitality, in the irrepressible enthusiasm," the crush of people everywhere and the intrusiveness into every moment of Lincoln's—and therefore Nicolay's—time was physically and mentally draining.[26]

Through it all, the secretary tried to accommodate and organize these requests. Seeking to oblige these groups while also running interference for Lincoln would have been more than enough, but he also had to cope with endless rounds of receptions and dinners. Three decades later, he described these events, undoubtedly ascribing to Lincoln and the crowds his own feelings about the ordeal. There were receptions arranged wherever the president-elect, and therefore his secretary, were available to the "public at large" so that "both ladies and gentlemen might have the opportunity to pass by him [Lincoln] and shake his hand." Reflecting back with a tinge of bitterness, Nicolay remembered those events as "a performance" that ranged from an "animal show" to a "grotesque ceremony of mock adulation."[27] Lincoln and his entourage were on display. Swollen hands, stiff, aching backs, and an all-encompassing fatigue became the norm.

Outside events were also grabbing the attention of the presidential party. On their arrival in Cincinnati, they learned that the newly established Confederate Congress, even before the arrival of their provisional president, Jefferson Davis, had sent peace commissioners to negotiate the formal recognition of their republic. No one knew what the fickle and hapless Buchanan would do. If he recognized the new Confederacy, the Union would be dissolved before Lincoln could be inaugurated. To the amazement of all, Buchanan stood firm for the Union.

The next day, as the party was leaving Cincinnati for Columbus, word arrived that the electoral votes of the thirty-three states, including those of the states claiming secession, had been counted during a session of Congress presided over by Vice President John Breckenridge. Thanks to the efforts of General Winfield Scott, the process was carried out without incident. Lincoln was now officially the president-elect.

From Columbus the train turned southeast to Pittsburgh. Nicolay described the arrival there in a letter to Therena dated February 15, 1861. Trying to put a good face on the increasingly stressful ordeal, he told her that "so far, we have got along reasonably well." He wrote that it was "disagreeable," with rain falling on the city. In view of the weather, he had hoped that no crowd would be waiting, but that desire had turned into a "vain illusion." The crowds were so thick that the party had difficulty leaving the train, much less leaving the station afterward.[28]

The stay in Pittsburgh followed the pattern that had emerged at every stop on the trip. In a February 15 letter to his beloved, Nicolay admitted that he had little time to himself, noting that newspapers he had purchased in Indianapolis to mail to her were still in his carpetbag "undirected." The crowds continued to be dangerously enthusiastic, with the secretary confessing that "it has been a serious task for us of his escort to prevent his [Lincoln] being killed with kindness."[29] Indeed, the crowds had been so uncontrollable that Lincoln was almost crushed in Columbus, Ohio. He was saved by the burly Ward Hill Lamon, who interposed himself between Lincoln and the crowd, allowing Lincoln to move behind a pillar until order could be restored.[30] For the non-robust Nicolay, throwing himself in front of Lincoln to protect his idol was a life-threatening act.

In his February 15 letter to Therena, he praised the preparations at Cleveland, noting "the arrangements have been good—better than we have found anywhere else."[31] But major problems lay ahead. Writing to Therena on February 17 from Buffalo, he conveyed how dangerous the security situation could become. Buffalo was unprepared to protect the president-to-be. "The usual thousands were awaiting our arrival," he declared, and while a path was made for Lincoln, the rest of the party faced the usual struggle to get safely off the train and away from the station. In the melee, he reported, "Major Hunter had his arm so badly sprained that it is doubtful" that he could continue the journey. And as if the scene at the rail station were not enough, the situation in town was worse. According to the picture he drew for Therena, chaos reigned at the hotel where the party was staying. The organizing committee "not only did nothing but didn't seem to care what to do." Taking charge, Nicolay arranged "pretty much everything." Afterward, he confessed that he was "feeling the effect of it to-day."[32]

Major Hunter's arm was broken, and he could not continue the journey. For the slender Nicolay, "elbowing" his way through the crowd must have been a daunting task and a frightening experience. His ability to step into the breach and take control of the arrangements from the welcoming committee was an exercise of his quick mind and organizational skills. There was no rest for the secretary in Buffalo. While Lincoln went off to church and then to a private dinner with the former president Franklin Pierce, the secretary had to entertain callers and straighten out details of the ongoing schedule.[33]

More bad news reached the party of the president-elect in Buffalo. General David E. Twiggs, a Georgian by birth, had surrendered the entire U.S. military command in Texas— including the federal arsenal at San Antonio and all federal garrisons, property, and men—without a shot. For his treachery, Twiggs would be commissioned as a major general in the Confederate army. With the surrender of these installations, the only significant federal properties remaining in the seceding states were Fort Pickens off the coast of Florida near Pensacola and Fort Sumter in Charleston Harbor. The aura of treason was everywhere.

Meanwhile, the Lincoln presidential traveling show rambled on, with Albany and New York City the next major stops. At Albany, an example of the crisis-driven political unity in the North, as described by Nicolay and Hay, could be found in the enthusiastic reception. The actor John Wilkes Booth was playing at the Gayety Theatre when the Lincoln entourage visited the capital of the Empire State. Surprised at the enthusiasm of the crowds greeting the president-elect in this bastion of the Democratic Party, Booth was told that the crowds were cheering for Lincoln, not as a black Republican but as the embodiment of the Union.[34] For the Southern sympathizer, it was the first realization that even Northern Democrats might fight to preserve the Union. While the president-elect was basking in the adulation of crowds in Albany, Jefferson Davis was inaugurated as the provisional president of the Confederate states, and Lincoln's old friend Alexander Stephens was installed as vice president. This event confirmed the seriousness of the Southern desire for disunion. In his inaugural address, Davis called for peaceful disunion in contrast to Lincoln's message of reconciliation and union. The country was edging ever closer to sectional separation and war. This event, occurring while the Lincoln party progressed toward the national capital, cast a pall on the celebrations.

The reception in New York City was perceptibly cool, but the presidential party moved on to its final stops at Trenton, New Jersey, and then on to Philadelphia and Harrisburg. Nicolay joined Lincoln for his visit to Independence Hall in Philadelphia, the birthplace of both the Declaration of Independence and the Constitution. Lincoln spoke on the significance of the historic events that had taken place there, another step in his evolving understanding of the Declaration and its meaning for all Americans. Lincoln concluded his stop at Independence Hall by raising the new thirty-four-star flag over this historic site. This flag had particular symbolism for the competing sections of the country, as the new star represented the free state of Kansas, admitted on January 29, 1861, after seven years of a bitter and bloody fight over whether it should be a free state or a slave state. The admission of Kansas as a free state confirmed the Deep South's fear that the expansion of slavery within the Union was at an end.

Death threats and strange incidents had continually marked this journey. Of particular note, Lincoln had received credible threats against his life as he traversed toward his destination. Baltimore, a city through which his train had to pass, was a hotbed of secession. The city and the surrounding eastern sections of Maryland were heavily invested in the institution of slavery and flush with pro-secessionist sentiment. A Chicago-based detective, Allan Pinkerton, had met with the president-elect and outlined threats against his life. Frederick Seward, son of the New York senator, also brought rumors of possible violence and assassination attempts. Private conversations behind closed doors ensued. Nicolay, initially kept in the dark, sensed that something was afoot. Always concerned for Lincoln's safety, he asked Norman Judd what was going on. Judd declined the request, noting that secrets were better kept by one person than by two. But later that day, the entire presidential party was privately informed of the plan to have Lincoln depart Harrisburg for Baltimore and Washington that night ahead of the rest of the presidential party in order to evade any assassination attempt.[35] Lincoln and his secretary arrived in the nation's capital, on separate trains a few hours apart, on Saturday, February 23, 1861, during one of the most intense, tumultuous, and unnerving times imaginable.

The original plan was for Lincoln to stay at a private house in Washington. While in Albany, Ward Hill Lamon confided this plan to Thurlow Weed. Weed objected to the arrangement, and he and Lamon agreed that Lincoln should stay at the Willard Hotel, Washington's most prestigious hostelry. Ever since Zachary Taylor had stayed there prior to his inauguration in 1849, the Willard had become the place for presidents-elect to stay. Weed then composed a letter to the management of the Willard, informing them that "Mr. Lincoln will be your guest." Weed also told them to provide rooms for Judge Davis and Ward Lamon.[36] Two days later, Lamon wrote the management of the hotel from Philadelphia in an attempt to clarify Weed's instructions. Lamon noted that "His private Secretary, Judge Davis & myself desire rooms adjoining Mr. Lincoln's."[37]

Regrettably for Nicolay, Lamon's letter arrived too late for Nicolay to be properly accommodated. In a February 24 letter to Therena, he complained of his poor housing arrangements, calling them "sorry accommodations," but then concluded teasingly, "Well, next week we hope to be in the White House, where perhaps, it may be better."[38] Perhaps not knowing that he had Thurlow Weed to thank for his accommodations, Nicolay was very put out about having to double up. But his accommodations in the White House were not that much better as he got to double up with John Hay for the next four years. To make matters worse, Nicolay was about to get a foretaste of the workload that would befall him in the Executive Mansion. A temporary office was established in Parlor Six at the Willard Hotel to accommodate the onrush of visitors and mail for the president-elect.[39]

Nicolay summed up his experience on the trip in his unpublished essay on the journey: "It is hard for anyone who has not had the chance of personal observation to realize the mingled excitement, elation and fatigue which Mr. Lincoln and his suite underwent, almost without intermission for the period of nearly two weeks during this memorable trip from Springfield to Washington."[40] Shortly after sunrise on February 26, the president-elect, his son Robert, and Nicolay were observed taking a long walk on the streets of the capital.[41] The sight of Lincoln and Nicolay strolling about the city would be a common sight for the next four years.

Nicolay had come through a whirlwind of activity on behalf of the president-elect, again demonstrating his organizing skills, patience, and endurance despite his physical frailty. He would get little respite from his labors as he accompanied Lincoln around Washington in the fortnight before the inauguration. Nicolay's visit to Washington in 1858, a decade after Lincoln had spent time there as a member of Congress, was of invaluable assistance in refamiliarizing the president-elect with the capital. Within days, he would be living in the White House as the private secretary to the president.

CHAPTER FOUR

Lincoln's Choice of Nicolay
The Importance of Being German

After returning to the Executive Mansion following his inauguration, the first official act of Abraham Lincoln as president was to sign the appointment of John G. Nicolay as his private secretary:

> Pursuant to the authority vested in me by the second Section of the Act of Congress of the third of March 1857, I hereby appoint John G. Nicolay of Illinois, Private Secretary to the President of the United States.
> Abraham Lincoln
> Washington,
> 4th March 1861[1]

It has never been clear why Lincoln chose the young and obscure clerk in the Office of the Illinois Secretary of State for this position. The choice puzzled both contemporaries of Lincoln at the time and historians over the years. The authors believe that Lincoln's appointment of Nicolay was based on a variety of reasons but due primarily to a political calculation based on Nicolay's connections with the German American immigrant community, most significantly the German American press.

Henry C. Whitney, a lawyer who traveled with Lincoln on the Illinois judicial circuit thought that Lincoln's law partner, William Herndon, should have received the appointment. In a letter to Herndon dated July 18, 1887, Whitney opined that Herndon should have been Lincoln's secretary "in the normal order of things." He was astounded that Lincoln had chosen an individual who was nothing more than "a mere clerk." Citing Franklin Pierce's selection of the young New Hampshire attorney Sidney Webster, Whitney asserted that Herndon could have served as "his [Lincoln's] private secretary & mentor," and by choosing Nicolay, Lincoln had deprived himself of a "confidential friend of astuteness and affection like you [Herndon]."[2]

John R. Sellers, in a biographical essay on Nicolay, offered an assessment of the choice that reflects those of many of Lincoln's contemporaries, including Whitney, as well as a wide range of modern-day historians. The allegation is that Nicolay "lacked the refinement and culture, the savoir-faire, expected of appointees to such an exalted position"—that is, that Nicolay lacked social standing. Nonetheless, Nicolay's "absolute loyalty" had always been recognized as an unquestioned asset, as well as his ability and readiness to "represent the commander-in-chief accurately in delicate political situations."[3]

While "absolute loyalty" would not have been sufficient for Lincoln to appoint Nicolay, it certainly was an attribute the young man possessed. He had to offer Lincoln much more to have first received the appointment as campaign secretary, which was the forerunner of his appointment as private secretary to the president. As noted by Carl Sandburg, Lincoln possessed a shrewd and calculating political mind that displayed "the cunning of a fox, with a wilderness sagacity, with natural instinct such as those guiding wild geese."[4] Lincoln's longtime friend Ward Hill Lamon was even more frank about Lincoln's attitude towards those who served him. Lamon was blunt when he wrote that Lincoln "did nothing out of gratitude and forgot the warmest devotion of his warmest partisans" when their services were no longer required. Lamon claimed that what Lincoln's followers did for him "was quietly appropriated as the reward of [Lincoln's] superior merit, calling for no return in kind."[5]

The image of the gentle, smiling Father Abraham, then as now, has always masked the mind of a calculating, self-serving politician whose every thought, every move, was tempered by the hard steel of ambition. Lincoln was no different from any other office seeker, then or now. He would not have appointed Nicolay as his private secretary if it did not help achieve his agenda in some important way. In 1860, the goal was the presidency. Nicolay would tell his daughter and others that he simply presumed that his appointment was based solely "on account of acquaintanceship" because he sincerely believed it.[6] The naiveté of her father's assumption underscores again the lack of political understanding the young secretary had throughout his life.

As Lamon noted, Lincoln "did nothing out of mere gratitude." After more than three years in close contact with Lincoln, Nicolay should have known this fact better than most people. There is no suggestion in Helen's biography or in her father's papers that he ever thought more deeply about the reasons why he was selected. Instead, he ruminated over the fact that W. D. Howells was selected over him to write the official campaign biography. Reflecting on this private bitterness that never left her father, Helen spent more time on the writing of the campaign biography than on why Lincoln gave her father a position that not only defined her father's life but was also the title, and justification, for her book.

If, in the world of politics, friendships meant little to Lincoln, neither did loyalty, since he, like all politicians, always had political followers who would blindly pledge themselves to their idol and place themselves at his service. Successful politicians, including Lincoln, are able to identify those individuals who could serve a variety of functions in their pursuit of political power and then discard those very same people while making them feel glad about it. Political success depended upon it. Nicolay needed a number of attributes before Lincoln would be willing to appoint him. His first attribute was his likeability. Lincoln liked Nicolay. Though not sufficient in itself for advancement, it was a necessary prerequisite. Some historians have remarked that Lincoln and Nicolay had quite different personalities. That certainly is true but such differences have never prevented friendships or even marriages between opposites. In fact, these men had much in common: family deaths, youthful isolation, self-education, and studied social climbing in a Western frontier state. This commonality of background would bind these two men in ways that neither Henry Whitney nor Ward Lamon could have understood, not having experienced the travails that Lincoln and Nicolay had gone through to get where they were.

The hours of playing chess in the secretary of state's office, where Lincoln could find respite from a difficult home life, and the demands put on him by both his law practice and political connections cemented the friendship. There is no evidence that Nicolay ever asked anything of Lincoln prior to his appointment. That alone would have impressed Lincoln, who was frequently asked for favors by friend and stranger alike. Lincoln also found that he could rely on Nicolay to be discreet, a quality the latter had demonstrated in his handling of the publication of the Lincoln-Douglas debates.

Coming from the frontier, Nicolay lacked a degree of "refinement and culture, [and] the savoir-faire," but those were qualities Lincoln never found to be particularly important. Lincoln's own "refinement and culture" came from years of practice, not family breeding, and with his homespun humor, physical awkwardness, and insecurity with the ladies, it would be hard to describe Lincoln as having savoir-faire. Many of Lincoln's associates were willing to overlook his social shortcomings because Lincoln was a prominent and successful attorney as well as a well-known politician. Upon reaching Washington, the Lincolns, who were among the upper echelons of Springfield society, were looked down upon socially by Washington's elite society, a fact that provoked the ire of the First Lady. Most significantly throughout his presidency, Lincoln promoted men on the battlefield and in his administration who sometimes lacked refinement and breeding, but these were men who could accomplish a goal—men who could fight and win, such as Ulysses S. Grant. Lincoln believed in promoting merit over class, while his adversaries in Washington and Richmond worried about protecting their class and distinction.

Nor was the position of private secretary to the president always filled by men of distinction. The first presidential secretary was Tobias Lear, a veteran of the Continental Army, who had served as tutor to Martha Washington's grandchildren and as Washington's private secretary beginning in 1784. Like his successors until Nicolay, he was college educated. Jefferson and Madison chose members of Virginia's prominent families for their secretaries. Starting with James Monroe, the private secretaries were the son, nephew, son-in-law, or brother-in-law of the sitting president. The only exception during this time period was Franklin Pierce's secretary, Sidney Webster. Most secretaries had received formal military or legal training. The typical age of the secretary was somewhere in their mid-twenties, with some presidential secretaries being as young as twenty-one. In short, while there were exceptions, the typical private secretary was a very young man without much experience, who usually earned his position and his "distinction" as the result of an accident of birth, marriage, or family connections and, like Nicolay, was totally beholden to his superior.

Nicolay assumed the position at the age of twenty-nine; thus he was older than most of his predecessors when they entered the office. Lincoln, having been self-educated, did not worry that Nicolay possessed little formal education. Lincoln saw a young man who, like himself, had pulled himself out of poverty and, like Lincoln, had obtained his law license by reading law books and passing the bar, rather than through formal legal training. This method was more common in the mid-nineteenth century than formal training at a college, especially on the frontier. Nicolay, like so many of his predecessors, was a lawyer. Like Franklin Pierce, Lincoln did not have a relative to whom he could turn. His eldest son, Robert, was just eighteen, and Lincoln wanted him to finish his formal education. Nor could he turn to any of his in-laws since many of the Todds disliked him personally and/or politically. Many of his wife's family were open secessionists and would join the Confederate army during the war. Lincoln needed a person he could trust but who would also be dependent on Lincoln for his position and future. Nicolay, who had demonstrated his admiration for and loyalty to Lincoln, fit that bill perfectly. While he may have been a "mere clerk" to Henry Whitney, to Ward Hill Lamon, who was more closely acquainted with Nicolay, he was "a very competent and clever clerk."[7] The young man had proven himself working in the Office of the Illinois Secretary of State under Lincoln's watchful eye. Competence does matter, and more significantly, Lincoln, who had no need of an alter-ego, as some of his contemporaries suggested, probably found Nicolay's self-effacing personality to his liking.

Until Buchanan, presidents had to provide the pay for their secretaries, which is one reason presidential relatives were often chosen. They could be expected to work for little or no compensation. James Monroe was the first president to file a complaint about the lack of support staff for the president.[8] It was not until the closing hours of Franklin Pierce's administration that the Office of Private Secretary to the President was created. The Civil Expense Appropriation Act, passed on March 3, 1857,[9] established the presidential staff and authorized salaries that would remain in place during Lincoln's presidency. It was this act Lincoln cited in his appointment of Nicolay. Section 2 of the act, along with providing an appropriation for the White House stationery, authorized the appointment of "one private secretary at annual salary of two thousand five hundred dollars."[10]

The position itself had not been especially taxing on Nicolay's predecessors. After an initial few months, during which the spoils of victory were shamelessly distributed among the party faithful, a presidential secretary would have a generally light workload. Even these appointments based on the "spoils system" were limited. The Virginia dynasty of Jefferson, Madison, and Monroe pulled their appointments from the same circle of Virginia and southern elites. John Quincy Adams lived to regret his decision not to replace his opponents in the government. Andrew Jackson made the art of political payoffs into a cardinal virtue. Van Buren and Buchanan had been limited in their spoils appointments because their immediate predecessors were from the same party. Nor was Congress a particular problem. Congress would meet from December to late spring and then adjourn to escape the sauna-like heat of a Washington summer. The calendar had a rhythmic cycle that created a life of its own.

Nor did war interrupt the duties of previous secretaries. In the seventy-plus years since Washington's inauguration, the country had been at war with a foreign power for less than five years. These wars had been fought with tiny armies supplemented by state militias. Generals were free to do what they wanted since no one could communicate with them in the field. Nor had these wars meaningfully affected the size or reach of the government. When Nicolay was appointed on March 4, 1861, no one could conceive of the changes that an industrially based, technologically advanced civil war would bring to Washington, the president, and his secretary. Lincoln assumed that his election was likely to bring on a war, but no one could conceive its duration or brutality, or even know for certain that armed hostilities would occur between North and South.

Yet, Lincoln saw in his assistant other attributes that for some reason were not readily apparent or appreciated by those around him or to anyone but a shrewd politician who had the "cunning of a fox." Lincoln got to know Nicolay intimately over a chessboard and through those long hours of conversation became thoroughly acquainted with his professional and personal background. More important, these attributes aligned squarely with Lincoln's agenda. Nicolay's background as a writer, reporter, editor, and newspaper owner was not lost on Lincoln. He was a talented writer. Though his February 1860 editorial endorsing Lincoln for president contained some politically awkward points, it was well written. He had honed his writing skills on the *Free Press*. Being a passionate reader, he efficiently assimilated the nuances of his adopted English language. Thanks to his command of the language, his editorial calling for the 1856 Decatur meeting of editors was quoted extensively by the *Chicago Press and Tribune*. Outside of his small coterie of friends and acquaintances in Pittsfield and Springfield, he had many contacts in the press, knowing a wide range of editors of both English- and German-language papers. After he sold the *Pike County Free Press,* he continued to take part-time reporting assignments that kept him connected to the newspaper business, which in the mid-nineteenth century was the only medium of mass communication. Since German, not English, was his mother tongue, he could communicate easily, both orally and in writing, with the editors of the German-language newspapers that flourished throughout the North but especially the Midwest, where the German immigrant population, and voters, were heavily concentrated. Who was better qualified than Nicolay to keep Lincoln informed about what was being said in the German-language press, both during the campaign and then during the Civil War, than Nicolay?

But Lincoln had more reasons for availing himself of Nicolay's knowledge of the German-language press. George Schneider was the editor of the *Illinois*

Staats-Zeitung, a leading paper for German Americans in the Northwest. Schneider had been one of the editors who attended the Decatur convention in February 1856. He was a delegate to the Bloomington convention that established the Republican Party in Illinois in May 1856 and to the first Republican Nominating Convention in Philadelphia in June 1856. He had worked with Lincoln at Decatur to formulate the outline of the platform later adopted by the Republican Party. In 1859, he was a strong supporter of William Seward for president, and his word carried weight throughout the German American community.[11] Schneider, like many other German Americans, supported Seward as a result of his staunch antinativist stands.

Lincoln decided that he needed to counteract Schneider's influence by purchasing a German-language newspaper of his own. On May 30, 1859, Lincoln bought the *Illinois Staats-Anzeiger*, located in Springfield and edited by Dr. Theodore Canisius.[12] The contract read:

This instrument witnesseth that the printing-press, and types by purchaser of John Burkhardt, belong to Abraham Lincoln; that Theodore Canisius is to have immediate possession of them, and to commence publishing in Springfield, Illinois a Republican newspaper, to be chiefly in the German language with occasional translations into English at his option; the first newspaper to issue in the ensuing month of June, and to continue thenceforward issuing weekly or oftener, at the option of said Canisius, the said Canisius bearing all expenses, [?] and taking all income and profits, save for pay; in political sentiment, not to depart from the Philadelphia and Illinois Republican platforms; and for a material departure in that purpose, or a failure of said paper to issue as often as weekly, or any attempt to remove said press, type, etc. from Springfield, or to print with them anything opposed to, or designed to injure the Republican party, said Lincoln may, at his option at once take possession of said press, type, etc., and deal with them as his own. On the contrary, if said Canisius shall issue a newspaper, in all things conformed hereto, until after the Presidential election of 1860, then said press, type, etc. to be his property absolute, not, however, to be used against the Republican Party, nor to be removed from Springfield without the consent of said Lincoln.

May 1859   *ALincoln*

ThCanisius[13]

Lincoln kept the purchase of the paper to himself. As Carl Sandburg stated, Lincoln told no one about this, "not even Herndon." Yet Lincoln could now "walk into its office, ask for favors and get consideration." So, while Lincoln controlled the content of the paper, Canisius "looked like the proprietor . . . and walked the streets of Springfield as such."[14] Lincoln now owned a newspaper he could not read unless the article was in English. The person he could depend upon to read the paper and make sure Canisius was doing his bidding was Nicolay. It is doubtful that Lincoln confided to Nicolay about his ownership of the paper since Lincoln kept this secret from everyone. Nonetheless, Nicolay would have been Lincoln's first, if only choice, to read Canisius's paper and report back to him about what Canisius was publishing as part of a general monitoring of the German-language press.

On December 6, 1860, Lincoln conveyed the paper and its assets back to Canisius. Canisius, never a successful businessman, thereupon went bankrupt. In a letter dated March 31, 1861, he wrote Lincoln seeking a consular position in one of the German states, preferably at the court of Saxony at Leipzig. Canisius asserted that he had labored "since four years . . . for your interest," as demonstrated by "the innumerable articles in my paper and the correspondence." Then the good doctor, who had lived off Lincoln's money for over a year and a half, informed the president, "No German has succeeded better to make you a favorite with our countrymen than I have." Then, not content with his prior statement, he wrote, none too subtly, "I could tell something about that [the story of Lincoln's owning the paper] also."[15] Dr. Canisius was appointed consul at Vienna.[16] Thus, Lincoln simultaneously rewarded Canisius and removed him from the country so that he would not disclose Lincoln's foray into the German American newspaper business.

Lincoln's investment in a German American newspaper highlights his awareness of the increasingly important political activities of recent German immigrants in the Midwest. Unlike their Irish immigrant counterparts on the East Coast, the German arrivals were not only literate but also politically sophisticated and well organized. They represented crucial votes in the states of Illinois and Indiana, which the Republicans had failed to win in 1856 and needed in 1860. The Germans had been moving towards the Republican Party, but they were wary of another faction within the party, the anti-immigrant nativists, recently members of the American, or Know-Nothing, Party. In the spring of 1859, a crisis occurred that affected the tenuous political alliances between the immigrant Germans and the party's anti-immigrant nativists. This crisis led to a potentially dangerous political encounter at the 1860 Republican National Convention. Meanwhile, candidate Lincoln was parsing phrases and otherwise tip-toeing through this political minefield.

The crisis arose in Massachusetts, then a stronghold of nativist feeling. At first, at the urging of the Know-Nothing Governor, Henry Gardner, and later by his Republican successor, Nathaniel Banks, the Republican-controlled Massachusetts legislature passed what was known as the "Two Year Amendment" to the Massachusetts constitution. It disenfranchised naturalized citizens for two years after their naturalization. Bay State voters ratified this provision in a statewide referendum on May 9, 1859.[17] Although the measure was aimed at the large Irish Catholic population in Massachusetts, which generally voted Democratic, the amendment enraged German Americans in the Midwest.

Most Germans had abandoned the immigrant-friendly Democratic Party due to the party's support of slavery and the Kansas-Nebraska bill. Now, they were being asked to swallow attacks against the foreign-born by their new political allies. Amid the fury, some German American editors called for a mass exodus from the Republican Party and the formation of a new political organization with German leadership.[18] While the German press debated the issue, Midwestern Republicans grew anxious. They rushed to denounce the Massachusetts amendment and reassure their German American adherents. In a letter dated April 30, 1859, and published in the *Chicago Press and Tribune* prior to the Massachusetts referendum, Senator James Grimes of Iowa denounced the action of the Massachusetts legislature, declaring, "I condemn it and deplore it without equivocation." Grimes then urged Republican voters to turn the measure down since they "owe it to their party" to see to it that it was defeated.[19]

After Massachusetts voters ratified the measure, the Republicans sought to shift blame to the Democrats for the embarrassing outcome. They claimed that the state's Democrats had conspired to vote affirmatively to embarrass the Republicans, who allegedly opposed the measure they themselves had placed on the ballot. William Herndon, in a speech delivered at a political rally in Springfield on May 15, made this implausible argument.[20] The *Chicago Press and Tribune* had done the same, but as scholar Frank Herriott pointed out, no one was buying the explanation, especially "the Germans and French and Scandinavians, Bohemians, Hungarians and Swiss, adversely affected." Herriott further noted, "Public confidence among the Germans in the reliability of the [Republican] party as to its pledges was rudely shaken by the conduct of the Republicans of Massachusetts."[21] In a letter to the *Illinois Staats-Zeitung* dated May 11, Congressman Elihu B. Washburne, a noted Illinois attorney and Lincoln associate, condemned both the Republican legislature and the Republican voters who had ratified it.[22] The Germans had nonetheless received a rude shock and, before it was over, would receive another at the upcoming Republican National Convention.

Meanwhile, on behalf of the German American editors and a fortnight before Lincoln purchased his paper, Dr. Canisius had asked Lincoln for his view of the Two Year Amendment and the fusion of the Republican and Know-Nothing Parties. Nicolay and Hay claimed that Lincoln wrote this letter "declaring his opposition to the waning fallacy of Know-Nothingism, in which he also defined his position on 'fusion.'"[23] Nicolay and Hay only reproduced part of the letter, but Herriot's long article on this response reprinted *in extenso* the editorial that appeared in the *Daily State Journal* of Springfield on May 18, 1859.

Noting that "Massachusetts is a sovereign and independent state," Lincoln declared that "it was no privilege of mine to scold her." Lincoln then professed that he would oppose the adoption of a similar measure in Illinois "or any other place I might have a right to oppose it." In concluding his comments on the Two Year Amendment, he noted that it would be "strangely inconsistent" if he commiserated with the plight of the black man while "curtailing the existing rights of white men, even though born in different lands, and speaking different languages from myself." On fusion, Lincoln merely noted that he was for it if brought about "on Republican principles." Dr. Canisius, who would soon be on the Lincoln payroll, characterized the response as "plain, straightforward, and directly to the point."[24] Undoubtedly, the young Nicolay seconded Dr. Canisius's evaluation.

Lincoln carefully parsed his public comments to straddle the political chasm of interests that defined the Republican coalition. It was not, as Nicolay and Hay would later describe, a "declaration of opposition to the waning fallacy of Know Nothingism." He did not condemn unequivocally the Republican-controlled Massachusetts legislature, as most of the Midwestern Republicans did, but instead wrapped his lawyerly denunciation in the flag of states' rights, saying that he would "not scold" the Bay State voters for what they had done. He then stated his opposition to a similar proposal in Illinois, should there be one, which there was not. Since Lincoln did not hold an office and the issue was not likely to arise in Illinois, where the German vote was very potent, he knew he would not have an occasion to oppose such a measure before the Republican Nominating Convention in 1860. Lincoln then linked the issue of denying newly naturalized citizens the franchise to the one common cause of the new party: opposition to slavery. He, personally, would not curtail the "existing rights of white men," even if foreign born. On fusion, Lincoln was equally obscure, stating that he only supported fusion on "Republican grounds," allowing the reader to interpret for himself what Lincoln's definition of those "Republican grounds" were.

Lincoln guarded his statement since he would need both foreign-born and nativist votes at the upcoming Chicago convention and for success in the subsequent election campaign. Privately, Lincoln was much more forthright about his opposition to nativism. These views were expressed in two letters he had written in the summer of 1855. On August 11, 1855, he wrote to the abolitionist Owen Lovejoy and laid out the political dilemma facing him. Noting that there was "not sufficient material (i.e. votes) to successfully combat" the Democrats without the nativists, he hoped that the Know Nothing faction would collapse of their own weight "without the painful necessity of my taking an open stand against them." Lincoln could not "perceive how any one professing to be sensitive to the wrongs of negroes, can join in a league to degrade a class of white men." Lincoln concluded by saying that he "had no objection to 'fuse' with any body, provided I can fuse on grounds which I think right."[25] Two weeks later, in an August 24, 1855, letter to Joshua Speed, Lincoln excoriated the nativists in a similar vein.[26] Obviously, these sentiments were well hidden from nativist and immigrant alike. By 1859, nativism had not collapsed of its own weight but had morphed into a significant segment of the Republican Party. Consequently, Lincoln's reply to Dr. Canisius on May 17, 1859, can be seen as both evasive and politically calculating, especially in contrast to his most serious competitor for the presidential nomination, the outspoken Seward.

Senator William Seward of New York was the presumptive Republican nominee in 1860. In an election speech in his home town of Auburn, New York, on October 21, 1856, Seward made manifest his unequivocal disdain for the Know Nothing movement. Seward inquired rhetorically, "What are its creed and its policy?" Answering his own question, Seward harangued that the creed of the nativists was to abridge "the political franchise of alien immigrants and Roman Catholics." He condemned the Know Nothings "because their movement is out of season and out of place." Going further, Seward decried Know Nothingism as contrary to both the principles of the Declaration of Independence and the U.S. Constitution. Seward argued that the republic was "based on the principles of rightful political equality of all the members of the state." Since the Know Nothings rejected these principles, he believed that the movement would be "regarded as one of the caprices of politics that a system of combination so puerile was ever attempted in the United States."[27] Seward was not going to finesse his position by saying one thing in public while concealing a different set of views he told friends in private. Many German Americans reciprocated Seward's principled and public stand on behalf of their rights by giving the senator their support. Not being an integral part of the German American communal experience, Nicolay did not, then or later on while writing the Lincoln history, fully appreciate their concerns. How could he honestly bring up the subject without contrasting his hero's prevarication against Seward's courage? Obviously, Nicolay's image of Lincoln would not have emerged unscathed. Consequently, the writers of the Lincoln biography had to spin his response to Dr. Canisius as courageous while simultaneously ignoring one of the most significant reasons Lincoln would win the Republican nomination.

By the spring of 1860, the Two Year Amendment controversy seemed to have gone away until it resurfaced as the party met in Chicago for three days beginning on May 16, 1860. There, a skirmish erupted over what constituted "Republican grounds" regarding the rights of the foreign born versus nativism. At a meeting at German House in Chicago prior to the convention, German delegates agreed to push a "Dutch plank" that would affirm their rights as Americans.[28] The party platform committee consisted of twenty-seven members, including four German Americans: Carl Schurz of Wisconsin, Gustavus Kaerner of Illinois, John A. Kasson of Iowa, and John P. Hatterscheidt of Kansas. The Germans thought that they had gotten their meaningful "Dutch plank" when the committee adopted the fourteenth plank, which read as follows: "The Republican Party is opposed to any change in our naturalization laws, or any state legislation by which the rights of citizenship hitherto accorded to immigrants from foreign lands shall be abridged or impaired; and in favor of giving a full and efficient protection to the rights of all classes of citizens, whether native or naturalized, both at home and abroad."[29]

The fourteenth plank was meant as a clear slap at the nativists for the Massachusetts Two Year Amendment. After the platform was read to the convention, D. K. Cartter of Ohio proposed that the platform be adopted without debate.[30] No sooner had Cartter completed his thought than there were objections to calling the previous question by Joshua Giddings of Ohio and other voices in the convention. John A. Andrew, the Republican gubernatorial candidate from Massachusetts, raised a technical question claiming that the rules required the platform to be printed and distributed. While the chair of the convention ruled that Andrew was incorrect and therefore his request was out of order, printed copies of the platform appeared on the convention floor. F. P. Tracy, a member of the platform committee from California, then objected to Cartter's call. Subsequently, the chair called for a voice vote on the issue of ending debate and ruled that the convention had voted to continue the debate. When Cartter objected, a roll call ensued, and by a vote of 301 to 155, the convention continued debate.[31]

Joshua Giddings offered a minor amendment to the wording of the second plank, adding the words of the Declaration of Independence regarding the equality of all men. This amendment was quickly voted down. Then, to the consternation of the German Americans, it became evident that many individuals wanted the platform debated in order to attack the plank regarding naturalization. David Wilmot of Pennsylvania proposed to strike the phrase "or any state legislation" from the fourteenth plank, justifying his position on the grounds of states' rights.[32] Judge Aaron Goodrich of Minnesota rose to say that no state had the power to change naturalization laws. To explain the thinking of the Platform Committee, Judge William Jessup of Pennsylvania noted that "a great number of Republicans are of foreign birth," who believed that in return for their loyalty and votes, the Republican party should affirm certain principles on their behalf. According to Judge Jessup, the German Americans felt that this affirmation should include a statement by the party that existing naturalization laws should not be tampered with, that the party did not support an alteration of the immigration laws by a state, and that the party did not approve any legislation impairing the rights of naturalized citizens.[33] Wilmot retorted that he was not arguing that states could change the naturalization laws but that states' rights allowed each state to determine the residency (i.e., voting) requirements of its citizens. Wilmot then stated that there must be a "misunderstanding," that the plank did not really "controvert the right of a State to thus modify the rights of foreign or native citizens, but merely wish to make a declaration that the Republican party, as a party, is opposed to it."[34] Wilmot then withdrew his amendment.

The German Americans knew that they had been had. This polite agreement to agree while really disagreeing only heightened their angst and made them wonder whether the Republican Party really was an option for them. Carl Schurz felt compelled to address the convention. He first reminded those gathered that German Americans had contributed 300,000 votes in the 1856 election and were prepared to do so again. Citing the party's 1856 platform in support of the "equality of rights among citizens," Schurz expressed concern that now the party was saying that the promise could be nullified by a state legislature. Then he questioned the convention, "Of what use, then, is a plank in a platform if its purpose thus can be frustrated . . . ?" Standing on principle, Schurz proclaimed,

"Gentlemen, the question is simply this, on one side there stands prejudice, on the other side, there stands right." He warned the party that cold political calculations as to which side could deliver more votes could never serve the party's interest: "the only thing we [German Americans] ask of you is this; that we shall be permitted to fight for our common cause; that we shall be permitted to fight in your ranks with confidence in your principles and with honor to ourselves."[35] Schurz's remarks were seconded by another German American delegate, Frederick Hassaurek of Cincinnati, Ohio.[36] After a second successful proposal to amend the second plank, the platform was unanimously adopted.

The platform debate highlighted the uneasy fusion between the German Americans and the nativists within the party ranks. Nicolay observed the debate from the gallery. However, he and Hay took no note of it in their history of Lincoln but instead focused on the amendment by Joshua Giddings regarding the Declaration of Independence. This raises a serious question about why Nicolay and Hay, but especially Nicolay, chose to ignore this consequential debate on the floor of the convention but instead focused on the rather insignificant amendment put forth by Joshua Giddings. The argument in the party over the rights of naturalized citizens was far more consequential.

There are several possible reasons why Nicolay and Hay would pass over this debate. By focusing on the immigrant plank, the authors would have had to admit the equivocal public stand Lincoln maintained as he tried to appeal to both sides in the controversy without offending the other. Also, the Giddings amendment, while it had no political import, fit into their post–Civil War narrative of Lincoln and the Republicans as emancipators. But it also suggests that Nicolay, though he could relate with German Americans and was an immigrant himself, did not identify with his fellow German Americans *as* an immigrant. Significantly, Helen Nicolay had very little to say about her father's German roots and nothing about an identification with the broader German community in the United States. Nor is there evidence that Nicolay wrote extensively on issues related to immigration as he did on slavery. Having grown up in America from the age of five, mostly away from the environs of a German communal experience, he viewed himself as an American even though he still was not a citizen. Immigration issues were not particularly important to him. Meanwhile, as the convention moved to select a nominee, the German Americans would have more reason for concern.

Seward was the favorite for the nomination, but he did not have a clear majority going into the convention. Nineteenth-century political conventions were tumultuous affairs in which any number of favorite sons would be placed in nomination. Few presidential aspirants received the endorsement of the party on the first ballot. The anti-Seward forces, which included the nativists, were seeking an alternative to Seward. When the presidential balloting was delayed after the platform controversy until the next day, it gave the anti-Seward faction one last chance to come up with an alternative.

The Republicans had a problem. Southerners referred to them as "a sectional party," and that they clearly were. In the 1856 election, the Democrats won the White House by capturing all but one slave state, Maryland, which had voted for the American Party, and four large northern states: Pennsylvania, New Jersey, Indiana, and Illinois. While Pennsylvania and Indiana gave majorities to Buchanan, the nativist vote had been the difference in New Jersey and in Lincoln's Illinois. To win the presidency, the Republicans had to retain all the states won in 1856 and add at least three of the four northern states whose electoral votes went to Buchanan. Faraway California and Oregon were considered, at this time, as safe for the Democrats but also electorally inconsequential.

Murat Halstead, a reporter for the *Cincinnati Commercial*, provided extensive reportage for the political conventions that occurred in the spring of 1860. He wrote a dispatch to his paper on the events of the second day of the Chicago convention. Writing about the prospective nomination of Seward, Halstead focused on the delegations of the states that had voted for Buchanan, noting that the consensus of these delegations was that the party's chances "would be immediately ruined" or, worse, suffer "the sting of political death."[37] The delegations from Pennsylvania, New Jersey, Indiana, and Illinois may have been posturing for their favorite sons, but these four states had also registered significant support for the nativist American Party in recent elections. These "doubtful" states had to be carried. P. Orman Ray summarized the situation in an address to the Chicago Historical Society on the occasion of the fifty-sixth anniversary of Lincoln's nomination. Commenting on the revelry of the Seward forces on the eve of the nominating vote, Ray noted that "soberer and sobering influences had been quietly at work against Seward"; he specifically mentioned the Republican gubernatorial candidates of Indiana and Pennsylvania, whose elections were dependent on the party nominating someone who would not harm their own chances for election. As Ray observed, these states "would have none of Seward because of his former hostility to the [Know-Nothing] party."[38]

Thomas H. Dudley, a delegate-at-large from New Jersey, described the pre-convention maneuvering. According to Dudley, the New England delegations represented by John A. Andrew avowed support for Seward but then stabbed him in the back by claiming that New England "preferred the success of the party rather than the election of any particular individual."[39] Andrew, a candidate for governor in a state with a sizable bloc of nativists, had his own agenda in defeating Seward. Dudley related that the three states with favorite sons each insisted that their candidate be presented to the convention as the alternative to Seward. A subcommittee was formed that included Lincoln friend and supporter Judge David Davis. The committee originally met in the "Cameron rooms late Thursday morning with Governor Reeder of Pennsylvania as chair."[40] With no resolution in sight, Halstead later reported that "there were few men in Chicago who believed it possible to prevent the nomination of Seward."[41]

Nonetheless, Seward's enemies made one last try at resolving the impasse. A meeting was held in David Wilmot's rooms beginning at six o'clock that evening, and remained in session for five hours. Horace Greeley, a dedicated foe of Seward's and credentialed as a delegate from Oregon, stopped by at ten o'clock to see whether there had been any resolution. At that time, there was none, and Greeley telegraphed his paper that all was lost.[42] While Horace Greeley lamented the inability of the insurgents to agree on a name, they finally settled on Abraham Lincoln after a canvas was made in the room and Lincoln was found to be the strongest candidate.[43] After the parties agreed on Lincoln, the participants moved about the delegations to secure Lincoln's nomination, working through the night.[44]

When the balloting for the presidential nomination commenced on Friday afternoon, Lincoln had the complete support of two delegations from the "doubtful" states of Indiana and Illinois. These delegations provided Lincoln with 48 of his 102 votes to Seward's 173½ votes on the first ballot. The real news of the first ballot was the defection of half of the New England delegates, who abandoned Seward without warning. This bode ill for the New Yorker and the German Americans who realized that these votes came from heavily nativist states. On the second ballot, Lincoln garnered an additional 79 votes, reaching 181 to Seward's 184½. Forty-eight of Lincoln's new votes came from another nativist stronghold when forty-four Pennsylvania delegates abandoned favorite-son Cameron, whose name was subsequently withdrawn. Lincoln also picked up Vermont's 10 votes as well as additional votes from Rhode Island and Connecticut. But the Lincoln wave would only have been a ripple had not the Pennsylvania delegation thrown their weight behind him. And so it happened. The coup against Seward, organized the previous night, was consummated when Lincoln surged forward and won the nomination on the third ballot.

While political promises from the Lincoln camp also greased Lincoln's way to the nomination, the open support of the nativists on Lincoln's behalf could not be reassuring to the German Americans. While Seward may have lost votes in the convention because of his "higher law" stance and his 1858 speech on the forthcoming "irrepressible conflict" between the sections, his open opposition to nativism sealed his fate. The man the German Americans had supported because of his principled and unequivocal stand on their behalf was defeated. Lincoln, the man who in May 1859 had parsed a lawyerly and tepid response to the Two Year Amendment, had won the nomination with the support of their enemies. The German Americans had also been disappointed again and went home wondering whether the Republican Party cared about their concerns or only their votes.

Although present at the convention in the midst of these events, Nicolay was not a participant in the nocturnal gatherings. Nor did he ever seem to grasp the motive behind the betrayal of Seward on the first ballot from the New England delegates. He did not understand how the different factions in the party worked with and against each other as part of the political dynamic. What he saw was only what he wanted to see: his hero being nominated for the presidency. He could report what he saw, but he was never what we call today an investigative reporter. For Nicolay, Lincoln's nomination was the way things should have been; there was no need to search for deeper explanations.

On the other hand, candidate Lincoln understood the problems he faced within his own party that had to be overcome if he had any hope of achieving the presidency. He did not concern himself with whether, as Carl Schurz had argued, prejudice or right would give him more votes; he just needed votes. Nor did he worry about Joshua Giddings's feelings about the Declaration of Independence. He needed the German vote and a lot more. Nativism, with its repercussions within the party, lingered in his consciousness throughout the election. It was the one issue that could split the party and cause him to lose critical states like Pennsylvania, Indiana, and Illinois. To win the election, Lincoln had to make sure that disagreements in the Republican coalition that surfaced at the convention over naturalization and the franchise did not surface again. At the same time, he had to reassure the German Americans that he was not a nativist without offending those who were.

Nor was the nativist-versus-foreign-born debate within the Republican Party overlooked by the Democrats, who published a German-language biography of Douglas during the campaign and disbursed subsidies to convince

German-language newspapers to advocate on their behalf.[45] The presence of a foreign-born German American as secretary to candidate Lincoln would go a long way to reassure the German American community, especially the influential German American newspapermen, that Lincoln was not a nativist. Nicolay's ability to speak and read the language was a valuable asset. After all, as Helen observed, her father had been brushing up on his German since coming to Springfield.[46] Nicolay's relative obscurity outside of Springfield and the German American newspaper community gave the nativists no cause for complaint or alarm. For Lincoln, who according to Lamon and others did nothing out of friendship but only out of political calculation, Nicolay's appointment was the first of many appointments he would make to mollify an ethnic voting bloc. In fact, when Nicolay was appointed as private secretary, he became, with the exception of Alexander Hamilton, the first foreign-born American to reach the inner sanctum of the national government.

Whitney's assessment of Nicolay as "a mere clerk" was born out of dislike for the private secretary and probably a bit of class and ethnic prejudice. "A mere clerk" could not have handled the responsibilities and stresses Nicolay faced as presidential secretary during the four years of the Civil War, greatly exceeding anything with which his predecessors had dealt. Ward Hill Lamon's assessment of Nicolay as "a very competent and clever clerk" is fairer and closer to the mark, but still misses it. Neither Whitney nor Lamon were politicians and did not see beyond the surface of the appointment, nor did they understand how the Civil War had begun to transform the federal government. Nicolay would become more than a private secretary. He would redefine the position and become the nation's first presidential chief of staff—in fact, if not in name. He was a trusted aide and confidant, one on whom Lincoln so depended that he would repeatedly dispatch him as a troubleshooter during his four years in the White House.

In the end, Lincoln chose trust, competency, efficiency, and cleverness over refinement and savoir-faire, qualities that were not particularly important to the homespun politician. What mattered most to Lincoln were the 300,000 votes that Carl Schurz had said the German Americans could deliver in November 1860. Nicolay's appointment was part of that calculation. Ironically, it is very likely that Nicolay never understood his ethnic advantage in obtaining the position as Lincoln's secretary. Nonetheless, with Lincoln, ethnic politics became important for the first time in national politics. All the other qualities Nicolay possessed—likeability, loyalty, efficiency, cleverness, trust, writing skills, and newspaper experience—could be found in others. Nicolay's background as a

German immigrant and his connections to the German American press, in particular, clinched the deal. The age of ethnic politics had dawned at the national level. He was its first beneficiary. For Lincoln, Nicolay's greatest asset was that he was German.

Once appointed secretary to candidate Lincoln, he could not be easily discharged without raising alarm bells among the sensitive German Americans that the appointment had merely been a ruse to secure their votes. This is one reason why Lincoln would demur on repeated calls for his secretary's removal during the Civil War. In this role, the young man from Essingen would give his full measure of devotion to Lincoln with impeccable service as private secretary.

CHAPTER FIVE

Private Secretary

A New Role, 1861

By the time of Lincoln's inauguration on March 4, 1861, on the east portico of the Capitol, the great Republican electoral victory of the previous November had been shrouded in the uncertain fog of secession and numerous threats to the life of the president-elect. Lincoln and his entourage had survived the long and arduous train trip to Washington, and now attention was focused on a successful, uninterrupted inaugural ceremony. Unprecedented security precautions were taken in Washington under the direction of General Winfield Scott to ensure the safety of the new chief executive and the uninterrupted completion of the ceremonial rituals that accompanied presidential inaugurations. Nicolay and Hay's biography of Lincoln described the security situation, in which "riflemen in squads [were] placed on the roofs of certain commanding houses along Pennsylvania Avenue . . . a battalion of District of Columbia troops [was] placed near the steps of the Capitol," riflemen were stationed in the windows of the wings of the Capitol, and at "the east front was stationed a battery of flying artillery."[1] Despite the many threats, the inauguration proceeded as planned with the new president telling the southern leadership that the "momentous issue of civil war" was in their hands. Afterwards, there was the usual round of balls and other festivities to celebrate the incoming administration.

The next morning, the immigrant boy from the Rhineland woke up in the bedroom he would share with his friend John Hay for the next four years in the northeast corner of the White House, officially known at the time as the Executive Mansion. In less than a quarter century, after experiencing personal loss, loneliness, and hand-to-mouth poverty, the boy who had kept accounts at the family mill, clerked in Aaron Reno's store in White Hall, apprenticed and ultimately became the sole editor and proprietor of a small frontier newspaper, wrote articles for frontier newspapers, and clerked in the Office of the Illinois Secretary of State had reached the apex of his career days after his twenty-ninth birthday. While he had mentors like Joel Pennington, the Reverend Carter, Z. N. Garbutt, O. M. Hatch, and Abraham Lincoln along the way, Nicolay had reached this point in his career largely through his own personal tenacity and perseverance. Despite lacking a formal education, he was a self-educated man in the best frontier tradition, a member of the bar of the State of Illinois, and a holder of patents. His ability to use the English language, as well as fluency in French and his native German, was well recognized. All of this had been achieved without family support, family wealth, or family ties. Yet, he remained a reserved, self-effacing individual. There is little evidence that he ever flaunted his personal experiences, connections, or success, yet he clearly disliked those whose egos required that everyone knew who they were and how rich, how educated, how successful, or how well-connected they purported to be. Such boastings did not impress Nicolay. Unfortunately for him, the Washington of March 1861 had an ample supply of these characters, with whom he had to interact on a daily basis.

Helen Nicolay provided a portrait of her father at this time. He was over five feet ten inches tall, with brown hair, blue eyes, a "particularly sensitive mouth . . . hidden by a moustache and small beard he wore from early manhood," and an "agile mind." Those characteristics could fit many men, but he was distinguished by a pencil-thin physique: "never in his life did he weigh more than one hundred and twenty pounds." His demeanor was notable for two things. His daughter wrote that "people who knew him in wartime commented on his 'slow smile.'" Although he "smiled frequently," he was seldom known to "laugh aloud."[2] Thomas H. Shastid described Nicolay as "not much of a joker. He merely broke loose at long intervals."[3] Nicolay is also described as having a "quiet movement," which he had learned from his sojourns into the forest as a lad.[4] "He was known as a man who was quick to take a hint," his daughter noted, "and (a most valuable quality in a private secretary) who 'never said anything worth quoting.'"[5] Historian James B. Conroy in his book on the Lincoln White House quoted a newspaperman who knew Nicolay and liked the secretary. The journalist described the secretary as having a "methodical, silent German way about him. Scrupulous, polite, calm, obliging, with the gift of hearing other people talk, coming and going to the Capitol like a shadow." Conroy further characterized Nicolay as "never drawing attention to himself, quick to respond to a request, committed to his job, devoted to the President."[6] These attributes gave Nicolay the ability to enter or leave a room or an assembly as if he were a shadow—unobtrusive, unnoticed, and unquoted.

One attribute the private secretary did not possess was the right to be called a citizen of the United States, for he had not yet become a naturalized citizen. Nicolay certainly knew that he was not a citizen, but he kept this fact to himself. Apparently, no one gave his citizenship status a second thought, especially O. M. Hatch or Abraham Lincoln. Everyone just assumed he was an American citizen. Nor did Nicolay discourage this belief. In 1858, on a patent application, he had checked the box stating that he was a citizen. His admission to the bar of Illinois certainly would have required citizenship as well as his admission in 1863, with the sponsorship of the attorney general of the United States, to present cases before the United States Supreme Court. He voted in elections. Yet, throughout both his tenure as private secretary and as consul at Paris, he was still legally a subject of the King of Bavaria. He did swear a loyalty oath to the United States on July 9, 1861, at a time when the government was trying to determine who was or was not loyal to the Union cause in the nation's capital.[7] However, affirming loyalty to the United States did not make him a citizen. Consequently, he holds the distinction of being the only foreign national to hold the position of the presidential secretary or chief of staff. Nicolay, according to the records of the Pike County Court House, became an American citizen on October 12, 1870.[8]

Helen tried to sidestep the matter, stating that since he came to this country as "such a small child," it "probably . . . never occurred to him that his citizenship could be questioned." Writing about her father's decision to secure citizenship, she rationalized that "when returning from Paris he reached the conclusion that American citizenship was something very precious to be surrounded by every possible safeguard."[9] It is somewhat implausible that a man who had served as Abraham Lincoln's right hand throughout the Civil War would only decide after an additional five years in Paris that "American citizenship was something very precious." The only possible safeguard that Nicolay could have was formal application for citizenship required of every foreign national to be recorded in the local courthouse.

But on that March day after the inauguration, the new secretary had more pressing concerns than his citizenship status. Nicolay had known long working hours and high pressure while working for Lincoln prior to their arrival in Washington, but life and work in the White House would be even more intense. Given his busy schedule, one can be thankful for his frequent correspondence with his fiancée, Therena Bates, back in Pittsfield, Illinois; these letters provide a window into his heart and mind as well as into the significant events unfolding in the nation's capital and within the Lincoln presidency. In his missives to Therena, he was generally unassuming, occasionally condescending, and often complaining (too much work, bad weather, unreasonable demands being placed upon Mr. Lincoln, not enough peace and quiet, and so on). His letters also frequently express concerns about Therena's health and his own, and are critical of opposition to Lincoln, as well as fiercely protective and always supportive of his boss's views and actions. He rarely boasted of his own importance or accomplishments. He was infrequently romantic, occasionally suggesting in a manner both teasing and taunting that Therena might have reason to be jealous of other ladies in Washington. But he did wander onto the path of passion now and then, and his loneliness at being a thousand miles away from his fiancée is at times quite evident. It is clear that in reality Therena was the only woman for whom he had deep feelings.

He described Washington society and some of his social engagements, but it is sometimes difficult to differentiate what he considered work-related activities from genuine free-time adventures. The letters to Therena, in sum, provide us with a revealing, insightful glimpse of life in the Lincoln White House and in Washington during extraordinary and perilous times, as perceived by a highly intelligent and observant young man who was both rather sure of himself and at the same time trying to find his way in the world. He often attempted to assure Therena that he was not in physical danger, either from sickness or secessionist threats to Washington, and that things would yet work out for the nation under Lincoln's wise and steady leadership. In addition to corresponding with Therena, he wrote to others and from time to time made notes to himself on various aspects of the events and crises impacting the country, particularly the ways in which Lincoln perceived and dealt with them. His notes and letters are intelligent, articulate, to the point, and generally written in quite beautiful, highly legible penmanship.

In penning his first letter to Therena from the White House, Nicolay prominently and proudly inscribed at the top, "Executive Mansion March 5th 1861 Washington, D.C." "As you can see from the heading of my letter," he proudly pointed out to her, "I am fairly installed in the White House." Declaring that "we had a gratifying and glorious inauguration yesterday," he informed her that it was a "fine display and everything went off as nicely as it could have possibly been devised." It was then another two days before he could again pick up the

On the day of his first inauguration, March 4, 1861, as his first official
act as president, Lincoln signed this order, in Nicolay's handwriting,
appointing John G. Nicolay Private Secretary to the President.
(Library of Congress)

pen to complete the letter. Seeking to calm her anxiety after the press reported
Lincoln's secretive arrival in Washington, he asked for "absolution" for not having written to her for more than a week, while also assuring her that "you need
have no apprehensions of danger to him [Lincoln] or those about him." As for
himself, "I consider myself quite as safe here as I used to be in the Free Press
Offices years ago."

Having reassured her about his safety, Nicolay proudly noted the fact that
Lincoln's first official act was to sign his appointment as private secretary. He
described his work as very taxing on both his "physical and mental energies"
but forecasted optimistically that "by and by" after the political appointments
were made, "I think the labor will be more sufferable." Going on to describe
his quarters, he commented on the very pleasant office space he and Hay were
assigned as well as the "nice large bedroom though all of them sadly need new
furniture and carpets." Knowing that Therena was back in small, quiet Pittsfield,
he concluded his letter by mentioning his recent social activities, including a
wedding, the inaugural ball, and two receptions, one diplomatic and the other

more general. Then he signed off as he would invariably do, not with a single romantic word but merely, "Your George."[10]

This would not be the last correspondence that the secretary would begin to write on one day and finish at a later date. He had not anticipated the magnitude and chaos that came with monitoring access to the President. Writing a quarter century later, he reflected on the bedlam "in the anteroom and in the broad corridor adjourning the President's office, there [due to] a restless and persistent crowd." These were, according to Nicolay's descriptive prose, the endless office seekers "in pursuit of one of the many crumbs of official patronage." This unruly horde, "ten, twenty, sometimes fifty," were a beehive of constant activity that "walked the floor . . . talked in groups . . . scowled at every arrival" and "wrangled with the doorkeeper." Not content to claw at or conspire with their fellows, these petitioners besieged members of Congress and "glared with envy" at the cabinet members . . . who pushed through the throng" to the presidential presence.[11]

On March 7, Nicolay also composed a letter to his former boss, O. M. Hatch. His tone here was a bit more brutal in describing the demands of his new position than what he presented to Therena. He complained to Hatch that "during the four weeks past," beginning with the arduous inaugural train trip, he "scarcely had time to eat, sleep or even breathe," and he went on to say that "the labor which has had to be undergone has been terrible. God knows how we shall get through that of the three months to come."[12]

The Republican ascendancy in 1861 not only represented a change in political parties, as the Democrats had been in power the previous eight years, but a new political coalition that had swept to victory in the North. Judgeships, every postmaster position in the country, collectors of the ports, every diplomatic post, and a veritable host of lesser offices and clerkships were the political plums to be obtained from the new administration. To claim their "rightful share" of the spoils came many people, political novices alongside the political hacks, who would all assert that if not for their efforts, Lincoln would not have been elected president. Contemporary political etiquette as spelled out in Washington travel guides reminded all citizens of their right to have an audience with the president. Nicolay was soon to learn how much of his time would become consumed dealing with a public clamoring to exercise their right to see President Lincoln.

An 1860 travel guide to Washington outlined its concept of access to the president.

[I]n the chapter upon etiquette, we have also explained the laws of courtesy governing the citizen in his approach to the elected chief of the government. It only remains therefore to announce that, while the President is a public servant, he is not the servant of each individual comprising that mythical tyranny, "The Public." Let it be understood that while every man who becomes President of the United States agrees to devote certain portions of certain days to miscellaneous hand-shakings and applications for opportunities to serve the republic, *his time is very precious,* and no one individual, unless charged with most extraordinary public business is entitled to more than two minutes conversation with him.[13]

The author of the travel guide later noted the expected code of conduct for the petitioners: "Business calls are received at all times and hours, when the President is unengaged. The morning hours are preferred. Special days and evenings are assigned, each season, for calls of respect, one morning and evening a week usually being assigned for this purpose."[14]

Another contemporaneous book, *Etiquette at Washington,* was more explicit in its description of access to the President.

Every citizen of the United States who visits Washington considers that he has a claim to visit the Chief Magistrate of the Union; and he is accordingly presented to him, and after *shaking hands* and conversing for a few moments, retires, delighted with the suavity of the President, and elevated in his own estimation.

Strangers who are awaiting an audience in the ante-room are frequently much annoyed at witnessing individuals who come along after admitted before them. The persons thus admitted are usually connected with the government, and hence the necessity for the preference. Members of the Senate, and Chairmen of Committees of the House, are immediately announced, and take precedence, with great propriety, because they are presumed to have official business which cannot be delayed.

Yet, with all this, we will venture the assertion that it is easier to gain an interview with the President of the United States than with the most petty noble in a monarchy.[15]

Two minutes, five minutes, ten minutes—it was all the same to the expectant and demanding office seekers. They wanted to see the president and receive what they thought they merited. In wartime, there were not only the plums of political office but also richly rewarding government contracts, inventions such as new armaments to be considered, military appointments, petitions for clemency from the judgments of military tribunals, and a host of minor distractions.

In normal times, the numbers of visitors to the White House might have been a manageable problem, but in wartime, which lasted the length of Lincoln's tenure, the problem of controlling, much less limiting, the number of people for their

Undated photograph of Nicolay, with his signature, during his time as Private Secretary to President Lincoln. (Library of Congress)

brief encounter with the president was daunting. There was a fence surrounding the White House but only manned by a single guard at the entrance. The gate was opened early in the morning and not closed until evening except on Sundays. There were no White House police or Secret Service to screen the public or halt the swarms of people who daily populated the upstairs in the Executive Mansion. Each individual merely walked past Edward McManus, the Irish doorkeeper, and went up the stairs to the second floor and, if he or she had one, presented a card and sat down in the waiting room until called.

Nicolay needed to prioritize and limit access to the president, as a modern chief of staff does, which meant that many who had enjoyed automatic access to the president in previous administrations—cabinet members, senators, congress-men—no longer had it. These necessary steps to protect the president earned the secretary the resentment of many, who urged Lincoln to dismiss him. Lincoln, who had difficulty saying no, came to appreciate his aide turned gendarme, who shielded him from the incessant clamor of a public who thought they were entitled to see their president whenever they wanted and, when possible, to extract offices and other favors from his hand. Nicolay served a very important function for Lincoln as a lightning rod for those who expected the easy access to the president that had existed through decades of peacetime but refused to understand that Lincoln had a war to manage. As a politician, the president could not turn them away, but he delegated this onerous task and therefore shifted the resultant resentments to his private secretary.

If the secretary and his assistants needed to screen and prioritize the daily rush of visitors, the voluminous mail that tumbled onto their desks each day proved to be less harrowing only in the sense that they did not have to confront the correspondents in person. An average of two to three hundred pieces of mail were received daily. Some mail quickly found its way to a proverbial dustbin of history, one of two huge wicker baskets flanking the sorting table. For cabinet secretaries and special personages such as Horace Greeley, there was a small pigeonholed cabinet, marked alphabetically.[16] The subject matter of the letters ran the gamut of human interest: requests for offices or political endorsements, requests for military appointments, requests for pardons or commutations, requests for information on lost relatives, ideas for patents, schemes to end the war (mostly from crackpots and seers), and poems and gifts—to give just a sampling of the mail's diverse content. One of the most interesting proposals made to the president during the war was an offer of war elephants from the King of Siam, whose unique proposal could not be dismissed out of hand. The king received a polite, if negative, response from Lincoln.

Another issue involving the president and the management of his affairs was his personal lack of organization. As an individual, Abraham Lincoln had many positive traits. One talent he did not possess, however, was the ability to keep his papers in order or, more important, to keep his papers at all. Historian David Herbert Donald summarized the problem while describing the chaos of the Lincoln-Herndon law office. According to Donald, it was a law firm without filing cabinets or even files, where documents were frequently lost by both law partners. Lincoln assumed Herndon would "manage the office, preserve the records, and keep the files straight." Instead, in one corner of the office was a bundle of papers with a note in Lincoln's handwriting, "When you can't find it anywhere else, look in this." Herndon took correspondence home with him, and Lincoln "frequently stuck correspondence" in what Herndon referred to as Lincoln's "desk and his memorandum book," better known as his stovepipe hat.[17]

As president, Lincoln could not afford to lose state papers or be allowed to carry them around Washington in his hat. Under Nicolay's direction, filing cabinets and files were set up. The presidential office was a model of organization

Undated studio portrait of Nicolay while Private Secretary to the President. (Library of Congress)

and efficiency that Abraham Lincoln could never have achieved alone. The secretary was, as some contemporaries sneered, "an efficient clerk." But without his capacity for organization, many of the documents we now have about Lincoln, his administration, and the Civil War may have been irretrievably lost. Another contribution to Lincoln's success was convincing the president to agree to limit his time with visitors. These contributions would have been significant in themselves, but in his four years as private secretary, Nicolay proved his usefulness to Lincoln in many other ways. Lincoln's dependence on his secretary went far beyond keeping the public at arm's length or the office in order.

To respond to the correspondence that did reach his desk, the president personally composed letters only on the most important matters or to select correspondents. For other replies, he would make notes outlining the appropriate reply[18] and trust either Nicolay or Hay to draft a response for his signature or allow his secretary to write the letter on his behalf. In the spring of 1861, when several western counties of Virginia were planning their own secession from Confederate Virginia, the leaders communicated with the White House on how best to proceed. It was Nicolay, not Lincoln, who wrote the sensitive response. John Hay, who kept a diary during the White House years, recorded on May 1, 1861, that the "Unionists of Western Virginia" had petitioned the president for assistance in their efforts to maintain a pro-Union government in their region.

John Milton Hay, six years Nicolay's junior, whose friendship from Pittsfield days resulted in Nicolay's request to Lincoln that Hay come to Washington as his secretarial assistant. (www.mrlincolnswhitehouse.org)

Nicolay was charged with the response. According to Hay, he "answered it cautiously today, leaving the door open for further negotiation."[19]

A workday in the White House for the president and his secretaries was filled with meetings, paperwork, and handling the endless stream of visitors and petitioners. In a letter written to William Herndon, as Lincoln's former law partner began compiling letters and interviews for his version of Lincoln's life, John Hay described the daily routines in the office, noting that the president "pretended to begin business at ten o'clock in the morning, but, in reality, the anterooms and halls were full before that hour." It was a perpetual struggle to "get him [Lincoln] to adopt some systematic rules. He would break through every regulation as fast as it was made" and then complain about the consequences. Hay handled most of the written responses for the president, since Lincoln "did not read one in fifty [letters] that he received" personally writing half a dozen a week. Hay also looked over the newspapers and supervised "the clerks who kept the records and in Nicolay's absence did his work also." As was his custom, as evidenced by Nicolay's mission to the publisher of the Lincoln-Douglas debates, the president preferred to send Nicolay or Hay as his representative on delicate errands, committing as little as possible to paper and rarely trusting such correspondence to the mails. When in Washington, Nicolay handled the overall supervision of the office, served as the chief liaison with the Congress, and received other important visitors to the White House. Among the visitors the secretary would host were delegations of Native Americans. At the end of the day, Nicolay and Hay took their meals at the Willard Hotel between "5 or 6," when the president took his at the White House.[20]

William Stoddard, who joined the White House staff on a permanent basis in July 1861, later described the layout of the White House and its second-floor working area:

At the head of them [the stairs leading to the second floor] is a spacious entryway and as we stand here, looking southward, to the right of us is the apartments which are used as sleeping rooms, but which hereafter will be turned into offices.

The fine broad hall that we next walk into runs the entire length of the building east and west. Yonder, across the hall, is a large room which serves as a citadel and place of refuge for Presidents to retreat into when they are too severely pressed in their own business office adjoining, on the east. Beyond that, in the southeastern corner of the house, is the private secretary's office, occupied now by Mr. Nicolay and his immediate assistant Mr. Hay. The large chamber on the north side of the hall is their sleeping-room. The northeastern room, next to its narrow room, corresponding to Mr. Nicolay's office on the other side of the hall, contains three desks. The two upright, mahogany structures in the further corners belong to Mr. Hay. The heavy-looking table-desk of drawers, green clothed and curiously littered, out here in front of the door, with its left elbow toward the fireplace is to be yours [Stoddard's] for several years to come. It is, in some respects, a kind of breakwater, and the duties attached to it will be almost entirely separated from those performed by the other private secretaries.[21]

What Stoddard failed to mention was that the living quarters of the Lincoln family were at the other end of the same floor. This meant that, when in the White House, the unpredictable Mary Todd Lincoln was often a looming presence just down the hall, day and night. There was almost constant bedlam in the crowded presidential anteroom. Manning the barricade was Nicolay with his tiny staff. First among his assistants was John Hay, his friend from those days a decade earlier in the office of the *Free Press*. Stoddard later recalled that "Nicolay and Hay never entered his [Lincoln's] office except on business" and "performed admirably well their manifest duty of keeping out of it as many intruders as they could, high or low."[22] Since the law only permitted Lincoln one paid secretary, Hay was given an appointment in the Department of the Interior and then assigned to the White House as Nicolay's assistant. Later, Hay would be given an appointment in the army as a major, later promoted to colonel, "with full pay and allowances for quarters, horses, and rations. He actually did some military duty with marked credit to himself" to support his duties.[23]

William Stoddard, or "Stod," twenty-six, was a former Illinois newspaperman

William Stoddard, "Stod" to Nicolay
and Hay, who assisted them in the
White House, especially with his ability
to get along with Mrs. Lincoln.
(www.mrlincolnswhitehouse.org)

working in the Interior Department. He had been born in 1835, growing up in Homer, New York, and was a graduate of the University of Rochester. Prior to coming to Washington, he, like Nicolay, had been an Illinois newspaper editor. In Stoddard's case, it was the *Central Illinois Gazette,* published in Champlain. His job in the Interior Department was to sign the president's signature to land patents. For some reason Mrs. Lincoln liked Stoddard, and as a consequence Nicolay and Hay were glad to turn over the responsibility of handling the First Lady to him as often as possible. Stoddard assumed the de facto role as Mrs. Lincoln's private secretary and the two got on reasonably well. Perhaps this was because the assistant did not live a few feet down the hall from the First Lady and could escape to his own private residence in the city after a day's work. Mary Lincoln biographer Ishbel Ross asserted that it was Stoddard who recognized the early signs of insanity in Mrs. Lincoln's behavior before the other men roaming the halls of the Executive Mansion.[24]

Stod had a good personal relationship with Hay. They often shared poetry and other literary endeavors. His relationship with Nicolay, though friendly, was clearly based on their professional interactions. Yet, Stoddard respected Nicolay, describing him as "a fair French and German scholar, with some ability as a writer and much natural acuteness." Notwithstanding these qualities, the secretary, "thanks to a dyspeptic tendency—had developed an artificial manner the reverse of 'popular' and could say 'no' about as disagreeably as any man I ever knew," but at the same time he "was of incalculable service in fending off much that would have been unnecessary labor and exhaustion to his overworked patron." In Stoddard's estimation, Nicolay's devotion to Lincoln was "his chief qualification for the important post he occupied . . . and his incorruptible honesty Lincoln-ward," measuring "all things and all men by their relations to the President." In the final analysis, Stoddard believed that for his devotion to Lincoln, Nicolay "deserves the thanks of all who loved Mr. Lincoln, even if at times they had reason to grumble at 'the bulldog in the ante-room.'"[25]

If Nicolay was a "bulldog" to Stoddard, to another critic he was the "grim Cerberus of Teutonic descent who guard[ed]" the presidential sanctuary. Cerberus was the multiheaded dog-beast from Greek mythology, better known as the "hound of hell." Noah Brooks, correspondent for the *Sacramento Union*, was less charitable toward Nicolay's strident manner. Brooks, who did much to ingratiate himself with Mrs. Lincoln and would be the prime candidate to succeed Nicolay as private secretary prior to Lincoln's death, described Nicolay to his California readers in a dispatch dated November 7, 1863. Brooks referred to Lincoln's staff as "snobby and unpopular" men, whom the supplicants in the anteroom "learn[ed] to love or dislike according to their treatment by his [Lincoln's] underlings." Brooks claimed that Nicolay had "a very unhappy time of it." The solution: "it would not be a bad idea if an inside guardian of affable address, as well as flintiness of face, were placed on duty here."[26] Brooks saw himself as that successor, but he never sat in Nicolay's chair to face the incessant clamor for but a "few minutes of the President's time."

William Stoddard did get to sit in Nicolay's chair when the private secretary and Hay were away on business. Then his appreciation for filling Nicolay's shoes became very acute. Describing the private secretary in his White House memoir, Stoddard recalled, "There is Mr. Nicolay, by the table, getting ready some paper or other for the President to sign. People who do not like him—because they cannot use him, perhaps—say he is sour and crusty, and it is a grand good thing, then, that he is." Reflecting on his own unpleasant experiences substituting for Nicolay or Hay, he warned his readers that "you will see what has become of any easy good-nature you sat down with." Stoddard then showed his professional regard for Nicolay by affirming the secretary's worth to Lincoln: "The President showed his good judgment of men when he put Mr. Nicolay just where he is, with a kind and amount of authority which is not easy to describe."[27] Hay also hated sitting in Nicolay's chair.

While Stoddard had great personal regard for Nicolay as office manager, their relationship was based primarily on their business affiliation rather than on any personal affinity, even though they had both been newspaper editors. He described his relationship with Nicolay as "of an entirely satisfactory character." After leaving the White House in late 1864, Stoddard confessed that he "saw little of Nicolay," who shortly before the latter's death sent Stoddard "a very cordial letter of remembrance and friendship which I was glad to get."[28] Nicolay and Hay would go to Stoddard's Washington residence to pass an occasional evening. It is clear from the carefully phrased "of an entirely satisfactory character" and the fact that the two men saw little of each other in the thirty-seven years between Stoddard's leaving the White House and Nicolay's death that the relationship was cordial but not particularly warm. In contrast, Stoddard reflected more positively on his relationship with Hay, describing it as between "the best of friends," and he recalled their daily association "with pleasure."[29]

By mid-1863, the pressures of work began to compromise Stoddard's health. To ease his workload, the Reverend Edward Duffield Neill,[30] a graduate of Amherst College and Andover Theological Seminary who worked as a Presbyterian minister and chaplain of the First Minnesota Regiment, was added to the office staff in January 1864. In addition to his religious background, Neill was an accomplished educator and author. Born in 1823, he would have stood out in contrast to the much younger team. In an 1885 speech to a convention of the Minnesota Commandery of the Military Order of the Loyal Legion of the United States, Neill talked about his year in Lincoln's White House, briefly mentioning his responsibilities. While he was not given the commission as secretary to sign land patents until Stoddard left Lincoln's employment, his primary assignment was "to read the mail and dispose of all letters addressed to President Lincoln. To this purpose "a mail bag was brought to my room . . . twice a day, well filled with letters upon various subjects."[31]

When Stoddard departed the White House to become marshal for the Western District of Arkansas, a fifth and final appointment was made to the secretarial staff. Charles Philbrick, who was a year older than Hay, having been born of New England parents while they were in Louisiana in 1837, had lived in Griggsville in Pike County since the age of two. He graduated from Illinois College and had been Nicolay's successor in the office of O. M. Hatch in Springfield. Philbrick was a friend of both Nicolay and Hay. In a letter to Nicolay dated October 28, 1862, Hay declared that Philbrick had a serious drinking problem and was drunk all the time. "Something must be done to reform him or he is gone up," Hay concluded.[32] Apparently, Philbrick conquered his demons, including his love of the bottle, since by the fall of 1864 he was working at the White House. Though friends with Philbrick, Hay appears to have had second thoughts about

Edward Duffield Neill, a Presbyterian minister who became another White House assistant brought in under the supervision of Nicolay. (www.mrlincolns whitehouse.org)

the choice. Writing to Nicolay about Philbrick, Hay confessed to finding out that being friends with someone and working alongside them could be two different experiences. "Taking dreary pleasure in seeing Philbrick eat steamed oysters by the ½ bushel" at meals was not something to which Hay looked forward.[33]

While the relationships between these five men were shaped by very different life experiences, they all managed to get along. It is notable that all the men who served with Nicolay and under his supervision had college degrees, the type of education of which the secretary could only have dreamed. Yet, none of them ever suggested that the self-taught Nicolay was poorly educated or that he was to be looked down upon as somehow inferior or intellectually deficient. There were other clerks who would come to the White House from the executive departments, but their role was only for a few days or weeks to help cover some emergency. And despite the popular mythology created to link the assassinated John F. Kennedy to the iconic sixteenth president, there was no Lincoln secretary named Kennedy. JFK had a secretary named Evelyn Lincoln, but that is as far as it went.

Another myth that grew up around this group of men is that they were all Lincoln's private secretaries. In signage at his grave in Lake View Cemetery in Cleveland, Ohio, as well as on the National Park Service website for his birthplace, Hay is proclaimed to have been "private secretary to Abraham Lincoln." The two books based on Stoddard's memoirs say that he was Lincoln's private secretary. An article in the *Illinois College Alumni Magazine* for summer 1997 is entitled, "Charles Philbrick, Private Secretary to Abraham Lincoln."[34] And, finally, Edward Neill's memorial on the popular website Findagrave.com lists him as "Private Secretary to Abraham Lincoln." Helen Nicolay was both emphatic and accurate in noting her father's unique position and title of private secretary to the president. After listing her father's aides, she asserted: "This accounts for the number of individuals whose families claim, quite incorrectly, that they were 'Private Secretary to President Lincoln.' Legally and officially my father was the only one. John Hay was known as his assistant. The others did clerical work and filled in as occasion demanded."[35]

Even before the routines of the office were firmly established, Nicolay found time to write Therena a second letter the week after the inauguration. It described the first Lincoln White House reception on Friday, March 8, 1861. Nicolay was delighted that old-time Washington residents labeled it "the most successful one ever known here. For over two hours the crowd poured in as rapidly as the door would admit them, and many climbed in at the windows."[36] Though he did not mention her on this occasion, Mrs. Lincoln was no doubt intimately involved in the details of the reception, having made it clear that she was coming to the capital "determined to set a high standard and prove her refinement" to Washington society. Many members of Washington's elite society "were open in their contempt toward the Lincolns," seeing the new president as an "uncouth frontier usurper who had come east to take his seat at the table."[37] The secretary would find out soon enough how demanding Mary Lincoln could be when it came to her expectations for public events in the Executive Mansion.

One problem that confronted everyone in the White House was that there were many in the North, and quite a few in Congress, who did not trust the First Lady. A native Kentuckian (like her husband), she was often portrayed as a source of treason within the White House. Her family, the Todds, were prosperous slaveholders. While Kentucky had remained loyal to the Union, members of the Todd family not only openly supported the Confederacy but also fought and died for it. Such false charges against a leader's wife in times of national stress are not unusual. Despite the ongoing tension and animosity between the First Lady and Nicolay and Hay during their time in the White House, nothing in the contemporaneous private writings of either man contain any hint of Mary Lincoln being disloyal to her husband or her country.

The animosity between Mrs. Lincoln and the secretaries continued after the president's death. In a letter dated July 21, 1866, Mrs. Lincoln wrote Alexander Wilkinson complaining that she had not received a medal being cast in her

husband's memory by a committee of French citizens. Her paranoia had conjured up a conspiracy among individuals on her ever-growing enemies list. She
claimed: "I have written in haste—hoping to hear soon from you. . . . I have a
great curiosity, to find out what has become of the medal—advertised to be sent
to me from France— Do make enquiries about it—if *Seward, Hay or Nicolay*
could stop its reaching me they would do so— They are a great set of scamps."[38]

There was no conspiracy. The medal presentation, with Victor Hugo representing the French people, occurred in Paris on schedule on December 1, 1866.[39]
Nicolay, by this time American consul at Paris, undoubtedly was pleased by the
honor the French people bestowed on Lincoln's memory and would have seen
to it that the medal got to the First Lady. A month later, Mrs. Lincoln acknowledged its receipt in a letter to an unidentified friend dated January 3, 1867.[40] The
secretaries got their final revenge in the Lincoln history. Undoubtedly, this was
with the full assent of their patron, Robert Lincoln, whose hostility toward his
mother was deep seated and outlived her death in 1882. In their monumental
work, Nicolay and Hay largely ignored Mary Lincoln. As her biographer Ishbel
Ross, among others, noted, "Mrs. Lincoln got no more than nine references [in
4,800 pages], three as Mary Todd and six as First Lady."[41] Getting along with
Mrs. Lincoln would be a constant challenge for Nicolay over the next four years.

In his second letter from the White House on March 10, 1861, Nicolay also
shared with Therena that it was too soon to "form much of an idea of how I
shall like it here." He teased Therena about the possibility of his running off
"with some beautiful and accomplished lady of the city." Perhaps not quite sure
how she would react, he somewhat reassured her by saying, "So far I have not
discovered many of them." As for his burdensome work load, he had a bit more
detail to share in this letter concerning help from his friend John Hay. "As the
existing laws do not provide for an assistant for me," he remarked to Therena, "I
have had John Hay appointed to a clerkship in the Department of the Interior,
and detailed for special service here at the White House [with President Lincoln's
approval], so that he gives me the benefit of his whole time."[42]

Despite the "almost overwhelming pressure of work which is upon me,"
Nicolay found it necessary to get away at times and try to have a social life in
his new surroundings. Even then, he found himself "haunted continually by
someone who wants to see the President for only five minutes. At present this
request meets me from almost every man woman and child I meet—whether
it be by day or night—in the house or on the street." A streak of reticence, even
shyness, is evident as he tells Therena that he attended a party early in his stay in

Washington that he "couldn't enjoy" because he knew so few people there; hence he felt compelled to "busy myself somewhat in getting acquainted—which is always work for me." He had the nerve to tell his fiancée, "There were a number of really very pretty girls at the party—I did not have the opportunity to judge of much more than their looks." Perhaps realizing that he had written more than Therena would want to know, even if he was only teasing her, he concluded his letter with this sentiment: "You cannot appreciate how much I would give for a quiet evening with you."[43] It is interesting to note that he signed his letters to those other than Therena "Yours, George" or "Yours, Nicolay," but to Therena he always signed off as "Your George."

About three weeks after his arrival in Washington, he composed an uncharacteristically long and, for him, romantic letter to Therena. When he was living and working in Springfield, a trip to see Therena in Pittsfield was not a major undertaking. Perhaps the reality of the distance between them, which now meant that far fewer visitations would be possible, was beginning to sink in. Yet even at his romantic best, he was guarded and on the reserved side. He started his letter by saying he blamed his reserved approach on "years educating myself to be a mere bundle of quiet and dignified imperturbability." Otherwise, he protested, he would "sit down tonight and write you a real love-letter—full of all the pathos and passion of which young men or rather boys in the foolish phrenzy [*sic*] of their first love are guilty." Although Therena would have welcomed a bit of "foolish phrenzy" from George, that would be expecting too much from him. He reassured her, as he had often reiterated, that "you are the only woman on earth to whom I turn in entire confidence—in whom I have an unshaken faith." He then went on to tell her, "you know that I do not cheat myself into the belief that you are perfect—or even near it. Nevertheless, it is a relief to have and express such faith as I have in you." Lovers usually don't see, much less discuss, one or the other's failings during the courtship, yet Nicolay is quite willing to tell his intended that she is not "even near" perfection. However, in conclusion, he wrote, "I could only find happiness with and through you."[44] The pressures and demands of his job would at times put strains on the couple and delay their marriage until he left the White House in 1865. Although his life would intersect with the lives of many others, his two greatest interpersonal commitments were to Abraham Lincoln (and the Lincoln legacy) and to Therena Bates Nicolay, followed by his relationship with his daughter, Helen, and his lifelong friendship with John Hay.

The newness of his situation, the press of his responsibilities, adjustment to his new urban surroundings, and concern about measles seem to have occupied

Nicolay's first few weeks in Washington, without much reference in his letters to the approach of civil war. He noted in a letter to Therena on March 20 that "the two little [Lincoln] boys have the measles," but that he, George, was "in good health, notwithstanding the fact that some of us have work and annoyances enough to make almost anybody sick."[45] A few days later, he learned that Therena had also been stricken with measles, a serious and sometimes fatal disease in the nineteenth century. He expressed his concern that she recover and that she not experience any damage to her eyes. Nicolay himself would battle eye disease and vision problems throughout much of his life. As for his impossible work load, he informed Therena in the same letter that he had come up with a plan: "Last night I got the President (it still seems queer to speak of Mr. Lincoln in that way although I am becoming used to it) to agree to let me have his business hours limited to from 10 in the morning to 3 in the afternoon." This schedule, Nicolay told Therena, "will relieve not him alone but all the rest of us, from a burden of labor which it would be impossible to sustain for a great length of time." He lamented that due to the press of business, "I have not yet spent a single hour in sight-seeing although there is much about this city that is well worth seeing. Good night! I send you many kisses!"[46]

It had taken Nicolay almost a month to convince the president to limit his access to the public. Lincoln hated saying no, but his secretary recognized that the exigencies of the moment did not allow for continuing to see everyone who wanted an audience with the president. The president had to budget his time. It was a crucial step in organizing the Lincoln presidency.

The timing of Lincoln's action, at his secretary's insistence, could not have come any later than it did. War clouds darkened ever more over the nation. Starting with his letter to Therena of April 7, 1861, Nicolay demonstrated an increasing preoccupation with rumors of war, although he was not yet convinced it would of necessity come, reassuring her that "I do not think that either the authorities or any considerable number of the people of either section want a civil war."[47] Four days later, he wrote to Therena specifically about "rumors of war" that focused on Washington's being in danger "by the secessionists against this capital." "Don't get alarmed," he told her. "The Southerners will I think need all their forces in their own country and will scarcely make an attempt so foolhardy as that of attacking this city."[48] However, many others, including President Lincoln, were very concerned about Washington's precarious defenses. A few days later, when "several were killed on both sides" in a riot in secession-leaning Baltimore on April 19, 1861, as the Sixth Massachusetts regiment marched through that city on their way to defend Washington, he remarked to Therena that "I believe [this to be] the first bloodshed in this civil war, and singularly enough it is the anniversary of the first bloodshed in the Revolution (the skirmishes at Lexington and Concord on April 19, 1775). A bit less certain of Washington's defensive situation than he was a few days before, he tried to reassure Therena that she need "not feel seriously alarmed although the apprehension of danger are pretty general."[49]

In reality, hostilities had already broken out in the early morning hours of April 12, 1861, when Charleston's batteries opened fire on Fort Sumter on orders of the Confederate government. As Nicolay and Hay summarized in their history, "In the bombardment of Sumter the insurgents . . . made active, aggressive war upon the United States."[50] On April 17, 1861, President Lincoln responded with a call for troops to put down the Southern rebellion, which in turn resulted in four more Southern states seceding from the Union and joining the Confederacy, including Virginia, just across the Potomac River from the capital. More defensive troops, this time from the Seventh New York Infantry, finally entered Washington on April 25, much to the relief of the Lincoln administration as well as the loyal people of the capital city. Describing the scene nearly a quarter century later, Nicolay and Hay cheered the arrival of more federal troops by remembering that "as they passed . . . they seemed to sweep all thought of danger and all taint of treason" out of the capital.[51]

Two days later, George was able to write to Therena, "Now pray at once give your fears [for his safety] wings and let them fly away." He also urged her to do her part for the Union effort—to not forget that "you are a good Republican, and have promised me to fight all secession democrats (Pa always excepted) with words if you can't with bullets."[52] Therena's father, Dorus Bates, was a staunch Democrat with Copperhead sympathies.

Nicolay received a strange request in a letter from Therena on May 11, asking him to burn her letters.[53] This request clearly perplexed him. Apparently Therena had her reasons and convinced George at some point to do her bidding, or perhaps her letters have been lost by other means. While the details are unknown, the sad fact is that precious few of Therena's many letters to George have survived. One can only speculate about their contents from the ways in which George's letters respond, and this situation has deprived posterity of a fuller understanding of their relationship.

Tragedy struck the White House on May 24, 1861, the day after Virginia's ordinance of secession was passed. President Lincoln ordered Federal troops to cross the Potomac and occupy Alexandria, now officially rebel territory. From the White House, the residents could see a particularly prominent rebel flag atop one of Alexandria's hotels. Among the officers participating in this action was Colonel Elmer Ellsworth, a young man who had studied law in Lincoln's office in Springfield before going to New York to raise a regiment of Zouaves. Ellsworth had been like a son to Lincoln and was a friend to Nicolay, and he had traveled on the inaugural train along with Lincoln, Nicolay, and Hay. On May 24, Ellsworth and his recruits, the Eleventh New York Infantry, along with other Union troops, entered Alexandria and forced Virginia's troops to withdraw. Remembering the flag defiantly floating in full view of the White House, Ellsworth was determined to take it down, only to be shot and killed in the attempt by the hotel's proprietor.

The president was deeply affected by Ellsworth's death; his body lay in state in the White House East Room, the first Civil War fatality to be mourned there. His funeral was likewise held in the White House. Honored as the symbolic, if not actual, "first casualty of the Civil War," Ellsworth became, in historian Joshua Zietz's words, "an instant hero throughout the North. . . . [H]is death became a rallying cry for the Union. He was celebrated in verse and song and memorialized in hundreds of newspapers."[54]

Nicolay had lost a close friend. Writing to Therena the day after learning of Ellsworth's death, he told her that he was "quite unable to keep the tears out of my eyes . . . until I have almost concluded that I am quite a weak and womanish sort of creature. . . . I had learned to value him very highly. He was very young— only 24 I think—very talented and ambitious, and very poor—a combination of the qualities upon which sadness and misfortune seem ever to play."[55] His description of Ellsworth could have fit himself a decade before: "very talented and ambitious, and very poor." Then in a bit of melancholia into which he would sometimes slip, he noted those "qualities upon which sadness and misfortune seem ever to play." The period of mourning was short, with the press of work and the activities of daily life working to assuage his grief.

Within a week his spirits had been lifted by an outing on horseback "in company with John Hay and Bob Lincoln who is here on a short visit from college. . . . We went across the Long Bridge over into Virginia where you know, many of our troops are now encamped." With appropriate pass in hand, they were able to ride up to Robert E. Lee's now abandoned plantation home, Arlington House, located in "one of the most beautiful situations imaginable—just opposite this city on a high sloping hill that rises up from the Potomac." George described to Therena how "in the garden we found an old negro at work who was born at Mt. Vernon before Gen. Washington's death. We asked him many questions—delighted him with introducing 'Bob'—the President's son—in whom the old darkey expressed a lively interest—and furnished him with a gift of small change. Altogether I don't know when I have passed so satisfactory and pleasant an afternoon."[56] Three years later, Mrs. Lee's garden would be the site of the first burials of Union dead in what is now Arlington National Cemetery.

While Illinois prairie summers can be hot and humid, Nicolay was complaining by early June about the humid Washington weather. There was little to write about regarding the "war," since not much was happening outside of drilling and other preparations for some future engagement, despite increased clamoring from some members of Congress and several Northern newspapers for immediate action to end "the rebellion." He complained to Therena on June 2, "It rained last night, and is so oppressively warm and sultry today, that I feel almost too languid and unnerved even to write. From what experiences I have had, and from what I hear about the climate, I fear we shall find it rather disagreeable here during the hot months."[57] He was able to escape the Washington heat and humidity for a few days in June for his first visit back to Illinois. It can only be assumed that he must have visited Therena in Pittsfield, but the only letter in his papers from this time was written to her from Springfield on June 7. It is not known whether he visited Pittsfield before or after this date. He addressed this letter, as he sometimes did, to "Dear Maggie" (his pet name for Therena) and teased, or perhaps tormented, her by recounting a picnic, presumably in Springfield, to which he had been invited. George would tell her about the "young ladies" present at the social event. With a lack of sensitivity for his love's feelings, he coyly informed Therena that should he "be taken captive by any pair of black or blue eyes, I will immediately communicate to you, so that you may come over and make a rescue."[58] Undoubtedly, all of this was in jest, but it demonstrates how insensitive he could be even with someone he truly loved, perhaps because of a lack of mentoring in the art of romance. After he returned to Washington around June 18, he wrote Therena registering a complaint that his overnight train ride from Chicago to Washington "did not add any delights to railroad traveling."[59]

It is apparent that neither Nicolay nor virtually anyone else in the country had, at this point, in their wildest imaginations any comprehension of the agonizingly long and appalling fratricidal war on which the country was about to embark. Most Americans, including the leadership of both sides, anticipated a quick and victorious end to the sectional dispute. This illusion was shattered at the First Battle of Bull Run. In mid-July, the president succumbed to the demands from Congress for military action and the press to march on Richmond. Lincoln ordered General Irwin McDowell to take his army south. On July 16, 1861, General McDowell began moving troops toward a Confederate force near Manassas Junction, Virginia, and a creek known as Bull Run. A full-fledged battle ensued, and it initially appeared to Washington onlookers who had made the thirty-mile excursion to watch the battle that the day was theirs. However, the arrival of Confederate reinforcements led by General Joe Johnston turned the Union victory into a retreat and then a rout, as soldiers and civilians made a chaotic flight back to Washington.

Nicolay had started writing a letter to Therena that afternoon but then put it down, undoubtedly in light of the panic and confusion in Washington caused by this defeat. Returning to the letter the next day, he informed her, "Our worst fears are confirmed. The victory that seemed in our grasp at four o'clock yesterday afternoon is changed to an overwhelming defeat—a total and disgraceful rout of our men."[60] Yet, the expected Confederate attack on the city itself never occurred. He followed up with another letter dated July 23 to give Therena some reassurance about the safety of Washington. Noting that the rebels had not pursued the Union troops from the battlefield, he proclaimed that the "preparations for the war will be continued with increased vigor by the Government."[61] Under the circumstances, it certainly sounded like a bit of bravado, but he knew his boss was determined to prosecute the war.

A few days later Nicolay again composed a letter to Therena, telling her, "Things remain here about as they were—there has been no further fighting, and the gloom and oppression of the late disaster is somewhat wearing off."[62] But two days later, he observed that the shell-shocked capital was "startled with the impression that the city was being attacked" when "one of our steamers which had gone on a pleasure excursion down the river, returned and was firing salutes on her way to the landing. Of course, there are constantly plenty of incidents on which to found rumors, and plenty of disturbed and lively imaginations to give them shape and utterance."[63] Life in the White House was providing other interesting experiences for Nicolay, in addition to talk of the war. He informed Therena on August 2 that "Prince Napoleon who is now in New York is coming to Washington and dines with us here at the Executive Mansion on Saturday (to-morrow) at 7 o'clock."[64]

As Lincoln's trust and dependence on his assistants grew, he would often seek the companionship of his secretaries when the burdens of his office would overwhelm him. On restless nights, and there were many as the war dragged on,

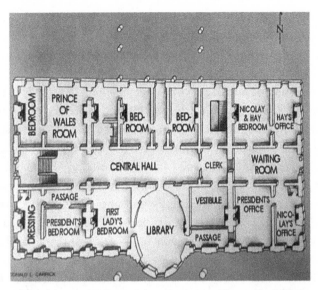

Plan of the second floor of the White House during the Lincoln
presidency. Note the Nicolay and Hay bedroom and offices
in the northeast corner. (Drawing by Donald L. Carrick,
www.whitehousemuseum.org)

Lincoln needed relief from the stresses of his responsibility. Helen described the
increasingly frequent scene as likely related to her by her father. As the burden of
office weighed down on Lincoln, his "hearty laugh was heard less often." Sleepless
nights would find the president pacing the hallway of the second floor. Finding
a light still on in his secretaries' bedroom he would "enter book in hand to enjoy
with them some odd conceit with which he sought to gain momentary relief."
After telling a tale or reading a story, perhaps chatting a few moments, Lincoln
would leave to continue his pacing. While John Hay would find "the tall spare
figure in his night shirt ... funnier than the jest he came to read," these nocturnal
visits intensified their love and devotion to the man of whom they would "speak
affectionately" as "'The Ancient' or 'The Tycoon' or if they were especially moved
as 'The American.'"[65] In those intimate moments, Lincoln was truly transfigured
into Father Abraham for these young men.

The president also shared conversations with his secretaries and sought their
opinions on quiet Sunday afternoons when the day's work had been done and
the threesome could relax without the interference of visitors.[66] The nature of
those conversations are also lost to history. Nicolay and Hay never revealed the

content of those quiet chats or of those midnight rendezvous. The president's willingness to share with them some private moments, to open up, if only a little, his inner feelings to them, speaks volumes about Lincoln's deep trust in their ability to hold his confidences without fear of revelation.

Lincoln rewarded his assistants with paid vacations, unheard of in the nineteenth century. Six months after he had left Illinois for Washington in the service of Mr. Lincoln, Nicolay was given the opportunity to spend a few vacation days at the seaside in Newport, Rhode Island, which he eagerly welcomed. Writing Therena, he described his first full day in town, during which he attended a Unitarian service and "heard a young preacher deliver an incoherent, unlicked and sophomoric sermon," and afterwards went down to the beach to frolic in the surf and enjoy dinner.[67] On the same day he described his Newport adventures to Therena, he also sent a similar account to John Hay of his first day there, with one addition: "I have listened to a stupefying sermon, taken a refreshing and invigorating bath in the surf, *and got an introduction to two pretty young ladies"* (emphasis by the authors).[68] Apparently, George did not feel compelled to tell Therena everything.

Nicolay could not avoid noticing the impact of the war, even when on vacation. He remarked to Therena that "the war has however ruined the summer resorts as well as everything else. I am told that during last summer and the year before there used to be five to six hundred carriages out on the drive every evening. Now not more than fifty."[69] As he was faced with returning soon to his work in Washington, he let Therena know that "I shall hate dreadfully to have to go back to my old treadmill again, and will consequently hold off as long as possible."[70]

Back in the White House, his vacation over, his thoughts increasingly turned to the war. The inability of anyone to see how it would play out and his own seemingly futile role in the course of things preyed on his thoughts. Very few people could yet grasp the suffering and death in the nation's future. A military man named William Tecumseh Sherman was predicting a long and bloody war, but most people thought him crazy. Nicolay shared his thoughts to Therena on September 8, 1861, and predicted that "we shall somehow get through it in the course of a year." Yet, he confessed that he could not "see very plainly the how and the where. In disturbed times like these the keenest human vision is necessarily blind to the accidents which always play such important parts in revolution."[71] Where Nicolay apparently saw chance and accident, an agnostic view of the workings of the universe, Lincoln, with a deepening religious viewpoint, came increasingly to see the war from a providential perspective. Lincoln ultimately concluded that although human understanding is limited, "the Almighty has

His own purposes," one of which may have been to require from the nation an atonement in blood, as John Brown had famously predicted, for the institution of slavery.[72]

While the daily routines of the office were established by the time of Stoddard's fulltime assignment to the White House in July, the demanding pressures that Nicolay faced day in and day out were beginning to wear on him by September 1861. He shared his candid feelings with Therena that "being here where I can overlook the whole war and never be in it—always threatened with danger, and never meeting it—constantly worked to death, and yet doing (accomplishing) nothing, I assure you grows exceedingly irksome, and I sometimes think even my philosophy won't save me. It is a feeling of duty and not one of inclination that keeps me here."[73] The war was dominating national life as well as his own perspective. "There is a sort of sameness in everything that surrounds us here" he wrote, "that makes it almost impossible to get one's self interested in anything but that which somehow pertains to the war, or the troubles of the country."[74]

His thoughts turned anxiously to the situation in Missouri, especially as it was close to Pittsfield and Therena. Demonstrating ignorance of the political repercussions of his action, General John C. Frémont had issued a proclamation in August 1861 unilaterally abolishing slavery in Missouri. This unauthorized decree nearly drove that state into the arms of the Confederacy. In a private journal entry dated September 17, 1861, Nicolay expressed his dismay and concern about Frémont's action and the effect it might have, especially on secessionist sentiments in neighboring Kentucky, a concern also expressed by Lincoln. In addition to Frémont's proclamation, which Lincoln asked him to modify, "His [Frémont's] alleged general mismanagement and incapacity formed the subject of a long session of the Cabt. And the next day, one week ago, the P.M. Genl. [Post Master General Montgomery Blair] and Q.M. Gen. [Quartermaster General Montgomery] Meigs went to St. L. [St. Louis] to look into the affair somewhat."[75]

As matters grew more serious, Lincoln sent Nicolay to Springfield, Illinois, to assess the situation. Upon his arrival in the Illinois capital, he composed a letter to Therena promising that he "will come over [to Pittsfield] as soon as I can, and hope to be able to stay a week or two when I get there."[76] A letter to John Hay, sent from Springfield on October 21, 1861, informed his friend, who was doing double duty in Nicolay's absence, that he planned to leave for Pike County that afternoon, hoping to stay two weeks. He reported to Hay that "I made a call on Mme l'Imperatrice [Madame Empress], but the Princesses were not at home, and so far I have only met Anne. Rhoda has two or three times dazzled my vision on the sidewalk. I meditate a pilgrimage thither." Hay apparently knew the

Springfield ladies in question, giving Nicolay's mysterious passage a salacious ring to it. Perhaps the secretary, who frequently teased his beloved about his wandering eye, may have been thinking about an afternoon tryst with a lady of the town. As in some of his letters to Therena, he liked to portray himself as the man about town, but the fact remains that there never was a serious rival to Therena Bates. Returning to more serious business in his letter to Hay, he added a postscript: "P.S. Fremont is 'played out.' The d__d fool has completely frittered away the fairest opportunity a man of small experience ever had to make his name immortal."[77]

After a quick visit to Pittsfield, Nicolay started the journey back to Washington. In Springfield, he wrote to Therena that "I already have a premonition of my Washington life, by meeting grumblers [in Springfield] on every hand, that even now disgust me with a harassing prospect of vexatious official duty, and make me wish myself back with you where I could hide myself from the annoyance."[78] After Nicolay reported back to Lincoln that public opinion was solidly against Frémont, the general was removed, and the crisis in Missouri abated.[79]

Frémont was not the only individual whom the secretary saw as damaging the war effort. On October 2, he commented to Therena that he was a "good deal oppressed with the quantity of bad and discouraging news which comes from the West." For explication, he declared that "pretty much everything appears to be going wrong there, if we may credit all the reports we get. And it seems to be in such a confusion that we are not able to tell at this distance where the fault lies."[80] He knew that he could not share everything going on in the Lincoln administration with her. Despite not assigning blame for the "bad and discouraging news" mentioned above, on the very day that he composed that letter to Therena, he also recorded notes of a private conversation with President Lincoln. Secretary of War Simon Cameron was becoming a problem. Nicolay attended most cabinet meetings and took notes, was an often-present figure in many of Lincoln's other meetings, and was, along with John Hay, a confidant with whom Lincoln liked to interact and from whom the president at times sought opinions.

Nicolay's notes of October 2, 1861, regarding a confidential conversation with the president about Secretary Cameron include these observations made by Lincoln:

Cameron utterly ignorant and regardless [unaware] of the course of things, and the probable result.
Cameron

Selfish and openly discourteous to the President.
Obnoxious to the Country.
Incapable either of organizing details or conceiving and advising general plans.[81]

Lincoln had hesitated adding Cameron to his cabinet in the first place, but had proceeded with the appointment and now was reluctant to dismiss him. Nonetheless, Cameron's deficiencies and political liabilities were becoming increasingly evident. In late 1861, the president requested reports from his cabinet for submission to Congress, along with his own annual message to the nation's lawmakers. Without authorization or consultation, the secretary of war inserted in his report the bold and controversial assertion that it was "clearly a right of the Government to arm slaves . . . and employ their service against the rebels."[82] Suspected by many of dishonesty, as well as of sloth and incompetence, Cameron by this unauthorized statement of policy crossed the line even with the patient and kindhearted Lincoln. The president sent him packing as minister to Russia in January 1862, St. Petersburg being the farthest diplomatic post from Washington.

While Nicolay was in Springfield, death again touched the White House. Senator Edward Baker of Oregon was killed in a fusillade of bullets at the Battle of Ball's Bluff on the Virginia side of the Potomac River at Leesburg. Baker, commissioned as a colonel with no military experience when the war broke out, had been a longtime close friend of Lincoln's, and the loss affected the president greatly. The political ramifications of this third Union defeat in the opening months of the war were significant for the Lincoln White House. The defeats at First Bull Run in July and Wilson's Creek in Missouri in August were harsh blows to Union morale and the hopes of an easy war against the South. When the bodies of Union dead from Ball's Bluff floated down the Potomac past Washington, this humiliation prompted the Republican-dominated Congress to establish the Joint Committee on the Conduct of the War, a congressional oversight committee that became the bane of Abraham Lincoln's existence and a meddling, counterproductive force in the Union war effort.

Yet even the members of the joint committee came to know the power of the president's secretaries. As Helen Nicolay noted, both her father and John Hay, while working in the White House, "did look very young, and not at all formidable, but those who tried to oppose them found that the President's secretaries usually carried their point."[83] The secretaries, especially Nicolay, continued to control access to the president. He may have acted like the "gatekeeper of Hell," as Noah Brooks derisively referred to him, but as every chief of staff of the modern era knows, access to the president must be carefully regulated. In return, Lincoln repeatedly demonstrated his appreciation for his secretary's doggedness.

A few days before Thanksgiving Day 1861, Nicolay wrote to Therena about an experience shared with John Hay that demonstrates his willingness to tell his fiancée about even embarrassing situations that befell him. Nicolay and Hay went with President Lincoln to review Union troops some "six or eight miles out" from Washington. Nicolay related to Therena that he suffered from overexertion: "I had tired myself out, lost my dinner, spoiled my pantaloons, and having got tangled in the road among a troop of cavalry had come pretty near getting our carriage broken to pieces—but I had seen the largest and most magnificent military review ever held on this continent."[84] The Union's military force looked impressive enough—and the secretary and others could not help but wonder why there was so little progress against the rebellion to show for it. However, as the coming year would reveal, performance on the parade ground did not equate to performance in the field.

Holidays in Washington seemed to cast a gloomy atmosphere over Nicolay's mental state. On the evening of his first Thanksgiving Day away from Therena, he penned a depressing note to her suggesting an attack of loneliness. Feeling his isolation from the traditional warmth of familiar surroundings on the holiday, he wrote that he was "very much afraid that my thanksgiving has been anything but profitable or satisfactory." He diagnosed his case as the "worse fit of the blues in six months" and that there was "an excellent prospect of its continuance for several days to come."[85] He fared no better on Christmas Day 1861, as he again noted to Therena in a depressed state that for Hay and him, it was just another ordinary day, with meals at Willard's and "without anything special to remind us that there are ever any such things as Christmas dinners with social 'sauce' . . . calculated to make one forget the drudgeries and 'unholy' days of life." Reflecting on his life, he wrote that "fortunately, in my fifteen years straying about the world alone, I have got pretty well used to it."[86] The phrase "fifteen years straying about the world alone" recalled his being callously cast out into the world by his older brother in 1846 after the death of his father without anyone to call a friend. But now, he was not totally alone; he had Hay at his side and Lincoln nearby. And there was his beloved, albeit geographically distant, Therena.

Even for his Christmastide depression in the capital in the midst of war, he had much to look back on with pride. He had come to Washington as the private secretary to the president of the United States, a remarkable feat for an immigrant boy who, as he himself noted, had been abandoned and left penniless at the age of fourteen. He had organized the Lincoln White House operation, making it an efficient if still overworked machine. He had convinced Lincoln to abandon the practice of his predecessors to allow every petitioner into the presidential presence—a necessary step for success, especially in wartime. He had proven himself as efficient, as dedicated, and, most important, as trustworthy as he had been in Springfield. Neither Nicolay nor Hay had fallen victim to the siren song of sycophants who would have used their "friendship" to gain political access or power. Nicolay was a man to be reckoned with, but he went about his business in a most unassuming way. He had achieved much and had not yet turned thirty.

CHAPTER SIX

War on Many Fronts, 1862

At the dawn of the New Year, no one really knew what 1862 would bring in terms of the war, but there was beginning to be a gnawing awareness that it would not be over soon. Despite the war, everyone in the capital was aware that New Year's Day was always the occasion for a presidential levee.

The 1860 guidebook *Etiquette at Washington*, states, "In Washington it is the custom for the most distinguished public functionaries to hold public levees, which are visited by both ladies and gentlemen. The custom of receiving New Year's visits has, within a few years, become quite general in Washington among private citizens. Visiting begins at twelve and continues till three o'clock and even later. . . . Full dress is appropriate on such occasions. The visits should be very short."[1]

Each year, the president had to endure the annual New Year's reception, first for the diplomatic corps, the Supreme Court, and the cabinet, and then the public. After a traditional late-morning New Year's Day presidential reception for dignitaries, the White House was opened to the general public from noon until two o'clock, creating a "jam most excessive; all persons, high or low, civil, uncivil, or otherwise, were forced to fall into an immense line . . . along the stately portico of the White House to the main entrance."[2] With Nicolay at his side, Abraham Lincoln shook the hands of well-wishers and the just plain curious for the next two hours. This ordeal would be repeated for the following three years.

With Cameron's departure to Russia, 1862 brought a new secretary of war to the cabinet. President Lincoln's appointment of Edwin Stanton encouraged Nicolay by the action taken "for the country." The secretary did not know Stanton

Mary Todd Lincoln as she appeared in 1861 as First Lady. She and Nicolay developed a largely adversarial relationship during their White House years, and Mrs. Lincoln urged her husband to replace him with Noah Brooks. (Library of Congress)

personally but nonetheless knew of his reputation, writing that "he is represented as being an able and efficient man, and I shall certainly look for very great reforms in the War Department."[3] Stanton, a Democrat, had been Buchanan's attorney general and a political opponent of Lincoln. But Stanton had a reputation as a no-nonsense individual who could get things done, and indeed he did.

But even this positive political news could not keep Nicolay from expressing complaints, if not cynicism, in his correspondence with Therena, beginning with his distaste for the weekly "executive receptions" that gave the general public the opportunity to meet and greet the president: "I suppose they [the receptions] are both novel and pleasant to the hundreds of mere passers-by who linger a day or two to 'do' Washington; but for us who have to suffer the infliction once a week they get to be intolerable bores."[4] The "infliction" would only worsen for Nicolay as First Lady Mary Todd Lincoln involved him in the detailed planning and execution of more White House events for which she had the highest expectations of perfection in every detail.

Mrs. Lincoln, who wanted desperately to make a dazzling impression on Washington society, had three things not working in her favor in the eyes of the capital city's social establishment. She was of southern (Kentucky) birth, was virtually unknown, and was an outsider who came to Washington directly from the frontier Midwest.[5] After nearly a year of public receptions and more intimate state dinners in the White House, Mary Lincoln decided to play hostess to a very large and elegant party in February 1862, in part to show off the new decorations in the Executive Mansion that had far exceeded her budget. Nicolay and Hay, who were by now referring to the First Lady between themselves as "the Hellcat" or "Her Satanic Majesty," found themselves at odds with Mrs. Lincoln on various issues, including her expenditures. Nicolay wrote to Therena on February 2, somewhat skeptical about Mrs. Lincoln's determination "to make an innovation in the social customs of the White House." "La Reine" (the Queen), as he sometimes referred to the First Lady, had "issued tickets for a party of six or seven hundred" instead of the "past dinners and receptions" that had been the standard social events at the White House. Evidently, he was skeptical of its success, noting, "how it will work yet remains to be seen. Half the city is jubilant at being invited while the other half is furious at being out in the cold."[6]

After the event, he confessed to Therena that "the grand party came off last night according to programme, and was altogether a very respectable, if not brilliant success." Yet his half-hearted admission about the success of the party could not go without a sniping comment that "many of the invited guests did not come, so the rooms were not at all crowded." And then, as he frequently did when writing Therena, he described the female attendees: "Of course, the ladies were all beautifully dressed having no doubt brought all their skill and resources to a culmination." Rarely content with superficial observations, Nicolay then offered Therena a critique of Washington's elite, which has a familiar ring to succeeding generations. He described how the Washington elite worshipped "power and position with the most abject devotion and cringe in most pitiable slavishness to all social honors and recognitions," even if, as the secretary noted, these people bought or begged for their invitations. While never admitting that he was a bit of a social climber himself, he judged the attendees as individuals who "will be forever happy in the recollection of the favor enjoyed because their vanity has been tickled with the thought they have attained something which others have not." After he described the visual effect of the evening in the East Room as "very beautiful" and the supper as "magnificent," the event ended not with a whimper but with a bang. A fight broke out among the servants, "damaging in its effect to sundry heads and champagne bottles. This last item is entre nous [between us]."[7] Added to these woes was Nicolay's dislike of Washington's winter weather: "wet, muddy—cold—nasty—slushy—slippery—You may add all the other disagreeable adjectives you can remember and not overdraw the picture."[8]

Tragedy would soon overtake these rather mundane concerns. Less than a week after the White House grand party, Nicolay informed Therena: "Since then one of the President's little boys [Willie] has been so sick, as to have absorbed pretty much all his [Lincoln's] attention, and the next-youngest [Tad] is now threatened with a similar sickness."[9] Childhood mortality was a painful fact of life in the nineteenth century. The Lincolns had already lost one son, Edward, in 1850, shortly before the boy's fourth birthday. On February 20, 1862, Nicolay recalled in a journal, which he maintained haphazardly, how "at about five o'clock this afternoon I was lying half asleep on the sofa in my office when his [Lincoln's] entrance roused me. 'Well, Nicolay,' said he, choking with emotion, 'my boy is gone – he is actually gone!' and, bursting into tears, turned and went into his own office."[10] The next day George wrote to Therena that the Executive Mansion was in mourning.[11] In the letter, he called Willie the "second son" of the president. Actually, the boy was the third son. Nicolay may have made the error because neither Lincoln nor anyone else had mentioned the existence, much less the death, of Edward Lincoln to him.

Whether Willie Lincoln's death helped steer Nicolay's or Therena's thoughts toward reflecting on religious faith is open to speculation. However, two days after writing Therena about Willie, George penned a long letter to her focused on his desire that she approach her own religious faith independently from his. From this one learns something about Nicolay's own views on religion. "You are entirely right in your conclusion that I desire you to follow your own good judgement and discretion in your religious views and actions," he wrote her, adding, "it is, in my opinion, entirely an independent and individual duty and responsibility." But for Nicolay, independence of thought was defined by a complete separation from organized religion or even spiritual advisors. "I will, however, take the liberty to caution you, that while you act independently of me in these matters" he counseled, "it is equally your duty to act independently (in forming your opinions) of all other persons and coteries."

Apparently, the sermons delivered by the Reverend Carter while George was the church organist had little effect on him. He urged Therena to regard all forms of spiritual advice "merely as so much argument; let nothing but your own mind and heart make up and render the final judgment." "Bitter as the conviction may prove," Nicolay asserted, "you will find that the boundary of the church, as well as the world outside, encircles all of human folly and weakness." He contended that church members and the men of the world occupied a plane that was "deplorably near the same level." Essentially a secular humanist, Nicolay felt that individuals could self-rationalize their way to the attainment of spiritual understanding. Condemning the superstition of the multitudes, he envisioned this spiritual purity for "only those who, like Moses, climb alone up the mount of sacrifice, through the clouds of Creeds, the thunder of Bigotry and the lightnings of Doubt, who shall see Divinity face to face with spiritual eye, and receive the true commandments." George thought that everyone should go it alone in understanding God.[12]

A few days later, on his thirtieth birthday, February 26, 1862, Nicolay admitted to Therena in a less serious mode that had fate been kinder to him (that is, than leaving him on his own at age fourteen), he might have "gained much skill, knowledge and experience which I now sorely need." On the other hand, he concluded, "while my years are thirty, my heart is but twenty." He also suggested, "I might pull one of the gray hairs out of my head, and write you a pretty page of sentiment about it; but shall assume that you prefer to forego the sentiment and join me in imagining that they are all yet as black and young as you first knew them."[13]

On March 23, 1862, Nicolay provided Therena an update on the progress of the war as he was able to give it. The administration was still awaiting news of the Union attack on "Island No. 10, but no decisive result seems to be reached yet." Island No. 10 was a sandbar in the Mississippi River near New Madrid, Missouri, that had been seized and armed by Confederates to block Union river traffic. Confederate forces did not surrender the fortified sandbar until April 7. Waiting for battle news was something that would prove a constant source of anxiety and stress for Lincoln and his staff throughout the war. George also informed Therena that the ironclad *Merrimack*—originally a U.S. Navy vessel but salvaged, rebuilt, and rechristened the CSS *Virginia* by the Confederacy—had "not ventured out from Norfolk since her famous fight with the Monitor [on March 9, 1862]. The chances of her reappearance are pretty closely watched."[14] There were fears that a Confederate ironclad had the potential of sailing up the Potomac River and shelling Washington with nothing to stop it. Secretary of War Stanton, easily agitated, predicted that such a ship "would soon send a cannon shot into the cabinet room."[15] In fact, the *Merrimack* never again left its moorings at Norfolk until being scuttled in May 1862.

Nicolay had reason for optimism on April 2, 1862. He had arrived in Springfield after a trip for the Treasury Department, and he would have some time off to see Therena in a few days in Pittsfield. Further improving his sometimes introspective and gloomy mood was the fact that he could report to his fiancée concerning recent Union victories on the Tennessee and Mississippi Rivers. "Truly these are great and glorious successes," he wrote to her. "In my opinion this finishes the rebellion in the West—they can never recover. . . . I feel better and lighter hearted about it [the war] than I have . . . for a year."[16]

At the same time that Nicolay was writing Therena from Springfield, the Battle of Shiloh was occurring several hundred miles away in Tennessee. Shiloh was the bloodiest battle to date and would be a sign that the war was getting costlier in terms of human lives. He went to the scene of the engagement only days after it was fought, before all the dead could be removed from the area. There he saw firsthand the results of a truly horrific Civil War battle. He could now give an eyewitness description to his boss of the frightful carnage that lay strewn on that field. Nicolay began to appreciate the true cost of maintaining the Union.

Despite the pressures of his responsibilities and the war, Nicolay also maintained connections with his siblings and was interested in the wellbeing of his brothers as well as his own financial future. In a letter to Therena on April 24, 1862, after he had again returned to Springfield, he told her about a farm he had purchased near Girard, Illinois, a few miles south of Springfield, on which he wanted his brother to live and farm. "I like my farm very much," he told her. "It is a good and pretty eighty acres of prairie land. . . . The place has a nice young orchard of about 100 apple trees. . . . The house is small and not good, but will do for a while. Altogether, it will make my brother a comfortable home and will I think pay well for the investment if in nothing else except the increase of value of the place itself."[17] The brother was likely John Jacob, who ultimately settled on another farm Nicolay purchased in Kansas, an area where many of John Jacob's descendants still live.

Back in Washington, resuming his duties, Nicolay's thoughts turned again to the progress of the war. This time he focused on the eastern theater in Virginia. Reporting on George McClellan's Peninsular Campaign, he was pleased to write Therena on May 4 that Yorktown, Virginia, had been evacuated by the rebels, leaving behind "over fifty pieces of cannon, large amounts of ammunition, camp equipage &c." He informed her a few days later that President Lincoln, joined by Secretaries Stanton and Chase, had taken the revenue cutter *Miami* to Fort Monroe, Virginia. Other military news also gave cause for cheer. Admiral David Farragut had captured New Orleans the week before on April 25, a victory that "will rank among the most brilliant exploits of history." "Verily," he proclaimed, "the present is full of hope and promise."[18] But this positive outlook on the progress of the war effort was short-lived.

By May 21, his views were already less optimistic as he expressed his growing disenchantment with General George B. McClellan to Therena: "I am beginning very much to fear that we will have to have a new General before we get any decisive results from the Army of the Potomac."[19] By June 5, Nicolay's criticism of McClellan had increased to such intensity that he wrote, "McClellan's extreme caution, or tardiness, or something, is utterly exhaustive of all hope and patience, and leaves one in that feverish apprehension that as something may go wrong, something most likely will go wrong."[20] His boss, the president, referred to McClellan as having "a case of the slows."

One of the things that often did go wrong with the war effort was the fact that rumor played a big role in creating both anxiety and intense speculation about what was on the horizon. Citizens in both North and South were hungry for information, and the slightest movement of troops or leaders could set minds wandering and tongues wagging. Newspapers of the day were sources of unverified stories, many of which proved to be fanciful in their reporting. Nicolay offered a great example of the rumor mill at work in a letter to Therena dated June 27, 1862. The president decided to leave the capital to visit West Point. Immediately, the Washington rumor mill went to work, setting off "a thousand rumors to buzzing as if a beehive had been overturned." He observed that the rumors included a reorganization of the cabinet, another shakeup in the military command structure, and another campaign to be launched. In the next century, this perpetual beehive of speculation would be christened the "Washington Merry Go Round" by columnist Drew Pearson. "You have no idea how rapidly rumors are originated and spread here," wrote the secretary, "nor how [much] importance even the coolest and most discriminating of our people attach to them." His impression, he opined, was that the president "merely desired and went to hold a conference with Gen. Scott about military matters"; he predicted that "no immediate avalanches or earthquakes are to be produced thereby."[21]

Nicolay was partially correct. The president had merely gone to West Point to confer with General Scott. No cabinet shakeup, no reorganization of the military chain of command, and no new campaign was in the offing. But on the other side of the Potomac, there was military news. General Robert E. Lee, who had assumed command of Confederate forces defending Richmond, launched a counterattack against McClellan on June 25, resulting in the Seven Days Battles. The first word of Lee's action swiftly reached Washington, and as so often happened, rumor and speculation filled the void created by the paucity of hard facts. While the president's trip did not generate an "immediate avalanche or earthquake," the fighting around Richmond did.

Nicolay penned Therena on June 29 that "there has been fighting around Richmond for three or four days." Stating that "having no definite dispatches upon which to base conclusions," he could not determine what had happened since "the news has been so completely kept from the public that up until this morning no one had a serious suspicion of what was going on." Individuals arriving in Washington from Fort Monroe did not have many hard facts either but merely added to the confusion with their own speculation. According to the secretary, "These [rumors] have been caught up here with great avidity and repeated with their usual additions and embellishments." Ever since his days at the *Free Press*, he preferred to deal in facts rather than rumors and thus waited impatiently for credible war news to be released to the public. Meanwhile, he reflected that the "suspense is terrible, but we have to learn to bear it very patiently here."[22]

While the stresses of work and war continued to bear down on him, Nicolay was no doubt happy to report to Therena on June 15 that Mrs. Lincoln had moved to a summer residence at the cooler, breezier Soldiers' Home on the city's northern outskirts. President Lincoln would make the commute back to the White House by carriage or on horseback. The Lincolns had talked for some time about following former President Buchanan's example of establishing a getaway residence at this relatively new institution for disabled veterans. The newness of the Lincoln administration and the pressures of the war had delayed this move in 1861, but now, following Willie Lincoln's death, Mary especially wanted to be away from the White House part of the time. "John and I are left almost alone in the [White] house," George told Therena, "and I am very glad of the change for several reasons."[23] Among those were likely increased privacy and the extended absence of the First Lady.

Nicolay spent his second Independence Day in Washington. Having time to write to Therena, he expressed thanks that the president was "away at the War Department, so that I have not been so much pestered with a large crowd here [at the White House]," but the news he shared was not good. A favorable outcome of the Seven Days Battles was not promising. Although "the victory was substantially with us" in the battle for Richmond, "Gen McClellan changed his position . . . constantly getting farther from Richmond. . . . Our loss is perhaps 15,000 killed and wounded. . . . Of course everybody here has been terribly blue about it for several days. . . . It is to be deplored that we lose the prospect of the early capture of Richmond."[24] It is likely that this setback, for which Lincoln blamed McClellan, contributed greatly to Lincoln's decision to remove McClellan from his command following the midterm congressional elections in the fall of 1862.

While Nicolay was often prone to negativity regarding the conduct of others and the war in general, he nonetheless had absolute faith in Abraham Lincoln's leadership and decisions. He had little patience for those who believed otherwise and who, taking the short view, were swayed by each twist and turn of the events of the moment. While he had mostly recovered from McClellan's inability to take Richmond a few days before, he now was despairing of the mood of many in Washington. Writing on July 13, he informed Therena that "the past has been a very blue week here" and that, except among the president and his cabinet, "I don't think I have ever heard more croaking since the war began than during the past ten days." He declared that he was "utterly amazed to find so little real faith and courage under public difficulties among public leaders and men of intelligence.... A single reverse or piece of accidental ill-luck is enough to throw them all into the horrors of despair." He admitted that he was "getting thoroughly disgusted with average human nature."[25] In short, he was showing his disgust with the politicians whose careers and egos depended daily on the shifting sand of events and public opinion. Fickleness and worry are part of a politician's stock and trade, but the secretary who could afford to live with an absolutist view of the world would have none of it.

Nicolay's wit and critical nature were on display in a clever letter he composed to Therena a week later in which he complained about bugs—big ones and little ones, figurative ones and literal ones—buzzing around in his office. Writing late on a Sunday night with the windows open for ventilation, he described the onslaught of "bugdom" attacking his gas lights: "The air is swarming with them, they are on the ceiling, the walls and the furniture in countless numbers, they are buzzing about the room, and butting their heads against the window panes, they are on my clothes, in my hair, and on the sheet I am writing on." It was, he maintained, "a not altogether inapt miniature picture of the folly and madness and intoxication and fate too of many big bugs, who even in this room I witness buzzing and gyrating round the great central sun and light and source of power of the government [presumably President Lincoln]."[26]

In the early summer of 1862, the president decided to treat Nicolay to a government-paid hunting trip to Minnesota. Lincoln appointed him secretary to a commission led by Commissioner of Indian Affairs William P. Dole to treat

Nicolay (right) and Indian Commissioner William P. Dole camped at Big
Lake, Minnesota, en-route to treaty negotiations with Chippewa Indians in
August 1862. The negotiations were delayed by an uprising of Sioux Indians
under Chief Little Crow. (From the Lincoln Financial Foundation Collection,
courtesy of the Allen County Public Library and Indiana State Museum)

with the Pembina and Red Lake bands of Chippewa (or Ojibwa) Indians that
summer. Meant largely as a pleasure trip, this assignment would be far different
from what anyone expected and would have a profound impact on the secretary.
In preparation for this journey, Nicolay used Lincoln's library card to check out
The History of Minnesota, written by his future assistant Edward Neill, from the
Library of Congress.[27] Friends from Pittsfield thought about joining him on the
trip, but he discouraged the idea, citing reports of Confederate snipers along the
banks of the Mississippi.[28]

It was mid-August when Nicolay met up with Commissioner Dole and Senator
Morton S. Wilkinson of Minnesota and started out for the negotiations. It was
on this brief trip that a photograph of Nicolay and Dole was taken. The photo
shows Nicolay standing with a hunting rifle in hand as Dole sits in a camp chair.
However, after only a day out on the trail, the party was forced to return to St.
Paul because of news that the Sioux had suddenly gone on the warpath. "About

this time a messenger reached us from Fort Ridgely, via St. Paul, who had been sent forward to warn us of the terrible outbreak of the Sioux," wrote the commissioner in his 1862 report. The group was warned that the Sioux were looking for the party to intercept it and seize "their money with which they professed to believe we intended to make a treaty with their enemies [i.e., the Chippewa]." The Sioux, it was said, also wanted to take possession of the party's goods and provisions.[29]

On August 17, four Sioux warriors were involved in an argument with a farmer. The dispute ended when the Indians killed the farmer, his wife, and two other men. The Indians returned to their village and reported the event, which caused consternation among the village leaders, including a chief named Little Crow, a Christian who had attended church that morning with his white neighbors. After a night of debate, the Indians decided to wage war, led by Little Crow.

The Sioux uprising was one of the bloodiest in American history. The Sioux made no distinction with regard to age or sex, and atrocities were widespread. Among the dead were many members of the congregation with whom Little Crow had worshipped. Most casualties occurred in the early days of the outbreak before settlers either knew there was a war or had time to prepare for it. Some Sioux, who did not agree with their brethren, did much to save many of their white friends. Estimates of the death toll have ranged from four hundred[30] to eight hundred, the number Lincoln reported to Congress in his annual address the following December.[31] More exaggerated reports by western newspapers placed the death toll at over two thousand.[32] In comparison, the Great Sioux War a decade later, which saw Custer's defeat at Little Big Horn, resulted in few civilian deaths. During the Indian wars, hysteria and exaggeration were commonplace in the press, as well as from settlers who fled from the region of the conflict but who had not experienced any immediate threat themselves and from traders who would later file claims, often overstated or totally false, for remuneration for losses from the government. Lincoln fell prey to this hysteria when he reported to Congress of a rumored Indian conspiracy linking all the Plains Indians in a general uprising.[33]

Because he was on the scene in the midst of the storm, Nicolay was particularly susceptible to the emotions around him. Demands were raised in frontier newspapers and official circles, including Minnesota governor Alexander Ramsey, for a genocidal response to the Sioux outbreak.[34] On August 27, nine days after the beginning of the uprising, Nicolay joined Commissioner Dole and Senator Wilkinson in sending a telegram to the president from the safety of St. Paul informing Lincoln of the conflict and noting that "a wild panic prevails in nearly one-half of the State."[35] In fact, a wild panic swept the entire frontier state.

On the same day, Nicolay telegraphed Secretary of War Stanton asking for arms and supplies. Whether he did this on his own initiative or was asked to do so by Minnesota authorities is not clear, but given his close affiliation with the president, who better to send the telegram? Nicolay's own panic spilled out across the page:

> Saint Paul, Minn. August 27, 1862
> Hon. E. M. Stanton
> The Indian war grows more extensive. The Sioux, numbering perhaps 2,000 warriors, are striking along a line of scattered frontier settlements of 200 miles, having already massacred several hundred whites and the settlers of the whole border are in panic and flight. . . . The Chippawas [sic], a thousand warriors strong, are turbulent and threatening, and the Winnebagos are suspected of hostile intent. The Governor is sending all available forces to the protection of the frontier, and organizing the militia, regular and irregular, to fight and restore confidence. As against the Sioux, it must be a war of extermination.[36]

By recommending a genocidal solution for the Sioux, the normally intellectual, reticent Nicolay was showing the level of his own panic and fear. The war lasted for about a month before the situation improved, as Minnesota rallied what forces were available. As the calendar deepened into September, tribal members became concerned about providing for their families during the winter months. Individual bands began to surrender at the forts or agencies. Little Crow, who became a fugitive, would be killed with his son while picking berries in a field the following summer.

At the outbreak of the war, the Chippewa had grown restless. Many tribesmen argued that they should join their ancient enemies, the Sioux, in the war against the whites. But lack of guns and ammunition caused the Chippewa to hesitate. It was with this background that Commissioner Dole and Nicolay went out to negotiate with the Chippewa, represented by one of their more formidable leaders, a chief named Hole-in-the-Day. Nicolay may have known the chief, or at least have been familiar with him because Clark W. Thompson, the agent for the Northern Superintendency commented in his report for 1862 that Hole-in-the-Day had visited Washington not as part of an Indian delegation but rather as an individual to petition for the removal of Thompson as agent.[37] In an article published in *Harper's Weekly* in January 1863, Nicolay described a perilous situation in which the commissioner and his party found themselves when attempting to meet with the chief.

> By-and-by they [the Indians] again began to move, and came down, in the same straggling procession, to a little valley in the village which had been indicated to them as the council-ground, and seated themselves in a long, irregular semicircle on the northern slope, facing the group of tents, and the soldiers and citizens on the other slope. They were scarcely half seated when two or three of them ran up to the river bank and shouted some signal or command in the direction of down the river. Judge the surprise of the whites present at seeing another party of Indians, nearly equal to that in front appear as if by magic from among the bushes on the roadside, and stretch a line across and take possession of the road a hundred and fifty paces in the rear!
>
> The trick of the red-skins was now plain; the party in front waited on the river bank until the other could make a circuit through the woods so as to take position in the rear. As no treachery had at first been suspected by the whites, they had out neither guard nor picket to warn them of the movement. Afterward they learned that still another party of Indians of about the same number remained concealed in the woods and did not show themselves until they recrossed the river.[38]

Commissioner Dole, experienced in Indian affairs, was able to extricate the party from this situation. It must have frightened Nicolay, who had no previous direct experience with Indians other than choreographed visits from Native American delegations to the White House. Although a good marksman, he had never been in a situation in which he might need to raise a gun against another human being, especially one in which his life would be at risk in turn.

Helen Nicolay noted that her father "recognized in Hole-in-the-Day a man of strong character and marked ability."[39] Indeed, in his article about the chief, her father used his literary skill to draw a majestic picture of this Chippewa leader. He had received "a six-chambered Colt revolving rifle" as a present from President Pierce during one of his trips to Washington. "It at once became his pet plaything, dearer to his savage heart than his prettiest squaw," wrote Nicolay in vividly descriptive prose, "in his muscular grasp its weight was but as a feather." Through daily practice, "with his quick eye . . . and his rigid muscles hardened in sun and storm," he continued, the weapon "became a sort of Jupiter's rod from which he shook out leaden thunder bolts at will."[40]

He followed this romantic description of the chief with a grisly account of Hole-in-the-Day on the war trail after Sioux who had desecrated his father's

Chippewa Chief Hole-in-the-Day with whom Nicolay interacted in treaty negotiations in Minnesota in September of 1862. (Minnesota Historical Society)

resting place. At the end of the expedition, the chief returned home via a public conveyance accompanied by a young boy who carried the severed heads of some of Hole-in-the-Day's victims in a bag.[41] In the end, the negotiations failed to get Hole-in-the-Day the gifts and annuities he wanted for himself and his people, but nonetheless the Chippewa stayed out of the fight.

While he had mixed feelings about the Chippewa chief, Nicolay had no such feelings toward the Sioux. Writing to a national audience months after his experience in Minnesota, he betrayed little sympathy toward those Indians: "The future disposition of the Indians of the State of Minnesota is one of the most perplexing minor questions of the day. In their present location, the feud of race engendered by the insurrection will only die with the generation that witnessed its beginning. Humanitarian impulses and humanitarian duties are forgotten in the fierce thirst for private vengeance. With one voice, the people of that state demand the removal or threaten the extermination of their dangerous neighbors."[42] There is little doubt the secretary fully endorsed the call of vengeance through what we call today ethnic cleansing.

Revenge was very much on the minds of the citizens of Minnesota. After the war was over, more than three hundred Indians were condemned to death by hanging. Nicolay called them the "ring leaders and worst offenders" and wrote,

"Before this paper is printed, some, at least, of these, will have expiated their crimes on the gallows."[43] There is no hint of mercy in Nicolay's words. However, Abraham Lincoln differed with his secretary. After listening to the pleas of the Episcopal bishop Henry Whipple, who courageously spoke for the Indians in the face of nearly universal condemnation, and after reviewing all the records of the military tribunals, Lincoln set aside the convictions of all but thirty-nine Indians. The condemned were, in Lincoln's mind, proven to have not only participated in the uprising but had been identified as committing rape or "proven to have participated in *massacres* as distinguished from participation in *battles*."[44] There are two letters regarding the execution of the thirty-nine Indians, with each name of the condemned clearly written out on the death warrant. One is in Lincoln's hand and the other in Nicolay's hand, signed by the president. The latter was the copy sent to General Henry H. Sibley ordering him to carry out the death sentences.[45] After an additional Indian received a reprieve, thirty-eight Sioux were hanged on December 26, 1862, in the largest legal mass hanging in American history.

The events in Minnesota had a profound effect on Nicolay. Helen proclaimed rather unabashedly, "my father entertained no sentimental illusions about the North American Indian," having "grown up too near frontier time in Illinois to regard them as other than cruel and savage enemies whose moral code, granted they had one, was different from that of the whites."[46] This is unlikely the case. The last Indian war in Illinois had been the Black Hawk War in 1832, the year of Nicolay's birth. While Nicolay certainly heard the stories told by his Pittsfield acquaintances, especially Colonel Ross, the Indian "threat" in Illinois was a thing of the past. He may also have listened to Lincoln talk about his experiences in the Black Hawk War over a game of chess. Given Lincoln's personality and his experience in the Black Hawk War, Lincoln's attitude may not have been as harsh toward the native peoples. It is unlikely that Nicolay had any reason to internalize his hatred of Indians until his experiences in Minnesota. When he subsequently went to Colorado, his views toward the native peoples hardened even further. While there appear to be no existing letters from Nicolay to Therena during this time, Nicolay did write Hay on September 8 from Fort Ripley, Minnesota. Nicolay, who knew that Confederate troops were not that far from Washington, wrote his friend, perhaps only partly in jest, that "I still think it is about an even chance whose scalp will be first—yours or mine."[47] He returned to Washington in the fall of 1862 after about two months in Minnesota. In the end, he had opportunity for the fishing and hunting he had anticipated.

Two important events happened while Nicolay was away. First, George McClellan, who had the military intelligence from the enemy and the advantage of more troops to destroy Lee's army, instead had won a strategic victory at Antietam Creek in Maryland on September 17 but had then allowed Lee to escape. Five days later, the president issued the Preliminary Emancipation Proclamation. Based on the authority given him by Congress by the passage of the Second Confiscation Act in July, Lincoln notified the rebellious states that should they continue to refuse to end the rebellion and return to the Union by January 1, 1863, he would abolish slavery in those states and enforce it with federal arms. The war was changing from a war for Union to a war for Union and freedom. The proclamation brought joy and consternation on both sides of the national divide.

However, Nicolay would have little time to contemplate the future. The pressure of his responsibilities kept him focused on more immediate concerns. A few days back at his White House routine in October, he was again complaining to Therena about dealing with the crowds of people, an aspect of his work for the president that seems always to have been among his least favorite duties. "The crowd still continues here as usual," he bemoaned, "and leaves me but little time for anything but to listen to their importunities and requests, and to invent and plead excuses and explanations for their disappointments. It is very irksome, very. Nothing of interest has transpired here during the week past."[48] Always at heart a writer, he did get some good news from the editor of *Harper's Magazine*, A. H. Guernsey, on October 24, accepting an article for publication that he had written about the Chippewa chief, Hole-in-the-Day. Nicolay was promised payment of "our regular rates—Five Dollars a page."[49] The six-page article netted him thirty dollars.

Two letters of interest were written by Nicolay on October 26, 1862—one to Therena and one to John Hay, on leave for a few days from his White House duties. He related to Therena how he had gone "riding yesterday evening, as I do frequently, and trotting rather fast down a little stony hill, my horse stumbled and fell down and rolled entirely over me. . . . Fortunately I received only one or two very slight bruises, I got on my horse again and rode home. . . . It was a very ugly tumble and one I shouldn't like to repeat." Nicolay then recounted an incident in the president's office from earlier that morning which annoyed the secretary immensely. Entering the president's office to announce the arrival of Edwin Stanton, he found "a little party of Quakers" surrounding Lincoln. The Quakers were praying over or with him. Nicolay referred to the scene as a "prayer meeting." Lincoln, he wrote, was "compelled to bear the affliction until the 'spirit' moved them to stop." In a statement that reveals much about his religious views, he concluded, "isn't it strange that so many and such intelligent people often have so little common sense?"[50]

While Nicolay had little use for prayer, his boss, with his own deepening sense of spirituality, could better appreciate not only the spiritual but also the political benefits derived from a moment of enforced piety. But the secretary's disparaging remarks about the efficacy of prayer may have also offended the recipient of his comments, as Therena remained devout in her religious practices. That same day, he wrote to John Hay that he had attended two parties the week before, including one "where I saw a whole bevy of new secesh [secessionist] beauties" and another party that "didn't pan out much," though the host "has got a reasonably good-looking wife."[51] While there is no evidence that he ever mentioned these particular beauties in his correspondence with Therena, he was nonetheless still indulging his roving eyes on the females of the species. He clearly knew how to target his letters to his respective audiences.

In the early November 1862 midterm elections, Lincoln Republicans suffered major losses in governorships and members of Congress. None of this surprised Lincoln, who had predicted earlier that year that "Democrats would fail to support his administration because it was too radical and Republicans because it was not radical enough."[52] Lincoln had not involved himself directly in the fall political campaigns. He was busy enough with the war efforts. He also desired not to be embroiled in the sometimes fierce factional struggles within his own party. Attacked from all sides following the election and with nothing more to lose politically, Lincoln did to McClellan what Nicolay had been hoping would befall the general he now referred to as "little Mac."[53] Nicolay composed a letter to Therena on November 9, rejoicing that McClellan had been removed as commander of the Army of the Potomac. "The President's patience is at last completely exhausted," he proclaimed, with the general's "inaction and never-ending excuses." Citing Lincoln's opinion of Little Mac as a "very superior and efficient officer," he explained the president's indulging the general in "whims and complaints and shortcomings as a mother would indulge her baby, but all to no purpose." Paraphrasing Lincoln's quote that the general had the "slows," Nicolay informed her that "He [McClellan] is constitutionally too slow and has fitly been dubbed the great American tortoise." All of this foreshadowed the treatment the general would receive in the Nicolay-Hay history. Then the secretary made another of his inaccurate political assessments. "It is barely possible that the secessionist element of the Democratic party," he opined, "will endeavor to make him a leader of an opposition movement and party, but I think his popularity is too fictitious for that."[54] Contrary to Nicolay's prognostication, in 1864 the Democratic Party would nominate McClellan as their presidential candidate on a peace platform. Four days later, McClellan's dismissal was still very much on George's mind, and he informed Therena that "there has not been the least excitement about it." Nicolay was relieved that McClellan "had the prudence and good taste to submit quietly to the president's decision, and to go home without saying anything on the way. Whether he will continue to behave himself properly or not, is of course yet a question, though I think he will. He can't himself help knowing something of how great a failure he has made, and what glorious opportunities he has wasted."[55]

Thanksgiving Day 1862, like the previous Thanksgiving, was a lonely disappointment for Nicolay, who told Therena that he had "just been down at Willard's [Hotel] and ate my dinner solitary and alone, as I would do on any other one of the three hundred and sixty five days of the year. . . . A real home Thanksgiving day and dinner would have been a social carnival in comparison." He also mentioned that a relative had recently arrived in Washington, his nephew John, and that Nicolay had been able to get him "discharged from the army and have obtained employment for him here in the Agricultural Department." "I hope to make something of him by and by," Nicolay shared with Therena, although he added, "for the present he needs instruction more than anything else."[56] The nephew was most likely John H. Nicolay who had enlisted at Bedford, Illinois, on August 23, 1862, and mustered into Company I of the Ninety-ninth Illinois Infantry. He was discharged on November 8, 1862, after less than four months in the army.[57] Earlier in 1862, Nicolay had assisted Therena's brother Dorus in receiving a commission as a second lieutenant in the Thirteenth U.S. Infantry. Dorus had initially enlisted as a bugler in the Second Illinois Cavalry in 1861.[58] Nicolay would also provide his friends a helping hand. One example of a request for Nicolay to wield his patronage influence for a nonrelative came from his former boss in the Illinois Secretary of State's Office, O. M. Hatch. Hatch wrote to him on March 11, 1862, seeking a position for George Browne of New York City, "my friend in my youth." Hatch was insistent: "George, I want this man to have a place—on my account, dam it. Some other gentlemen obtain favors. I ask this of you."[59] While we do not know how Nicolay responded to this pressing and perhaps awkward request from a man to whom he was truly indebted, he was very open about using his influence to assist his relations, so it would not be surprising if Nicolay also accommodated this and similar requests.

On December 7, he wrote to Therena that as he was writing her, a message had come up from Mrs. Lincoln inviting Messrs. Nicolay, Hay, and Stoddard to dine with her at five o'clock that evening. He found the invitation "startling" and was "at a loss at the moment to explain it." Not eager to attend the dinner with Mrs. Lincoln present, Nicolay nonetheless explained that "etiquette does not permit any one on any excuse to decline an invitation to dine with the president. I shall have to make the reconnaissance, and thereby more fully learn the tactics of the enemy."[60] Unfortunately, the results of his "reconnaissance" are unknown.

Union troops were finally on the move in December 1862, and Nicolay was cautiously hopeful, telling Therena that "we are perhaps again on the eve of great events." "There is so much of chance in war that all speculation based on single movements or battles," he warned, "is vague and unreliable." Trusting in the "wisdom of our leaders, in the valor of our troops, and the favor of the god of battles," he assured her that he would "sleep in the firm faith that the conflict of today . . . [would] vindicate and establish our cause."[61] Eager to see for himself what might be transpiring on the front, he made his way to Fredericksburg, Virginia, for four days and even entered the largely deserted town for a few hours, where he witnessed Union soldiers "in the houses in some instances, apparently helping themselves to what they desired. The place was still within easy reach of rebel batteries, and as there was a reasonable expectation that they would commence shelling it at almost any moment, I only stayed long enough to ride through two or three of the principal streets, and to get off and drink a cup of coffee with some officers who were lunching in one of the houses."[62] Fortunately for Nicolay, he left the city itself before the massive defeat suffered by Union forces under Burnside's command on December 14. Burnside ordered repeated suicidal, and unsuccessful, attacks on the well-entrenched Confederate forces on Marye's Heights just west of Fredericksburg. It was one of the most devastating Union defeats of the war, and it sent President Lincoln into a deep depression. The bloody disaster helped precipitate, or at least exacerbate, a crisis in Lincoln's cabinet, which shared the wrath of the northern public alongside Lincoln. For the northern people, it was evidence of the administration's weakness and incompetence.

Another crisis erupted as the administration was coping with the fallout from Fredericksburg. It was no secret that there were personality as well as political differences among cabinet members. Lincoln, however, was willing to tolerate, or even encourage, what David Herbert Donald has called "creative friction among his advisors."[63] Things spun out of control, however, when Secretary of State Seward tendered his resignation to Lincoln on December 16, having learned of a Republican caucus of senators out to discredit him, fueled largely by information from Secretary of the Treasury Chase. The senators had been convinced that Seward was the real problem in the administration and had to go. Lincoln shrewdly called a meeting of the senators, who had visited him earlier and lodged their complaints against Seward, and his own cabinet, at the same time and place. At the meeting, the cabinet denied some of the things that Chase had been saying. Consequently, Chase was essentially forced to walk back his main accusations that important matters had not been discussed by the cabinet and that there was a lack of unity in the cabinet. The next morning Chase handed the president his resignation. Lincoln took both Seward's and Chase's resignations and said he would accept neither. Both men remained in the cabinet, and, as Lincoln stated, they balanced each other out, just as a young Lincoln had learned in Indiana how to carry pumpkins while on horseback. "I can ride now," Lincoln told Senator Ira Harris of New York, "I've got a pumpkin in each end of my bag."[64]

Nicolay wrote to Therena on December 23, 1862, that "We had a Cabinet crisis last week," but "the President determined that he would retain both Mr. Seward and Mr. Chase, meddlesome outsiders to the contrary notwithstanding." Taking Seward's side in the dispute, Nicolay declared that "Mr. Seward particularly has achieved a triumph over those who attempted to drive him out, in this received assurance of the President's confidence and esteem." The president's secretary left out any mention of Secretary Chase. After spending another Thanksgiving alone, Nicolay was able to tell Therena that he had "just received and accepted an invitation to eat a Christmas dinner at Mrs. [Samuel] Hooper's the wife of one of the Boston members of Congress."[65] On Christmas Day, he composed a holiday tiding to Therena, writing, "I send the accompanying little box of trinkets with 'A merry Christmas'" but also with "a heartier wish that I might be with you to enjoy it."[66] What was not in the correspondence was the gift Therena wanted more than anything else, a marriage proposal.

Another year in Washington was coming to a close for the secretary. He had seen the fruits of war at Shiloh. There was no way to erase the memory of the mangled bodies he saw left on the battlefield. That haunting memory would fuel more bitterness against the South in the pages of the yet-distant history. His hunting junket to Minnesota had turned into a nightmare that he would long remember. From each of these experiences, he had brought back information

and insights for his boss to ponder. For all of his distaste for the throngs of petitioners, lobbyists, military men, and politicians who daily made his world seem
miserable, Nicolay still ran an efficient, well-oiled operation in the White House
and continued to enjoy the confidence of the one man who mattered, Abraham
Lincoln.

CHAPTER SEVEN

Emancipation, Euphoria, and Frustration, 1863

As the new year of 1863 began, John George Nicolay could not have imagined how many momentous events would transpire for the nation and how many diverse experiences on a personal level would be his. He certainly did not expect that the agonizing war to preserve the Union would still have no end in sight by the time 1863 came to a close. Nor could he have imagined the pressures, crises, and criticisms that the president whom he so admired and faithfully served would face in the year ahead with such resolve, calmness, and, at times, almost despair.

New Year's Day 1863 is a pivotal turning point in American history. As with so many other events during the Lincoln administration, John George Nicolay was an eyewitness. He was present at the signing of Lincoln's Emancipation Proclamation, an executive action taken as a war measure to free the slaves in those areas of the United States still in rebellion against the authority of the Washington government. This proclamation was not intended to free slaves in the states that remained loyal to the Union, nor in selected areas of the Confederate states that had already been pacified by Union troops. In reality, the slaves were theoretically freed by this proclamation only in areas in which the United States currently had no practical means of enforcement, but the word soon reached the slave population, many thousands of whom, instead of waiting for Union troops to enforce their freedom, took their freedom by their own efforts. Perhaps of greatest importance, the document was a clear indication that slavery throughout the United States was being set on a path to ultimate extinction.

But before Lincoln could attend to the business of emancipation, he and his secretary had to endure the annual New Year's reception. After a traditional late-morning presidential reception for dignitaries, the White House was opened to the general public from noon until two o'clock, during which time Abraham Lincoln shook the hands of well-wishers and the just plain curious. As he had done the year before, Nicolay endured this ordeal at Lincoln's side.

Unquestionably, there was quite a lot of excitement in the air as the crowds talked and speculated about the promised proclamation freeing the slaves. Lincoln had warned the rebellious states he would sign it if they did not end the rebellion. But with the disastrous battle of Fredericksburg having occurred just over two weeks before, it may have seemed to many an inauspicious time to issue such a proclamation. On January 2, William Rosecrans would win the Battle of Stones River over Confederate General Braxton Bragg, giving fresh hope to the Union cause, but that was a day off in the future.

Sometime after two o'clock, the president made his way upstairs to his executive office to sign the Emancipation Proclamation. Nicolay recollected that "it was not known at what hour the President would sign it, and therefore no concerted or formal meeting took place to witness it." In 1900, an inquiry was addressed to John Hay, then secretary of state under President William McKinley, regarding who was present at the signing of this central document of American history. Hay referred the matter to Nicolay, whose response was replicated in Helen's biography of her father. According to Nicolay, there was no authoritative list of those who watched President Lincoln place his signature on the proclamation, but he did recall that it was his "strong impression that neither Mrs. Lincoln nor any other lady was present." According to his daughter, he also related in an interview that it was he who handed Lincoln the pen used in signing the document.[1]

The actual signing of the proclamation, but not the proclamation itself, was downplayed by Nicolay and Hay in their biography of Lincoln: "No ceremony was made or attempted of this final signing. Those who were in the house came to the executive office merely from the personal impulse of curiosity joined to momentary convenience." The group, consisting of "less than a dozen persons," witnessed the signing of "one of the greatest and most beneficent military decrees of history."[2]

Inexplicably, there are no extant letters or notations by Nicolay to his fiancée Therena or anyone else regarding this momentous event. The Emancipation Proclamation itself was celebrated by Nicolay as "vast" in its consequences, and it is highly probable that he was the author of an editorial appearing in the *Washington Daily Morning Chronicle* on January 2, 1863. A copy of this unsigned editorial was cut and pasted in a scrapbook that he maintained of his own writings. While the editorial did favor "successful and prosperous colonization" of the freed slaves, its main point was that "To-day, the principle of right and justice and liberty has dealt its antagonist [slavery] the mortal wound from which it can never recover; and there remains but the struggle of arms for the integrity of the Republic, in which the God of battles [a phrase often used by Nicolay] will as surely give us the victory." The editorial concluded with unbounded praise for this historic action:

> [S]hall not the President's act of to-day become a great moral landmark, a shrine at which future visionaries shall renew their vows, and a pillar of fire which shall yet guide other nations out of the night of their bondage? And for this New Year's gift, the man who has wrought the work, amid the doubts of friends, the aspersions of foes, the clamors of faction, the cares of Government, the crises of war, the dangers of revolution, and the manifold temptations that beset moral heroism, Abraham Lincoln, the President of the United States, is entitled to the everlasting gratitude of a despised race enfranchised, the plaudits of a distracted country saved, and an inscription of undying fame in the impartial records of history.[3]

The editorial itself foreshadowed the hyperbolic tone of the Nicolay-Hay history twenty-five years later. There was great personal satisfaction for Nicolay in this historic occasion. Although never more than a foot soldier in the antislavery cause, he had a profound aversion for the peculiar institution. The secretary was further gratified to receive a letter expressing positive reaction to the Emancipation Proclamation from Horace Greeley, who had been in Washington and had hoped to see the president before departing but was not able to do so. Greeley asked Nicolay "to say for me to the President that his message fully satisfies the expectations of his friends, and is received with general enthusiasm."[4] It was not the reaction to the Emancipation Proclamation by Lincoln's friends, however, that concerned Nicolay. "I think we have great dangers to apprehend from the treasonable attitude which the Democratic party of the North is everywhere preparing to assume," he confided to Therena on January 11. He predicted that "under the subterfuge of opposing the Emancipation Proclamation," the Democrats would seek to undermine the war effort. "It is a very bold issue for them to make," he thought. While he did think they could not succeed, he rightly foresaw that "they may give us great trouble."[5]

Another personal moment of significance and achievement for Nicolay came on January 20. On that date, he was admitted as an attorney to practice before the United States Supreme Court, his sponsor being none other than the attorney general of the United States, Edward Bates. While he never argued a case before that distinguished body (or any court), his membership in the bar of the Supreme Court would strengthen his qualifications for his appointment as marshal of the Supreme Court in 1872, a position he would hold for nearly fifteen years.

Nicolay, admittedly not a very faithful church attender, did write to Therena on January 25 that he had "walked up this morning to the Senate Chamber to hear a sermon by M. D. Conway," then a Unitarian minister and editor of the *Boston Commonwealth*. Conway was "an Abolitionist, but one of the most eloquent men of the country. I should be willing to go to Church every Sunday, if I could hear a sermon of equal power."[6] Since he still held strong discriminatory views toward African Americans while opposing the institution of slavery, he saw no merit in the abolitionist viewpoint at this time. Nonetheless, he heartily approved of the homily. Like Lincoln, he had adopted a more moderate position and had personally avoided association with the abolitionist label, which even after the Emancipation Proclamation was viewed as being at the radical end of the antislavery spectrum. A complicating factor for any member of the White House staff showing any sympathy to the abolitionist cause was the political situation in the border states, particularly Kentucky and Delaware, which remained loyal to the Union while clinging steadfastly to the institution of slavery.

While the signing of the Emancipation Proclamation is not mentioned in any of Nicolay's extant letters to Therena, he did write to her of a few parties and receptions he attended in the winter of 1863, including "a little reception given by Mrs. Lincoln to Tom Thumb and his bride."[7] As for the progress of the war, reports in the first half of 1863 were not very encouraging. Ambrose Burnside's "Mud March" was another disaster for the Army of the Potomac, leading to Burnside's resignation. "The telegraph brought us news night before last of another serious reverse in Tennessee—an entire brigade which Rosecrans sent out to reconnoiter having been routed, killed, and taken prisoner." Nicolay informed her on March 8, "it is very hard not entirely to lose one's patience at this succession of adverse accidents which seems to have no end."[8] Updating her on the war news on March 19, he described more setbacks: "Our reverses still seem to continue. . . . Admiral Farragut attempted to pass the batteries at Fort Hudson with his fleet, but was disabled and driven back. . . . I had supposed our fleet would have made an attack on Charleston or Savannah before this, but the delays seem never-ending."

As if the war news were not bad enough, Washington's weather proved especially foul: "The spring weather has been so terribly bad that we need not expect a movement from the Army of the Potomac yet a while."[9] The capital had been hit with an unusually heavy amount of snow, with a storm Nicolay claimed was "almost a perpetual snowstorm, with all its inclement attendings" that had lasted two weeks. The sun had finally appeared but with "a very feeble and sickly luster," and good roads were "only a thing we remember" as the city was buried in large drifts.[10] Washington, a city even in modern times ill-equipped to handle a mild snowfall, was totally immobilized, making Nicolay's walks to the Willard Hotel for his meals an ordeal.

There is generally little romance in George's nearly three hundred letters to Therena while he was in Washington. One can only wish to see the letters she sent to her George to have a fuller context of his correspondence. There is a curious mention of Therena's concern about her aging, to which he responded in a letter dated April 12, 1863. "Pray what has been the cause of your looking five years older [than when I last saw you?]" wrote the concerned lover. "As I cannot come to see and judge for myself," he pleaded, "please have your photograph taken and send it to me so that I may determine the question here."[11] Perhaps she was growing weary of waiting for marriage and fearful that by the time they tied the knot, the bloom may have faded from the rose in George's eyes. Apparently her fiancé was sufficiently troubled by her remarks about losing her looks that he wanted a new photograph sent to him, but he seemed in no hurry to rush to her side or to make the matrimonial leap, which would have been nearly impossible, given his living arrangements in the White House. Their wedding would have to wait.

A few days later, he shared with Therena his frustrations over another failed Union attempt—this time to launch an assault on Charleston with a fleet of nine ironclads under the command of Admiral Samuel F. DuPont. Five of the ironclads were seriously damaged or at least disabled early in the attack, and DuPont had decided to withdraw. Nicolay felt that DuPont had abandoned the attack too soon, and that a much-needed Union victory "was partially thrown away by the subsequent withdrawal of the whole iron-clad fleet, leaving the enemy undisturbed."[12] Such letters to Therena expressing frustration and disappointment at Union military failures would be all too common, yet they were interspersed with occasional good, even humorous news.

He composed a fascinating letter to Therena on April 29, 1863, that shows how laughable and yet frustrating the interaction with the public that Nicolay was required to endure could be. To spare Lincoln the potential waste of time and energy resulting from easy public access to the White House, Nicolay did his best to screen out the "crazies." He recounted that "a plain looking but also very rational looking man" had been brought into his presence by the doorkeeper. The gentleman was on a mission to save the Union on instructions from God. He had been to see both the governor of New York and General Henry Halleck. Both men had directed the man's attention elsewhere, hoping that the fellow would just go away. Confronted by Nicolay, the man announced, "I am commissioned from on high." "In a very matter-of-fact and businesslike way he stated the object of his call," reported the secretary. The mission was simple and straightforward: the man was there to see the president because God had sent him to end the war. To this end, he told Nicolay, the governor of New York had "promised to raise as many men of the militia of the state as I need." Having received the governor's promise, the man declared that he had come to Washington because even though "no power was competent to stop or impede my progress, yet I desire to act with the approval of the authorities." On meeting Halleck, he was informed that "he [Halleck] could not give me any men or assistance, that nobody but the President had authority to act in the case." So, here he was.

The man's plan was simple. He would take "only two thousand men, go down South, and get Jeff Davis and the other leaders of the rebellion" and deliver them to an insane asylum. Why an insane asylum? Because, as he explained, "they are plainly crazy, and it is of no use to be fighting with crazy men." The secretary informed the man that the "President would give him no men, nor authority of any kind—and that whatever he did in the matter he must do on his own responsibility." The man, according to Nicolay, went away peacefully, "saying that he should write at once to the Governor of 'York State' to raise and organize his force for him, and proceed with his work."

"All this transpired with as much gravity and method as if it had been a little conference about any matter of routine business," the secretary reported, "and an observer would have thought that I was as crazy as the man himself, from the perfectly serious and natural manner in which both he and I talked the matter over." But "lunatics and visionaries are here so frequently," he went on to say, "that they cease to be a strange phenomena [*sic*] to us." Judging from his description of how he handled such situations, it appears that the secretary's conduct was the antithesis to his critics' claim that he always acted the crabby German. Though having a reputation for not suffering fools well, he assured Therena, "I find the best way to dispose of them is to discuss and decide their mad projects as deliberately and seriously as any other matter of business." Given cases like this, the man offering the president-elect armor for his trip to Washington was not so crazy. But these "lunatics and visionaries" provided Nicolay and Hay with necessary comic relief from the stresses of the office. Assuredly, the two had a good laugh over a meal or during a late-night conversation about the latest Don Quixote.[13]

In his letters, Nicolay also often described to Therena the suspense the White House staff experienced in Washington while awaiting word of the outcome of various military engagements. After the wet roads of April had dried sufficiently, hope was placed in General Hooker's advance with the Army of the Potomac across the Rappahannock River, "both above and below Fredericksburg," in early May. On May 3, Nicolay wrote his fiancée about the Battle of Chancellorsville. As often occurred, actual news from the battlefield was scarce, so "for the present, we content ourselves with a silent prayer," while as usual, "the city is full of rumors . . . ranging from brilliant success to disastrous defeat, usually according to the wishes and sympathies of their retailers."[14]

The next day he started a follow-up letter to her. "We have been in terrible suspense here for two days," he wrote, as there still was not "yet any definitive information on the subject." An officer who had escorted the body of General Hiram G. Berry, killed in action on May 3, reported that "the enemy have again recaptured the works and heights at Fredericksburg." "We do not as yet however," he bemoaned, "get any confirmation of the intelligence, which would be very bad if true." As George finished these words, the funeral procession for General Berry was passing by his window "with draped banners and bands playing dirges." Military funerals were an all too common event during these years. As sometimes happened, the busy secretary had to put down his pen to pick it up again. He finished the letter two days later on May 6. But all he could report was another defeat for the Army of the Potomac, noting that "in the bitterness of disappointment, I can add no comment."[15] Perhaps the only good news from the Union perspective to emerge from the major defeat at Chancellorsville was the loss of General Lee's acknowledged "right arm," Thomas "Stonewall" Jackson, who was shot by friendly fire and died a week later.

There was finally some good military news to share with Therena. Ulysses S. Grant had produced several notable successes in the area of Vicksburg, Mississippi. Most notably, Union forces had successfully crossed the Mississippi River below Vicksburg and were poised to lay siege to the city. Nicolay commented that it was "really glorious and inspires new satisfaction and hope among all." But the secretary hesitated, not ready "to vent our exultation, as we know from sad experience how often performance finally falls short of promise." Should Grant "capture Vicksburg and the rebel army in it," he predicted, "our pleasure will only be kept within bounds by the sorrowful recollection of how many of our brave have given their health and life to win the proud victory."[16]

Unknown to Nicolay at the time he penned those words was that one of the brave boys who gave his health for the Union cause was well known to him. The siege of Vicksburg became much more personal when he learned in early June that Therena's brother Dorus, then serving in the Thirteenth U.S. Infantry as a first lieutenant but who went by the nickname "Major," had been injured in battle at Vicksburg and lost an arm. Major was sent home to Pittsfield to recover. George attempted to console both his fiancée and future brother-in-law by reminding them that the loss of an arm need not diminish Major's effectiveness as an officer. "Having chosen the profession of arms, and made this much sacrifice," he opined, "Major should rather be encouraged by this event to strive for a higher accomplishment and usefulness as an officer." Seeking to bolster their spirits, he concluded, "I trust Major will remember that he is just at the beginning of a useful and honorable career."[17] However, Dorus did not make a career out of the military, resigning his commission on January 25, 1865.

Even as military events moved along, Nicolay felt compelled to take up the pen to defend his president and his own conduct as private secretary. On June 19, 1863, Nicolay responded, in classic form, to a letter from the *Chicago Tribune,* which had written to Nicolay a few days earlier. Nicolay quoted their concern in his response:

"By the way, we [the Tribune Company] are told the President said to Senator Sumner recently, that he had not seen a copy of the Chicago Tribune for four months. Now as it is mailed regularly we wish to know whether it is received at the White House. If it miscarries we will have that corrected. If he does not want it—declines to read it—we will discontinue sending it. Please answer. Yours Respectfully, Tribune Company"

To this let me answer:

The Chicago Tribune is received very regularly, opened and kept with other papers on the newspaper table in my office; it is very regularly examined by myself, and especially sought after by the Western men who happen here. That so far from desiring to place the Tribune under ban in the Executive Mansion the President requests me to say that he will be very glad to receive it here so long as in your kindness you may please to send it. And to this much from him let me add a word on my own responsibility. Excepting the Washington City Dailies, in which he carefully reads the telegraphic dispatches, the President rarely ever looks at any papers, simply for want of leisure to do so. In this the Tribune fares as well as, and no worse than all others. Still I think that during the two years of his stay here, he would have been attracted to your journal more frequently as to an old and familiar friend, if it had not in that time contained so much which he had a right to expect it would at least have left unsaid.

I can assure you of what you ought to be able to guess, that the President's task here is no child's play. If you imagine that any man could attempt its performance, and escape adverse criticism, you have read history in vain, and studied human nature without profit. But was it not to be expected that those of the President's friends, who knew him long and intimately—who understood his integrity and his devotion to the country and the cause entrusted to his charge—would at least abstain from judging him in the blindness of haste, and condemn him in the bitterness of ill-temper? It does seem to me that this much was due to generosity and charity for the fiery trial which he is called upon to pass through here, if not to political or personal friendship.

Let me repeat that these are exclusively my own thoughts and not the President's, and even I would not have written them, if I could, without misconstruction have otherwise answered the implication in your note to which you specifically requested a reply.

Let me add that I desire to continue reading the Tribune—reserving only the privilege of finding as much fault with it as it finds with the Administration, which I know is unselfishly endeavoring to do its whole duty in the crisis.[18]

Nicolay's response demonstrates how the private secretary could use his language skills to turn the pen into a sword, cutting deeply into the sinews of his protagonist's ego. Always steadfast in the defense of his president and friend, he was especially so when the antagonist was seen as a traitor to the president's cause.

Ironically, it was Joseph Medill, the *Tribune*'s editor, who had been instrumental in the *Tribune*'s editorial boldly proclaiming "The Winning Man, Abraham Lincoln" that appeared just before the Republican Convention met in Chicago in May 1860. But since Lincoln had taken office, the increasingly radical Medill had become disenchanted with Lincoln's slow action, even writing him a personal letter in February 1862 pleading, "Mr. Lincoln, for God's sake and your Country's sake rise to the realization . . . that this is a Slave-holders rebellion." Medill had softened his criticism of Lincoln after the Emancipation Proclamation was announced, calling it "the grandest proclamation ever issued by man." But after the Union disaster at Fredericksburg, Medill had concluded that "the war is drawing toward a disastrous and disgraceful termination." Medill ranted shortly thereafter that Seward must be ousted from the cabinet, that he was "Lincoln's evil genius" and "has kept a sponge saturated with chloroform to Uncle Abe's nose."[19] Clearly Joseph Medill could dish out both praise and sharp criticism of the Lincoln administration, and clearly Nicolay had little tolerance for Medill's attacks on his boss.

Early in the summer of 1863, Lincoln provided his secretary with another government-paid junket, this time to the Rocky Mountain West and the Great Basin. Nicolay was appointed as secretary to another Indian commission, this time to negotiate with the Ute Indians of the Colorado Territory. Prior to leaving on this trip, Nicolay consulted Francis Parkman's *The Oregon Trail*, John C. Frémont's *Crossing the Sierra Nevada in the Winter of 1843-44*, and J. Quinn Thornton's two-volume *Oregon and California in 1848*, checking them out from the Library of Congress on July 2.[20] Before departing the capital city, he received a warrant from the Treasury Department for $5,000 for expenses for the trip and the work of the treaty commission.[21] The money was for the purchase of food and other supplies to sustain a council with thousands of Indians as well as presents for the leading chiefs. The plan also included a trip to Carson City, Nevada, to select a site for a federal mint.[22]

Undoubtedly, Nicolay was grateful for the opportunity to get away from the White House. He had not been home to Illinois to see family or his fiancée for several months. Therena's brother Dorus was still recuperating in Pittsfield. His African American servant named Rosey had carried him off the battlefield and accompanied him to Pittsfield. There despite the displeasure of many, including undoubtedly her Copperhead father, Therena taught Rosey to read and presumably to write. Helen noted that "he became enshrined" in John Hay's *Pike County Ballads* as the character Banty Tim.[23] Curiously, Helen failed to mention that the fictional narrator of the piece, a "Sergeant Tilmon Joy," based on her uncle Dorus, tells the story of how he was carried off the Vicksburg battlefield by Banty Tim. Yet, the ballad is not so much about Rosey's heroic action at Vicksburg as it is about "Joy's" defense of Rosey when a local group of whites in "Spunky Point, Illinois" (i.e., Pittsfield) demand that the African American leave town.[24] Perhaps Helen, and maybe her father, felt embarrassed by Hay's literary foray into the life of Pittsfield and the Bates Family.

As preparations for his western adventure got underway, events were unfolding that would prove to be highly significant for the outcome of the war, and Nicolay continued to chronicle them in his letters to Therena. Grant continued the siege of

Vicksburg. Reporting on the war in the East, George told Therena that on June 21 "Lee's army has moved up toward Harper's Ferry, though precisely where, or for what purpose, I think is not yet definitely settled." Though Harpers Ferry was not that far from Washington, he assured his fiancée that "I do not think we are in the least danger here, or even in any danger of having our communications with the North interrupted." In the same letter, he took the opportunity to attack Illinois Democrats for their "eternal disgrace" of "passing an anti-war resolution at their late State Mass Meeting. . . . It does seem as if they were endeavoring to sound the lowest depths of infamy and moral treason."[25]

He had more war news to report to Therena on June 30. "It appears pretty evident that Lee has taken the most of his army into Maryland and Pennsylvania," he informed her; but no one knew exactly where the Confederates were headed. "[P]erhaps the design [is] taking Baltimore or Washington," he speculated. Critical of the response of Pennsylvanians to the invasion, he questioned "whether as the danger presses her [Pennsylvania] she will arouse herself to more vigorous action is yet a problem." Another problem was yet another change in the command of the Army of the Potomac. Nicolay reported that Joe Hooker had "at his own request" asked to be relieved, and George Meade was appointed in his place. In the midst of these events, there was, according to the secretary, "a pretty daring raid" by the rebels "within ten or twelve miles" of Washington, causing "quite a little panic" in the city.[26]

The first five days of July were extremely stressful for the secretary since while there was an awareness that a significant battle had been fought, no one had reliable news about what was happening. On Sunday, July 5, 1863, Nicolay told Therena what he knew about the great battle that had just taken place on the rolling farmland near Gettysburg, Pennsylvania, about eighty miles almost due north of Washington and only about fifty miles from Baltimore. For Confederate forces under Lee's command to penetrate this far north was risky and fraught with peril for both sides, and yet a substantial victory here promised hope of ultimate victory for the winner. While he would have no way of knowing the full significance of the engagement that had just taken place between these two great armies, Nicolay was able to grasp the situation well enough to inform Therena that "the army of the Potomac has met and measured the enemy." After briefly noting that fighting had started on Wednesday "where a considerable engagement ensued without much advantage to either side," he reported that on the following two days the "enemy attacked again . . . and were repulsed with great disaster to them." In a surge of optimism that the outcome "looks more hopeful than it has ever done before with this army," he confided that "we are watching the final result with the most intense anxiety." George speculated that "the turning point of the whole war seems to be crowding itself into the present. It seems almost impossible to wait for the result." While waiting for definitive results, time seemed to stand still as "hours become days and days become months in such a suspense."[27]

Definitive news finally reached Washington confirming the Union victory at Gettysburg. At almost the same time, the city also received the news about the fall of Vicksburg on July 4 where the Mississippi River, in Lincoln's words, "now flowed unvexed to the sea." On July 12, 1863, Nicolay reported to Therena about the Union army's follow-up of Lee's retreat from Gettysburg and his own plans to head west, including spending a few days with her. He was not quite sure where Meade's army was, perhaps "somewhere between Williamsport and Hagerstown [Maryland]." His comment that "public feeling has been wonderfully improved and buoyed by our recent successes at Gettysburg and Vicksburg" undoubtedly reflected his emotions as well.

Then he turned to his forthcoming trip to Colorado. He laid out his itinerary, "a day or two at Springfield," a "visit with brother Jacob in Macoupin County; and a few days with Therena starting on July 20 or 21." After his stay in Pittsfield, he intended to head west to Atchison, Kansas, where he would pick up the Overland Stage to Denver. But the trip would not be all business: he confessed to Therena that he would probably stop for a few days along the way for buffalo hunting. Once he reached Denver, he would join a party led by Territorial Governor John Evans that would go "somewhere about 250 miles southwest of Denver to hold a treaty with the Ute Indians." Plans for the trip also included a possible excursion farther west to Carson City, Nevada, but Nicolay did not give Therena any specifics, merely stating that "whether I shall return [to Washington] from there or go further west I have not yet fully decided."[28]

While planning for his lengthy trip to the West occupied much of his time following Lee's retreat from Gettysburg, Nicolay later realized what had been lost for the Union cause by Meade's failure to engage Lee's army decisively before the Confederates managed to slip back into Virginia and relative safety. President Lincoln, while initially announcing a victory by Union forces at Gettysburg "such to cover that army with the highest honor" and giving thanks to God for the "joyous news,"[29] was also bitterly disappointed that General Meade had not pursued Lee's army more vigorously. Lincoln was not pleased with Meade's congratulatory order to his men that their task was to "drive from our soil every vestige of the presence of the invader." "Drive the invaders from our soil! My God! Is that all?" Lincoln exclaimed in great distress. The president saw in Meade's attitude "a dreadful reminiscence of McClellan. The same spirit that moved McC. to claim a great victory because P[ennsylvania] and M[aryland] were safe." He moaned, "Will our Generals never get that idea out of their heads? The whole country is *our* soil."[30] Nicolay and Hay replicated Lincoln's frustration in their history because whenever the president expressed such feelings, they were deeply imbedded into their own consciousness for the future.

Recent events, including Lee's invasion of Pennsylvania and the carnage at Gettysburg, had placed considerable stress and strain on the Lincoln adminis-tration. Adding to these woes, Mary Lincoln was thrown from a carriage whose driver's seat had been suspiciously unscrewed, causing the driver to lose control of the equipage, which flipped over and resulted in Mrs. Lincoln cutting her head on a rock—a cut that soon became infected and required days of around-the-clock nursing care for the First Lady. To make matters worse, deadly antidraft and race riots broke out in New York City and other urban areas of the North as the Union's need for additional military manpower was now greater than the number of enlistments. Despite the recent victories in the field, these events cast a shadow over the work of the Executive Mansion as the secretary made his goodbyes and headed west.

On July 16, Nicolay finally left Washington for Colorado, with a stop in Pitts-field. To facilitate Nicolay's travel, Secretary of War Edwin Stanton had written a document instructing army officials to provide him with "transportation and subsistence when required" during his journey.[31] He proceeded west along the Platte River route to Colorado. In a report written at the conclusion of his trip dated November 10, 1863, the secretary noted his twofold instructions to act as a special agent and secretary to the commission and to report on the "capabil-ities and material progress of that Territory."[32] He claimed that the journey to Denver on the overland stage, "traveling day and night," gave him "reasonable opportunities for noting the character of the country transversed."[33] What he neglected to mention was that he stopped along the way to indulge in his love of hunting.

By early August, his party had arrived at Fort Kearney, in central Nebraska.[34] There, he took time out from his travels to participate in a two-day buffalo hunt. He drafted a letter to Hay, telling him of the hunt and confessing that he was "considerably fatigued" upon his nighttime arrival at Fort Kearney. "I found some of the officers of the Fort still up, made myself known to them," he wrote, and to his delight they all "at once improvised a buffalo hunt next morning." Nicolay clearly enjoyed the thrill of the hunt. Going up the Platte Valley, a party of "about thirty" had a "relaxed two day hunt—killing altogether some twenty buffalos." Declaring it "altogether about as enjoyable a trip as I ever took," he noted that "the chase is very exciting sport . . . with a continual popping of revolvers in all directions is a very pretty sight."[35]

The same night, he tried unsuccessfully to tamp down his enthusiasm when he reported to Therena that he and his companions had "arranged to start a buffalo hunt" and that "we organized a chasing party . . . killing about six of them." "The next morning we went out again," he proudly proclaimed, "finding another herd . . . of which we killed fourteen." In all, "it was a very exciting sport." He added that he "had as fine a hunt as well could have happened—and have had just the experience I wanted."[36] Intoxicated with the exhilaration of the hunt, Nicolay could allow Denver to wait a day or two. But like many sportsmen of the nineteenth century, Nicolay and his friends likely left the carcasses to rot on the plains, taking neither hide nor meat nor any other part of the animal that provided the Plains Indian with his sustenance. The fresh air and open landscape must have been invigorating to him compared to the cramped and dirty capital. Being an outdoorsman, he would have been looking forward to encountering the wildlife of the Rocky Mountain West, so different was it than that found during his boyhood in Illinois. His plans would not be thwarted by events as had happened the previous year in Minnesota.

Nicolay arrived in Denver on August 16 after a long stagecoach ride, which he described to Therena as "a very hard one." He declared that the terrain of western Kansas and eastern Colorado was "almost literally a desert, and the heat and dust during portions of the trip were very severe." Apparently, the stage was a bit crowded with "six passengers and a [black] baby." But his travails were not over upon reaching Denver. Barely settled into his hotel, he had to evacuate as a Colorado wind, "blowing strongly and steadily towards our hotel," threatened to spread a fire from a neighboring blacksmith shop.[37]

Upon his arrival in Colorado, he found that the treaty negotiations had been delayed from the first of September to the first of October. This gave Nicolay an entire month to satiate his passion for exploration and hunting before the treaty negotiations finally commenced "on the Conejos river in the San Juan Valley."[38] He did not regret the delay. On August 25, he informed Therena: "after we leave here [Denver] it is uncertain how often or when I can send you a letter. If the hunting and fishing is good, I may stay over there two or three weeks."[39] A few days later, he wrote Hay that "I am growing fat on trout and sage hens and luxuriating in hot sulphur baths without price."[40] While he never grew "fat" on anything, he continued to report on his time in the Rockies. "I can't undertake now to describe what I have seen," he wrote Therena after a visit to the Garden of the Gods and Camp Creek, "except to say that it seems to me that the world cannot produce any more beautiful natural scenery."[41]

The primary group of Ute Indians at the treaty negotiation was the Tabeguache band. Describing the Indians as "very active, intelligent and energetic, very successful in hunting and formidable in war," he nonetheless showed his condescension toward them, for, according to the secretary, they "were well-armed and, for Indians, tolerably clothed." "They seemed very friendly, and entirely well-behaved," perhaps, Nicolay suggested, because some of them may have been a part of a delegation that had visited Washington the previous year. Nicolay exhibited his sense of racial superiority, stating that the visitors to Washington had "an opportunity to see with their own eyes the wonders of civilization, and the great numbers and strength and resources of white people and the government."[42]

Native American delegation at the White House Conservatory (undated) with Nicolay in the center of the back row. (Library of Congress)

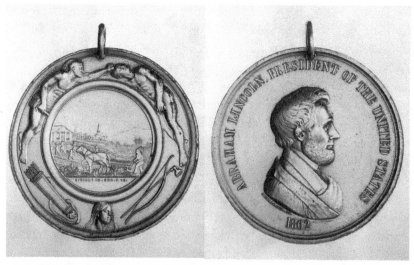

Lincoln Indian Peace Medal, front and back, 1862, silver, 62.5 mm diameter. Nicolay
carried copies of this medal to present to leaders of Native American tribes with
whom he was negotiating in 1862 and 1863. These medals were highly valued by Native
Americans and their importance was understood by American presidents.
Lincoln's unrealistic hair may be an indication of a "rushed job" to prepare
a Lincoln medal in time for Nicolay's trip to Minnesota in August 1862.
(American Numismatic Society, numismatics.org)

Nicolay may have known one or more of the chiefs attending the conference
since he had hosted several Native American delegations at the White House.
Having seen him at the Executive Mansion, the Native Americans would have
recognized Nicolay as a man close to the president. His connection to the president served an important function at the conference. Acting in his capacity as a
representative of the president and "with solemn injunctions to observe perpetual
friendship to the government," Nicolay presented seven Indians, considered
"most friendly" by Governor Evans, "silver medals sent for the purpose."[43] The
medals presented on this occasion were undoubtedly the peace medals with
Lincoln's image that were first minted in 1862.[44]

However solemn the pledges for peace and friendship, Nicolay, like the rest
of the commission, knew that the treaty negotiations were merely a necessary
charade to bring peace to the West. In his report, the secretary reflected on the
future: "The problem of the future maintenance of these Indians occupied the
attention of the commission. It was apparent to them that a very few years will

elapse before all the available and desirable spots in the mountain region, where they now subsist by hunting, will be invaded and occupied by white emigration and settlement for purposes of agriculture and mining, and that such settlement will destroy or drive away the game, thus completely cutting off their present means of living. The Government cannot always continue to feed them, and it must therefore teach and assist them to gain their livelihood." He recommended that the government teach the Indians to become herdsmen, not farmers.[45]

Nicolay concluded his report by providing some cogent advice to the governing powers in Washington. He urged that should it "prove satisfactory to the government," the treaty should be ratified "within the present year, if possible." "To sell their lands and receive the compensation agreed upon is with the Indians, a plain, practical, matter-of-fact transaction," he wrote, "the consummation of which they cannot comprehend there should be any cause or necessity for delay." Noting that the Indians were "poor, ignorant, and weak, while the government is rich, wise and powerful," he warned that, power difference notwithstanding, the government "should not permit delays to excite their suspicion and distrust, but by promptness and certainty, inspire them with confidence and respect, as well as compel fear and obedience."[46]

Nicolay had already experienced one Indian war and did not want to see another. As his report amply displayed, neither his prejudices against the Native Americans nor his paternalistic attitudes toward them had been softened by his trip to Colorado; however, he had come to realize that the Indians had legitimate concerns that must be addressed. A repeat of the events that had occurred in Minnesota the previous year would be devastating to all concerned.

As for the mineral and agricultural wealth of the new territory, Nicolay produced an enthusiastic report. He noted that the arable land in the state needed extensive irrigation, and he was not optimistic about the state's capacity to grow cereal grains. Instead, "in natural advantages for raising and herding stock, horses, mules, cattle, sheep, etc., the country seems to compensate for its limited capacity to grow cereals."[47] He went on to argue that "mining, however, is evidently destined to be the chief business of its people."[48]

On the trip, he also had an opportunity to assess the leading men of the Colorado Territory for his boss. Chief among these were Governor John Evans and Colonel John Chivington. Evans, a Lincoln appointee, had been in office for a year and a half. Chivington, the hero of the Union victory at Glorieta Pass, New Mexico, in March 1862, was a former Methodist minister from Indiana whose hostile views toward the native peoples would have reinforced Nicolay's racial prejudices. The politicians did not miss a chance to curry favor with the Lincoln administration, especially with their plans to ask for Colorado statehood in the offing. In a letter to Nicolay at the end of November, John Pierce, a Colorado acquaintance, informed the secretary that a mountain in the Rockies had just been named for the president.[49]

Nicolay did not return to Washington until November 6, much later in the year than expected, due to scheduling problems of the governor and Indian agents. Unlike the previous year in Minnesota, the negotiations had proven successful as a treaty was entered into with the Tabeguache band. The treaty was ratified by the Congress the following year.[50] His report promoted investment in Colorado while deprecating the arid territory's agricultural future. It had provided him ample opportunity for hunting and fishing. Given the delays, he had to forgo his excursion to distant Nevada.

Nicolay thoroughly enjoyed his sojourn to the Rockies and planned a follow-up trip to Colorado in the summer of 1864, but he got no farther west than Fort Kearney, Nebraska, before turning back. Delays in getting started, rumors of Indian troubles farther west, and general discomfort aborted his plans. The following November, his friends Governor Evans and Colonel Chivington launched an unprovoked attack on a friendly Cheyenne village on Sand Creek, indiscriminately slaughtering and then mutilating the Cheyenne, without regard to age or sex. There was a national outcry over these acts of savagery. Chivington hurried back to his native Indiana while Lincoln removed Governor Evans from office the following spring. The knowledge and insights into the politics of the territory gained from Nicolay's 1863 trip would prove invaluable as Lincoln sorted through this problem.

Like Stoddard, Hay hated sitting in Nicolay's chair, especially when Nicolay went west to Colorado in late July 1863 and remained there for over three months, well beyond the original plan. By September 27, Hay was lamenting Nicolay's absence, noting that his friend was "in the mountains getting beef on his bones and I am a prisoner here."[51] A month later, on October 29, Hay was still complaining. "Saw [future President James] Garfield & [General David] Hunter. Hunter is just starting for the West on a tour of inspection," Hay wrote in his diary. "I would give my chance for—to go with him but Nicolay still stays in the sunset & I am here with a ball and chain on my leg."[52] Nicolay returned to Washington on November 6, undoubtedly refreshed and in no hurry to return to his duty as first gendarme but regrettably with no more "beef on his bones." And it is doubtful that Nicolay troubled himself over Hay's discomfort back in Washington while on this memorable excursion.

Lincoln, Nicolay, and Hay in the only known pose of them together,
taken November 8, 1863, by Alexander Gardner in Washington,
D.C. The photo has been altered over the years by historians and
biographers to show only Nicolay and Lincoln or Hay and Lincoln.
(From the Lincoln Financial Foundation Collection, courtesy of the
Allen County Public Library and Indiana State Museum)

While their difficult relationship with Mary Lincoln continued, a duty that
Nicolay and Hay were always glad to perform was providing the president with
companionship. The president rarely went about Washington unless he was
accompanied by Nicolay or Hay when either of them was in the capital. Hay
recounted the day in his diary on November 8, 1863, two days after Nicolay's
return from Colorado, that he, a Mrs. Ames, the president, and Nicolay were all
at Alexander Gardner's photo studio. "We had a great many pictures taken. Some
of the Prest. the best I have seen," Hay opined. Then in a moment of pride, and
a bit of conceit, Hay wrote that "Nico and I immortalized ourselves by having
ourselves done in a group with the Prest."[53]

At some point, Nicolay hired an artist to paint the figures in the Gardner photo (see p. 161) and include a background of the Lincoln White House office. Nicolay, when consul to Paris, had postcards made of this image (a "carte-de-visite") which he made available to the public, producing both a modest income and proving his close connection with Lincoln, who was a beloved figure in France. Note that Hay remains in the picture. (From the Lincoln Financial Foundation Collection, courtesy of the Allen County Public Library and Indiana State Museum)

The iconic photograph immortalized the secretaries as associates of the president, as Hay had predicted. It is the only known posed photograph of the three men together. That Lincoln agreed, or perhaps made the suggestion, to have his photograph taken with his assistants testified to his personal closeness to these two young men. The only other individual Lincoln posed with in studio portraits was his son Tad, including the only known photographs of Lincoln wearing spectacles. The photograph of the secretaries with the president was not only an irreplaceable memento, but both men used it to demonstrate their close relationship with the martyred president decades after his death.

The original photograph did not have a backdrop. Later Nicolay demonstrated his consciousness of the photo's importance to him and his career by hiring an artist to paint a backdrop as if the photo had been taken in the Executive Mansion. And then, when Nicolay had moved to Paris, he authorized E. Talone to make a *carte-de-visite,* or photographic card, of the altered photo, which was then offered for sale.[54] Not only would the sale of the *cartes-de-visite* bring the

American consul at Paris a little extra money, it also advertised his close relationship with the beloved Lincoln to the French people. No other photo with either Nicolay or Hay posing with Lincoln is known to exist. There are versions of this photo in which either Nicolay or Hay has been cropped out from the original, leaving only the other with Lincoln.

The next day, November 9, 1863, Nicolay and Hay went to the theater with the president. One or the other or both frequently accompanied the president to the theater, with or without the presence of Mrs. Lincoln. On this occasion Mrs. Lincoln was also there to see a performance by a member of America's leading family of thespians. That evening, John Wilkes Booth performed the starring role in *The Marble Heart*. Afterward, Hay noted the presence of the famous actor in his diary, writing that the play was "rather tame otherwise."[55] Lincoln was so impressed with the famous actor's performance that he sought a meeting with the star, which Booth avoided.[56]

Shortly thereafter, the president asked Nicolay and Hay to accompany him to Gettysburg for the dedication of the National Soldier's Cemetery to be held on November 19. The bodies of the Union dead at Gettysburg had been gathered together for final burial. The president had been asked to make "a few appropriate remarks." Lincoln had received a formal invitation to participate in the event on November 2,[57] but a final decision that the president, accompanied by Nicolay, Hay, and several dignitaries, would be present was not confirmed until November 17. "After breakfast on the 19th my father went to the upper room in Mr. Will's house [i.e., the home of David Wills] where the president had spent the night," Helen wrote over eighty years later, "and remained with Mr. Lincoln" until he departed for the cemetery. "It was during this time," she continued, "that Mr. Lincoln finished writing his address."[58] Since they were the only two present, it remains unknown whether Lincoln discussed the draft with Nicolay.

What Nicolay's dutiful daughter failed to mention in this account was that Nicolay and Hay had stayed out quite late the night before and gotten drunk in the process of doing one of the things expected of them—seeing to the president's best interests by courting influential Republican voices important to Lincoln's renomination in 1864. In Gettysburg, Nicolay and Hay targeted an important Pennsylvania Republican journalist, John Weiss Forney, publisher of the influential *Washington Sunday Morning Chronicle* and secretary of the U.S. Senate, who had become rather inebriated and was pleased to have the two Lincoln staffers join him in consuming quantities of whiskey and singing together in his room. Somehow, Nicolay was able to pull himself together the next morning in time

Lincoln finishes his Gettysburg Address, November 19, 1863. The President is
in the center, hatless, looking down. Immediately left of Lincoln is Nicolay.
Above and to the left of Nicolay, the top portion of John Hay's head is visible.
The speech was so short that Lincoln was finished and preparing to sit down
before the photographer had the camera ready. (Library of Congress)

to assist Lincoln as required; Hay slept in and was later able to find "a beast" to
ride out to the cemetery for the dedication.[59] There is evidence that Nicolay and
Hay were present for the speech. In a photograph showing Lincoln having just
finished the address, Nicolay can be seen seated in the front row slightly to the
president's right. Hay is seated behind Nicolay.

Edward Everett of Massachusetts was the keynote speaker. Everett had been
a congressman, governor, ambassador, secretary of state, U.S. senator, and vice
presidential candidate and was known as one of the most gifted orators in the
country. Everett's Gettysburg speech commenced at about noon and lasted about
two hours. Following a musical interlude, President Lincoln rose to address the
crowd. The speech was brief, lasting less than three minutes.

Years later, Nicolay and Hay wrote in their 1890 biography of Lincoln that
"It was a trying ordeal to fittingly crown with a few brief sentences the ceremonies of such a day, and such an achievement in oratory [as Edward Everett

had just delivered]." In their recollection of Lincoln's delivery, Nicolay and Hay asserted that any "passing doubt" about Lincoln's ability to make an appropriate speech "vanished with his opening sentence." In their opinion, "the President pronounced an address of dedication, so pertinent, so brief yet so comprehensive, so terse yet so eloquent." In a work that is noted for its unequivocal ode to Lincoln's greatness, the president's assistants were correct when citing "the best critics" who "have awarded it an unquestioned rank as one of the world's masterpieces in the rhetorical art."[60]

In the view of Nicolay and Hay, the "best" critics would have been those who praised the speech at a time when the Gettysburg Address had yet to be recognized as the immortal work that it is. "Contrary to the often made statement" that the address "was little appreciated by those who heard it," Helen, still trying to portray the speech as universally well received at the time it was given, declared, "the Associated Press report shows that during the short period of its delivery, he [Lincoln] was interrupted six times by applause."[61] Helen may have found clippings of this positive report on the speech among her father's treasured memorabilia.

Yet, the greatest compliment regarding Lincoln's speech came neither from the partisan Republican press nor the Democratic press, which condemned it as unworthy of the occasion, nor from Nicolay and Hay, but from Edward Everett, who wrote Lincoln, "I should be glad, if I could flatter myself that I came as near to the central idea of the occasion, in two hours, as you did in two minutes."[62]

But what exactly did Lincoln say in one of the shortest speeches he ever gave? There were different versions of the speech: the one the president had prepared, the one he actually gave as recorded by an Associated Press reporter, and a final revised copy he had made. Nicolay and Hay discussed the speech in their history, but questions remained about the various versions. In 1894, Nicolay clarified what actually happened:

> The newspaper records indicate that when Mr. Lincoln began to speak, he held in his hand the manuscript first draft of his address which he had finished only a short time before. But it is the distinct recollection of the writer, who sat within a few feet of him, that he did not read from the written pages, though that impression was naturally left upon many of his auditors. That it was not a mere mechanical reading is, however, more definitely confirmed by the circumstance that Mr. Lincoln did not deliver the address in the exact form in which his first draft is written. It was taken down in shorthand by the reporter for the "Associated Press," telegraphed to the principal cities, and printed on the following morning in the leading newspapers.

It would also appear that a few, but only a very few, independent shorthand reports or abstracts were made by other correspondents. For all practical purposes of criticism, therefore, the three versions mentioned at the beginning of this article, namely: (1) The first draft; (2) the Associated Press report; (3) the revised autograph copy, may be used as standards of comparison.[63]

In this article, Nicolay overcame his natural reluctance to write himself out of events and placed himself on the podium within a few feet of the president.

As the year drew to a close, Nicolay became aware of disloyalty within the cabinet itself when he met with a Mr. Flannigan, editor of the *Philadelphia News,* on December 19. He made a note only to himself about this White House meeting, no doubt sensing that this was information too sensitive even to share with Therena at this point. Flannigan had hoped to meet with Lincoln, but as the president was not available, he chose instead to "talk politics" with Nicolay.

Flannigan shared with Nicolay that Salmon Chase, Lincoln's secretary of the treasury, had designs on the presidency and "is actively at work through his friends in Phila[delphia]." Flannigan informed Nicolay that he had been recruited to "do the press-work for two papers to be published in Chase's interest . . . both bought by Jay Cooke & Co."[64] Nicolay and Hay treated Chase with considerable disdain in their 1890 biography of Lincoln, stating that "he regarded himself as the friend of Mr. Lincoln, even making protestations to this effect to others." While Chase "undoubtedly thought" his friendly feelings toward Lincoln were sincere, Nicolay and Hay insisted that Chase's estimation of Lincoln involved "so poor an opinion of the President's intellect and character . . . that he could not believe the people so blind as deliberately to prefer the President to himself."[65] While Nicolay and Hay asserted that "there never was a man who found it so easy to delude himself" in their four years in Washington, it is likely they found others who could match Chase's narcissistic delusions, but their venom against the treasury secretary for challenging Lincoln was usually unrestrained and singularly focused.

In retrospect, Nicolay concluded that Chase's desire for the presidency was no surprise to Lincoln. "He [Lincoln] had his own opinion on the taste and judgment displayed by Mr. Chase in his criticisms of the president, and of his colleagues in the Cabinet; but he took no notice of them."[66] Indeed, the politically astute Lincoln took notice of nearly everything; he just did not make public note of it, a point Nicolay never seems to have grasped. The Lincoln cabinet was, as historian Doris Kearns Goodwin has so aptly named it, a team of rivals. Lincoln would have heartily endorsed an axiom made popular in our time: "Keep your friends close, and your enemies closer." The Chase campaign for the presidency was short lived. Within a few weeks, Chase publicly disavowed any attempt to have himself nominated, and by early summer of 1864, he was no longer in the cabinet after Lincoln accepted Chase's third offer to resign.

As the year 1863 wound down, Stoddard recorded an incident in which Nicolay's stern manner proved its usefulness. It was a situation half comic and half serious but showed the lengths to which individuals would go to get their five minutes with the president. Nicolay and Hay had to bar a persistent petitioner from the president's sickbed. It was December 1863, and Lincoln had the only significant illness during his presidency, a mild case of smallpox. The inhabitants of the White House were quarantined and a notice posted on the doors that none should enter. Nonetheless, an office seeker managed to breach the inner sanctum of the White House. The trespasser was "eager to unfold the fact that he is an important office-seeker," who, Stoddard revealed, was "sure of his success if he could see the President, his papers of recommendation are so overpowering strong." When told the president had smallpox and could not receive visitors, the invader, solely concerned about securing an appointment, assured everyone that he had been vaccinated. "It requires something like engineering to get the fearless adventurer out of the White House," Stoddard recalled, "for he really is a man who is of some value," but he ought to know, Stoddard continued, "that another man, in enduring pain and fever and intolerable irritation ought not be intruded upon." "Perhaps," Stoddard cynically recorded, "he was thinking less of that, and more of the fact that Mr. Lincoln could appoint him to-day and die tomorrow." "There are more like him," Stoddard lamented, but "the quarantine is usually too much for them. And for those who do get through the barricade, there is the impassable Nicolay who has a fine faculty for explaining to some men the view he takes of any untimely persistency." Exasperated by his memory of such incidents, Stoddard concluded: "it is of no use to employ verbal needles upon such pachydermatous natures."[67] It was a silly interlude that brought an end to a busy year.

Indeed, 1863 had proven to be a momentous year for Nicolay. On its first day, he had been present at Lincoln's side for the signing of the Emancipation Proclamation. In the same month, he had been admitted to the bar of the Supreme Court of the United States. He had been at the president's side through the grueling month of May 1863, when Union fortunes sunk to a new low after the defeat at Chancellorsville on May 5. He was present supporting the president through those dark uncertain days when the outcome at Gettysburg was not assured. Like all loyal Unionists, he celebrated the twin victories of early July. Gettysburg concluded with the retreat of Lee's army beginning on July 5, and on the same day, news reached Washington that the Confederate bastion of

Vicksburg had fallen, cutting the rebellious states in half. It seemed that the tide of the war might finally begin to turn in the Union's favor. But then, little else happened on the war front in Virginia for the remainder of the year. Although the Confederate siege of Chattanooga had been lifted, there was little progress on the western front as well.

Throughout 1863, Lincoln had given public and private acknowledgment of the trust and support he had for his secretary. Nicolay's many public appearances—on the streets of Washington, at the theater, at public levees, and in many other venues at the president's side—gave ample though unspoken confirmation of Lincoln's continuing confidence in his secretary. Entrusting Nicolay with a second Indian negotiation reaffirmed Nicolay's role as the dependable voice of the president himself. This assignment had also made a public statement that the president had every confidence in Nicolay's abilities, despite the failure of the negotiations with the Chippewa. The Sioux War had changed the facts on the ground, and in that climate, trust between the Chippewa and the representatives of the government was at a very low point.

In contrast, the negotiations with the Ute Indians had been a success. In his annual report, Commissioner Dole had commended Nicolay's role "as secretary whose valuable services in effecting the treaty deserves special mention."[68] While in Colorado, Nicolay, who loved the outdoors, had been able to enjoy the fresh air, the limitless skies, different wildlife, and general excitement of a government-financed junket to the Rocky Mountain West for several months, leaving Hay to handle the chores in the White House.

The end of 1863 did not bring any hope that the long, bloody war would soon end. The Army of the Potomac did nothing to capitalize on its victory at Gettysburg, and many in the North began to feel that those who had made the ultimate sacrifice on its bloody fields may have done so in vain. In Tennessee, the siege of Chattanooga had been lifted on Missionary Ridge and Lookout Mountain, but little progress had been made in the western theater since the fall of Vicksburg. In early December, the president confided to Nicolay his frustrations with the disappointing performance of the Army of the Potomac.[69] Also, at this time, Lincoln faced problems in Missouri, as well as difficulties with the Peace Party in the North, whose leaders included Clement Vallandigham, a former congressman from Ohio. Vallandigham's disruptive activities had been replaced by the unrelenting lobbying of Fernando Wood, the former mayor of New York City and now a congressman. These problems made life difficult for everyone in the White House as the calendar turned to 1864.[70]

CHAPTER EIGHT

Victory and Tragedy, 1864–1865

New Year's Day 1864 started off with an even busier public White House reception than usual. "I have just run away a little while from the reception which is going on below to write you 'A happy New Year,'" Nicolay penned Therena, "and to get a brief respite from the interminable crowd which is besieging the Presidential doors. I have not seen anything like it on New Year's since I have been here."[1] Even with the twin victories of Gettysburg and Vicksburg, the war was not going well. It was closing in on its third, increasingly bloody year without resolution for either side in sight.

Two items of great importance were on the mind of Lincoln and his administration, both of which would have significant consequences for his secretary. When Lincoln gave his annual address to Congress the previous December 8, he attached to it his Proclamation of Amnesty and Reconstruction. In this plan, Lincoln hoped at least some of the seceded states would seize the initiative to rejoin the Union without coercion, and he wanted to make it as easy as possible for them to do so. The proclamation contained a "Ten Per-Cent Plan," which would allow a seceded state back into the Union once 10 percent of its citizens on the 1860 voter rolls took an oath of allegiance to the Union and agreed to support emancipation. The president, believing Florida was a likely candidate for inauguration of this plan, decided to send John Hay on a mission to help accomplish it. If Hay could assist in gathering fourteen hundred valid signatures, Florida could qualify, and the Confederacy would be on the rapid path to extinction.

To accomplish his task, Hay was commissioned as a major in the U.S. Army and sent off to Florida on January 15, 1864, leaving Nicolay without his friend and White House roommate and with more work to do in Hay's absence. Now it was payback time for the Colorado trip, and Nicolay's turn to handle the work at the White House while Hay was away. The second great issue was actually of paramount importance to the amnesty and reconstruction plan, that being Lincoln's renomination and reelection in 1864, without which little else mattered.

However, the war and other issues had to be put aside temporarily as the secretary had to contend with the First Lady yet again. Mrs. Lincoln and Nicolay often clashed over arrangements for state dinners. The first concern for the secretary was appropriate attire. "There is an amusing list in my father's handwriting, of what gentlemen should wear on occasions of ceremony," Helen reminisced:

Coat:
  Black dress
  Blue   "   bright buttons.
Pants:
  Black—white in summer.
Vest:
  Black
Shirt:
  (Here the paper was left virgin white.)
Gloves:
  White or straw kids.
Boots:
  Boots or shoes.
Cravat:
  White.[2]

Then there were the receiving lines at these state dinners. "How very tall the President looks, standing there in the foreground between his two private secretaries," Stoddard recalled. "That is their customary post of duty upon reception evenings, and we know by experience that it means an evening of hard work."[3] The secretaries flanked the president, the first to announce to the president who he was about to greet, the other to spur the just-announced guests to move along and not seek to extend their "few moments" with the president about some item dear to their heart or pocketbook. This proved a difficult task when the president usually greeted people with "How do you do?" or, more ominously, "What can I do for you?"[4]

Nicolay turned to the State Department for directions when the dinners involved members of the diplomatic corps. Protocols and precedents had to be observed with utmost care. "The detail that bored my father most of all," Helen revealed, "was the seating of guests at state dinners where 'unbreakable' rules of precedence loomed large, yet occasionally had to be side-stepped because of personal or political feuds." The inevitable last-minute cancellations "of course upset the whole apple cart," requiring a hasty reorganization of the seating chart. Nicolay's lifelong attention to detail saved the situation on numerous occasions. His daughter reported that he kept "his neat diagrams of the banquet tables, ladies' names in decorative red ink, the gentlemen's in black, accompanied by lists of the guests originally invited, and of those who finally came."[5] No detail escaped his notice, and state dinners in the Lincoln era met the expectations of all but the most demanding critics. What is most ironic about this duty for the immigrant from Germany was that when members of the diplomatic corps were present, he had to be deferential to the titled members of European nobility. His family allegedly left the Palatinate because his brother Frederick Lewis did not like standing in the rain while a member of the royal house passed by. Now, the youngest Nicolay was politely smiling and shaking hands with the representatives of Europe's monarchs. But his real nightmare at these dinners was not the protocols of the State Department or the rivalries of cabinet members and politicians or the late cancellations but Mrs. Lincoln, who sought to exercise her authority in ways that could bring political embarrassment or worse to her husband. Consequently, she often came to loggerheads with Nicolay over seating arrangements and guest lists.

A particularly unpleasant clash occurred in early 1864. On January 18, Nicolay composed a letter to "My dear Major" John Hay while Hay was on military service in Florida; in it he complained about the problem he was having with the First Lady over invitations to a formal White House cabinet dinner. One of his responsibilities was to see that invitations were properly sent for such events and that the events themselves ran smoothly. Salmon Chase's very attractive daughter Kate, recently wed to Governor William Sprague of Rhode Island, was not on Mary's list of favorite people for several reasons, including Chase's aspirations to be the Republican nominee for president in 1864. Nicolay discovered to his dismay that Mrs. Lincoln had unilaterally scratched off Chase, his daughter, and her husband from the guest list Nicolay had prepared. "I referred the question of 'snub' to the Tycoon [Lincoln]," he informed Hay, who after "a short conference with the powers at the other end of the hall [his wife] came back and ordered" that the treasury secretary, along with his daughter and son-in-law, be reinstated to the guest list. Almost immediately, "there . . . arose such a rampage [from the First Lady]," Nicolay reported, "as the House hasn't seen for a year." "Stod fairly cowered at the violence of the storm," mused the secretary, "and I think for the first time begins to appreciate the awful sublimities of nature."[6] However, Mrs. Lincoln was not about to forgive, much less forget, that the secretary was the root cause of her displeasure.

A few days after the event, Nicolay again wrote to Hay that he believed he had emerged from the cabinet dinner with "flying colors." He had called the president's attention to the fact that Mrs. Lincoln had stricken the Chase and Sprague names from the guest list. Because of Nicolay's action, "Her S. [Satanic] Majesty" had been compelled to reinstate them. In retaliation, the First Lady had "made up her mind resolutely not to have me at the dinner." She then struck him from the guest list, as she had determined that, with William Stoddard's help, she could manage the details of the dinner without Nicolay's usual involvement. Nicolay told Stoddard to plead ignorance of the necessary information to be of assistance and also to inform her that it really was Nicolay's business. One can imagine how inwardly gleeful the secretary must have been when he informed Hay that Mary Lincoln soon "backed down, requested my presence and assistance—apologizing, and explaining that the affair had worried her so she hadn't slept for a night or two." "I think she has felt happier since she cast out the devil of stubbornness," he wrote facetiously, and "the dinner was got through with creditably."[7] And significantly, Nicolay was at his usual place at the table.

Mrs. Lincoln had proven to be a problem for the secretary throughout the Lincoln administration. Relations with Nicolay had been good in Springfield, where her interaction with him would have been occasional and mainly social. But after he arrived in Washington and lived down the hall from her, his relations with the mercurial First Lady deteriorated. Her disposition could change in an instant, and when her temper flared, she could be both verbally and physically abusive. She ran up very large debts for her husband by redecorating the White House well beyond the budget allocated by Congress. Mrs. Lincoln engaged in moneymaking schemes and was very willing to use government funds for purposes not earmarked. She made scenes in public and was known to make well-publicized comments injurious to her husband's government while exercising poor judgment in her associations. All of this troubled Nicolay, the frugal, proper private secretary absolutely devoted to the president.

Since nineteenth-century First Ladies were expected to be a bauble in their husbands' social firmament and little more, Mrs. Lincoln had to depend on Nicolay and Hay for secretarial services for the considerable correspondence she received during the war. Nicolay and Hay lived just footsteps away from the Lincoln's private family quarters, leaving little privacy for any of the White House's residents. It must have been awkward at times for Nicolay and Hay to be within earshot of the episodes of marital discord between the first couple. Worse yet, the public business of the president was conducted within listening distance of the First Lady, who would interject her opinions or questions. Working and living in these close conditions would test anyone's nerves. Hence the importance of Stoddard's ability to get along with Mrs. Lincoln and serve as her secretary, as assigned by Nicolay, which was a great relief to Nicolay and Hay.

According to Mary Lincoln biographer Ruth Randall Painter, Nicolay maintained a "correct but distant relationship with her." As the private secretary, he had no choice for the sake of his boss and his position. Hay, on the other hand, left little doubt about his feelings.[8] Nicolay, however, could play both sides of the street in his relations with the First Lady. He was not above playing to her fantasies when it was called for. When Mary Lincoln fired the venerable doorkeeper, Edward McManus, in January 1865, allegedly for spreading rumors about her, the old man subsequently showed up in New York in the company of Thurlow Weed. In a letter to Abram Wakeman, Mary noted that "Nicol, himself says that E's [Edward McManus's] mind is positively deranged. I have suspected it for some time."[9] In Helen's biography, where she mistakenly referred to him as Edward "Moran," she wrote that the man could be "trusted equally with state secrets, or with the diplomatic management of the President's young son Tad."[10] That description could only have come to Helen from her father, who had also, according to Mary Lincoln, declared that McManus was "deranged." But McManus was gone, and Nicolay probably saw no purpose in disagreeing with, and quite possibly inciting, the First Lady on that point.

Trying to deal with Mary Lincoln's volatility and schemes while handling the office in Hay's absence put a strain on the secretary. Lest Hay worry that all was business in Washington, Nicolay informed him that "Society flourishes—I couldn't begin to count the parties on all my fingers. They are beginning to double up."[11] As he had been in Springfield, Nicolay, with his gift for languages and his knowledge of politics, music, and literature, would be a welcomed guest. While party guests invariably sought to squeeze tidbits of information from the presidential secretary, he frustrated every query, pleading ignorance and otherwise evading a meaningful answer.

It was at about this time that Therena made a trip to Washington to visit relatives[12] and, one would assume, her fiancé, sometime in late January and/or early February 1864. Evidence for this visit is found in Nicolay's brief mention of her trip home in a letter to her dated February 12. A few days later, he wrote her again, saying, "As over a week has elapsed since you started home and I have not yet received a letter from you I am beginning to fear you have been delayed on the way." This visit from Therena would also explain a gap in his usually more frequent correspondence to her in late January and early February, and her return home to Illinois may also help explain his feelings in a letter to her dated February 21, 1864. "I have had the blues badly several times this past week," he complained, adding, "It seems as if the circumstances surrounding my position were getting worse by the day." With all the stress and overwork, he began "seriously to doubt my ability to endure a great while longer. 'Nous verrons [we'll see].'"[13]

Nicolay's cynical side came out in force while writing a letter he sent to John Hay, who was still in Florida. "I infer that you are living in metaphorical clover," he wrote caustically, "while we poor devils are eating husks of hard work in the national pig sty." He then reported to Hay on the political undercurrents in the capital. Salmon Chase and his supporters "were busy night and day and becoming even more and more unscrupulous and malicious." The Chase forces were circulating "a scurrilous anonymous pamphlet" seeking to undermine the president. Senator Samuel Pomeroy of Kansas, who was upset at Lincoln regarding the distribution of patronage in his state, proposed that Chase form campaign committees throughout the country. In the meantime, Chase supporters in Congress were described by Nicolay as "malicious and bitter" while refraining from openly attacking the president. "Corruption intrigue and malice are doing their worst," he proclaimed, "but I do not think it is in the cards to beat the Tycoon."[14] Within days, George appeared to be back to his old self, writing Therena a newsy letter including information on Secretary Chase's not-so-secret interest in becoming president in 1864.[15]

Around the time of Therena's visit, another tragedy struck the White House. In those days, communication between the White House and Capitol Hill was by messenger, a function performed by Nicolay, Hay, and sometimes Stoddard. Consequently, that these men had instantaneous access to the halls of Congress was of paramount importance. Stoddard described the method of moving messages to the other end of Pennsylvania Avenue while relating a humorous story concerning the "two younger secretaries":

There are many public messages going, almost daily, it seems, from this end of the avenue to the other, but they carry only part of the electric current of influence which travels the same road all the time.

It is Nicolay's business or Hay's, or that of both, to carry those messages as a rule, and they have a two-horse cab in which to ride to the Capitol. When those horses were first procured, the two younger secretaries were seized with the idea of perfecting their horsemanship by taking early morning saddle exercise, but in less than a fortnight they gave it up. Gallops before breakfast were too much like cavalry service without pay or rations.[16]

Later Stoddard would join the two-horse cab express and entered the halls of Congress with what Stoddard referred to as his "paper latch-key." On presentation of his credentials as presidential messenger, Stoddard described how he was escorted by the sergeant-at-arms of the House of Representatives: " Forward marches the Sergeant-at-Arms to your side, and in a moment more your paper latch-key is before the Speaker, and with its further treatment by the House you have nothing to do. The doorkeepers have made you free of the legislative chambers heretofore, but from this day forward you are legally entitled to the 'privilege of the floor,' to come and go at will, except when the Senate is in executive session, the theory being that you are supposed to be always on business for the President and cannot be questioned as to its nature."[17]

The horses used for these excursions to Congress were maintained in the stable next to the White House, where the West Wing is today. Also stabled there were the president's horse and Tad's ponies. On February 10, there was a disastrous fire in the White House stables. The carriages were saved from the fire, but "Tad [Lincoln] was in bitter tears at the loss of his ponies, and his heaviest grief was his recollection that one of them had belonged to Willie." Cooper, the stable hand, suffered the greatest loss—about $400 worth of gold and paper money, and expressed his strong opinion that arson was involved, as he had been gone from the stables for only an hour when the fire broke out and everything had been in good order when he left. Nicolay informed Hay: "Mrs. L[incoln] had discharged her coachman [Patterson McGee] today, and Bob [Robert Lincoln] who is here suspects him of the work. Quien sabe! [Who knows?]"[18]

Three days after the fire, Congress passed an appropriation of $12,000 to rebuild the stable "forthwith."[19] The act did not provide for compensation for the loss of personal property including the president's. Nonetheless, two days after the appropriation became law, Nicolay sent a letter to Thaddeus Stevens, chairman of the Committee of Ways and Means of the House of Representatives, requesting reimbursement for his considerable out-of-pocket expenses, beyond a partial government subsidy, for "carriage, horses, harness, repairs, horsefeed and coachman's wages" that were in "almost constant use" to "carry messages from the President to Congress, and to visit the various Departments, &c." "As the government only pays me an annual salary of $2,500" and "as I lost horses in the late burning of the stables at the Executive Mansion," he informed the congressman, "and as the great rise in prices has so largely increased this class of expenses, I cannot longer afford to bear this private expense for the public service." Not only did the secretary want "a new pair of horses" but also "about one hundred dollars per month," or twelve hundred dollars a year, to maintain them.[20]

The price of horses had escalated exponentially as the war progressed. Both armies consumed horseflesh at a horrific rate on the battlefield. Any horse was becoming harder to procure. While Congress passed an act compensating Union soldiers for the loss of their horses under certain circumstances later that year, the act would not have applied to Nicolay's situation. The outcome of his request is not known, nor is it known whether he fought this battle on his own or sought the intervention of the president. It is questionable whether Stevens, a frugal Radical Republican, would have lent a sympathetic ear to either Nicolay or his boss.[21]

Stevens was fully acquainted with the secretary, as was much of Washington. Nicolay and Hay took their meals at the Willard Hotel since the White House dining room was the exclusive realm of the first family. While coming and going from their meals, the secretaries were daily confronted by men seeking access or favors. The hotel's lobby was infamous for gatherings of such men. Eventually, during the Civil War, a new term entered the political lexicon for these men in the Willard lobby: "lobbyists." Nicolay and Hay were particularly deliberate in keeping these men at arm's length. Thomas H. Shastid repeated his father's reminiscences of Nicolay, noting that the secretary "was always a modest, perhaps even diffident man." Shastid's father had recollected that "when in his boyhood, he and Nicolay of nights had walked together [in] Pittsfield, Nicolay would so far as possible, shun the streets whereon the elite of the village were most likely to be passing—so shy, so very, very painfully shy he was."[22] While he could not "shun the streets" where the elite of Washington traversed, Nicolay tried during his time in the capital to be as unobtrusive and unnoticed as possible when out and about by himself.

While Hay was in Florida, Lincoln made a major shift in the command of the Union armies. With the Republican Party convention and the presidential election looming, Lincoln wanted to do everything possible to be reelected and

bring the war to a successful close, guaranteeing both union and freedom. Bringing General Ulysses S. Grant from the western theater of the war to the East was
something Lincoln had contemplated for some time, and now he felt that the
time had come. By promoting Grant to the rarified rank of lieutenant general
and placing him in command of all Union armies, Lincoln hoped to put an end
to Robert E. Lee's continued military successes and comebacks. When Secretary
of War Stanton called Grant to Washington, Nicolay was on the scene as a keen
and interested observer, hopeful of good things to come for the Union cause.

Nicolay offered observations of Grant's coming to Washington and attending
a White House reception in memoranda dated March 8 and 9, 1864. He was astounded that "by some sort of negligence there was no one at the Depot to receive
him [Grant] but he found his way to Willard's [Hotel] with the two members of
his staff who accompanied him." The memorandum continues:

Reception tonight. The weather was bad, but the "Republican" having announced
that Grant would attend the reception it brought out a considerable crowd. At about
9½ p.m. the General came in—alone again excepting his staff—and he and the President met for the first time. The President expecting him knew from the buzz and
movement in the crowd that it must be him; and when a man of modest mien and
unimposing exterior presented himself, the President said, "This is General Grant,
is it?" The General replied "Yes!" and the two greeted each other more cordially, but
still with that modest deference—felt rather than expressed by word or action—so
appropriate to both—the one the honored Ruler and the other the honored Victor of
the nation and the time. The crowd too partook of the feeling of the occasion—there
was no rude jostling—or pushing or pulling, but unrestrained the crowd kept its
respectful distance, until after a brief conversation the President gave the General
in charge of Seward to present to Mrs. L. at the same time instructing me to send
for the Secretary of War. After paying his respects to Mrs. Lincoln the General was
taken by Seward to the East room where he was greeted by cheer after cheer by the
assembled crowd, and where he was forced to mount a sofa from whence he could
shake hands with those who pressed from all sides to see him. It was at least an
hour before he returned, flushed heated and perspiring with the unwanted exertion.

After a promenade in the East Room—the Prest with Mrs. Seward and Gen Grant
with Mrs L. the party returned to the Blue Room and sat down. The President went
up stairs and returning in a little while sat down near where the General the Sec of
War and myself were sitting.

"Tomorrow," said the Prest to the Genl. "at such time as you may arrange with
the Sec of War, I desire to make to you a formal presentation of your commission
as Lieut. Genl. I shall then make a very short speech to you to which I desire you to

reply, for an object; and that you may be properly prepared to do so I have written what I shall say—only four sentences in all—which I will read from my mss. as an example which you may follow and also read your reply, as you are perhaps not as much accustomed to speaking as I myself—and I therefore give you what I shall say that you may consider it and from [sic] your reply. There are two points that I would like to have you make in your answer: 1st To say something which shall prevent or obviate any jealousy of you from any of the other generals in the service and secondly, something which shall put you on as good terms as possible with the Army of the Potomac. . . . One o'clock tomorrow was finally fixed as the hour, after which the General took his leave, accompanied by the Sec of War.

—The President, as I learned in a reply to a question to him, is contemplating bringing the General east to see whether he cannot do something with the unfortunate army of the Potomac.[23]

Likely unintentionally, since Nicolay rarely included himself in these scenes, the secretary highlighted his stature in the Lincoln White House as being more than "a mere clerk." As he described the scene, "The President went up stairs and returning in a little while sat down near *where the General the Sec of War and myself were sitting*" (authors' italics). To be sitting and presumably conversing with Grant and Stanton highlights the fact that Nicolay was recognized as a person of consequence, not a mere paper shuffler. Decades later, in writing the Lincoln history, both Nicolay and Hay attempted to expunge their roles in the Lincoln administration from the pages of history. Yet, in this memorandum, meant for Nicolay's eyes only, he clearly let his guard down to give posterity a glimpse of how his contemporaries viewed him as a significant person in the events of the day.

Nicolay was also present the next day when General Grant received his commission from the president and recorded the following in a memorandum dated March 9, 1864:

The Presentation ceremony of Gen. Grant's commission as Lieut. General, took place today at 1 PM. in the Cabinet Chamber. The newspapers give the proceedings and addresses in full. Both the President and the General read their remarks from mss. The General had hurriedly and almost illegibly written his speech on the half of a sheet of note paper, in lead pencil, and being quite embarrassed by the occasion, and finding his own writing so very difficult to read, made rather sorry and disjointed work of enunciating his reply. I noticed too that in what he said, while it was brief and to the point, he had either forgotten or disregarded entirely the President's hints to him of the night previous.

But no doubt of greater interest to the secretary was his noting an event of the same day in the same memorandum. "During this afternoon, Gov. [Salmon P.] Chase sent the President a copy of his letter to Judge Hall of Ohio withdrawing his name from the Presidential canvass."[24]

Nicolay had reason for optimism; a new, fighting general was in command of the Union armies, and Lincoln appeared no longer to face competition for the 1864 Republican nomination from Chase, or any other candidate. To make matters even brighter for him, his friend, roommate, and coworker John Hay arrived back in Washington from his lengthy assignment in Florida. Hay arrived by train early in the morning of March 24 and went immediately to the White House. "Finding Nicolay in bed at 7 oclock in the morning," Hay recorded in his diary, "we talked over matters for a little while & I got some ideas of the situation from him."[25] Undoubtedly, Nicolay did his best to bring Hay up to speed as soon as possible with all that had transpired in the White House and intrigues in Washington since his last letter to Hay.

Having aligned his planned departure for a trip to New York with John Hay's return to the White House, Nicolay informed Therena on March 25 that he was leaving that evening for New York since Hay had returned from "an agreeable trip down south. He will remain on duty here in his old position for the present."[26] Nicolay was heading north to accomplish a couple of things for Lincoln. He was assigned to determine the pulse of Republican leaders in New York concerning Lincoln's bid for renomination and reelection, including hand-delivering a note from the president to Thurlow Weed and trying to sort out some alleged traitorous activities emanating from the New York Custom House. "I have been mainly occupied with seeing and talking with politicians in regard to the next Presidential election," he wrote Therena on April 1 from New York's Astor House, "about which there seems to be more diversity of views and interests here than anywhere else in the country." He also reported that the general consensus was that "Lincoln's re-nomination and re-election is considered almost a foregone conclusion." He noted that even "those who were dissatisfied with that result and who therefore adopt the belief very reluctantly and unwillingly" were prepared to go along.[27]

About this time, Nicolay received an encouraging letter from John Evans, governor of the Colorado Territory, thanking him for informing him that President Lincoln had signed on March 21 the congressional "Enabling Act" that allowed Colorado to proceed with an application for statehood. Evans also informed the secretary that Colorado was sending "a delegation to the Baltimore Convention who are unanimous for Mr. Lincoln's nomination."[28]

After returning to Washington, Nicolay responded to an inquiry from Therena about when he might next be able to visit her. He also tried to reassure her that heated political passions back in Illinois during an election year should not pose any physical danger to him. Not knowing when or if he could get away, he assured her that he would have "no objection to notifying you when I may conclude to come West." As to possible threats against his personal safety from the heavily Democratic and Confederate-sympathizing elements of Pike County, he insisted that "while of course the Copperheads in Pike necessarily dislike me more because of my close personal relations to the President, I have no idea their animosity would be so intense as to move them to seek my personal injury." Reminding her of his many antislavery editorials during his *Free Press* days, in which he dealt their views "hard blows," he did not think "they treasure that up against me." He assured her, "At all events, when I get ready to come out to see you, I shall not delay or defer my visit on that account." It is not known whether Nicolay penned that last sentence out of stubbornness, a trait he was sometimes known to exhibit, bravado, or the simple conviction that no harm could possibly come to him since he was right and in their hearts his adversaries, having received "hard blows" from his editorial pages, knew it. In any event, no harm ever came to him on his visits back to Pittsfield. Updating her on the news in Washington, he told her, in a classic and somewhat inexplicable understatement, that "little that is of interest has transpired here, except that the Senate the other day by a vote of 38 to 6 passed the resolution proposing an amendment to the Constitution of the United States abolishing slavery."[29]

In the second half of April 1864, Nicolay seemed to be experiencing frustration if not outright depression, assuming that his letters to Therena are a true indicator of his outlook. His frustrations bubbled to the surface as he complained to her of "the multitude of little things" that absorbed his attention such that "at the end of a week I can't see that I have accomplished much, and yet there is never an opportunity for doing the things I have most at heart. This everlasting frittering away of hours and days is one of the many very disagreeable features of life here." He also informed her of the "disgraceful" capture of Fort Pillow by Confederate forces under the command of Nathan Bedford Forrest and the subsequent massacre of defenseless African American prisoners, which would "create much uneasiness in Kentucky and Tennessee." Like many White House staffers since, he had nothing good to say about the Congress, which he described as "timid, vascillating [sic] and idle—to say nothing of its being selfish and corrupt. It is fortunate that the fate of the country does not hang entirely on its action." The only thing that seems to have brightened his life in the past week was his attendance at the opera: "I have gone every night, and have been well repaid by the very excellent music and singing."[30] His mood, as expressed to Therena a week later, did not seem to have improved. On April 24, he grumbled about recent "high winds, which blow almost like a hurricane, and fill the air with clouds of dust. So Washington weather goes—rain or desert—cold or heat—always a disagreeable extreme that adds to the annoyance of its people, and increases their [and apparently his] ill-temper." He even shared that he had attended recent parties and receptions, but found that they had "grown stale, flat, and unprofitable." To make matters worse, as he complained in a letter of May 1, he had been "quite sick . . . owing to imperfect digestion. . . . I shall take extra care of myself for a few days and hope to have no more trouble with it." As for spending time with Therena back home in Pittsfield, he lamented, "I see no early prospect of getting out West on a visit. Congress is not making any headway with its work, and it is but little over a month now until the Baltimore convention."[31]

By mid-May, Nicolay's outlook had clearly improved, and he penned a lengthy letter detailing to Therena his encouragement over General Grant's fighting style against Lee: "he has steadily whipped him and driven him back." Meanwhile, "Sheridan with his cavalry force has made a raid around the rear of Lee's army, destroying railroads, trains, depots of supplies, and capturing even the outer works of the City of Richmond," and "Sherman has advanced and compelled the enemy to evacuate Dalton, Ga." He had nothing but high praise for Grant and predicted: "The whole situation is so encouraging that we hope he may be able to totally destroy the rebel army and capture Richmond." "The President is cheerful and hopeful," he confided, "—not unduly elated, but seeming confident, and now as ever watching every report and indication, with quiet, unwavering interest." He was thrilled to see what he believed to be "the signs of final and complete victory every day growing so bright and auspicious!"[32] But apparently the four very full pages of military news in George's latest letter, encouraging as it was, must have left Therena wondering whether she was still important to him, as he said nothing about her or that he wished to see her. Nor did he offer up even a smoldering ember of anything resembling romance.

A week later, Nicolay wrote her again, this time focusing on Lincoln's pending nomination at the Baltimore convention coming up in June. Then, almost as an afterthought, he ended his letter by asking, "What did you mean when in your letter before the last you wrote that you thought we were slowly but surely drifting apart?"[33] Romantic courtship was not George's strong suit, and he seemed generally oblivious to Therena's emotional needs. But whatever difficulties had come between them were apparently remedied or patched over, as no mention was made in any of his subsequent surviving letters to this episode, and their relationship continued.

Meanwhile, the politically astute Lincoln had much on his mind since he did not take his own renomination, much less his reelection, for granted. While, in retrospect, the war was inexorably moving in favor of the Union, the Northern public at the time was frustrated. By this time, the Confederacy was split in half, and the blockading naval forces were daily tightening the stranglehold on the South's access to the outside world. Even though large swaths of the Confederacy had fallen under Union control, the war dragged on, and the long lists of dead and wounded continued to appear in the newspapers. War weariness was a spreading cancer in the North.

Amid the malaise of the Northern voters, the Republican National Convention in Baltimore convened on June 7. The party was split by a small group of Radical Republicans, content with neither the progress on the proposed constitutional amendment to abolish slavery nor progress on the battlefield. They had already formed their own party, nominating John C. Frémont, the Republican standard bearer in 1856, as their candidate. While not a serious threat to Lincoln's renomination, it caused concern about the possible effects on the election outcome. To make matters worse, the regular party held its convention in the midst of the bloody battles of Grant's Overland campaign.

The party adopted the name National Union Party as a means to expand its base by attracting the War Democrats. Lincoln dispatched his trusted secretary to the convention to monitor events and report back to him regarding developments. Nicolay was there as presidential liaison, communicating the president's wishes to the convention. He would meet with politicians and even with state delegations; however, he was not in any sense a political operative during the parley. Securing Lincoln's nomination was not in question, as no serious opposition surfaced. Nonetheless, two problems vexed Nicolay as he made the fifty-mile journey to the convention.

The first dealt with the vice-presidential nomination and the second, the seating of a radical delegation from Missouri. The first order of business for Nicolay was to meet with the Illinois delegation, including Congressman Burton C. Cook, who informed him that though there were three or four disaffected members, the unit rule would be enforced, and all of Illinois's votes were therefore pledged to Lincoln. Cook assured the secretary that "the delegates will in good faith do everything they can for Lincoln." He was questioned by Cook as to the president's preference for a running mate, "either personally or on the score of policy—or whether he wishes not even to interfere by a confidential indication." Nicolay did not know the answer since a vice-presidential preference was not part of his instructions, nor would he, as usual, act independently and hazard an opinion. Therefore, in a letter sent by express train, he asked John Hay, "Please get this information for me, if possible."[34] Hay passed Lincoln's wishes on to Nicolay: "Wish not to interfere about V.P. Can not interfere about platform. Convention must judge for itself."[35] Apparently as unaware of behind-the-scenes discussions as he had been at the 1860 Chicago convention, he informed Hay that it was his opinion that "Hamlin will in all probability be nominated V.P. . . . Andy Johnson seems to have no strength whatever."[36] Despite Nicolay's prediction, Andrew Johnson of Tennessee, a War Democrat, was made Lincoln's running mate.

The other issue that concerned Nicolay was the Missouri delegation. Missouri sent a twenty-two-man delegation consisting of Radical Republicans who opposed Lincoln's nomination. Nicolay wired his concerns to Lincoln about the Missouri delegation. The secretary could neither understand nor tolerate opposition to his president. Lincoln instructed Nicolay to let the delegation be seated. When the nominating ballot concluded, there were only twenty votes cast for another individual, Ulysses S. Grant. These were all cast by the Missouri delegates, but the president won because he had avoided a floor fight and a cause célèbre among the radicals who had remained loyal to the party.

Had Nicolay been a political operative with the authority to make decisions, he would have likely ordered a floor fight. Such a fight over the Missouri delegation could have led to further defections in the party and unraveled the near unanimity for Lincoln. At the conclusion of the balloting, the Missouri radicals, having made their statement of opposition to Lincoln, then made Lincoln's nomination for a second term unanimous. Before adjourning, the party also adopted a platform that specifically referred to slavery as the cause of the Civil War and called for the passage of the amendment already ratified by the Senate the previous April. The resolution read as follows:

3. Resolved, That as slavery was the cause, and now constitutes the strength of this Rebellion, and as it must be, always and everywhere, hostile to the principles of Republican Government, justice and the National safety demand its utter and

complete extirpation from the soil of the Republic; and that, while we uphold and maintain the acts and proclamations by which the Government, in its own defense, has aimed a deathblow at this gigantic evil, we are in favor, furthermore, of such an amendment to the Constitution, to be made by the people in conformity with its provisions, as shall terminate and forever prohibit the existence of Slavery within the limits of the jurisdiction of the United States.

Lincoln, Nicolay and other conservative Republicans had now been enlisted in the abolitionist movement.

With the convention successfully behind him, Nicolay prepared for another trip west, part vacation and part tending to business for Lincoln. Included in his agenda was a much-needed visit to his fiancée. However, his trip to the Rocky Mountains was cut short. Delays in getting the needed conveyances and rumors (which proved false) of the Arapahoe Indians on the warpath stymied the adventurers. Nicolay and his companions journeyed as far west as Fort Kearney before a plague of mosquitos finally convinced them to abandon the trip.[37]

When the Baltimore convention concluded, it was not certain that Lincoln would be reelected. Four days before its convening, Grant had launched assaults on Confederate lines at Cold Harbor, resulting in some of the worst carnage the Union army experienced in the bloody Overland campaign. The lists of dead and wounded appeared throughout the North, causing many to consider the idea of letting the South go its way.

Back in Washington at the "Maison Blanche" (as he referred to the White House in correspondence with Hay) after his abortive trip,[38] Nicolay was troubled that the upbeat mood following the president's renomination in Baltimore a few weeks earlier had been replaced by pessimism, not only among Lincoln supporters but also of the president himself, who now doubted his reelection. Lincoln penned a private memorandum on August 23 contemplating his defeat as a real possibility and the course he would have to take to save the Union before the inauguration of the new president.[39] "There is a rather bad state of feeling throughout the Union party, about the condition of things" Nicolay revealed to Therena on August 21. The lack of any military success and the "necessity of the new draft" had the politicians in a panic mode. His contempt for the political class was apparent when he declared that recent events had "discouraged many of our good friends, who are inclined to be a little weak-kneed and croakers." Reassuring himself as well as Therena, he added, "I think however, that it is mainly anxiety and discouragement and that they will recover from it." He admitted that "The

Democrats are growing bold and confident, and will be very unscrupulous, but I still [do] not think they can defeat Mr. Lincoln."[40]

His confidence seems to have vanished four days later when he wrote a letter to John Hay who was vacationing in Illinois. The missive sounded the alarm that crisis was upon them, although all was not yet lost. "Hell is to pay," declared a despondent Nicolay. Henry J. Raymond and the Union Party National Committee had met with the president earlier in the day and urged peace overtures to the Confederacy, he reported, but "the Tycoon sees and says it would be utter ruination." "Weak-kneed and d—ded fools like Chas. Sumner are in consultation for a new candidate," warned the secretary, so "everything is darkness and doubt and discouragement." Yet, he had faith that "if the President can infect R[aymond] and his committee with some of his own . . . patience and pluck, we are saved."[41]

The Democratic Party was the beneficiary of this war weariness but was bitterly divided between War Democrats and Peace Democrats. The Democrats, meeting in late August, nominated George McClellan on a peace platform. However, the party's platform made no mention of the peculiar institution or the proposed constitutional amendment abolishing slavery then before the House of Representatives. According to Nicolay and Hay, the Democratic nominating convention had originally been scheduled for July 4, 1864, but party leaders decided that time was on their side and postponed the convention until the end of August. This strategy appeared to be working to the Democrats' advantage. "As in the field of theology there is no militant virtue unless there is an active evil to oppose it," Nicolay and Hay would later declare, "so in that of politics a party without an organized opposition appears to drop to pieces by its own weight." Lincoln himself was quoted by Nicolay and Hay as saying, "At this period we had no adversary and seemed to have no friends."[42]

Once the Democrats met and produced a platform that "promised the millennium,"[43] Nicolay felt a great sense of relief. He was delighted at the seeming disarray in the Democratic ranks and sent a letter to Therena upon his return from New York on September 4. News had reached the capital the day before that the rail center of Atlanta had finally been captured by Sherman. Fort Morgan, guarding the approaches to Mobile Bay, had also been captured after an extended siege. George predicted that the news "will stimulate . . . a very potent enthusiasm." Adding to the positive news was his assertion that the peace platform was "disgusting to many honest War Democrats." He then struck an unusual religious note. "The Lord preserve this country," he wrote, lamenting that it would "be a dark day for the nation" if the Peace Democrats were elected. "I cannot think," he confessed, "that Providence has this humiliation or disgrace and disaster in store for us."[44]

As time moved closer to the election, Nicolay became even more enthusiastic and optimistic about Lincoln's chances for reelection. He wrote to Therena, "The political situation has not been as hopeful for six months past as it is just now. There is a perfect revolution in feeling. Three weeks ago our friends everywhere were despondent, almost to the point of giving up the contest in despair. Now they are hopeful, jubilant, hard at work and confident of success." He listed several reasons for this upswing in Lincoln's prospects, including Union success and growing optimism on the battlefield with Sherman's capture of Atlanta and Grant's determination to finish the war in Virginia, the split in the Democratic Party over McClellan's equivocal support for the peace platform, recent election results in Vermont, and finally, investor support of a new loan to the government of $30 million, which drew "three times more bidders than there were bonds for sale.[45]

Nicolay was then off briefly to New York for more business on behalf of the president in mid-September. Prior to leaving Washington, he received an unexpected letter dated September 20 from the capital's provost marshal drafting him into the Union army, effective September 26.[46] On his return to Washington, he informed Therena that he had secured a draft substitute. He assured his beloved that "if I had offered myself [I] would have been rejected by the surgeon" but thought that paying for a substitute would "forestall any evil or ill-natured criticism by Democratic demagogues"[47] To make sure that there was no such criticism, Nicolay apparently planted a story in the *New York Times*. On the same day Nicolay wrote Therena, a news item appeared in the newspaper. The brief article noted that "though erroneously enrolled" in Washington, the president's secretary was not subject to the draft in the district but in his home in Illinois, "which has more than filled its quota." It was reported that Nicolay, being "incapacitated by illness from serving," had nonetheless "sent a substitute to the enrolling office, who was duly accepted and mustered in." Only a person with a journalistic background such as Nicolay's would have known how to get this information into print.[48]

These statements were both self-serving and untrue. There was no way for the president to spare his secretary from military service with so many Union homes mourning their dead in the summer of 1864. Nicolay, the accomplished horseman, marksman, and outdoorsman who could shoot buffalo from a galloping horse, would have met the standards for military service. In 1864, the Union army needed bodies, any body, to fill its ranks. Perhaps recalling his brush with combat in Minnesota and the horrific scenes of the dead at Shiloh, Nicolay had no desire to win military honors like John Hay. Purchasing a substitute was a legal option for those who could afford it, and despite his oft-repeated protestations of poverty, Nicolay could afford it. In the letter, he informed Therena, "He cost me $550—was accepted and mustered in, and I doubt not will do my fighting to the best of his ability." The sum of $550 was a lot of money in 1864, slightly over 20 percent of his annual salary. It is noteworthy that in Helen's account of this incident, she omitted the amount her father paid, while quoting the remainder of the sentence. According to Helen, the substitute, an African American named Hiram Child, died in battle doing her father's fighting "to the best of his ability."[49]

A check of the American Civil War Database, which replicates available Civil War service records in the National Archives, lists only one African American by the name of Hiram Child. He enlisted on September 27, 1864, in the 22nd Infantry, U.S. Colored Troops.[50] Nicolay's letter to Therena is dated two days later on September 29. In it, he noted that he found his substitute "the day before yesterday"—that is, the very day of Hiram Child's enlistment. These facts strengthen the circumstantial evidence that this Hiram Child was Nicolay's substitute. The American Civil War Database cites *The History of Pennsylvania Volunteers, 1861–1865* as an additional source of information. Child could have been from North Carolina but living in Pennsylvania at the time of his enlistment. He had to be in the North, probably looking for work in New York at the time, in order for Nicolay to find him. However, if this Hiram Child was Nicolay's substitute, he survived the war, being mustered out on October 16, 1865. Helen undoubtedly got her information from her father. Given that her father harbored the prevailing racial and class prejudices of the time, it is unlikely that he cared about, much less ascertained, the fate of his substitute. Decades later, while relating the sad tale of that poor man, who died "doing my fighting," he could proclaim his sympathy for the man and his race to his daughter in the comfort of his Washington home.

His draft notice was not the only incident to mar the memory of the trip. In the same letter in which he discussed his draft situation, Nicolay confessed to Therena that he had lost a valuable keepsake she had given him. His watch had been stolen and "while it was of no great value it was still somewhat annoying to lose it in that manner." "But what troubled me the most," he confessed, "is that the watchguard you gave me was attached to it and was also stolen with it."[51]

With the New York trip and its attendant problems behind him, Nicolay looked forward to a more relaxed fall. In early October, with his thoughts very much focused on the November presidential election, he was able to write to Therena that "the political news from all directions was very encouraging." State elections in Indiana and Pennsylvania were about to be held, and "our friends are very hopeful of carrying both by a small majority," which would bode well for Lincoln's victory in those states. He was able to conclude that "it is very generally conceded that the President will be re-elected in November unless the popular feeling should greatly change in the interim."[52] But in Missouri, political factions were troublesome to Lincoln. The Radical Republicans in that state had not yet publicly committed to Lincoln, and there was concern that McClellan might carry the state. Lincoln decided to send Nicolay to Missouri to get a clearer picture of the situation and to see what could be done to bring the state's Republicans of various stripes to unite behind Lincoln's reelection. Lincoln knew that this trip would also place Nicolay near his home voting precinct in Springfield on Election Day, and give his often harried secretary some time with his fiancée. Nicolay was no doubt delighted to inform Therena that he would be coming for a visit, "endeavoring to visit a week—perhaps or more."[53]

By October 17, he had completed his work in Missouri and had written Lincoln to inform him that he thought things were "gravitating towards an understanding—temporary at least if not permanent—which will unite the vote of all the union men on the electoral and State ticket."[54] Now he had time to visit Therena and then make it to Springfield for Election Day, November 8, 1864. He arrived in Springfield in time to vote—although he was not yet a citizen. Undoubtedly, he cast his ballot for Abraham Lincoln of Illinois. That night, Lincoln was reelected to a second term.

In a letter to John Hay two days after the election, Nicolay revealed that when he attempted to cast his ballot, an election official challenged his right to vote, and he had to get two men to "swear for me." That inconvenience aside, he was able to express his relief to Hay that the election brought "the right result for the nation." "The waiting at the telegraph office for tardy news—the lunch at midnight over Watson's furnished by the ladies—the jubilee at Representative Hall, reminded me," he recalled, "very much of four years ago," even if the events were but "faint imitations of the glory of those departed days [election night 1860]."[55] Back in Washington by November 30, Nicolay dispatched a brief note to Therena to tell her, "Of course I find a large pile of letters here for me, and numbers of things to look after, so I only write this to let you know I am here."[56]

Nicolay settled back into his work routine, which included getting copies of the president's annual address to Congress on the state of the Union ready for distribution. He also found time to tell Therena that "I have finished the

"Blithedale Romance" [written by Nathaniel Hawthorne in 1852] since my return, and while I do not think the last part as good as the first, yet on the whole
I find it a most exquisite and delightful bit of reading."[57] When Congress re-
convened on December 5, 1864, Lincoln announced his choice for his fifth, and
final, nomination to the United States Supreme Court. Chief Justice Roger B.
Taney had died on October 12, but Lincoln wanted to take his time in naming
a new chief justice and waited until nearly a month after the election to arrive
at a final decision. Nicolay informed Therena that along with the president's
annual message to Congress came the nomination of Salmon P. Chase to be
the new chief justice. Chase was confirmed by the Senate on the same day his
nomination was submitted. Ignoring the political popularity of the decision by
the president within the Republican Party and the calculation of Lincoln to give
Chase less opportunity to be a voice of opposition, Nicolay instead focused on
Lincoln's magnanimity. "Probably no other man than Lincoln would have had,
in this age of the world," Nicolay gushed, "the degree of magnanimity to forgive
and exalt a rival who had so deeply and so unjustifiably intrigued against him."
He worshipfully added, "It is however only another most marked illustration of
the President in this age of small men."[58] The apotheosis of Abraham Lincoln,
codified in the Lincoln history a quarter century later, was already underway.

Nicolay, not surprisingly, had a high view of the executive branch of the government, at least when it was headed by his friend and hero, Abraham Lincoln. In
good measure due to Congressional interference with and meddling in Lincoln's
handling of the war, the secretary had adopted a rather cynical attitude toward the
national legislature. He permitted his disdain for Congress be known to Therena
on occasion, as in his letter to her of December 11, in which he complained that
"scarcely anything of interest transpired during the last half of the week just
past." Congress had voted itself a pre-Christmas recess of a few days, which he
attributed to that body's "usual habits of indolence and of letting everything take
its own time at the beginning of a session." He went on to tell her that Sherman's
army was marching through Georgia toward the coast but that the only real news
they had of his activity was from the rebel newspapers. These papers "promise
their people every day that he is to be stopped, and surrounded, and annihilated,
but do not indicate how or where."[59]

On December 16, 1864, George updated Therena on war both in the White
House and in Georgia and Tennessee. "About three days of the week have been
taken up with a row with my particular feminine friend here [Mrs. Lincoln],"
he informed her, "but I have got through it without any serious damage, or even
loss of temper [which was not always the case]." While Mary Lincoln and Nicolay

never seemed to hit it off, it is fair to say that he knew that the First Lady could be helpful at times to Lincoln but as often could be a distraction and an embarrassment. It seemed to him that she was often demanding, petty, and contrary when it came to her dealings with him, and he had no sympathy for her lavish expenditures and attempts to pad her accounts. When he determined that a second term as President Lincoln's private secretary was not what he wanted, surely Mary Lincoln was a factor in this decision.

But at least now there was good news from Union military action in the South: "Sherman is before if not in Savannah, and [General George] Thomas seems to have defeated Hood at Nashville. The Anaconda [Plan] is beginning to squeeze the rebellion."[60] Two days later, he wrote Therena again. The letter starts off with a strange query: "Why don't I deserve a letter?" It is likely that question was sparked by an expression of frustration, if not outright irritation, on Therena's part with her beau's inattentiveness. After raising the question, he moved on to the latest military news. He confirmed the virtual destruction of the Confederate Army of Tennessee by General Thomas outside of Nashville and that Sherman's army was poised to take Savannah, Georgia. "There remains but the army of Lee to be caught and overcome," he opined, "and the military strength of the rebellion is at an end. I think this result will almost certainly come within the next year." Nicolay sensed that the war was getting closer to the end, expressing the "hope that we may even gladden our next fourth of July with the rejoicings over the great event."[61] On the next Independence Day, he would celebrate the dawning of peace and unity for his country but under quite different circumstances than he could then imagine.

On December 23, Nicolay sent a private note to Simon Cameron, whose business acumen was more impressive than his record had been as Lincoln's first secretary of war. Cameron was interested in purchasing the *Baltimore Sun* as part of an investment group that Nicolay was invited to join, more for his journalistic expertise than his financial standing. He wrote to Cameron, who had returned from his stint as American minister to Russia, that "I am ready to join you and others in the enterprise of buying and publishing the 'Baltimore Sun,' if it can be obtained on the terms you mentioned to me." He ended with a postscript: "Please say nothing to any one at present about my proposed connection with the affair."[62] He was already contemplating moving on after Lincoln's second inauguration but was not yet ready to go public with his intentions. But before the *Baltimore Sun* transaction could be fully explored and implemented, a whirlwind of events in 1865 would send him in another direction entirely.

On Christmas Eve 1864, Nicolay wrote to Therena that Congress had adjourned for the holidays, noting "the eagerness with which the members rush off to their several homes." The weariness with which Nicolay now approached his job jumps off the page at the reader: "they [members of Congress] expect a happier Christmas there, than . . . in this labor-ridden and care-burdened town, whose very atmosphere seems infected with some subtle poison fatal to all peace of mind or repose of body."[63] After nearly four long years, the pressures were getting to him. The demands of office seekers, contractors, military men, inventors, crackpots, and the always fickle, sometimes panicky, and generally narcissistic politicians on his time and patience were becoming intolerable. He knew it was time to go. But as yet he did not know the answers to key questions: when should he leave and what should he do next?

As if that were not gloomy enough, his letter to Therena on Christmas Day gives a glimpse of the melancholy nature of a young man who still felt like a loner and outsider in some respects and yet who took solace in hope of a brighter future with her at his side. He reflected on another solitary Christmas, expressing not only a sense of loneliness on what has always been a family-oriented holiday but also a sense of personal deprivation going back to childhood. Permitting a rare insight into his innermost feelings, he wrote a poignant epitaph to a lost childhood:

The day seems to signify little more than any other mere holiday, or day of rest from ordinary cares and labors. I have been so long astray in the world—cut off from all those close and endearing associations of home and kindred, that I feel rather like a traveler in a strange land, who sees the pleasures and enjoyments of people about him, but at the same time feels that he himself has no part or right in them. I have indeed a sort of dim and indistinct recollection that in Germany, while yet a child, I was able to enjoy that perfect illusion which cheats care, and gives us a foretaste of perfect happiness. Whether it was the superstition of childhood, or the subtle influences of home and kindred, I am not now able to analyse; but I do know that the feeling, whatever produced it, was left on the other side of the sea. Still I have not lost faith in the potency of the charm, although I have learned from sad experience, that alone I have no power to evoke it. But by and by, when I shall have founded a home of my own, I shall install you wizard-in-chief, and trust to your skill to surround the Christmas Holidays with all the brilliant and delicious enchantments of the olden fairyland!

Your

George[64]

The childhood Christmases that he could only imagine were when he was sur-rounded by a nurturing and complete family unit, "on the other side of the sea." His father and older siblings were too busy surviving in America to pay much attention to young George. After Christmas 1845, the last one his father lived to see, he was alone in the crowd, a man "who sees the pleasures and enjoyments of people about him, but at the same time feels that he himself has no part or right in them." He wanted to belong, the way he had been a part of something until the day his brother kicked him out of the mill. He knew that he was part of something bigger than himself while serving Lincoln, but what he yearned for was a more intimate, personal relationship. Some day, with Therena as "wizard-in-chief" in a "home of my own," it would be her responsibility to "surround the Christmas Holidays with all the brilliant and delicious enchantments of the olden fairyland!" It was a dream that was at once beautiful and profoundly sad.

He had promised Therena that he would write her at least two letters a week during his time in Washington, and on December 30 he complained of having been so busy that "you must content yourself with even a technical adherence to my two-letters-a-week rule—though I should be compelled to write both on the same day." On December 26, General Sherman telegraphed the president, presenting him with the city of Savannah as a Christmas present. Washing-ton received news "to cheer us on Christmas morning—or rather on Monday morning, which was kept as Christmas." The administration hoped to "be able to celebrate our New Years with rejoicings over the fall of Wilmington, but that expedition turns out a failure."[65]

The 1865 New Year's levee must have been as busy as ever, though there is no mention of it in Nicolay's letters. But it was a happy event. The war was moving toward its final, successful conclusion, and with it, the prestige of the Lincoln Administration and its representatives was on the rise. The cumulative effect of General Winfield Scott's Anaconda Plan was squeezing the last breath out of the Southern resistance. Within a fortnight, Fort Fisher, North Carolina, would fall to Union forces and the port of Wilmington, North Carolina, would be effectively blockaded. The Confederacy's last port had been sealed off from the sea. The Union blockade was now effectively complete.

One of Nicolay's first assignments in 1865 was to attend two funerals, in Phil-adelphia and Trenton, of political note: those of the former vice president (un-der Polk) George M. Dallas, who had died on New Year's Eve, and of Lincoln's American minister to France, William L. Dayton, who had died in Paris on December 1. Dayton had beaten out Lincoln for the Republican vice presidential nomination in 1856 and had worked diligently and successfully to prevent French intervention on behalf of the Confederacy. Robert Lincoln and Secretary of State William Seward joined him at Dayton's funeral. George informed Therena that he went at President Lincoln's request, as Lincoln determined "that this mark of respect was due to these deceased gentlemen for their eminent worth and high public service."[66]

Nicolay's assignment as Lincoln's representative was also a "mark of respect" for his secretary. Nicolay was, to some degree, a representative of the Lincoln administration wherever he went and was encouraged to attend various receptions and other social engagements, some of which he enjoyed and others he found tedious. He told Therena in a letter dated January 13, 1865, that "the gayety of the winter is getting pretty well underway, and there is so much of it, that as usual it will soon cease to be play and become hard work." He informed his fiancée that the day before he attended a dinner party at the postmaster general's home, a party at the mayor's home, and a dance at the National Hotel. Tomorrow's social schedule, he wrote, would be relatively light, with "nothing but the reception at Speaker [of the House] Colfax's."[67]

Two major events of great significance had Nicolay's attention in January and early February 1865. Lincoln's address to Congress in December 1864 brought up the issue of getting an antislavery amendment passed as soon as possible. Such a constitutional amendment had, after all, been part of the Republican Party's 1864 platform. A joint resolution for the abolishment of slavery had passed the Senate but not the House. Lincoln wanted action before the war actually ended, lest his Emancipation Proclamation, a war measure, be overturned by the Supreme Court.

By the end of January 1865, the Lincoln administration had acquired enough votes from Democratic congressmen through patronage or coercion to push through a constitutional amendment to abolish slavery throughout the United States and send it to the states for ratification. The secretary was in the House gallery as the eyes and ears of Lincoln, preparing in his mind a detailed description of events for the president.[68] In describing the passage of the amendment by the House of Representatives on January 31, 1865, Nicolay and Hay quoted a congressional source years later in their Lincoln biography that "the success of the measure had been considered very doubtful, and depended upon certain negotiations the result of which was not fully assured, and the particulars of which never reached the public." Undoubtedly, Nicolay and Hay had been privy to those "certain negotiations." More significantly for Nicolay, the institution that he had hated all his life, slavery, would soon be a thing of an ugly past. Curiously, the extant letters to Therena are also silent on this momentous event. The amendment would now be passed to the states for ratification, which was certified as completed on December 18, 1865, a few months after Lincoln's assassination and Nicolay's move to Paris.

Another major event of early 1865 was a peace conference or, as Nicolay expressed it, "an informal conference about matters with a view to reaching a peace." On board the *River Queen* docked at Fortress Monroe at Union-held Hampton Roads, Virginia, on February 3, 1865, President Lincoln and Secretary Seward met with Lincoln's old friend, Confederate vice president Alexander Stephens, former U.S. senator and now Confederate senator Robert Hunter, and former associate justice of the Supreme Court and now Confederate assistant secretary of war John Campbell. While there is no indication that Nicolay was present at this conference, he knew enough about the meeting's substance to write to Therena the next day: "The President told them [the Confederate commissioners] that he could not entertain any proposition or conversation which did not concede and embody the restoration of the national authority over the states in revolt." Nor would the president back down from his public comments about slavery, nor could he "agree to any cessation of hostilities, which was not an actual end of the war and a disbandment of the rebel armies." The Confederate delegation "neither offered or declined any distinct point," reported Nicolay. Consequently, the conference came to naught.[69]

Still very much on his mind was what he would do once Lincoln was inaugurated for a second term. Several things were converging in his mind. He no doubt sensed that Therena was growing restless and at age twenty-eight (well beyond the age at which most women were wed at that time) wanted to get married. Meanwhile, his relationship with Mary Lincoln had deteriorated even further. Nicolay and Hay were secretly referring to her as "Her Satanic Majesty." It was known that Mrs. Lincoln was strongly pushing her husband to make a change in the White House staff that would replace Nicolay with Noah Brooks. Additionally, Nicolay often worried about his health, given both the daily rigors of his job as private secretary and the physical and emotional climate of Washington. He also could use more money than his position paid if he ever intended to settle down with Therena. None of these factors diminished his admiration for and total support of Lincoln and his policies, but he did have much to ponder. Yet, by this time, he had essentially made up his mind to leave the employ of the White House after Lincoln's second inauguration on March 4.

"Do not think that because I have written nothing about it," George reassured Therena on February 10, 1865, "[that] I have not engaged in considering the question as to where I shall stay and what I shall do after next fourth of March." They had discussed the matter the last time he was in Pittsfield, "but I have not yet reached any definite conclusion," except for being "pretty well resolved not to remain here in any present relation after that time." He also informed her that he had little interest in remaining in Washington. He had not seriously brought the matter up with the president, "although I have once or twice alluded to the subject in our conversation," he reported, but the president "does not wish to be troubled with the question . . . in any way." For the moment, the secretary was unable to determine his future course. He ended this letter of personal uncertainty with praise for his president and boss: "[Lincoln] is the wisest and safest man the nation could have at its head at the present time."[70]

Nicolay found himself caught up in a whirlwind of social events and hard work at the White House as the inauguration approached. He sent a missive to his fiancée on Valentine's Day with a rather unromantic listing of his problems: he had a cold, he needed more sleep, and his burdensome workload and over-scheduled social calendar had left him feeling "quite stupid today, and generally disgusted with myself and everybody about me. Don't feel in the least alarmed at this report of myself."[71] On February 26, his thirty-third birthday, he was in better spirits, as he wrote to Therena with excitement about "constant tidings of victory" announcing the fall into Union hands of Charleston; Fort Anderson, the last of the forts protecting Wilmington; and finally Wilmington itself. "The impression begins to gain ground," he noted, "that Lee must abandon Richmond and endeavor to make a stand somewhat further south. Rebeldom seems to be losing and suffering in all quarters."[72]

The second inauguration of Abraham Lincoln as president of the United States went off well from Nicolay's perspective. "The ceremonies passed off yesterday in as pleasant a manner as was possible," he confided to Therena. Using his talent as a writer, he wrote a dramatic account of the ceremony. While "the morning was very dark and rainy, and the streets were very muddy," he observed, a sudden change in the heavens occurred "when the President appeared on the East portico to be sworn, [and] the clouds disappeared and the sun shone out beautifully all the rest of the day." The celebrations of the inauguration also went off smoothly. Describing one of the last receptions in the White House that he would attend as private secretary, he noted that it "was without exaggeration the largest crowd that has been here yet." Sensing final victory in the air, everyone

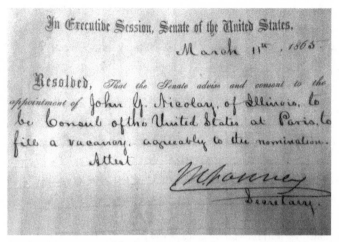

In Executive Session, Senate of the United States,

March 11ᵗʰ, 1865.

Resolved, That the Senate advise and consent to the appointment of John G. Nicolay, of Illinois, to be Consul of the United States at Paris, to fill a vacancy, agreeably to the nomination.

Attest

Documentation of the U.S. Senate's confirmation of Nicolay's
appointment as Consul of the United States at Paris, March 11, 1865.
(Library of Congress)

wanted to be near the soon-to-be-victorious president. As great as Inauguration Day was in Nicolay's eyes, now the dreaded "office-seekers will swarm in upon us like Egyptian locusts for two or three weeks; but I do not think the President intends to give them much encouragement."[73]

As Lincoln prepared for a second term, his attention turned to his secretaries. Lincoln liked and appreciated his secretaries, but the wartime stresses that had been placed on the White House were believed to be things of the past in the coming years. Having no love for either Nicolay or Hay, the First Lady continued to crusade for her friend Noah Brooks. When offered the consulship at Paris as a reward for his services, Nicolay hesitated but finally acceded to accepting the post. His last day as secretary was not officially set when he accompanied Lincoln to the second inauguration. Sitting on the rostrum near the president, he heard Lincoln call upon the war-torn nation to bind up its wounds, with "malice toward none" for a "just and lasting peace."

On March 12, George shared news with Therena that he suspected she may have already heard: that he had been appointed by President Lincoln and confirmed by the Senate as consul at Paris, at an annual salary of $5,000 (twice what he made as private secretary to the president). It was all so new that he had not determined his precise calendar, but he told his fiancée, "The probability is that I will not start there for two or three months yet, and that meanwhile I shall see you and ask you to be ready to go with me. While I have not yet fully decided this point, it will be as well for you to be quietly getting your wardrobe ready for the trip."[74] This was the change, indeed promotion, that he needed and that would enable him at long last to take a wife.

Nicolay's trip to Cuba, beginning in late March 1865, was to be a well deserved break and would give him time to begin planning the transition to his new role as consul at Paris. There was a new job ahead with which he had to familiarize himself, and there would be an apartment to rent in a foreign city. There would be many things to bring to a close at the White House, including gathering his notes and the president's papers that would someday be key to writing a history of Lincoln and his administration. There would be goodbyes to say or write to family and friends, including his friend, mentor, hero, and employer Abraham Lincoln. There would be many details to work out to make the transition from Washington to Paris a smooth one. Not least there would be Therena, his ever-patient fiancée, whom he could now support in a home of their own, even if in a foreign land. There was so much to think about and so much to do in a relatively few weeks, and yet it was quite exciting to ponder the possibilities.

On March 25, Nicolay checked out Edmond Texier's two-volume *Tableau de Paris* from the Library of Congress, the last book to be checked out under Lincoln's name. A week earlier, he had borrowed Emile Bonnechose's two-volume *Histoire de France*.[75] As usual, the secretary wanted to read up on his forthcoming adventure, this time to France. Consequently, these hefty books were to be his reading material as he set sail to Cuba for a vacation approved by his boss. As he embarked on his trip, Nicolay said good-bye to Lincoln, not knowing that he would never greet him again. Lincoln had become in many ways the father-figure he had lost when he was only fourteen.

On the day Nicolay left for Cuba, Lee attacked Fort Stedman in a desperate but unsuccessful attempt to break Grant's siege of Petersburg. This event led to a chain of military actions that culminated in the fall of Richmond on April 3 and Lee's surrender to Grant at Appomattox Court House on Palm Sunday, April 9, 1865. The Confederate government's flight signaled the beginning of the final collapse of Confederate resistance.

As part of his Cuban itinerary, he was present on his return as Major Robert Anderson raised the American flag over the ruins of Fort Sumter on April 14,

1865, four years to the day after Anderson had been forced to strike the colors. Early the next morning, Nicolay resumed his trip. When the steamship *Santiago de Cuba,* on which the secretary was returning to Washington, left Charleston, South Carolina, on Saturday morning, April 15, 1865, word of Lincoln's assassination had not yet reached those on board. As they neared Hampton Roads, Virginia, the next day, the steamship took on a pilot at Cape Henry to help guide them along the route to Washington. It was from him that Nicolay and others on the ship were stunned to hear, as he later related to Therena, "the first news of the terrible loss the country has suffered in the assassination of the President." He continued:

> It was so unexpected, so sudden, and so horrible even to think of, much less to realize, that we could not believe it, and therefore remained in hope that it would prove one of the thousand groundless exaggerations which the war has brought forth during the past four years. Alas, when we reached Point Lookout at daylight this morning, the mournful reports of the minute guns that were being fired, and the flag at half-mast left us no ground for further hope. I went on shore with the boat to forward our telegrams, and there found a Washington paper of Saturday giving us all the painful details.
>
> I am so much overwhelmed by this catastrophe that I scarcely know what to think or write. Just as the valor of the Union arms had won decisive victory over the rebellion, the wise and humane and steady guidance that has carried the nation through the storms of the past four years is taken away, and its destiny is again shrouded in doubt and uncertainty. My own faith in the future is not shaken, even by this sad event; but will the whole country remain as patient and as trusting, as when it felt its interests safe in the hands of Lincoln?
>
> It would seem that Providence had exacted from him the last and only additional service and sacrifice he could give his country—that of dying for her sake. Those of us who knew him will certainly interpret his death as a sign that Heaven deemed him worthy of martyrdom.
>
> You will readily infer that my own personal plans may be entirely changed by this unlooked for event. We hope to reach Washington by 4 p.m. today. I will write again as soon as I can, but may not learn anything definite for some days.
>
> Your
>
> George.[76]

Arriving in the mournful capital city in mid-afternoon on the day after Easter, he wrote to Therena on the following day from the White House about what he experienced:

Dear Therena,

Our ship arrived safely at the Navy Yard at about 2½ p.m. yesterday. I cannot describe to you the air of gloom which seems to hang over this city. As I drove up here from the Navy Yard through the city, almost every house was draped and closed, and men stood idle and listless in groups on the street corners. The Executive Mansion was dark and still as almost the grave itself. The silence, and gloom, and sorrow depicted on every face are as heavy and ominous of terror, as if some greater calamity still hung in the air, and was about to crush and overwhelm every one.

This morning the house is deeply draped in mourning, and the corpse is laid in state in the East Room where great crowds are taking their last look at the President's kind face, mild and benignant as becomes the father of a mourning nation, even in death. The funeral will take place tomorrow.

Your

George.[77]

He related more detail in his later writings concerning the expressions of grief shown in Washington and the nation in general over Lincoln's death. "Within the hour after the body [of Lincoln] was taken to the White House," he chronicled, "the town was shrouded in black." The signs of mourning were seen not only in the expected places, "but still more touching proof of affection was seen in the poorest class of houses, where laboring men of both colors found means in their penury to afford some scanty show of mourning."[78] The news "fell like a great shock" on the national scene, Nicolay related. "It was the first time the telegraph had been called upon to spread over the world tidings of such deep and mournful significance," he observed. Northern exultation over the surrender of Lee's army and the end to the rebellion would be swept away by a tide of tears. Hating "the arrogance of triumph," Lincoln would have been glad, Nicolay intoned, to know that "his passage to eternity would prevent too loud an exultation over the vanquished."[79] Even the former Confederacy, according to Nicolay's later reminiscences, shared the grief of Lincoln's premature death: "As it was, the South could take no umbrage at a grief so genuine and so legitimate; the people of that section even shared, to a certain degree, in the lamentations over the bier of one whom in their inmost hearts they knew to have wished them well."[80]

At noon on Wednesday, April 19, 1865, the first of many funeral and memorial services was held for the martyred president, this one taking place in the East Room of the Executive Mansion. There Nicolay sat to the right of Lincoln's casket, a place of honor near his friend, hero, and mentor. As William Coggeshall described the scene: "At 12 o'clock President Johnson, escorted by the venerable

Preston King [Republican leader and former senator from New York] and the members of the Cabinet, entered and took their places on the right of the coffin. Private Secretaries Nicolay and Hay, and Capt. Robert Lincoln, the President's eldest son, and only member of the family present, then Gen. Todd of Dakotah[81] and relatives of the family, were seated near the foot of the catafalque."[82]

Secretary of the Navy Gideon Welles recorded in his diary that "the funeral on Wednesday the 19th was imposing and sorrowful. All felt the solemnity, and sorrowed as if they had lost one of their own household. By voluntary action, business was everywhere suspended, and the people crowded the streets. The Cabinet met by arrangement in the room occupied by the President [Andrew Johnson] at the Treasury. We left a few minutes before meridian [noon] so as to be in the East Room at precisely 12 o'clock, being the last to enter."[83] Mary Lincoln was too distraught to attend this, or any other event for her departed husband,

The only known photograph of Lincoln in his casket. Discovered by Edwin Stanton's son in his deceased father's papers in 1887, he sent the photo to Nicolay thinking he might want to use it in his writings about Lincoln. The photo remained in Nicolay's possession and after his death it ended up with some of his papers given to historical archives in Springfield, Illinois. It was rediscovered and made public for the first time in 1952. See chapter 11, note 9 for additional information. (Library of Congress)

and would remain secluded in the White House in deep mourning for over a month after Lincoln's body was removed to the Capitol and later taken by train home to Springfield.

We will never know what memories may have passed through Nicolay's thoughts as he looked on Lincoln's corpse at the funeral in the East Room. He had just completed four years as private secretary to the president during the most tumultuous and stressful period of American history. For all those years, he had been at Abraham Lincoln's side as the president's assistant, rendering him impeccable and unimpeachable service. His association with Abraham Lincoln had defined his life and would shape his future.

Nicolay later described the White House funeral as "brief and simple—the burial service, a prayer, and a short address; while all the pomp and circumstance which the government could command was employed to give a fitting escort from the White House to the Capitol, where the body of the President was to lie in state. . . . [A]nd to associate the pomp of the day with the greatest work of Lincoln's life, a detachment of colored troops marched at the head of the line."[84] Nicolay did not board the president's funeral train on its long journey back to Illinois, largely replicating in reverse his inaugural train trip in February 1861.[85] He traveled separately with John Hay to attend the committal services at Springfield's Oak Ridge Cemetery on May 4. As Nicolay turned away from the cemetery on that solemn spring day, he knew that, at age thirty-three, the defining chapter of his life was drawing to a close.

CHAPTER NINE

To Paris and Back
The Search for Significance

Spring 1865 was a watershed time in Nicolay's life. In the space of two and a half months, his life changed dramatically. First, he lost his friend and mentor, Abraham Lincoln, to an assassin's bullet. He resigned his position as private secretary to the president and left Washington, where he had lived for four tumultuous years. He would not reside in the city again until 1872. He would finally marry Therena and depart with his bride to Paris to take up his new position as the American consul. Upon returning with his family in 1870, he would still be searching for a permanent focus in life.

On April 20, 1865, Nicolay officially submitted his resignation as private secretary to President Andrew Johnson, to be succeeded by Edward Neill. He had concluded that moving ahead with the consulship in Paris was his best course of action; he had already been confirmed unanimously by the Senate for that position and saw no reason to decline it despite his uncertainty and distress immediately following Lincoln's assassination. No doubt Therena was eagerly awaiting his decision about his future, which would have everything to do with her future. In the heart of his letter to President Johnson, he simply stated, "The death of President Lincoln having terminated the necessity for my temporary continuance in the discharge of its duties, I respectfully ask permission to resign the office of Private Secretary to the President of the United States."[1]

Nicolay, like Mary Lincoln, would remain in the White House throughout May; there, he and John Hay spent much of their time gathering and organizing Lincoln's presidential papers. Andrew Johnson generously allowed Mrs. Lincoln to remain in the White House until she, along with her more than fifty trunks of possessions, was prepared to leave. In the meantime, the new president took an office in the Treasury Building and lived in a guarded house at 15th and H Streets.[2]

Nicolay did not leave any contemporaneous record of whether he ever attended a session of the military tribunal that tried the Lincoln conspirators. The trial began on May 8, as Nicolay returned from the Lincoln committal service in Springfield. Testimony began on May 12. While Washington was consumed by the daily accounts of the trial, he may have been too occupied with wrapping up his affairs or too burdened with grief to dwell on the details of the conspiracy that murdered his idol. The verdict in the trial was never in doubt, given the fever-pitched emotions of the time, only the ultimate fate of each conspirator. By the time the trial ended and the sentences were pronounced on June 30, Nicolay was at sea on his way to Paris.

Despite his resignation letter, Nicolay still seemed reluctant to inform Therena how, or if, his plans for the short term included her. His letter to her dated April 24, 1865, does not even mention the fact that he had tendered his resignation as private secretary, but it does give insights into his thinking about the country, if not any hint as to his thoughts about his fiancée:

Dear Therena,

After the funeral of the President on Wednesday last, I felt entirely too depressed in spirits to write you a letter. Words seemed so inadequate to express my own personal sorrow at the loss of such a friend as the President has been to me, and my deep apprehension of the new troubles and difficulties in which it would involve the country, that I could not bring myself up to the task of attempting to portray them in language.

I trust that I do not yet, and probably shall not for a long while, realize what a change his death has wrought in my own personal relations and the personal relations of almost everyone connected with the government in this city who stood near to him, and this state of feeling is very much enhanced by the unsettled condition of the country. So far the new President has very favorably disappointed the expectations of almost every one; he has been quiet, steady, and content to let the government run along under the healthy and strong impetus it had at Mr. Lincoln's death—the very wisest policy he could have pursued under the circumstances. I have seen and talked with him twice, and all the indications of his personal appearance are very good, except that I think he will not have very great physical endurance, and is in some danger of wearing himself out.

He has not yet come into the Executive Mansion, but has his business office in the Treasury Department, and does not intend coming here till after Mrs. Lincoln goes out, which will not be for two or three weeks yet. Major Hay and I are still here arranging the papers of the office, which has kept us very busy.

Your

George.[3]

About this time Nicolay received a letter from a friend, James C. Derby, urging him to move forward with plans for a biography of Lincoln. "You above all others are the man and have the material for a perfect history of his Administration, and the people will anxiously look for it from your hand as soon as possible," Derby wrote. If needed as a further incentive, his friend assured him, such a project would result in "fame, honor, and money."[4] The Lincoln biography would have to wait. There was so much work to do back in Washington, and it is unclear whether Nicolay even had time to see Therena during his trip to Illinois for the Lincoln burial. It fell to Nicolay and Hay to continue gathering up and organizing Lincoln's papers as well as their own papers and possessions to make way for the new president and his staff.

Nicolay drafted a letter to Therena from Springfield on May 5 with some bad news, at least for her. He informed her that he was "sorry to say that I think I shall not be able to take you to Paris with me this time—but this I will talk over fully with you while at Pittsfield. I am still trying to get ready to sail about the first of June."[5] At some point in May, whether by letter or in person, apparently Therena made it clear to "her George" that if he intended to remain "her George," he had better rethink the plan about her not going to Paris with him. Whatever the exact circumstances, Nicolay got the message. According to Pittsfield resident Thomas H. Shastid, he finally proposed to Therena after nearly losing his nerve. "Even in 1865, after he had won an international reputation at the White House as a man of magnificent ability," wrote Shastid, "he came very near to going back to Washington without her." He "would in fact have done so had not some of his old-time admirers so twitted him about his timidity," Shastid's chronicle continued, "that, at last, in desperation, he rushed into Therena's house, [and] gasped out a proposal." Therena "instantly accepted," since she "had been waiting for him for years and years and years."[6]

The groom was not too shy, however, about planning the wedding. The meticulous secretary left few details to the bride's discretion other than her maid of honor. Having delayed his departure for Paris from his original June 1 schedule, Nicolay penned his instructions for the wedding to his fiancée from the Executive Mansion on May 30.

Undated photograph of Therena
Bates, presumably taken to provide
Nicolay with a keepsake prior to
their marriage on June 15, 1865.
(Library of Congress)

Dear Therena,

We will be married on Thursday, June 15, and sail for Europe from New York on the "City of London" on the 24th of June.

We will have the ceremony performed either at your house (in the presence of a few friends) or at the Congregational Church, by Mr. Carter, at six or seven o'clock in the evening, and then go out to Mrs. Garbutt's, and have a party or reception from eight to ten or eleven o'clock, as you may desire.

Major Hay will be groomsman and you must select a bridesmaid for him. If you think Dr. and Mrs. Hodgen desire to stand up with us, we will also ask them to do so.

I will meet you at St. Louis at some time between the 10th and 13th of June. From there taking Dr. Hodgen and Delphinia with us, we will go up to Pittsfield so as to get there on the 14th or 15th. Major Hay will also meet us in St. Louis and either go up with us, or go by Springfield to invite and bring with him a few friends from there. If you could manage to have Dan or Lieut. Dorus at St. Louis at the same time, he could go up the Mississippi and bring Aurelia and her husband from Louisiana.

By this plan no one but your bridesmaid and Mrs. Garbutt would need to know anything about the affair until the 14th or 15th. I think Mrs. Garbutt would keep the secret. Don't you think it possible to find a bridesmaid who would also do so? I should very much like to surprise the people and gossips of Pittsfield with the event. You can speak to them about it (I mean Mrs. G and your bridesmaid) before you go to St. Louis, where of course you will have to stay some days for preparation.

Or rather the better way would be to take your bridesmaid with you to St. Louis. Tell Mrs. Garbutt not to worry herself about any extravagant preparation; and we will save her what trouble and expense we can by bringing cakes, confections and berries from St. Louis with us, in such quantities as you may suggest.

Make out a list of Pittsfield people to be invited—only let it be large enough. Let the house be filled to overflowing—a perfect jam—and everybody will be entertained and delighted. We will send out the invitations on the 14th or 15th in something like the enclosed form—but we will have no regular wedding cards, my range of acquaintances outside of Pittsfield being too large to make it convenient to send to all.

After the wedding we will stay at Mrs. Garbutt's until we leave Pittsfield, which will be next day by way of St. Louis or on Sunday by way of Naples. I have thought the matter all over and can devise no better plan than this. I am decidedly in favor of having a large party and Mrs. Garbutt's house is decidedly the best place to have it in. I will be interested to see how successfully you will be able to execute the programme.

I would have written before but waited to hear from New York about the time of sailing.

Your

G.

P.S. Lest this letter should fail to reach you I will send a copy of it by tomorrow's mail also. Write me as soon as you receive it, directing your letter here as usual.

Your

G.[7]

Clearly George had realized that it was time to marry Therena. It also seems clear that he was calling the shots and expected things to be done according to his specifications. Probably she knew him so well by this time that none of this came as a shock to her. At last, there was light at the end of her long spinsterhood tunnel.

The surprise invitations that went out shortly before the wedding and reception simply read:

Mrs. P. B. Garbutt will be pleased to see you
on Thursday evening, June 15, from 8 until
11 o'clock, to meet Mr and Mrs Nicolay.[8]

Helen Nicolay gave a bit more detail of the wedding of her parents, which was held at Therena's parents' home in Pittsfield. The rushed nature of the ceremony complicated the arrangements to procure a presiding clergyman. Reverend

The Pittsfield, Illinois, home of Mrs. P.B. Garbutt where the Nicolay-Bates wedding reception was held following a small private ceremony at the home of Therena's parents, Dorus and Emma Bates. (Photograph by Allen Carden)

Carter, Nicolay's first choice, was unavailable as he was away from Pittsfield at the time. A second minister they contacted was ill, and a third, a Reverend Burnham, agreed to perform the ceremony; he was delayed half an hour due to a strong thunderstorm but finally arrived. The couple was married in front of a small company, and then the much larger reception at Mrs. Garbutt's home proved to be "a great success" and "went down in local history as the first time ice cream was served in Pittsfield to a large evening party."[9] The wedding reception also included "ornamental cakes" and other refreshments costing $81.70, from the "Confectionary and Ice Cream Saloon" of Charles Burkin in St. Louis, whose motto was "Parties and Families supplied at short notice," which was a good thing since the order was placed on June 13 for the June 15 event.[10] Thomas H. Shastid documented this recollection of the nuptial celebration: "A letter from Mrs. Sarah Bates Utt informs me that the first ice-cream ever served in Pike County was served at the marriage of her aunt, Therena Bates and John G. Nicolay on June 15, 1865. The finally relenting anti-emancipation, anti-Union Dorus Bates (Sarah's grandfather) provided his daughter, Therena, and her *fiancé* with, for Pittsfield, a most elegant wedding. Hence, the presence, on that occasion, of ice-cream—something which was talked about all over Pike County for many weeks."[11] George and Therena were at long last husband and wife.

His new boss, John Bigelow, former consul at Paris and now minister to France, had written to Nicolay from France on March 31, 1865, giving him a bit of orientation and general encouragement about the job awaiting him. Bigelow informed the consul-to-be that "you can live here satisfactorily as a batchelor [*sic*]" and "for $2500 to $3000 . . . you can have a nice apartment, keep a manservant, entertain when necessary." He was glad Nicolay was coming, since the workload at the consulate was considerable. "I think the labors of the consulate proper are about five times as great as they were before the war," Bigelow opined, "but with proper organization and assistance they do not involve necessarily any great increase of labor to you."[12] If there was anyone who could devise "proper organization," it was his new protégé.

In one sense, his work as consul began weeks before he left for Paris, as he began receiving letters while still in Washington from office seekers hoping to be part of his consular staff. One such petitioner, Atwood Wright of Baltimore, modestly informed Nicolay that his "loyalty, morality, and knowledge of business" could be verified "from gentlemen in this city [Baltimore] or Washington." Another hopeful staffer, August Goisons, a French-born immigrant currently serving in the U.S. Navy and obviously hoping to get out of that assignment as soon as possible, composed his letter to Nicolay in French to demonstrate his fluency.[13] It appears, however, that Nicolay made no commitments for staff changes until he arrived in Paris and learned who was already in place at the consulate.

Nine days after the wedding, the Nicolays departed New York for Paris on board the Inman Line ship, *The City of London*. In 1865, the average Atlantic crossing from New York to Liverpool was nine days, a week shorter than it took a generation earlier, when George had first come to America.[14] It must have been interesting for him to reflect on his journey of some twenty-eight years before, when as a child he crossed the Atlantic Ocean from Europe to the United States. Now he was returning to Europe as an American diplomat (although to no one's knowledge but his, he was still not a citizen of the United States). The Inman Line, no doubt seeing strategic value for the company, had offered in a letter of May 26,

1865, to provide Nicolay and Hay complimentary passage to their diplomatic posts. Perhaps Nicolay or Hay had allowed some personal information to leak, for Inman Line agent E. S. Sanford in this same letter stated, "If Mr. Nicolay has increased his family by taking a wife, let me know,"[15] the implication being that the Inman Line would, in such a case, also cover Mrs. Nicolay's passage.

His best friend and groomsman at his recent wedding, John Hay, was on board the same ship, also heading for a new position in Paris. Hay's role, completely separate from Nicolay's, was to be secretary of the Legation of the United States at Paris. Hay would spend about a year in Paris before moving on to another diplomatic post in Vienna. Unlike the newly married Nicolay, Hay was not ready to settle down, especially abroad. Hay, a future ambassador to Great Britain and secretary of state, confided to a friend, "I think it [Paris] will be a pleasant place for study and observation. I shall no doubt enjoy it for a year or so—not very long, as I do not wish to exile myself in these important and interesting times."[16] On the other hand, Nicolay was prepared to settle in with Therena at Paris for as long as his political appointment and significantly improved salary might last.

The Nicolays carried with them a letter of introduction from Horace Greeley to his sister Mrs. Esther C. Cleveland, a resident of Paris. Greeley's letter asked his sister to "know and advise my friend Mrs. J. G. Nicolay, who will make her first experiments in housekeeping in your city, and who will greatly profit by your experience and thrift. . . . I pray you to be as wise and good to her as you possibly can." However, Therena, being both shy and independent, never delivered the letter.[17] The American Consulate was located at 79 rue de Richelieu, and the Nicolays' first home in Paris was at the Hôtel Chateaubriand near the Arc de Triomphe, about two and a half to three miles from the consulate, and according to historian Joshua Zeitz, "a twenty minute ride by carriage or an hour's walk, depending upon the time of year."[18] At this hotel, the couple rented a large room and took their meals with other guests in the hotel's dining room. Neither a luxury hotel nor a flophouse, the Chateaubriand served the Nicolays reasonably well for several months. The hotel also had a few annoyances and amusements provided by some of the hotel's clientele and the very frugal proprietors, Monsieur and Madame d'Asterac. On one occasion, Nicolay wrote about a new family that had moved into the hotel with "a dark dirty colored dog that makes a horrid noise, and which the woman holds up for the edification of the boarders at dinner. Was there ever any habit so filthy and disgusting?"[19] He eventually determined that he and Therena should have a place of their own, in part because, as he complained to his wife who was away on a trip, "my stomach, having patiently endured boardinghouse abominations for ten years, is becoming rebellious."[20] Another and more important reason for a move was not mentioned by the consul in this letter. Therena was already four or five months into her first pregnancy, and the Hôtel Chateaubriand was no place to raise a family.

The consul settled into the routines of married life, spending evenings at home with his pregnant wife. The former bon vivant of Springfield and Washington was now a husband and future father. The consulate, where Nicolay worked, and the legation, where Hay was employed, were several blocks apart so their daily contact was limited. According to biographer John Taliaferro, Hay, who remained a bachelor, "did not hesitate to partake of the pleasures of Paris."[21]

The Nicolays were living in France's Second Empire, ruled over by Napoleon III, and on his watch Paris was being transformed around them by a major urban renewal project spearheaded by Baron Haussmann. The crooked lanes and dilapidated buildings of the old Paris were being replaced by broad, straight avenues and new apartments, shops, and public buildings. Nicolay had mixed reactions to Paris, which he called "a great city, having much to admire and more to condemn," finding it only "finitely curious and interesting." He described Paris in a letter to a friend as a "sort of delta in the great stream of human life, rather an aggregation of debris, than a fresh healthy organic structure of vital and intelligent forces." While he appreciated the city's location relative to travel in Europe as central and convenient, he concluded that "as a place to live in or die in—well it may do for Frenchmen, but an American possessing taste, intelligence or ambition will want none of it." Apparently the frontier Midwestern American by upbringing was not impressed. What seemed to disturb him most of all, however, was the Parisian weather. Sometimes he found it too cold in the summer, complaining of having to wear an overcoat and stoke the fireplace on occasion in August. If the summers were too cold, he found the winters dreary. "During the winter weather in Paris, the day is a myth. I am not exaggerating when I say that the sun sets every morning at seven o'clock, and that the rest of the twenty-four hours is a night of clouds and fog."[22]

As busy as he had been as President Lincoln's private secretary, he surprisingly found his duties as the American consul at Paris to be quite time consuming, varied, but often tedious. "Practically every traveler from the United States called," wrote Helen many years later, "and usually asked 'a small favor' before he went away." The new consul soon became "an expert on sightseeing tours, leisurely or rapid to suit demands." Helen revealed that her father had "once boasted that he had shown Paris 'thoroughly' to an American in four hours." Receiving a calling card "bearing the name 'Mr. Fillmore,'" Nicolay "realized with something of a start" that the visitor was the former president Millard Fillmore, whom George had visited on his first trip to Washington in 1853, then getting his five minutes with a president.[23] Nicolay, who enjoyed travel, sightseeing, and observing the cultural and social scene, was unable to engage in many of these activities during his first six months in Paris. He confided to a friend in December 1865 that "I have been devoting myself to business, and have not as yet had much Parisian experience. Even of the theatre I have as yet seen but little. . . . As for the music I can't as yet say much."[24]

What was it that kept him so occupied on the job? From the moment he arrived in Paris, he was besieged by letters requesting assistance of one kind or another. Some requests were fairly routine, such as asking that mail be held for pickup at the consulate. Other requests were more complex and/or bizarre. One letter from a Mr. Valentine Haefner of Potosi, Missouri, claimed that he should have been awarded a prize offered in Paris for a cure for cholera, but the French had not delivered on their promise. Haefner's cure was to prescribe an application of "fresh animal blood" to the cholera patient because cholera victims, in his opinion, died "from want of positive Electricity." According to Haefner's specifications, within three hours of taking his cure, "the cholera symptoms will have subsided." Acknowledging that one of his patients died while under his treatment, Haefner was quick to point out that the patient had not followed his instructions and had in fact died not from cholera but from an overdose of opium. Haefner's entreaty to Nicolay was to help him secure the well-deserved prize.[25] While there is no documentary record of Consul Nicolay's response, if any, one can surmise that Haefner's claim to the prize continued to go unfulfilled. The consul quickly discovered that the crackpots and schemers who had filled his days at the White House could turn up anywhere.

Unusual requests also came from prominent individuals. One such request came in a letter from the well-known German American artist Albert Bierstadt, who claimed that one of his paintings on display in a famous Paris gallery was not in the proper location for optimal viewing; he asked Nicolay to please do something about it.[26] Even Chief Justice Salmon P. Chase of the U.S. Supreme Court sent a request to him seeking confidential information about a young man who was courting a woman known to Chase. Roscoe Conkling, the influential senator from New York, wanted to purchase furniture from France and have it shipped to the United States. He asked Nicolay to research packing, freight, and insurance costs. The senator informed Nicolay that his request "may be vexatious—if so, have no hesitation in neglecting it. . . . I shall esteem it a favor—but if it will annoy you, don't hesitate to decline it."[27] Undoubtedly, it annoyed Nicolay. However, he could ill afford to offend a Republican U.S. senator, especially someone like Roscoe Conkling, since Nicolay's position as consul was a political appointment dependent on staying in the good graces of Washington's powers-that-be.

A Parisian sanitarium for the mentally ill asked Nicolay what to do about a young American man who had been left there for care three years ago and then apparently abandoned by his family. Another letter asked for help in finding a pair of spectacles; yet another sought assistance in locating a missing husband.[28] He was even asked for advice on how an American might obtain a patent in France. In April 1867, the consul received a letter with a small request: would he kindly send a list of mailing addresses of every chamber of commerce in the United States to the vice president of *La Campagnie de Canal de Suez* so that they could send information about how their canal would be able to facilitate the transit of merchandise and passengers between the Mediterranean Sea and the Indian Ocean?[29]

Other duties facing Nicolay included responding to scores of letters of introduction asking that he provide information, assistance, and various forms of hospitality to American visitors in or on their way to Paris. One such letter was sent by the famous detective Allan Pinkerton asking that an acquaintance of his who had provided "very faithful service" to the Army of the Potomac during the late war and who was a "thorough Republican" be appropriately entertained by the consul upon his arrival in Paris.[30] Not only letters but also packages were often forwarded to the American consulate with instructions to hold them for the arrival of their owners. On one occasion a large box of guns arrived, causing curiosity and likely some concern.[31]

American expatriates living in Paris, of whom there were several hundred in the 1860s, also required the services of the consulate. Paris was the recognized art capital of the world at the time, and American artists made up a sizeable proportion of the foreign artists studying and producing art there. Added to that number were American diplomats and their families, as well as businessmen and other Americans simply disillusioned with American life and culture, who had made Paris their home. Americans living in Paris would sometimes gather together for special events like the Thanksgiving celebration held in Paris on December 7, 1865. In attendance were Nicolay, Hay, Ambassador Bigelow, Major-General J. M. Schofield, and others. The party included addresses and remarks by many of the participants as well as a poetry reading and singing.[32]

As consul, Nicolay was called upon to perform civil marriage ceremonies for Americans that would be legally recognized in France, as well as in the United States. Most of these weddings were held at the American Consulate. In later years he expressed his dislike of performing these weddings because "the responsibility was so great."[33] He also found himself giving legal advice to Americans concerned about dying in Paris, including dealing with wills of American citizens. On occasion, the consulate was required to take possession of the effects of Americans who died in Paris without a will.

There were other ongoing duties that consumed the time and mental energy of the consul. A major duty of the consulate was to record French exports to the United States, done through quarterly reports from Nicolay to Assistant Secretary of State Frederick W. Seward, son of Secretary of State William Seward. While it may have appeared that his direct supervisor was the American minister to France, John Bigelow, it was actually Frederick Seward, who played a more active role in keeping tabs on Consul Nicolay and his performance. A careful record

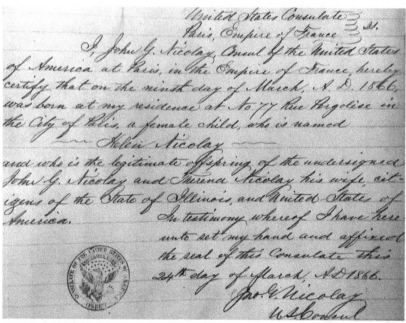

Registration of Helen Nicolay's birth in Paris, France on March 9, 1866 in the Consular Record Book, in Nicolay's own handwriting. He falsely stated that he was a citizen of the United States at the time of Helen's birth. (National Archives)

keeper, Nicolay was also responsible for recording the marriages and births of Americans throughout France, as well as recording last wills and testaments.

Another task that fell under his responsibilities was the management of a fund that had been established for "relief of destitute American seamen" who found their way onto French soil. It was also his duty to certify personal property consisting of household effects and furniture being shipped from France to the United States for the private use of the owners; apparently such documentation was needed to avoid American tariffs. He signed every official document: "John G. Nicolay, Consul of the United States of America at Paris in the Empire of France." Although it was an impressive title, the scope of the work was at times tedious, and he yearned to have the time and proximity to sources to begin what he knew would be the long process of writing the Lincoln biography. While in Paris, as time permitted, he began writing to individuals back in America who could give him information and verification of various events in Lincoln's life and presidency of which he was not fully aware.[34]

The recording of births was an especially important consular responsibility. Since the First Congress, American law had established the principle that the child of an American father born overseas was a natural-born citizen as defined in the Constitution.[35] One of the births recorded in the consular record of 1866 was of special significance to John George Nicolay and his wife, Therena Bates Nicolay:

I, John G. Nicolay, Consul of the United States of America at Paris, in the Empire of France, hereby certify that on the ninth day of March, A.D. 1866, was born at my residence at No 77 Rue Pergolese in the City of Paris, a female child, who is named
——Helen Nicolay——

and who is the legitimate offspring of the undersigned John G. Nicolay and Therena Nicolay, his wife, citizens of the State of Illinois, and United States of America. In testimony whereof I have here unto set
my hand and affixed the seal of this
Consulate this 24th day of March, AD 1866.
Jno. G. Nicolay
U.S. Consul[36]

Since in 1866, the citizenship status of the mother was not considered, Helen was not an American citizen, having been born in France to a father who was still a foreign national. However, there is no known record that Helen Nicolay ever rectified this anomaly in her citizenship status.

Nicolay's life was forever changed by the arrival of baby Helen. In his thirty-fourth year, he had become a father. His daughter was named for his mother, Helena. George had the family and "home of his own" that he had written Therena about at Christmas in 1864, nearly a brief year and a half before. It is not clear why it took him two weeks to record his daughter's birth, for fatherhood was a role in which he would delight. In return, Helen would be devoted to her father and his work and memory throughout the length of her eighty-eight years.

Always concerned about the health of Therena and himself, and now his child, Nicolay reluctantly relocated wife and daughter in Switzerland in the summer of 1866 due to threats of cholera, which often plagued Paris in warmer weather. Returning to his duties at the consulate, he also began searching for better living arrangements. Writing Therena on August 18, he described his delight in receiving a letter from her that included a photograph of Helen, which he showed to "all the ladies at the house [their Paris hotel]," who were "very much pleased with it." He noted Therena's comment that "Helen is taking of bread and milk. Is she not too young yet to begin eating solid food? Are you sure it is good for her?"[37] Clearly, he was a proud but perhaps overly concerned father.

One of the benefits scholars have of Therena and Helen's cholera-avoiding stay in Switzerland in the summer and fall of 1866 is a letter that George penned to his wife with a description of his workday back in Paris, which, for the moment, appeared less than overwhelming, as perhaps his organizational skills were again working magic. He got up at eight, had coffee and a croissant, and then headed to the office to arrive by ten. At around one, he went to Byron's Tavern for "breakfast," consisting of "cold roast beef, bread, butter and water spiced only with an occasional small radish" and "a glance at the *London Times.*" Returning to the office, he stayed until about "four-thirty," meaning that he was working no more than five and a half hours per day.[38] Apparently, Nicolay was a man so hardened by routine that he didn't allow himself to indulge his palette in the culinary delights of Paris.

While Therena and Helen were in Switzerland, Nicolay began to worry about the security of his employment as consul, a plum patronage position. The political situation in Washington was complex and chaotic, as President Andrew Johnson was rapidly falling from favor with many congressional Republicans. It was Johnson, after assuming the presidency, who had confirmed his position and on whose good graces Nicolay depended to remain as consul at Paris. Charges were being made against Nicolay, including a diatribe written to the State Department by a Mrs. Mary Livermore that the consul was "intensely radical" and was considered by many Americans in Paris to be "both careless of and utterly inefficient in, the discharge of his official duties." A mitigating notation was made, however, by a State Department official that Mrs. Livermore "Craves the position for her husband."[39] In October 1866, the consul received a letter from Assistant Secretary of State Frederick W. Seward, with a list of concerns that had come to his attention and to which he wanted Nicolay to have the opportunity of responding. However, Nicolay was not given the identity of his accuser. The all-encompassing charge made was dereliction of duty, which consisted of paying "little attention to the duties" of consul, assigning clerks the bulk of the duties while "doing little more than signing papers, spending but an hour or two in the office each day," and finally, giving the "general impression . . . you are negligent and inefficient." He was also charged with "speaking disrespectfully of the President [Andrew Johnson], even to the extent of claiming he had 'gone over to the rebels.'" Frederick Seward was not stating that he believed these serious charges but rather that he hoped that Nicolay would "be able to give such explanations as will be satisfactory."[40]

Such accusations were not only painful to Nicolay but they also threatened his family's livelihood and could tarnish his credibility as Lincoln's future biographer. In the same season, he learned of the death of his only sister, Catherine, who had to some degree stepped in to care for him following their mother's death.[41] Prior to Therena's and Helen's return to Paris, he composed a disheartening and pessimistic letter to his wife about his employment situation. Incapable of being underhanded and duplicitous himself, the straight-shooter, in-your-face Nicolay had a hard time dealing with back stabbers. He suspected that his accusers were the "Gibbs coalition."[42] "While, I should say they would be powerless to do me injury" he wrote, he was not completely sure because of the political unrest back in the states. He then advised Therena to be prepared to "migrate at short notice."[43]

Since it was not his nature to roll over and play dead, he shot off a letter to Seward in which he systematically refuted the allegations made against him. Perhaps his greatest defense was his appeal to Seward's "personal knowledge of the manner in which I discharged my official duties [as Lincoln's secretary] in Washington." The whole situation, in which he was unable to confront his unknown accuser(s), was distressing to him, and the charges against him caused "passing chagrin that such accusations should appear on the public records; but a moment's reflection reminded me that I could not have a greater compliment to my official character than that the malice of the accuser has been unable to trump up anything else than allegations so trivially absurd, so utterly untrue, and so easily disproven."[44] While it would not be surprising if he had developed negative opinions about President Johnson, given that Lincoln's successor had moved further and further from Lincoln's views concerning the former slaves and their wellbeing, Nicolay would have been prudent enough not to speak openly about this.

When Therena and Helen returned to Paris in the autumn of 1866, the Nicolays left the Hôtel Chateaubriand for an apartment of their own at 73 Avenue de la Grande Armée, a few blocks away. It was here that the new family of three settled in for the remainder of their time in Paris, with the exception of travels and interludes in Switzerland for Therena and the baby. To his relief, and no doubt to Therena's as well, a letter written by Frederick Seward on November 19, 1866, arrived, approving some staffing recommendations made by Nicolay and concluding, rather matter-of-factly, that his recent letter "seems to fully and clearly refute the charges made against you, and it is accepted by the Department as satisfactory."[45] However, just when he thought he was out of danger, rumor had it that his health was failing and that Seward had received a letter from an American in Nice, France, offering to take over the Paris consulate. A Mr. Jacob R. Freese was convinced that, "greatly to my regret . . . the health of our present Consul there [in Paris] (Mr. Nicolay) was so very delicate that he would probably be obliged to relinquish the duties of his office ere long." Freese then went on for four pages extolling his own virtues for the post.[46] Then, as now, there was no lack of individuals who had no moral impediment to destroy the reputation and career of others in order to promote their own agendas.

Nicolay remained on the job and was able to make a visit to other parts of Europe, including his native Germany, in the fall of 1867. This trip was apparently his wife's idea, as she confided to her mother in a letter dated August 14, 1867, that "I think George's health is better than it was before we went to Switzerland." She informed her mother that she planned to encourage him to take a trip to Vienna to visit Hay. She also shared with her mother about their forthcoming trip to Pittsfield so that the Bates family could meet the newest addition to the clan.[47]

Given his penchant for travel, it likely took little coaxing from Therena to get George to pack up and go visit his good friend John Hay, now installed as chargé d'affaires in Vienna. He departed in late September 1867 and wrote in good humor about his baggage having decided to take a trip of its own, leaving him stuck in Munich with little but his umbrella and the hope that the missing bag would show up. It did—the next day—after having first strayed to Lake Constance on the Swiss border. "Verily, the wonders of modern travel [by rail] are not all written," he told Therena. He also asked his wife to "Kiss baby for me and tell her Papa missed her at breakfast this morning."[48] Two days later he arrived in Vienna, writing to Therena that Colonel Hay "is very pleasantly situated in the very heart of the city, and is as comfortable in every way as a man can be without a wife and baby." Apparently unimpressed with European cities, he told Therena that Vienna was "a queer old city" with narrow dark streets: "The effect is peculiarly gloomy and dungeon-like."[49] Clearly the German-born Nicolay had become thoroughly Americanized when it came to an urban landscape.

Returning to Paris, he was plagued by his chronic dyspepsia, severe enough to prevent him from joining Therena and Helen on a trip home to Illinois for Christmas. When his wife and child returned to Paris, he concluded that he needed to recuperate in the warmer climate of Italy. Unfortunately, he made a serious mistake in not requesting an extended absence from the consulate, for which he had a physician's certificate, in advance. This resulted in a letter of reprimand from Frederick Seward, who told Nicolay, "The [State] Department cannot but look upon your action . . . with regret and disapproval, insomuch as you did not forward the physician's certificate and ask that your absence might be sanctioned, instead of waiting until complaint was made of it." While not wanting to appear "harsh," the assistant secretary of state insisted that Nicolay keep the State Department "promptly and fully informed" of his movements beyond the normal reaches of his consulate.[50]

The election of 1868 did not bode well for Nicolay's continued employment as American consul at Paris. Although Ulysses S. Grant's Republican administration was elected, the consul received a letter from J. R. Biggs, assistant clerk of the House of Representatives, that he was possibly being set up for dismissal. "If you want to remain at Paris, as Consul, you will have to take immediate steps to secure your position," Biggs warned him. The American consul at La Rochelle had his eyes on a promotion to Paris, and his scheming, wealthy mother was busy in Washington greasing the wheels for her son's rise to this position. Her strategy to get her son promoted by the incoming president included a smear campaign against Nicolay consisting of the following points: "that you have fallen into the habits of a drunkard; that you go away to Italy for months at a time without leave, pretending to be all the time at Paris; that you have the venereal disease, etc." Biggs went on to explain why he was warning Nicolay. Biggs had met him "once or twice on transient business that I happened to have with Mr.

Lincoln." He warned Nicolay not only because he detested "such an intrigue . . . attacking your character without the privilege of defence," but also because he respected Nicolay as "a decent and honorable man personally." Biggs, who knew the plotters and details of the calumny against Nicolay, asked him to accept his confidence and "preserve [it] inviolate."[51]

Despite a subsequent letter to Nicolay from Senator James Harlan, the father-in-law of Robert Todd Lincoln, informing him that President Grant "assured me that he had no intention of making a change" in the Paris Consulate,[52] the axe fell, as Nicolay suspected it would, once the Sewards were out of the State Department, replaced by the new secretary of state, Hamilton Fish. In a State Department dispatch dated May 18, 1869, he learned that he would be replaced as consul by John Meredith Reid.[53] At least this was not the son of the scheming mother who had attempted the smear campaign against him. As for John Hay, his position in Vienna was also tenuous. Despite his earlier protestations against a long stay in Europe, Hay had changed his mind. He was able to secure an appointment as secretary to the American legation in Madrid through the assistance of friends.[54]

Now the question facing Nicolay was what to do next. It was clear that he, Therena, and Helen should return to the United States and that he must eventually find a livelihood to provide for his little family, although he had apparently

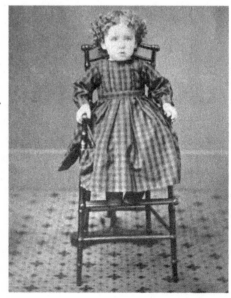

Helen Nicolay, age 3, photographed in Paris in 1869 shortly before the family returned to the United States. (Helen Nicolay Collection)

saved enough of his consul's salary to tide them over for a while. At least back home he would be that much closer to doing the research necessary to write the biography of Abraham Lincoln that he held as a cherished dream. After returning to the United States in the spring of 1869, he was able for a time to focus on restoring his often frail health, which by now included growing difficulty with his eyesight. The family spent some time in Florida at an old home on the St. John's River and removed to New Hampshire to escape the heat of summer. He visited his brother John Jacob, who was farming land that Nicolay had purchased near Scranton, Osage County, Kansas, to which, he stated, the family could always relocate if nothing else developed.[55]

An opportunity did present itself in July 1870 for him to become head of the editorial department, as well as general manager, of the *Chicago Republican,* a failing newspaper that was to be revitalized by some new investors and his journalistic expertise. Such an offer appealed to his old newspaper days, and the fact that his old boss and friend O. M. Hatch was one of the paper's directors made it even more attractive.[56] When Hay returned from his diplomatic assignment in Madrid, Nicolay asked him to join the paper's staff. "I could get along with Nicolay more easily than with almost anyone I know," Hay wrote, but declined the offer.[57] After three months on the job, however, Nicolay was physically exhausted and concluded that the newspaper, which continued to lose money, would take more effort than he could provide. In his letter of resignation, he stated, "I have neither the strength nor the courage to undertake to dig my way through such an avalanche of expense. . . . I need not tell you how much I am pained at the necessity of this determination on my part."[58] On a more positive note, Nicolay finally became a naturalized citizen of the United States on October 12, 1970, through the Pike County Circuit Court of the State of Illinois.

Reviving his writing skills, he submitted two series of articles to the *New York Times:* one dealt with conditions in the South following the Civil War, and the other concerned his descriptions of Paris. He hoped that these efforts might lead to a permanent position on the editorial staff of the *Times,* but the only opening involved night work and would not be a good fit for a family man in frail health. Nicolay sent some poems to the *Atlantic Monthly* for publication but received a disheartening reply suggesting that he submit prose articles instead. He was most eager to devote time to starting the Lincoln biography; however, he knew he first had to have a job that would enable him to support his family, and he seriously was not ready to "give up and retire to Kansas."[59] In the meantime, he decided he would like to return to Springfield, Illinois. He purchased a forty-acre farm

Nicolay's naturalization certificate noting that he had become a citizen of the United States on October 12, 1870, at the Pike County Court House in Pittsfield, Illinois.
(Library of Congress)

near the Illinois capital in the autumn of 1871. "Here at least, he could be near old friends, live cheaply and store his Lincoln material until he should be able to use it," Helen observed. Physically unable to endure the stresses of farming, he leased most of his land to a neighbor, keeping only the house and the surrounding property for his family's use.[60]

In June 1872, Nicolay became aware that the American minister to Colombia had obtained a seat in Congress and the position in Bogota would be open. He decided to seek the office by writing to both Vice President Schuyler Colfax and Senator James Harlan for assistance, but his efforts proved unsuccessful.[61] Looking back, he could see how fortunate it was that the Bogota appointment did not come through for him, since in December of that year, he received an ideal position as marshal of the United States Supreme Court. "A most excellent appointment," the *Philadelphia Public Ledger* editorialized, recalling that "Mr. Nicolay," while serving President Lincoln, "was noted for his courtesy of deportment, and for the extreme energy with which he labored to fulfill the requests of all persons who applied to him for information."[62]

Actually, Nicolay had not been appointed but rather elected to the position. An article in the *New York Times* described the process, noting that there had been "scores of applicants." The Justices of the Supreme Court cast numerous ballots until there were only four candidates remaining. Of the eight justices then serving,[63] five had been appointed by Lincoln, including Chief Justice Chase. Besides the former secretary, the finalists included D. R. McKee, a Washington-based journalist with the Associated Press, Frederick A. Schley of Maryland,[64] and Robert C. Kirk of Ohio. As the balloting continued, it became a contest between Nicolay and McKee, each with three votes, and with Schley and Kirk receiving one vote apiece. The tie was broken when the justices who had backed Schley and Kirk switched their votes to Nicolay on the final ballot.[65]

It is not difficult to determine which justices switched their votes and put Nicolay over the top. Chief Justice Chase and Associate Justice Noah Swayne were both from Ohio. In all likelihood, Swayne supported Kirk, a former lieutenant governor of Ohio and ambassador to Argentina and Uruguay. Chase unquestionably was Schley's supporter. Frederick A. Schley had been the editor of the *Frederick (Maryland) Examiner* during the Civil War.[66] Over the course of the war, Schley had become an increasingly radicalized Republican and, in the process, disenchanted with the Lincoln administration. As a result, he became one of three men who formed a state correspondence committee to advance the "Chase for President" movement in Maryland.[67] Chase owed Schley a debt. At some point, Chase and Swayne, who may have been using Schley and Kirk as placeholders until they saw how the voting was going, got together and decided to throw their support to Nicolay on the final ballot. In doing so, Chase put aside his many personal and political differences with the former secretary and his boss. Without Chase's support, Nicolay would never have received the fifth and deciding vote to become marshal of the Supreme Court.

The process had been so unabashedly political that the *New York Times* denounced the result as showing "how much like seeking a lottery prize is seeking public office."[68] Yet, Nicolay probably never realized that it was Chase who made his appointment possible. While the papers reported that Schley was one of the finalists, Nicolay likely did not know who Schley was or his connection to the chief justice since even the dispatch to the *New York Times* was unable to identify Schley, other than noting that he was from Maryland.

Once again oblivious to the political machinations surrounding him, George may have thought, as he had when Lincoln appointed him campaign secretary, that it was somehow his due. Ironically, Nicolay and Hay would savage Chase's reputation in their Lincoln history, likely without Nicolay's awareness that it was Chase who, in the final analysis, gave Nicolay the means to write that history. Thus, Nicolay became the second marshal of the Supreme Court, succeeding Richard C. Parsons, a confidant and political ally of Chief Justice Salmon P. Chase, who had served in the position since 1866 and had resigned to run for Congress.

Parsons, who in later years would admit that while marshal of the Supreme Court he had continued his law practice representing the Pacific Mail Company against the government in court, described the position as an "office of trifling pay which required but a portion of my time."[69] But for Nicolay, two great needs were met in this one position. While the pay was "trifling" to the prosperous Parsons, Nicolay could comfortably support his family, and because the duties of the position were not demanding, he would have time to devote to the Lincoln biography, including summers off when the court was not in session. Most significant, he would have proximity to important records and influential people in Washington that he would need to make the Lincoln project a success.

Nicolay had found significance in Paris as a husband and father. Finally, three and a half years after returning from Paris, the details of his life were falling into place as he had hoped they would. Now, he could commence work on his life's ambition, the monumental biography of Abraham Lincoln.

CHAPTER TEN

Crafting the Lincoln Legacy
Abraham Lincoln: A History

From the time that Nicolay had his heart set on writing Lincoln's biography for the 1860 presidential campaign, only to have that assignment given to William Dean Howells, it would be three decades until his dream was realized with the publication in 1890 of the massive ten-volume work on Lincoln he coauthored with John Hay. Nicolay and Hay had contemplated writing such a biography even before Lincoln's death when they were both playing key roles in the administration and rooming together in the White House. They believed they had an inside view of their hero and his presidency and counted on someday using the Lincoln papers to document their story.

The proposed Nicolay-Hay biography must have been public knowledge, for in Nicolay's scrapbook, dated 1865, is an editorial from the *Pittsburgh Evening Chronicle,* which may have caused both Nicolay and Hay amusement and irritation. "Mr. Hay should stick to verse writing," the paper editorialized, and "Mr. Nicolay is a brilliant writer, in his way but his specialty is airing sweet nothings." The editors proclaimed that "it was only the other night we were reminded of the fact that few men begin until they are forty." Then, snidely coming to their point, they declared, "And we are decidedly opposed to any one learning at the expense of Abraham Lincoln."[1] Although the editorial was dismissive of both men's talents and their relative youth, the newspaper from Pittsburgh had little to fear. Nicolay and Hay would be accomplished authors in their fifties by the time their Lincoln history was published, a quarter century later.

As might be expected, shortly after the death of Abraham Lincoln, both literary and lecture efforts were undertaken to provide the public with accounts of the martyred president's life. Iowa senator James W. Grimes was a frequent

Lincoln critic over the conduct of the war. Sometimes exasperated with what he saw as Lincoln's interminable procrastination, missteps, and inadequacies, Grimes had once declared that Lincoln and his administration "were a disgrace from the beginning." On April 16, 1865, the day after Lincoln's death, Grimes in a letter to his wife, Elizabeth, wrote disparagingly but with a great deal of foresight. "Mr. Lincoln is to be hereafter regarded as a saint," he wrote, "all his foibles and faults, and shortcomings, will be forgotten, and he will be looked upon as a Moses who led the nation through four years of bloody war and died in sight of peace."[2] Senator Grimes was prophetic but less insightful with regard to the imagery. Former slaves would remember Lincoln as their Moses, who led them out of the bondage of slavery. White Americans would remember Lincoln not as Moses but as a Christ figure, who was martyred on the holiest weekend of the Christian calendar, Easter, which commemorates the redemptive passion, death, and resurrection of Jesus the Christ. The memory of Lincoln would be wrapped in the Easter imagery of Julia Ward Howe's popular Civil War anthem, *The Battle Hymn of the Republic.*

Early accounts of Lincoln's life were developed without reference to the massive collection of Lincoln papers sitting in the White House at the time of the president's assassination but instead in response to an outpouring of national grief and bewilderment. As early as Easter Sunday 1865, the day following Lincoln's death, sermons, eulogies, and soon thereafter biographies of the assassinated President were everywhere. Even in Europe, Dr. Theodor Canisius, former editor of Lincoln's German-language newspaper in Springfield, published an 1867 Lincoln biography in German entitled *Abraham Lincoln, Historiches, Charaktarbild,* based on his brief business connection to the fallen president. For the next half century, people with the slightest link to Lincoln would attempt to cash in on his legacy with books and speaking tours. Aptly described by Lincoln Papers librarian David C. Mearns of the Library of Congress as "extravagant, unrestrained, [and] wholly uncritical," these early adulations were "products of the tinsmiths of mythology, but Robert Lincoln liked them very much."[3] While Robert Lincoln may have appreciated the high esteem with which his father was being remembered due to these lofty and frequently trite, unsubstantiated, and even outrageously false stories, the studious Nicolay could only have shuddered at what was happening to the authentic collective memory of the man he had known intimately and admired unequivocally.

History provides many examples of attempts by family members and supporters of deceased persons of note to create and control the image and reputation of the departed, however unrealistic such portrayals might be. Such situations also provide opportunities to build careers and fortunes by linking oneself, even remotely, to the famous person. In the case of Abraham Lincoln, one of the most peculiar examples of this was Dennis Hanks, a first cousin of Lincoln's mother, Nancy, who bore a striking physical resemblance to Lincoln which, according to biographer David Herbert Donald, "he carefully cultivated—even to the point of wearing a stovepipe hat—and the combination of Lincolnian mannerisms with Dennis's shambling gait and countrified accent was a ludicrous spectacle." Yet, his connection to Lincoln was such that "he acquired a reputation as an inexhaustible source of anecdote. After the assassination, Dennis became something of a celebrity."[4]

Robert Lincoln wanted his father's reputation to rest on something more substantial. Immediately following the president's death, Robert had requested help from David Davis, a family friend and Lincoln appointee to the Supreme Court, to assist in settling Lincoln's affairs, including disposition of Lincoln's presidential papers. The collection was massive: correspondence to and from the president alone involved some 42,000 individual pieces of paper, to which were added reports, speeches, memoranda, and other miscellaneous documents. Organized by Nicolay and Hay as best they could between mid-April and early June 1865 under Robert Lincoln's authority, these papers were transported to Bloomington, Illinois, and placed in a bank vault under Justice Davis's supervision. Lincoln's papers were regarded as the property of the Lincoln family. This was nothing unusual, as presidential papers since Washington's time had been considered without question the private property of the president's family.[5]

Robert Lincoln's actions effectively sealed Abraham Lincoln's papers for the foreseeable future. As early as April 27, 1865, he was already declining a request to view the papers from Charles Eliot Norton, a gifted writer who had supported Lincoln and his policies in the *North American Review* and wished to write a definitive biography of the fallen president. Responding to Harvard professor Francis James Child, who had written to Robert Lincoln on behalf of Norton, Robert replied that while Lincoln's presidential papers "have been carefully collected by the [president's] Priv. Secretaries and sealed and deposited in a safe place," no one would have access to them for several years.[6] With both Nicolay and Hay assuming diplomatic assignments in Europe beginning in July 1865, nothing would be done with the Lincoln papers for some time to come. Thus, the earliest biographical accounts of Lincoln's presidential years relied on sources other than the Lincoln papers and were accordingly deficient in scope, perspective, and, all too often, reality.

Lincoln's former law partner, William Herndon, was among the early petitioners denied what Robert Lincoln considered to be premature access to his father's papers. Herndon was an unsentimental realist, a religious skeptic at best, and no fan of Mary Lincoln; he was utterly dumbfounded by the emerging superficial and saintly portraits of the man he had known so well in their Springfield law office for several years. He was determined to do his best to set the record, or at least his version of it, straight. If he could not have access to Lincoln's papers, Herndon would go in search of other sources of information, including interviewing people who had known Lincoln well—or at least made such a claim. Herndon's portrayal of Lincoln exposed the newly canonized secular saint as having feet of clay and being thoroughly human. In the eyes of Lincoln family members and their supporters, Herndon's lectures and writings in the newspapers of the day were disconcerting, as he "impugned the legends of domestic felicity, scorned reports of orthodoxy, and generally made himself a painful and probing nuisance."[7] Yet, Herndon's close relationship with Lincoln as the president's last law partner gave Herndon a level of credibility that was difficult to dismiss.

William Herndon's lecture on Lincoln's love affair with Ann Rutledge, which received significant coverage in the *Chicago Tribune* on November 28, 1866, and was also available for sale in printed form, incensed Mary Lincoln and had Robert Lincoln fuming and scheming over how to stop Herndon from doing further damage to the Lincoln family's reputation. Herndon essentially concluded that Ann Rutledge was the only woman Lincoln had ever truly loved, that her untimely death drove him to the brink of insanity, and that Mary Todd Lincoln was more of a consolation prize than an object of Lincoln's passionate affection. Robert Lincoln traveled to Springfield in late 1866 to see whether he could convince Herndon to cease and desist, telling him that despite his supposed good intentions, all understood the Ann Rutledge story to reflect poorly on Mary Lincoln. Robert's entreaties were unsuccessful. "All I ask," he then wrote Herndon, "is that nothing may be published by you, which after careful consideration will seem apt to cause pain to my father's family, which I am sure you do not wish to do."[8] Herndon would have much more to say and print that would cause discomfort to the Lincolns and those who desired to idolize them. Herndon's mischief helped motivate Nicolay, Hay, and Robert Lincoln to move ahead with a more orthodox and flattering biography of the Great Emancipator, although the project proceeded very slowly.

Once he became marshal (i.e., office manager) of the United States Supreme Court on December, 16, 1872, Nicolay could at last pursue more systematically the compilation of information and collection of documents necessary for the

Lincoln biography, as his new position required only about four hours a day, once his assistants were in place. He saw the work on Lincoln that he and John Hay envisioned as the antidote to Herndon and all the other deficient and distorted writings about their hero. Yet, he knew this effort would require years of work. It is unclear at exactly what point Robert Lincoln promised Nicolay and Hay that they were the chosen ones to write the biography with the use of the Lincoln papers. It is difficult to sort out what may be hope on Nicolay's part from a firm commitment on Robert Lincoln's part, but Nicolay and Hay, as Lincoln's private secretaries and assistants, appeared to have the inside track. Before his father's papers were made available to anyone, Robert Lincoln appeared nearly as eager as Nicolay to move forward with the project, writing to Nicolay that "Herndon has so clearly falsified the record that I think it time he was squelched."[9] Nicolay's desire to move ahead with the biography and not get sidetracked with continued inquiries about every aspect of Lincoln's life is evident in his reply to the pastor of Springfield's First Presbyterian Church, who inquired about Lincoln's religious beliefs. "Intending no discourtesy to yourself," Nicolay responded that he intended to save his comments for the time when he could write about it in the Lincoln history as "fully and carefully as possible."[10]

After settling in to his new job in Washington, Nicolay returned to Illinois for a lengthy visit in the spring of 1873. Therena's mother, Emma Bates, had died in Pittsfield on January 26 of that year and his oldest brother, Frederick Lewis, had died the previous year. The trip's main purpose was to attend to family matters in Pike County. While there, Nicolay wrote to Robert Lincoln in Chicago indicating that he was unaware of any progress being made concerning access to the Lincoln papers and hinting that he was eager to start working on them. The secretary asked whether Robert had followed through on his expressed intentions to move the papers to Chicago and have work completed on "their examination and arrangement." If so, Nicolay offered, he would try and arrange his schedule so he could go to Chicago and "look them over."[11]

Nicolay was becoming impatient to move forward with his Lincoln history, especially after Charles Francis Adams had recently published his eulogy of William Seward, delivered before the New York State Legislature, in which Seward's role in the Lincoln administration was significantly magnified and Lincoln's was severely diminished. A brief quote from the oration demonstrates Adams's disdain for the deceased President:

> I now come to a point where what appears to me to have been one of his [Seward's] greatest qualities, is to be set forth. It is impossible for two persons in the relations

of the President and the Secretary of State, to go on long together without taking a measure of their respective powers. Mr. Lincoln could not fail soon to perceive the fact that, whatever estimate he might put on his own natural judgment, he had to deal with a superior in native intellectual power, in extent of acquirement, in breadth of philosophical experience, and in the force of moral discipline. On the other hand, Mr. Seward could not have been long blind to the deficiencies of the chief in these respects, however highly he might value his integrity of purpose, his shrewd capacity, and his generous and amiable disposition.[12]

While Charles Francis Adams was the son and grandson of two presidents, he was also a Boston Brahmin. The elitist attitudes rooted in class, educational, and likely regional prejudices that permeate this assertion would have infuriated Nicolay. The Adams speech only spurred his growing frustration with Robert Lincoln's delays. "The contemptible assertations and insinuations of Chas. Francis Adams, and the late death of the Chief Justice [Salmon P. Chase]," Nicolay insisted as he wrote to Robert, "demonstrate the necessity of promptly beginning the collection and arrangement of the materials which John [Hay] and I will need in writing the history we propose."[13] Impatient with Robert Lincoln's inaction, he had already begun the process of "accumulating a vast library of manuscript collections, books, articles, and government documents, in anticipation of the heavy work that lay ahead."[14] In addition to the Lincoln papers and the documentation he was collecting, Nicolay and Hay had other, more personal sources from which to draw information for the Lincoln biography. John Hay had kept a diary during his White House years, and while Nicolay did not do likewise, he did write a number of personal memoranda regarding important meetings and issues of the day. Then there were his letters to Therena, which provided another chronicle of the Lincoln years. President Lincoln himself had offered to assist Nicolay and Hay when the time would come for them to write the biography, and it is likely that the two secretaries long ago "had probably made their intentions known to Robert Lincoln."[15]

Yet by March 1874, nearly a decade after Lincoln's death, only minimal progress with the Lincoln papers had been made. The papers had finally been transferred from Bloomington to Chicago, and Robert Lincoln had actually opened and examined one box of them, only to put the massive project aside. Nicolay wrote to Robert on March 3, 1874, urging that he not be left out of the process. "I am satisfied that the task is in every way a longer and more perplexing one than either of us yet fully appreciate," he observed, "therefore it will need all the time and patience that the both of us may be able to give it." Fearing that a clerk might discard some innocuous looking scrap of paper that might have significance, he urged that he not only be present "at the first overhauling of the papers," but also emphasized "the only good rule is to save everything." Nicolay then went on to articulate his strategy for gathering source materials for the Lincoln history. He proposed to bring together the Lincoln papers and shape them into "a permanent methodical and convenient arrangement for reference and use." In addition, he would "glean the files and records" of the various executive departments, along with the captured Confederate archives, "the personal and private papers of cabinet officers," and "leading army and navy officers whose careers gave them official prominence or personal intimacy with your father's administration." On top of all this, he would attempt to interview members of Congress who had worked with the president. "I do not flatter myself that this is a trifling work," he admitted, "but I know that no one has better advantages with myself for doing it." Indeed, what Nicolay proposed would be a monumental task.[16]

John Hay, closer to Robert Lincoln in age and clearly more affable than George, may have had more leverage with the president's son and, consequently, was able to share some good news with Nicolay later in the spring of 1874. There were publishers in New York very interested in their project, and Robert Lincoln now promised Hay that the two former secretaries could have access to the Lincoln papers whenever they were ready to get to work. In the summer of 1874, dozens of boxes of the Lincoln papers were shipped from Illinois to Nicolay at the capitol in Washington and stored in his office there. The Supreme Court met in a lower level of the capitol, and Nicolay's protected and essentially fireproof office proved to be a safe repository for the treasured documents.[17]

At last, Nicolay had access to the documents he needed, but there were other concerns with which he now had to deal. While he considered Robert Lincoln to be a good friend, Nicolay was nonetheless jealously protective of the assumption, if not the outright promise, that he, along with Hay, had been chosen by Robert to write the definitive biography of Abraham Lincoln using the Lincoln papers. Although it is not possible, as noted earlier, to pinpoint the precise time when the agreement was reached, or exactly how the arrangement was made, Nicolay began to fear that Lincoln's eldest son, often besieged by others for information, might give in and allow material from the Lincoln papers to fall into others' hands first. "Having chosen me as your father's biographer," he wrote to Robert in an undated note in 1874, "you must not cripple me at the very outset by giving my trump card to another player."[18]

In a long letter to Robert Lincoln dated July 17, 1874, Nicolay urged him in rather strong terms not to give access to his father's papers to others before he and Hay had examined them. Robert, along with Judge Davis, wanted to prove Lincoln's leadership of the government, contrary to Charles Francis Adams's assertion that it was really Secretary of State Seward who was in control of policy early in the administration. Robert knew that his father's papers could prove otherwise, but Nicolay feared that releasing documents from the Lincoln collection every time something was written or said publicly with which Robert (as well as Nicolay and Hay) might disagree would "be extremely injudicious" and would make them appear as "mere partizans [sic] and camp followers," whereas "by judicious reticence" they would hold "the immensely higher and more authoritative position of historical arbiters, and possessors of the decisive historical record." To do otherwise would be "the most rash and inconsiderate step two such sensible men as yourself and Judge Davis could possibly devise."

Nicolay next revealed how strongly he felt about Robert allowing only him and John Hay to do the job for which they were qualified and why it was so important for them to do it. His judicious foresight would be vindicated when their history became the authoritative biography of Lincoln, a monumental work that would set the standard for future Lincoln scholarship, if not objectivity, and which would indeed give Nicolay and Hay recognition as "possessors of the decisive historical record." Ever fearful that Robert would assign the writing of his father's biography to another, Nicolay pleaded with him again, "I beg you to not think of us as mere boys but as men who have reached reasonably mature powers." Robert's father, Nicolay declared, "is our ideal hero" and "we wish to delineate the grandeur of the era in which he lived, the far-reaching significance and influence of the events he led, and how to set him in history as the type, the Preserver and Liberator of the People." According to Nicolay, the former secretaries wanted to portray the president as "the master-spirit" who "held, guided, controlled, curbed and dismissed" the men around him, "with perfect knowledge of men, and almost prophetic forecast of events." "This we believe," Nicolay concluded, "a logical presentation of the proof will demonstrate."[19]

Robert Lincoln acquiesced to Nicolay's request on this occasion, but further struggles would lie ahead in Nicolay and Hay's ongoing relationship with the president's son as the project proceeded. One awkward situation was reflected in a letter John Hay wrote to Richard Watson Gilder, editor for the Century Company and a Lincoln devotee, years later in 1886. Apparently, Gilder wondered why, in the Nicolay-Hay serialization of some of the Lincoln material in his magazine, so

Robert Todd Lincoln in
middle age. (Library of
Congress)

little was said about the president's father, Thomas Lincoln. "Everything shows that the only weak link in the chain is Thomas Lincoln," Hay responded. "His grandson [Robert Lincoln] is extremely sensitive about it." Hay went on to state that the authors "can't dwell on that," since Robert Lincoln felt "sorry for the old man and does not think it right to jump on him."[20] Robert may have had some reservations about dwelling on the relationship between his grandfather and father. Nonetheless, Hay may have been pointing the finger at Robert when the real reluctance to talk about the relationship came from Nicolay and Hay. The relationship between Thomas Lincoln and his son was so bitter that Abraham refused the pleadings of his stepmother to visit his father while the elder Lincoln was on his deathbed. Robert, who sometimes had a difficult relationship with his father, may have had some sympathy for his grandfather. More important from Nicolay's and Hay's perspective, the unhappy and bitter relationship between Thomas Lincoln and his son would not have found a place in the glowing account of the life of Abraham Lincoln being composed by them. It was in their minds best glossed over, and so it was.

Thus began the arduous, painstaking, but exciting process of going through the Lincoln papers, work done largely by Nicolay, who had more interest in the actual research aspect of the project than Hay did. He was the senior partner and initiator in this massive literary effort to preserve and shape the public's memory of the sixteenth president. On the other hand, John Hay, while he was a very willing and highly capable partner in the project, had numerous other professional and financial interests over the years, as well as a financially advantageous marriage. For Hay, the Lincoln project was one of many items on his life's agenda, whereas for Nicolay, the Lincoln project was at the center of his life's aspirations. The work ahead of Nicolay was enormous, requiring years of effort before any actual writing could be undertaken.

Describing the task before Nicolay, David C. Mearns, the director of the Reference Department of the Library of Congress charged with the custody of the Lincoln papers collection when they were opened to the public in 1947, had nothing but praise and admiration for Nicolay's accomplishment in organizing the documents. "Mr. Nicolay undertook the gigantic task of putting them in order," wrote Mearns, and "relating them to other documents in his keeping." "For him, the most important task of all, was devising . . . plans for a comprehensive treatment of the Lincoln period," Mearns related, asserting that "necessarily, it was a one man job, and necessarily it was slow, but the tall-browed Mr. Nicolay was not deterred by its proportions." Having handled the Lincoln papers himself, Mearns spoke as an expert when he stated, "Only those who have seen the Lincoln papers can fully appreciate the difficulties which confronted him [Nicolay]."[21] Since Nicolay had served as Lincoln's private secretary and what would today be called "chief of staff," he was uniquely qualified for these tasks as he had handled many of the papers at the time of their origination and had been an eyewitness to the events with which many of the documents were associated.

While continuing his work as marshal of the Supreme Court, Nicolay tried to find time for his research and writing. Family responsibilities, illnesses, and personal tragedy were ever present priorities. A son, named George Bates Nicolay, was born to George and Therena on August 25, 1877. Sadly, the Nicolays endured a parent's worst nightmare when their infant George died on October 22 of that same year. On August 18, 1880, Therena's brother, Dorus E. Bates, committed suicide. Dorus, who had lost an arm during the siege of Vicksburg, may have been a victim of what is now identified as post-traumatic stress disorder, or PTSD. Two years later, on October 22, 1882, Therena's father passed away at the age of seventy-seven on the fifth anniversary of infant George's death. For Nicolay, the greatest personal tragedy of all occurred on November 25, 1885, when his beloved Therena passed away.

Through it all, he moved forward with a dogged determination, first with assistance from Therena, and following her death with daughter Helen's aid. He fervently desired that he and John Hay would produce a work vindicating the Lincoln they knew. They believed Lincoln to be among the wisest, kindest, and most effective leaders the nation, perhaps the world, had ever known. Occasionally his forays into the Lincoln papers produced unexpected results, such as his discovery of $62.50 in currency as reimbursement for overpayment of "sundry accounts" by Mr. Lincoln to B. B. French, the commissioner of public buildings. "The letter had evidently been hurriedly laid aside without taking out the bills where they have resided ever since," the scrupulously honest Nicolay immediately wrote to Robert Lincoln informing him of the discovery and asked whether he should send the money to him now or keep it for him until Robert's next visit to Washington.[22]

In the fall of 1875, a frustrated Nicolay wrote to John Hay explaining that his work of examining, classifying, and prioritizing the Lincoln papers for their Lincoln history had been delayed because two of his assistants were out sick, leaving him with the work of three people.[23] Additionally, there was no end to distractions that Nicolay and Hay endured from the public, sometimes from those sincerely wanting to assist the researchers with personal recollections or documents, and other times from people simply seeking opportunities to cash in on a scam. "They were offered alleged manuscripts, and Lincoln signatures for a price," Helen recorded.[24] Most of these offers turned out to be fraudulent. None of them met the authors' high standards. "It gave them satisfaction," Helen later wrote, "to be able to say when their book was finished that not a statement in it had been made without written proof."[25] In spite of these and other challenges, by the end of 1875, Nicolay had sent Hay "a first installment of material."[26]

Over the next several years, Nicolay gave time and attention to the Lincoln papers, and he and Hay began writing the Lincoln history as they felt ready and could find the time. Hay biographer John Taliaferro described Nicolay as the "engineer" of the project, conducting interviews, researching the archives, and "delivering his yield to Hay."[27] There were always more sources to track down, verify, and place into context, as well as more inquiries from the public to which they responded, along with many they determined to be unworthy of a response. There were always expenses for the project, which Hay helped Nicolay cover with a check, "$200 here, $100 there."[28] Hay had married Clara Stone on February 4, 1874, and soon settled in Cleveland to assist his father-in-law, the railroad and banking magnate Amasa Stone. Consequently, Nicolay and Hay regularly corresponded regarding the book, sending each other chapters for criticism and revision. Each man also made occasional visits to the other to better coordinate their efforts.

Meanwhile, since 1864, the War Department had been actively gathering, compiling, and publishing Civil War documents for the massive *Official Records of the Union and Confederate Armies*. One of President Rutherford B. Hayes's early actions following his inauguration in March 1877 was to instruct the new secretary of war, George Washington McCrary, to give Nicolay special permission to borrow printed documents from the War Department dealing with the Civil War. Secretary McCrary's letter dated March 19, 1877, to Nicolay, only five days after McCrary was installed as secretary, informed Nicolay that the "Department has uniformly refused to permit [the completed volumes] . . . to be used by any individual, because of the manifest injustice of discriminating in favor of one author to the exclusion of many. . . . An exception, will however, be made in your case provided you will agree to return the books as soon as practicable, and not permit them to be used by any other person."[29] Secretary McCrary may have had misgivings about the fairness of doing this, but President Hayes had spoken.

The official records were clearly put to use. Relaying an encouraging progress report to Hay three months later, Nicolay reported, "I have found quite important mss. [manuscripts] in the Rebel Archives of the War Department." He reported that he was going over "the doings of the Buchanan Administration between the election and inauguration of Lincoln," having completed the first draft of "about twenty chapters." He would send them to Hay for his review, as each author had his work checked by the other.[30]

As 1880 approached, Nicolay was attempting to work on two major literary projects simultaneously. He was able to use some of his research to prepare a one-volume manuscript entirely of his own composition entitled *The Outbreak of Rebellion*. For this work, he found a receptive publisher in Charles Scribner's Sons, which published the book in 1881 as the first volume planned in a series by various authors called "Campaigns of the Civil War." Shortly after receiving Nicolay's completed manuscript, Scribner's editor Edward L. Burlingame wrote Nicolay of his "admirable success" in writing a volume containing "a thoroughly graphic and masterly narrative of such a time." The publisher's congratulations continued: "What I especially appreciate and admire very heartily is the perfect proportion and perspective you have given to a period which . . . must be familiar to you."[31]

Ten days later, he received another letter from Charles Scribner's Sons, which Nicolay acknowledged contained a check "for six hundred dollars payable to my order, the same being payment in full for my manuscript, *The Outbreak of Rebellion.* Thanking you for your promptness I remain, Yours very truly Jno. G. Nicolay."[32] Nicolay's book and the succeeding volumes of the series, which included titles written by such Civil War notables as Abner Doubleday, A. A. Humphreys, and Jacob Cox, were a commercial success. All titles were written by participants in the campaigns about which they wrote. Nicolay's volume, which dealt with the events and decisions leading up to the First Battle of Bull Run, was a unique record by an eyewitness to many of the events occurring in the White House following Lincoln's inauguration. The book also mentioned the unauthorized behind-the-scenes negotiations conducted by Secretary of State Seward until Lincoln asserted his authority.

In late 1881, while working on the papers and biography of the nation's first assassinated chief executive, Nicolay must have been emotionally moved, as was the nation, by the lingering death watch for the second American president to fall by the hand of an assassin—President James Garfield. Shortly after Garfield's death, Nicolay wrote to Garfield's widow, Lucretia, to assure her of "my high admiration of your husband's character and career," as well as "my own and Mrs. Nicolay's profound sorrow and sympathy in your great loss." Most of his letter, however, was taken up with offering "a few suggestions which are prompted by my own experience in the care and handling of the papers of President Lincoln." Again, we see glimpses of what he was undertaking. Confirming the wisdom of the advice he had given Robert Lincoln years before, he advised Lucretia Garfield:

> My urgent advice to you is, not only that your husband's papers should be carefully preserved, but that you should at an early period institute some methodical and systematic examination and arrangement of them. In his long and varied public career, a great accumulation of original manuscripts, letters and other material for biography and history must have taken place. Only those who have undertaken similar labors have the remotest conception how painfully tedious and difficult it is to examine and prepare such material for the biographer's or historian's use. Hurry in such a task is utterly impossible, and one mind must practically accomplish the greater part if not the whole, in order that unity of plan may be preserved. Every document, leaf and scrap must be deliberately scrutinized to ascertain its date, relation and historical value, and a convenient method of handling and reference must be devised. Not only this; but, concurrently, newspapers and public documents must be searched, or persons written to, to find explanations and supply omissions.

Nicolay also made it clear that he was trying to be helpful but was not seeking the job of organizing the Garfield papers, nor did he have anyone to recommend. He did set out a list of criteria for the right person to do the job, however, and in

Therena Bates Nicolay in
an undated photograph,
possibly early 1880s. (From the
Lincoln Financial Foundation
Collection, courtesy of the Allen
County Public Library and
Indiana State Museum)

the process he was really describing himself in his relationship to Lincoln. Mrs. Garfield should, Nicolay urged, select one of her departed husband's "confidential friends who is intelligent, discriminating, and thoroughly loyal to your husband's memory; in addition he ought to be familiar with his personal history, his temper and habits of thought, his methods of labor and study, and if possible, familiar with the papers and materials themselves. In such a task personal knowledge is of infinitely more value than mere literary ability or experience."[33]

Nicolay turned fifty years old on February 26, 1882. He was in Palatka, Florida, where the Nicolays often spent time in winter, at an old, once-elegant home made available to them. His wife and daughter were home in Washington as he wrote to Therena, noting his amazement at the passing of this milestone and demonstrating both denial about his age and a sense of satisfaction with life. Like many reaching the mid-century mark, he wondered, "I think there must be some mistake about it—the family tradition." He admitted, however, that he no longer serenaded young girls, did not dance as much, and saw "gray hairs in the looking glass." But then he reflected on the important things in his life. What is the difference after all if the years do come and go so long as we three [George,

Therena, & Helen] are all reasonably well, and happy and prosperous," but surely for George, the most significant thing of all was that they were still together.[34]

In March 1882, he received the first of many letters he and John Hay would be sent from the *Century Illustrated Monthly Magazine* (hereafter *Century Magazine*) of New York. Having twice tried unsuccessfully to find him at his office in the U.S. Capitol, the Century Company's editorial department was now soliciting by letter an article to be written by Nicolay about the White House—the "historical, social and political aspects of it." Apparently, the editors really wanted this article, promising, "We could make the commission quite well worth undertaking from a financial point of view." But of even greater importance was the request "whether there would be any chance for us to arrange for the publication of some of your [pending] Lincoln book in the magazine. . . . Moreover, our publishers would take great pleasure in putting the imprint of The Century Co. upon the work in book form." The editors also mentioned that they had been in similar contact with John Hay regarding the Lincoln material, "of course with proper compensation in both cases."[35] This relationship with the publishing company would be a long-term, usually amiable, though occasionally contentious, association that would culminate in publication of the Lincoln history.

Nicolay waited two weeks before responding to the Century Company's letter. Perhaps playing "hard to get," he declined the request for an article on the White House, saying, "it will be impossible for me to take the necessary time for the work, which would otherwise be most agreeable to me." He also informed the editors that "we have as yet no definite plans concerning the publication of the Lincoln book, and deem it too early to adopt any."[36] Apparently, he reconsidered not long afterward, at least as far as the White House article went, for on July 3, 1882, he wrote to the editor: "I have begun work on the White House paper though I am not as far advanced as I had hoped to be by this time." He cited "the illness of both my wife and daughter" as contributing factors to the delay, and asked, "When must you absolutely have it, and when must the illustrations be begun, and must I choose them?"[37]

While working on his literary projects, Nicolay took time in December 1882 to respond to Therena's eighteen-year-old nephew Frank Bates, son of her brother Daniel, who had written to Uncle George from Pittsfield asking about employment opportunities in Washington. Nicolay discouraged his nephew from looking for work in the nation's capital, saying, "This city has become one of the most difficult places in the country to find work in, of any kind." He told Frank that for every job there "are twenty here seeking it," and if "by a lucky chance they do get a situation, living is so expensive that, although they appear to get good wages they have nothing left after paying for their board and clothes." Nicolay then admonished Frank to "remember in whatever you undertake to try and make yourself able to do it better than others." Perhaps relying on his own experience as a young adult in a new situation as Lincoln's secretary in Springfield and Washington, he offered this advice: "Be very particular about your companionship. . . . seek the society of the educated, the upright, the industrious, the well-to-do; men who are engaged in steady useful occupations."[38]

As time and inclination allowed, Nicolay and Hay made slow progress on their Lincoln history. Both men suffered from vision problems, making the rigorous process of writing and editing a grueling task. Sometimes each man wrote a chapter, sometimes a series of chapters almost reaching the span of an entire volume. When a chapter was completed, they passed it back and forth, editing and polishing the text several times. Much later in the process, as actual publication neared, Nicolay would do the proofreading—painstakingly—nine times: "three times in galley, three times in page proof, and three more after the pages had been cast."[39]

By the summer of 1885, the two authors had completed about 100 chapters out of a project that would eventually encompass 224 chapters in ten volumes. The Century Company was unrelenting in wooing Nicolay and Hay for an agreement to be their publisher. As early as 1880, the company's Richard Gilder had contacted them with the idea of publishing their work in serial form for at least a couple of years before their Lincoln volumes would be published, an idea that Nicolay and Hay initially dismissed.[40] In the spring of 1885, Roswell Smith, the president of the Century Company, wrote to Hay calling their project "an exceptional book" and told him, "We want your Life of Lincoln—we must have it." Later in the letter he repeated this sentiment: "The Century Co. wants it, and the Century Co. must have it, and if you will trust us to publish it, and are not satisfied with the 10% [royalty] we will agree with you upon the terms of a contract by which we shall divide the profits."[41] Nicolay was still wary of the publisher's desire first for serialization, telling Hay that "we could not afford to have the pith of our work consumed" in such a manner and that "they [the Century Company] clearly are not ready for such a job as ours." Nicolay favored the idea of "dropping negotiations and buckling down with a will to write another volume. It would not be advisable for us to mortgage our time in advance. Neither your health nor mine justifies it. We could write two volumes a year, but we could only do it with voluntary work, and not under compulsion."[42]

However, the *Century Magazine*'s success with a series of Civil War articles, which doubled the magazine's circulation and brought in a million dollars in revenue,[43] along with the 1884 release of William Stoddard's *Abraham Lincoln: The True Story of a Great Life*, caused Nicolay and Hay to realize that perhaps it was time to begin to publish their work, even if in serial form. Knowing that they were still some years away from completing the entire Lincoln history, serialization in the *Century Magazine* would allow them to get some of their work out to the public for a couple of years while they completed the remainder of their history.

The Century Company was not to be denied. The editors viewed the serialization of the Lincoln biography as the natural sequel to their Civil War series.[44] In June 1885, editor R. W. Gilder sent Nicolay a letter with two good reasons why a serialized version of the Lincoln history would be a good idea. "If your object is that Lincoln's story should reach this generation, how could it be better accomplished?" the editor queried. He further argued that a serialized version prior to publishing the Lincoln story in book form would be "the opportunity of correcting possible errors and enriching the volumes with material elicited by serial publication."[45] That same month, another letter from Roswell Smith seemed to close the deal. Addressed to John Hay, Smith informed him that the company "want[s] it first for the magazine and then in book form" but then conceded that if Nicolay and Hay only wanted to see publication in book form, "we still want the book."[46] The dealmaker was a check for five thousand dollars.[47]

John Hay was no stranger to the *Century Magazine* by this time. Hay had written a novel, *The Bread-Winners*, a not particularly flattering story about his adopted city of Cleveland. Beginning in August 1883, *The Bread-Winners* was being serialized anonymously in the *Century Magazine*, and it had become "The Sensational Novel of the Year," according to one journal.[48] The story took a decidedly anti–organized labor stance, and Hay's authorship was not definitively revealed until after his death in 1905.

In July 1885, Nicolay was vacationing in Bethlehem, New Hampshire, and had invited R. W. Gilder to join him there to peruse the Lincoln manuscript chapters that he and Hay had written to date. Four days into the visit, Nicolay wrote to Hay that the Century editor had been avidly perusing the text. He "is visibly interested," observed Nicolay after the editor had proceeded to "about the middle of the reading" and had "pointed out only one page that he suggested could be condensed."[49] Gilder was impressed, and a contract for the Lincoln history, first in serial form, was getting closer by early August. Nicolay responded to a letter from the editor that a proposed "three years' schedule" could commence in the fall of 1886, provided their health held up.[50] Gilder wrote a friend the following November: "This summer I spent a couple of weeks up in the mountains by appointment; there met Nicolay, and read . . . about half [of what the coauthors had completed to that point]." Gilder was impressed that what gave the Nicolay-Hay work "its great value" was that it was "the only authorized life of the greatest man this country has ever produced . . . and not only the greatest, but by far the most interesting." Furthermore, the editor exclaimed, "in this history, wherein the story of his life and great work is completely told for the first time, Lincoln looms up an even greater and more important figure than he has hitherto been supposed to be."[51]

Helen was, by this time, playing a growing role as her father's assistant. Several of the letters that Nicolay sent regarding the Lincoln project were dictated by him to his daughter. Her assistance on the Lincoln project, as well as other literary projects, particularly as her father's eyesight worsened, was both vital and much appreciated. As early as 1880, when she was just fifteen years old, Nicolay presented his daughter with a special leather-bound edition of *The Outbreak of Rebellion* in which he inscribed the following:

From the author to his daughter
Helen Nicolay
As an acknowledgement of her careful and correct work in copying the entire manuscript of this book for the printer, in the winter of 1880.[52]

The Nicolay family lived in a substantial home just a couple of blocks from the U.S. Capitol, on land now occupied by the John Adams Building of the Library of Congress. Their home was described by Helen as having "large square rooms." Her father's study was on the second floor, and in it "was the huge desk that my father had used in the White House," purchased at an auction of government surplus. The November 1863 photograph of Lincoln, Hay, and Nicolay, the one with the interior of the Executive Mansion added, hung on the study wall. Believing that "windows were made to let in the light, not shrouded in dry-goods," her father did not allow drapery in the house, except in the guest room, "whose furnishings were considered strictly a woman's business." The regimen in the household, which "was geared to the writing of the Lincoln book, called for breakfast at seven-thirty," after which her father did some writing before heading off to work.[53]

The late summer and fall of 1885 saw letters going back and forth between the publishing house, Nicolay, and Hay regarding details of the pending contract on the Lincoln book in serial and book forms. In the fall, contract negotiations were finalized and signed. The postscript of a letter from Gilder to Nicolay on November 2, 1885, cheerily notes, "We are all much gratified by the completion & signing of the contract. Mr. [Roswell] Smith says you and Hay are 'our kind' of people, & that [it] is a pleasure to have dealings with Lincoln men."[54]

Nicolay's response was delayed for several days, due to "a slight illness of my own, and a rather serious one of Mrs. Nicolay for a few days past." Nicolay "heartily" concurred with Gilder concerning their mutual satisfaction of having signed the contract for the Lincoln history, and saw the agreement as "the full realization of my hope and expectation from the beginning." Nicolay believed that he and Hay were producing a work that "has not only found a publisher, but the right one. . . . The quick and hearty agreement which was reached, indicates not only unity of views and confidence now, but is an assurance that we shall not disagree in the future."[55]

The joy of a signed contract with a reputable publisher for the Lincoln history quickly gave way to grief as tragedy struck the Nicolay household. On Wednesday, November 25, 1885, forty-nine-year-old Therena Bates Nicolay, devoted wife and helpmate of twenty years, succumbed to the "rather serious" illness Nicolay had described in his letter to Gilder a few days earlier.[56] The funeral was held at the family home two days later and was "largely attended," according to one newspaper account, which continued: "The death of Mrs. Nicolay, wife of the Marshal of the United States Supreme Court, on Wednesday, was not a surprise to those who knew of her critical condition for several days previous, but the announcement was a painful shock to a large number of friends who were not aware of her illness. Her sweet quiet ways and high intellectual qualities had greatly endeared her to all who knew her, and her death will throw a cloud of sorrow over many pleasant circles, while to that of the family, where she was always at her best, the loss will be simply irreparable." Other obituaries referred to Therena as "a worthy Christian lady and admired by all," as "an amiable, faithful, motherly woman who gave up her whole life to the welfare and interests of her husband and children," and as "the unwedded companion of his [Nicolay's] humbler days and the sharer of his somewhat conspicuous later life in Washington and in Paris." One obituary noted, "Mr. Nicolay has the deep sympathy of his many friends."[57] Therena was laid to rest in Georgetown's Oak Hill Cemetery beside her infant son, George. The loss, indeed, was "irreparable."

Little documentary evidence survives concerning Nicolay's grief at the death of his beloved Therena, and his process of emotional recovery. Helen quoted a letter he sent to Hay shortly after Therena's death: "You can best appreciate my loss when I tell you that since the day you assisted at our wedding she has kept my life young and enabled me to smile complacently at my gray hairs. Now I am sundered from the past by a chasm which can never be bridged. . . . But another and immediate loss will be the absence of her cheer and help in our work. For ten years past she has neglected no opportunity to contribute by her mind and hand to its progress. . . . If our volumes ever reach the full dignity of the binder's art, they will be in some degree a monument to her zeal and labor as well as our own."[58]

In another letter to John Hay two weeks after Therena's death, Nicolay shared that despite his great loss, life would go on since it was "better to cling to the plans and ambitions of the past, shattered and diminished as they are, than to face the dreary blankness of an entire want of purpose. . . . For the present Helen and I are filling up the hours with the habitual daily routine, and as much work as is compatible with health. I suppose too the sooner I get back to business of whatever nature, the nearer I will get to a normal mental and bodily quiet."[59]

Unlike the obituary writers, John Hay knew Therena well. In responding to Nicolay's first letter after Therena's death, Hay wrote a brief but poignant and heartfelt testimonial to Nicolay's one and only true love: "She asked so little for herself—she was so full of help and brightness for others. . . . There is no one outside of my own blood whose death can be such a loss as hers. I have not such another friend left in the world to lose."[60] In fact, John Hay did have "such another friend." His name was John George Nicolay.

Helen, twenty years old at the time of her mother's death, stated simply, "We carried on as best we could."[61] In response to a letter from Roswell Smith only ten days after Therena's passing, Nicolay thanked him for "your kind words of sympathy and personal friendship." He also reassured the publisher that he was not going to let the work fall by the wayside in his grief: "I have already been trying to put into practice your suggestion of renewed work as a means of forgetfulness, and for a week past have to some extent succeeded in losing myself, so to speak, in the chapters which I have in hand."[62]

In late December 1885, Nicolay received a letter from R. W. Gilder thanking him for receipt of the first twenty-four chapters of the Lincoln history, stating, "It is not without considerable emotion that I receive this first instalment [sic] of your great work." The editor also informed him that Hay's first seventeen chapters had also just arrived. The next day Nicolay was sent a check for $10,000, a hefty payment to any author in that day, for his portion of the author's fee for serial publication, scheduled to begin later the following year.[63] His longstanding dream of bringing the authentic Lincoln he had known and revered to the attention of the American reading public was about to be realized. Word of the Nicolay-Hay Lincoln project was spreading, and in March 1886, Nicolay received notification that he had been elected to the American Historical Association (AHA), organized just a year and a half earlier at Saratoga, New York, with George Bancroft as president. He responded quickly, saying that it gave him "great pleasure to accept," and he sent in the lifetime membership fee of $25.[64] In the same month he was elected to the AHA, Nicolay also received notice of his selection for membership in the Northwestern Literary and Historical Society of Sioux City, Iowa. These invitations must have been very gratifying to him. Since 1874, he had been a founding member of the Literary Society of Washington, D.C. Now, he was to be counted among the nation's intellectual elite. He had disproven the mocking criticism of that Pittsburgh editor of years before that he was an intellectual lightweight, not fit to write a biography of Lincoln.

Preparation continued for the launch of the serialized portions of the Lincoln history. A letter from Nicolay to Gilder in June 1886 indicated that he and Hay were ready to commit both the serial version and the full-book version of the Lincoln history to the Century Company, provided that certain conditions were met:

I. If upon your examination of the manuscript thus far written, The Century is satisfied with the character and quality of the work.

II. If we are satisfied with the price and terms to be offered.

III. If mutual agreement can be reached upon the style and mode of publication—that is, size, typography, arrangement of volumes, and kindred points.

IV. (And most important) That we shall be held only to reasonable diligence, consistent with health in completing the manuscript, and not be required to finish it at an arbitrary date.

If we keep our health, we think we can have it done at the period proposed, namely November 1888. Ill health, on the other hand would necessarily delay us beyond that time.[65]

Apparently, agreements were reached, since the proofs of the first magazine installment were received by Nicolay in October 1886, due to be published the following month. To the frequently ill Nicolay, whose eyesight was giving him increasing difficulty, health was always a major concern, perhaps even more

John George Nicolay in an undated photograph, possibly in the late 1880s, as the Lincoln history was being completed with John Hay. (Library of Congress)

so following the death of Therena. Two years later, Hay, who had ongoing eye problems himself, would write to Gilder that "I have corrected my proofs" for the installment, "and sent them on to Nicolay. . . . Nicolay has to work rather slowly on account of his eyes."[66] With Helen's assistance, Nicolay would push forward.

The ever-critical Nicolay liked what was presented to him. His usual reserve was cast aside as he gave an uncharacteristically effusive response to the editor of the Century Company, "It is not without emotion that I have examined these first pages of our work in actual magazine form," Nicolay confessed. As he wrote, "Seeing them thus, about to be launched into the great ocean of literature," he could see that his labor was about to bear its first result even though the complete work was still three years in the future. At this moment of triumph, he willingly confessed that he was "not unmindful of the debt of friendship" he owed the Century Company "for the thought and care bestowed upon their favorable presentation." He also took the opportunity to praise Clarence King's introductory article in the October 1886 issue of the *Century Magazine*.[67]

When the first installment of the Lincoln history appeared in the magazine's November 1886 issue, it was well received and gave Nicolay the satisfaction of having his and Hay's work praised by Roswell Smith, who wrote Nicolay that, "The quality of the biography so far has exceeded anything we had the right to

John Milton Hay, lifelong friend
of John George Nicolay and collaborator with him in the writing
of *Abraham Lincoln: A History*.
(Library of Congress)

expect, and the reception by the public has been all that we could have desired."[68] Nicolay responded to Smith two days later: "Your words of commendation are very gratifying. Under such warm appreciation something of the long years of waiting and work through which our chapters have grown from purpose to performance is made to disappear."[69]

The serialized version of the Lincoln history required an ongoing effort of proofreading and revision, even as Nicolay and Hay pressed forward toward completion of the project in book form. Nicolay's stress is apparent in a letter to Gilder in February 1887 and appears to be triggered by his own health issues as well as what he regarded as inadequate turnaround time given for the proof pages. "You will do me a great favor," he remarked with a curt tone, if the proofs could be sent "giving us plenty of time to read, revise and verify." Acknowledging his health problems, he noted that the extra time is "especially essential."[70] Despite the stresses of deadlines and eye problems, Nicolay on occasion gave evidence of a sense of humor. He saw the need for revising his chapter of the serial install-ment called "Congressional Ruffianism," which included the caning of Senator Charles Sumner. After proofreading his submitted text, he concluded in a letter to Gilder that he had condensed the story to the disadvantage of Sumner. While fully explaining what happened to Sumner's assailant Preston Brooks, Nicolay confessed that he had "sent the principal hero to bed without his supper," and the enclosed revision was needed to prevent Massachusetts from "coming down solid and ransacking the Century office."[71]

In addition to the serialization of portions of the Lincoln biography and the pending publication of the entire ten-volume work, the Century Company sent out feelers to Nicolay and Hay in March 1887 concerning the proposed publication of "The Works of Abraham Lincoln. Letters, Speeches, State Papers &c. Complete Collection." Nicolay responded to Roswell Smith that he and Hay had not discussed such a project with anyone else, that the project as proposed would be massive, approaching half a million words in Nicolay's estimate, and that he felt a more concise project—"a useful volume of short letters, reminiscences, and anecdotes intermingled . . . which I would class under the general title of "Personal Traits of Abraham Lincoln"—would be more reasonable. But given "the mountain of work still before us . . . we are not in a condition even to lay out or seriously consider such a supplementary task."[72] As it turned out, Nicolay made extensive notes for the volume he proposed but died before having written it up for publication. Helen edited her father's notes into book form and published it under the banner of the Century Company in 1912, using the very title her father had suggested in his letter to Gilder in 1887: *Personal Traits of Abraham Lincoln.*

As work proceeded on the Lincoln history, three major issues became obvious to the publishers and were delicately raised without indicating to Nicolay and Hay that the publishing house was in any way dissatisfied with their work. These issues are the same ones which modern readers of the work surely notice quickly and which are likely even more problematic for modern historical scholarship and readers' sensibilities than they were at the time the work was written.

First, the Lincoln history is less a biography of Abraham Lincoln than a history of his times and particularly the events occurring during his presidency. Lincoln frequently disappears from the narrative, sometimes for a number of chapters or scores of pages, as the work shifts its focus to the military and political events of the Civil War. Second, virtually every political issue is viewed unapologetically from a Northern perspective. "We are forced by our consciences to tell the truth," Hay wrote in a firm response to Gilder's concerns about how the reading public, North and South, would receive such a viewpoint. Notwithstanding the editor's concerns, Hay finished his comment by noting, "and every time the truth is told you will hear them yelp."[73] The third issue is the approach the authors took toward Lincoln. It was one of unflinching devotion and praise, with virtually no probing, questioning, or criticism of his actions, beliefs, or motives. Where Lincoln is discussed, it is a work of hagiography, and this is surely what Robert Lincoln, Nicolay, and Hay intended.

Richard Watson Gilder, editor at the Century Company, and point person for the Nicolay-Hay Lincoln history, first in serialized and then in book format, in his office in New York. (From Letters of R. W. Gilder, 1916)

These issues were first raised in the mildest of ways by Gilder in two letters to Nicolay dated March 30, 1887. "Sometimes I feel jealous of every paragraph that hasn't Lincoln in it," the editor wrote, "but of course I am not a fool, and know how necessary and desirable it is to illuminate the general theme." Gilder also sent Nicolay a copy of a response he had written the same day to a critic of the serialized version of the Lincoln work appearing in the *Century Magazine*. J. A. Mitchell of New York City had complained about aspects of the Nicolay-Hay effort, and Gilder wanted Nicolay to see his response to Mitchell, in which he defended and affirmed the authors' work, while acknowledging some validity to Mitchell's observation. Responding that the "story, as told by the two secretaries, cannot be impartial as if narrated by an historian of some subsequent age," the editor asserted that "the public will discount any unconscious partisanship." Furthermore, he wrote, "their facilities [for writing a Lincoln biography] . . . are incomparably beyond those of any contemporaneous writer." As if to encourage the authors further, Gilder excerpted in his letter to Nicolay a positive review he had received from the *Beacon,* a Boston newspaper, which stated, "The fact remains that this biography is infinitely the most important publication of our day, not merely as to thoroughness, but also in its national and world-wide significance."[74]

Over the course of their association with the Century Company, the two authors' responses to their editor differed in tone. Nicolay's letters to Gilder were mostly businesslike. Hay, on the other hand, was more prone to sarcasm and humor in corresponding with the editor. "Perhaps it might help here and there to say Old Abe was a pirate, a liar, and a dog's meat man," a clearly irritated Hay wrote at one point. "I would do anything to please my publisher."[75]

Nicolay's eye problems caused him to lose patience with the schedule and quality of work done by the publisher's proofreaders on several occasions. There were times when he claimed, "My eyesight is in a condition making it impossible to read or write except for brief moments—I am obliged to do all my work with the help of an amanuensis [his daughter]."[76] And while his vision sometimes improved, he hated straining his eyes attempting to figure out what editors and proofreaders were doing to his work. Telling Gilder that the proofreaders appeared to be "a most careless and incompetent lot," he protested, "I wish you would also hint to your proofreaders that fully one-half of the corrections over which I am obliged to torment my eyes are plain and palpable [many of them typographical merely], and ought to have been corrected or at least marked before the proofs came to me."[77]

Nicolay's irritation over the proofreaders' "slovenly carelessness" got the best of him as he complained in a letter to the publisher of their "simply atrocious" handwriting, which was "as hard to decipher as if it were hieratic Egyptian or Chocktaw [sic]picture writing." He pleaded desperately, "Do for God's sake send the perpetrator to a school of penmanship."[78] Part of the annoyance he experienced may have had less to do with the proofreader's penmanship than with the criticism aimed at his authorship. As time passed, he became ever more invested not only in the completion of the project but also in his control of the end product.

In December 1887, Nicolay experienced a career change to full-time author. After fifteen years of service, he was given word of his replacement as marshal of the United States Supreme Court. He left little record of his feelings about the matter. Nicolay wrote to Robert Lincoln on New Year's Day 1888 indicating that his departure was not voluntary, and he reported that "there was no reason given for the change . . . except that, as I suppose some of the judges had got tired of seeing the same face. . . . At least they have assigned no other intelligible motive." He had served under the aegis of two chief justices and five presidential administrations. On his way out, he arranged for the Lincoln papers to remain safely stored in the Capitol Building.[79]

Another hint of what may have happened to Nicolay's career at the Supreme Court is found in a typewritten transcript of what appears to be a newspaper story filed away in the Nicolay papers at the Library of Congress. It is simply headed, "Not to be used before December 23rd [1887]." The article informs readers that Nicolay was being replaced as marshal of the Supreme Court but "the reason for it is not very obvious." However, it suggests that while no fault could be found with the marshal, "the fact" that Nicolay was now receiving substantial annual compensation as an author had "doubtless something to do with the change."[80] The article incorrectly identifies Nicolay's successor as the same Richard C. Parsons he had replaced. It is likely that the Democratic Cleveland administration filled the position as a piece of patronage, since a prominent Kentucky Democrat, John Montgomery Wright, was named to succeed Nicolay, serving in the position until his death in January 1915. Whatever the reason for his dismissal, it gave Nicolay more time for the book.

As Nicolay and Hay transitioned from the serialized publication of portions of the Lincoln history to actual publication of the complete ten-volume set, an agreement was reached in May 1888 concerning the venture between the two authors and the Century Company. Without restating the details arrived at earlier, Nicolay wrote to Frank Scott saying that they agreed with the scheme of publication, while adding three points: He and Hay wanted about fifty Civil War military maps included, noting that "we shall be somewhat particular about their style and workmanship." Second, the authors were insistent on a "full and accurate" index. Finally, the authors "favor and urge the completion and issue of all the volumes together."[81]

Meanwhile, readers of the serialized version of the Lincoln history raised complaints and/or suggestions, sometimes to the *Century Magazine* and occasionally to Nicolay or Hay directly. Coming from a New York reader, E. H. Simons, was a concern, written to Nicolay in May 1888, about the constant use of the words "rebels" and "traitors" in reference to the South. Simons also objected to calling Robert E. Lee not "General" Lee but usually just "Lee"; he noted that Lee was "particularly denounced for his traitorous conduct." Simons acknowledged that what was written "may, in a certain sense, be true," but suggested that "a warmer recognition of Lincoln's greatness among the Southern people" would be furthered if the terms "rebels and traitors were not applied at this late day. Is it not time for bye-gones to be bye-gones?"[82] Neither Nicolay nor Hay were interested in national reconciliation on those terms.

As the serialized Lincoln material was scheduled to end after the February 1890 issue of the *Century Magazine*, R. W. Gilder continued to pressure Nicolay and Hay to produce the "Personal Traits" work as a follow-up to the Lincoln history. Pointing out that "there is some disappointment that Lincoln himself does not shine on every page of the History," the editor apparently used this criticism to goad Nicolay into moving ahead with the "Personal Traits" volume, hoping to serialize it in the *Century Magazine* after the "Lincoln History" serialization had run its course in early 1890. Gilder believed that such a follow-up work, focused just on Lincoln's personal traits, would "be of great service to us in holding our audience . . . —we would breathe freely. The future would be ours as the past has been. . . . I should dearly love to know whether you are in the mood and mind to go on with that part of your great scheme pretty soon."[83] Nicolay and Hay were not in such a mood and mind, desiring instead to tackle compilation and editing of the "Complete Works" of Lincoln as soon as the Lincoln history was ready for publication in book form. Neither Nicolay nor Hay would live to see the 1912 publication of *Personal Traits of Abraham Lincoln*, as assembled by Helen from her father's notes.

Less than a month after Nicolay informed the publisher that the "Personal Traits" project was not going to happen anytime soon, Nicolay and Hay had perhaps their most serious conflict with *Century Magazine*. Their treatment of the war material, according to Gilder, was overly detailed and would be redundant with much of the information contained in a forthcoming Century publication specifically on the Civil War. "I must ask you kindly to curtail," Gilder wrote in a letter addressed to both Nicolay and Hay, "so far as the Magazine goes, all that you possibly can with regard to the purely military part, so that we will not be publishing simply a new War Series." The "war" editors, working with both the Nicolay-Hay material and the new book by Robert L. Johnson and Clarence C. Buel entitled *Battles and Leaders of the Civil War*, were, according to Gilder, "extremely anxious about the matter. They feel that it would never do to let it [the Nicolay-Hay material on the war] go out [in serialized form] as now written. It would not satisfy, scientifically speaking, the contemporaneous audience." Perhaps wanting to soften his position a bit, the editor wrote the next day that concerning the required omissions, "All these points can come up later on book publication. Our great object now is simply to omit military details [in the serialized version] wherever possible."[84]

Apparently, the matter was settled satisfactorily, for the serialized magazine segments continued, and Nicolay and Hay each received their annual payment of $5,000 apiece at year's end, 1888.[85] Earlier that year, Nicolay and Hay had received from the Century Company a "MEMORANDUM AS TO THE ISSUE OF THE LIFE OF LINCOLN IN BOOK FORM," which included details of the timing of release, a format of ten volumes containing about 1,200,000 words, priced at $3 per volume or $30 for the complete set, a desire to include between 250 and 300 illustrations, and a 10 percent royalty of 30 cents per volume.[86]

As Nicolay and Hay wrote their history, they continued to encounter questions about what to do with personal reminiscences submitted to them concerning events of many years before. Individuals who wanted to be part of the Lincoln legacy offered the publisher and the authors stories, sometimes true, often exaggerated, and some patently false that linked them to the sixteenth president. In early 1889, Roswell Smith sent Nicolay a printed recollection from a Union officer named Hewitt about actions involving Forts Henry and Donelson that referenced a telegram from President Lincoln. Based on his knowledge of the situation and research in the War Records, Nicolay told Smith that Hewitt's "memory is greatly at fault in at least some of his particulars." Smith's version of the story, he added, was "improbable," and Nicolay cautioned him thus: "We do not think it would be good policy to invite such reminiscences. We have found nearly every one of them worthless for history."[87] Nicolay's unfailing authentication of every word and document that went into the history is a testament to his determination to publish an epic work that would survive the scrutiny of time. Nicolay and Hay were especially proud of the fact that their history was based on nothing less than solid, well-documented scholarship. "Can you remember things?" Hay once asked Gilder in a letter. "I have to rely exclusively on documents. I would not trust my recollections in the slightest matter of historical interest."[88] There would be no place for hazy reminiscences in their Lincoln history.

Letters went back and forth in 1889 between Nicolay, with input as needed from Hay, and the Century Company with regard to editorial details of the Lincoln History. One issue was whether or not the earlier memorandum outlining the release of the volumes and the financial arrangements with the authors contained merely suggestions or carried the weight of a serious agreement. Nicolay and Hay took the details of the memorandum at face value, and now Frank H. Scott, the publishing house's treasurer, wrote to Nicolay, "We infer from your letter that you have considered our memorandum of May last as to book publication more literally than we had intended." It was not however, designed to be a contract or agreement."[89] Not one to shy away from confrontation when provoked, Nicolay quickly responded. While admitting testily that the correspondence was not a contract, the legally trained Nicolay viewed it as "an agreement" or, better put, an understanding. "It was not in this spirit that we have thitherto conceded every modification which the Century Company required and added much to our care and labor," he lashed out at Scott, protesting, "We have considered its word [i.e., the Century Company's] as good as its bond, and we prefer to continue our dealings on the old basis."[90] Scott, perhaps sensing the danger of antagonizing Nicolay at this point in the project, emphasized their common ground and attempted to smooth over their differences. Asserting that "we are and have been all along practically agreed upon the main points as to the issue of your book," Scott responded in a conciliatory manner, "and we feel that there should be no difficulty in settling the remaining details."[91] Amends were made on both sides, and 1889 ended happily with the final payment of $5,000 each to Nicolay and Hay for their serialized work, accompanied by a flattering letter from Frank Scott.[92]

As 1890 was ushered in, Nicolay and Hay received a congratulatory letter from Gilder regarding their completion of the serialized work on the history of Abraham Lincoln, the final installment of which would appear in the February 1890 issue of the *Century Magazine*. No doubt Nicolay and Hay were pleased to read the editor's words. "There is no doubt in my mind, and I trust there is none in yours," the Lincoln devotee penned, "that not only Lincoln's fame, for all time, has been more firmly established by your labors." Not content to leave his praise there, he went on to remark that "people now living . . . have had the opportunity of knowing the man," which would not be the case for many if the book had not been in "serial publication."[93] While writing congratulatory words to the authors, he was also keenly aware that subscriptions for the *Century Magazine* had declined steadily throughout the serialization of the Lincoln history. Nonetheless, the Century Company was able to sell five thousand sets of the Lincoln history by subscription.[94]

A gratified and somewhat mollified Nicolay responded a few days later, remarking that "our expectations of its favorable reception have been fully realized." He assured Gilder that "The friendly criticism . . . has enabled us" to produce a better work. Nicolay also acknowledged the publisher's "personal good will," but then he unsheathed his rhetorical stiletto, unable to resist taking a parting shot at some of the criticism they had received, even from the Century Company itself: "As to possible accusations of partisanship, we stand in no awe of them. We deny that it is partisanship to use the multiplication table, reverence the Decalogue, or obey the Constitution of the United States. When logic, morals and law all unite to condemn the secession and rebellion of 1861, he will be a rash critic to pronounce censure upon any who helped put down that secession and rebellion, or who venture truthfully to record its incidents."[95]

Approximately half of the Nicolay-Hay Lincoln material had appeared in serialized form in the *Century Magazine* every month beginning with the November 1886 issue and concluding with the February 1890 issue. Now the final preparations were needed to get the whole project ready for publication in book form. Proofreading was a tedious but necessary part of the process that Nicolay occasionally found distressing, especially when he felt the pressure of time constraints. His frustration again erupted in a letter to the publisher in June 1890 about the way in which material for proofing the Lincoln volumes was being sent to him. Complaining that the publisher had sent "a cart-load of proofs . . . all at once," the clearly angry and frustrated Nicolay declared, "it is this 'spurting' business which makes the trouble." Authors could not hire proofreaders while publishers could hire compositors "any five minutes," Nicolay protested, demanding, "Send us proof regularly, not spurtically [sic]."[96]

Even if it were the culmination of his life's ambition and now nearly completed, the whole Lincoln project was beginning to wear thin on Nicolay, especially when his editor was again pressing him for the Lincoln "personal traits" volume even before the Lincoln history had been released. Nicolay was honest and remarkably transparent as he acknowledged to Gilder that "I am completely fagged out, physically and mentally, and don't see much use in books." There was still much to be done for the final preparations for the Lincoln volumes, and after nearly two decades of assembling, planning, thinking, and writing, Nicolay had reached the point of exhaustion. Another book would have to wait; he needed a break from it all.[97] Before 1890 came to a close, the Century Company had released the ten-volume Nicolay-Hay *Abraham Lincoln: A History*.

Nicolay, clearly eager to know how the work was being received by literary critics, began cataloging the American and British newspaper and journal reviews the Lincoln history received starting in November 1890. From that point through September of 1891, his handwritten list of "Newspaper Notices of the Book" contained twenty-four entries, which were listed chronologically and categorized as "very favorable," "favorable," "generally favorable," and "generally favorable—criticism."[98]

A major controversy erupted in 1891 following the death of Lincoln's first-term vice president, Hannibal Hamlin, on July 4 of that year. Not long before his death, Hamlin released a testimonial, used by the Century Company, in praise of the

Nicolay-Hay Lincoln biography in which the former vice president, who had been an avid reader of many Lincoln biographies by that time, stated "I think Maj. Nicolay's and Col. Hay's book is the life of Lincoln that will remain." Giving the work his imprimatur, Hamlin noted "that the statements contained in it are accurate," confirming and strengthening the impressions he had with regard to Lincoln's character. "I think those who did not know him [Lincoln] will . . . get a fair estimate of what he was."[99] The controversy concerned the question of how and why Hamlin was dropped from Lincoln's reelection ticket in 1864. In the Nicolay-Hay account, Lincoln sent Nicolay written instructions that he did not wish to "interfere about V.P. . . . Convention must judge for itself." The account continued, "This positive and final instruction was . . . communicated to the President's most intimate friends in the Convention. It was therefore with minds absolutely untrammeled by even any knowledge of the President's wishes that the Convention went about its work of selecting his associate on the ticket."[100] Alexander K. McClure, a journalist and leading Pennsylvania Republican, attacked the Nicolay version of events and claimed that Lincoln was responsible for dropping Hamlin and adding Johnson to the ticket. The disagreement between Nicolay and McClure became fairly heated. Nicolay called McClure's version, aired in a published review of the Lincoln history, "so pitifully weak. . . . Anyone who wants to believe McClure's preposterous assertion rather than Lincoln's word, will of course do so even if Lincoln were to rise from the dead. I maintain that Lincoln did not write a falsehood. McClure insists that he did. That is the controversy in a nutshell."[101]

After the publication of the Lincoln history, Nicolay took a break from writing to rest and restore his health. By late 1892, his interest in more writing and editing had returned, and he and Hay were able to write to Frank Scott, now president of the Century Company, that they were at last "ready to proceed with the publication of the *Complete Works of Abraham Lincoln* upon the general plan outlined in your letter of Oct. 24 [1892]." It was Nicolay's plan, "subject to further conference with Hay," to publish the Lincoln documents "in as strictly chronological order as possible. This would intermingle speeches, letters, state papers, and miscellanea irrespective of topics, and obviate all necessity for further classification."[102] In 1894, the Century Company published Nicolay and Hay's *Abraham Lincoln: Complete Works,* a two-volume set that was, in reality, far from "complete," although it was the best available compilation of Lincoln documents at that time. Nicolay next undertook a concise condensation of the Lincoln biography into one volume, to be called *A Short Life of Abraham Lincoln.* A major motivation for creating this shorter volume was the less than stellar sales of the enormous ten-volume set. Although five thousand copies of the entire set were sold by subscription not long after the set was released, sales thereafter lagged considerably behind the Century Company's hopes, and in 1895 the publisher notified Nicolay and Hay that due to disappointing sales, individual volumes of the Lincoln history would thereafter be sold at a discounted price.[103] Nicolay was nearly finished with his one-volume condensation of the history, *A Short Life of Abraham Lincoln,* when he died in 1901. With Helen's assistance, the Century Company published it the following year.[104] However, it was no more a biography than the larger history was, with much of its content reflecting the same broader historical narrative.

John George Nicolay, who had given the full measure of devotion throughout his life to Abraham Lincoln, had at long last fulfilled his dream of bequeathing to future generations his understanding of the true greatness of the nation's sixteenth president.

CHAPTER ELEVEN

The Apotheosis of Abraham Lincoln

Assessing the Lincoln History

The attention of visitors to the Capitol Building in Washington, D.C., is often directed to a work of art at the top of the great rotunda. There, visible through the oculus, is a painting entitled *The Apotheosis of George Washington*—that is, Washington ascending to the heavens to become a god. Completed in 1865, the year of Lincoln's assassination, the artist was an Italian-Greek painter and immigrant named Constantino Brumidi. As he sought to enshrine Washington among the demigods of history with a brush, so did Nicolay and Hay seek to enshrine Abraham Lincoln with the pen.

Abraham Lincoln: A History is a milestone in bringing to the reading public an authoritative, yet very personal view, of the Lincoln whom Nicolay and Hay had known and whose image they wanted to perpetuate. But it was far more than a biography of one man, it was also a history of many significant events that impacted the life of Abraham Lincoln as well as the entire American Republic. The subtitle—*A History,* rather than *A Biography*—reflects the intention of the authors to write a history of Lincoln and his times, with Lincoln and his leadership as the unifying theme and thread that holds the massive work together. While Lincoln would be absent for pages on end, his presence is not far away, and he often reappears strategically and magisterially. The editors at the Century Company were initially concerned about this approach, noting in their correspondence with Nicolay that the authors' historical emphasis often seemed to overpower the Lincoln biographical focus. Eventually, the publisher appeared to drop this concern.

Of all the numerous contemporary reviews of the work, perhaps the best written, as well as the longest, was by former journalist, Republican activist, Union general, senator, and cabinet member, Carl Schurz. During the war, he had met with Lincoln in the White House. From these visits, he had become acquainted with both Nicolay and Hay. After serving in the Hayes administration as secretary of the interior, he returned to journalism, editing the *New York Evening Post* between 1881 and 1884. He abandoned the Republican Party in 1884, joining other Liberal Republicans, called Mugwumps, in support of Democrat Grover Cleveland.

Schurz often contributed articles to *Harper's Weekly* throughout the 1890s.[1] His review of the Nicolay-Hay *Abraham Lincoln: A History* in the June 1891 issue of the *Atlantic Monthly,* which was characterized by the *New York Times* as a "striking review,"[2] was a masterful summary of the life of Lincoln. In spite of his political differences with the authors, he penned a perceptive and overall positive, yet appropriately critical, review of their effort. Since Schurz knew and interacted with Lincoln on numerous occasions, his viewpoint is all the more meaningful. The review begins with a realistic yet sympathetic critique of the work:

Messrs. Nicolay and Hay undertook a peculiarly difficult task in writing a biography which at the same time was to be a complete history of the greatest crisis in the life of this republic. . . .

While the authors of this comprehensive biography of Lincoln could hardly be expected completely to overcome the difficulties inherent in their undertaking, they have indeed succeeded in producing a work which, both as a biography and a history, is of high value. They enjoyed the great advantage of having been eye-witnesses to many of the occurrences they relate; of having stood in confidential relations to not a few of the foremost personages of the time; of having been intimate daily companions of Lincoln himself during his presidency; and of commanding a mass of documentary material hitherto not accessible to other writers. Of this advantage they have made excellent use in bringing out new facts of historic importance, and in shedding new light upon others which were only imperfectly known. We cannot follow them in all their reasoning, nor accept their judgment in every case as impartial, least of all in their treatment of some of the persons grouped around the principal character. In their presentation of Chase's conduct, for instance, they transgress all the limits of fairness. But, on the whole, the merit of the contribution they have made to the history of a most important period cannot be too highly acknowledged.

It is to be regretted that a somewhat diffuse style has swelled what should be a popular book into a formidable bulk of ten stout volumes, which only persons of means are able to buy, and from the reading of which only a man of leisure will not recoil. Especially when speaking of their hero, the authors seem to lose all restraint. On every possible occasion, the reader is reminded, with great redundancy of phrase, what high quality of Abraham Lincoln's mind or heart came into play when he said this or did that, while the naked story might safely have been left to point its own moral. Only in the treatment of a few facts and circumstances in Lincoln's life, which might be regarded as capable of unfavorable interpretation, the book is less explicit and straightforward than might be desired. It is not surprising, however, that in the hands of Nicolay and Hay, a biography of Lincoln should have drifted into the tone of a eulogy. In the days of their early manhood, and during the most eventful period of his career, they had been his private secretaries, and lived with him almost like members of his family. What they will always regard and be proud to remember as the most interesting part of their lives they had spent in the closest intimacy with him. They had shared his hopes, his labors, his triumphs, his anxieties, his sorrows. They had known his aims to be high and his motives to be pure, when his acts were fiercely assailed. They had been under the strange charm of his sympathetic nature, his large humanity, when his manners were held up to ridicule, and his character was belittled and traduced. Their story of him could hardly be anything but a work of filial love, painting every strong and noble feature in idealizing colors, and with reverential tenderness covering whatever might look like a blemish.

But Abraham Lincoln's fame needed neither the reiterated enumeration of his virtues and abilities, nor any concealment of his limitations and faults. It was rather the weird mixture of qualities and powers in him, of the lofty with the common, the ideal with the uncouth, of that which he had become with that which he had not ceased to be, that made him so fascinating a character among his fellow-men, gave him singular power over their minds and hearts, and fitted him to be the greatest leader in the greatest crisis of our national life.[3]

Schurz was not the only one to praise this monumental work. In his review in the *New York Tribune*, William Dean Howells, Hay's friend and Nicolay's rival for the honor of writing the 1860 Lincoln campaign biography, wrote "the labor of a generation and the affection of a lifetime have, indeed, joined in raising to the memory of the greatest American of our days a monument worthy of his fame."[4] Henry Adams, grandson of John Quincy Adams and a scholar in his own right, declared the history "a work the equal of which I know not in any literature," and recommended that Nicolay and Hay be awarded honorary degrees from Harvard. However, Harvard president Charles Elliot disagreed, noting that since Nicolay and Hay had been participants in many of the events described, the authors could not be considered historians.[5]

Not everyone shared Schurz's, Howell's, or Adams's appreciation for what the former secretaries had accomplished. No doubt aware that their work was designed, in part, to counter his more earthy version of Lincoln, William Herndon criticized the work's portrayal of the sixteenth president as a secular saint. The irascible Herndon, still disappointed he was denied access to the Lincoln papers, was quoted as saying, "I will bet you a chicken cock that Nicoly [*sic*] & Hay's book will tire out the public by its length and unimportant task." Herndon accused the authors of having "suppressed many facts—material facts of Lincoln's life," including his family background, his love for Ann Rutledge and his near insanity over her death, his skeptical views about religion, his later break-up with Mary Todd, and finally, his "misery with Mary Todd" as his wife. Herndon concluded that these things "have been purposely suppressed" by Nicolay and Hay, who chose to handle Lincoln's life "with silken gloves" because they were writing their biography "under the surveillance of Bob Lincoln" and were, in Herndon's opinion, "afraid of Bob." Instead of giving the public the real Lincoln, Herndon snidely asserted, the biography was "weak and wordy stuff."[6]

Herndon's criticism had some merit. The biography was under the sponsorship of Robert Lincoln, who controlled access to his father's papers and was vitally concerned about his father's historical image. The biographers did gloss over or entirely omit some aspects of Lincoln's life. The biography was meant as political hagiography, but it was also much more, being the first scholarly life of Lincoln and his administration based on verifiable documentation and eyewitness accounts and not a spurious collection of anecdotes meant to enhance the reputation of the author. The former secretaries did not have to prove their intimate contacts with the fallen president. Their association with Lincoln was an unquestionable fact.

The work itself is immense, comprising 4,800 pages of text divided into ten volumes. It is a history of the events of Lincoln's life with Lincoln as the central character. Its prose is almost chronicle-like, written in a matter-of-fact style. This is understandable when one recalls Nicolay's training as a news reporter and editor. There are occasions of soaring prose, most reserved for their hero. Each chapter is more or less freestanding with little or no transition from one chapter to the next. From the writing style, it is impossible to detect which portions of the work were written by Nicolay and which were composed by Hay. However, from the correspondence between the publisher and Nicolay, it is known that Nicolay wrote a majority of the chapters, with Hay's input. According to Helen, "They seemed to take a mischievous delight in keeping it a secret."[7] The end product was an effective collaboration, although Nicolay was the driving force, principal organizer, researcher, and author of the work.

The volumes are exceedingly well-documented, with the authors excluding unsubstantiated material, especially the mountain of unreferenced anecdotes that had accumulated in publications since Lincoln's death. It is the first scholarly biography of Lincoln. The footnotes are many, detailed, and sometimes ponderous. It is the first biography of Lincoln to use the Lincoln papers. Many details about Lincoln's life that have found their way into later books and documentary films about Lincoln first made their appearance in these pages.

No attempt was made to present a historically balanced picture of Lincoln. Instead, Lincoln is too perfect, and the depiction of his godliness is virtually without blemish. When writing of Lincoln's youth, Nicolay and Hay stated that they were "making no claim of early saintship for him. He was merely a good boy, with sufficient wickedness to prove his humanity."[8] However, their treatment of his later life, especially Lincoln's handling of the presidency, belies their claim. The work goes well beyond "saintship" into a form of apotheosis or deification. Where others see Lincoln as vacillating, they call it deliberation. When Lincoln finally makes a decision, it is at precisely the opportune moment. Where others are portrayed as either panicking or naively optimistic, Lincoln is always calm and deliberative. When a cabinet member, general, or political ally causes a political crisis through words or actions, Lincoln is always depicted as receiving the news in a nondramatic, steady-handed, and generally patient and forgiving manner.

Even the greatest of men have their shortcomings, but it is impossible in these volumes to find any in Lincoln, especially during his presidency, when Nicolay and Hay were closest to him. To understand to what extremes this adulation of Lincoln was taken, one only has to recall that even the Evangelists described Christ as being exasperated and occasionally angry with his followers, especially the Apostles. In Christian theology, Christ alone has both a human and divine nature, but Lincoln's human nature seems to have vanished in the Nicolay-Hay volumes. This storyline satisfied the expectations of Robert Lincoln. It also appealed to a primarily Northern audience, whose remembrance of Lincoln, the president and national martyr, were still fresh in the collective living memory.

Arrayed in conflict against this perfect man was the imperfect world and the imperfect men around him. Every day, Lincoln had overcome the incompetence and malevolence of others. Lincoln became the tragic Greek hero, an Atlas, who carried on his shoulders alone the success or failure of the war. In some manner, everyone else tried to pull the great man down, to divert him from his task.

Lincoln's opponents were treated critically, their shortcomings exposed to the world. Individuals who were perceived as serving Lincoln well were treated favorably, but critically, while those whom the authors viewed as having opposed or failed Lincoln and his agenda were targets of much criticism, if not outright venom. The work brims with exasperating minutiae on military matters, including battlefield positions and maneuvers, as well as dispatches from commanding officers, that leave most readers lost in the details. The inclusion of overly intricate maps of various battles, too small and complicated to be readily deciphered, may have been well-intentioned but is frustratingly ineffective. A summary of military events could have provided context for the history while saving hundreds of pages of text. The insertion of so much military material is inexplicable since Nicolay had virtually no military background except as a member of the Springfield Zouaves. Hay's experience in the military was laudatory but very limited. Perhaps this emphasis can be explained by Nicolay's obsession with detail, learned during his days as a newspaperman. Though the volumes contain numerous high-quality portraits of persons mentioned in the narrative, regrettably, they were not always appropriately placed in the text. However, this fault may lie with the editors at the Century Company rather than with Nicolay or Hay.

One historically significant photograph that Nicolay had in his possession was not included in the book. This was the only known photograph of Lincoln lying in his coffin. The picture had been taken in New York City on April 26, 1865. Secretary of War Stanton had ordered copies of it destroyed, but Stanton's son Lewis sent Nicolay the only known copy in 1887. The younger Stanton found the photograph in his father's papers and thought Nicolay might want to use it. For perhaps multiple reasons, Nicolay chose not to do so.[9]

There is no mention of either Nicolay or Hay in the first person anywhere and less than a dozen third-person references in the work for each man, even though one or the other or both were present for many of the events detailed, a rare occurrence for political biography when the authors were involved in many of the chronicled events.[10] Yet the authors could not refrain from inserting some French phrases on occasion without providing translation, an indication that they may have viewed their primary readership as the educated elites, not the general public.

In a letter to Nicolay dated August 10, 1885, Hay described the philosophical underpinnings of the Lincoln history. "The war is gone by. It is twenty years ago," Hay wrote, "Our book is to be read by people who cannot remember anything about it. We must not show ourselves to the public in the attitude of two old dotards fighting over again the politics of their youth." Hay expressed his surprise that Nicolay's *The Outbreak of Rebellion* had been criticized for a "tone of aggressive Northernism," which Hay described as "perfectly fair and candid." Hay did not want the Lincoln history to be a "stump speech" or have the "present tone of blubbering sentiment." He intoned, "We ought to write the history of those times like two everlasting angels who know everything, judge everything, tell the truth about everything, and don't care a twang of their harps about one side or the other." However, Hay noted, "there will be one exception. We are Lincoln men all through."[11] Indeed, they were. In a postscript, Hay directed Nicolay to destroy the letter (which he obviously did not do) since "it would be too great a temptation for any reporter who should pick it up."[12] Written a full decade into the history's composition, the letter reveals the image-conscious, diplomatic Hay justifying the deification of their hero.

Lincoln's boyhood was described in almost messianic terms. Depicting a time when neither author knew Lincoln, they described him as "evidently of better and finer clay than his fellows, even in those wild and ignorant days." Calling the Lincoln household "happy and united . . . under the gentle rule of the good stepmother,"[13] they glossed over Lincoln's sometimes difficult relationship with his father. The authors continued to describe young Lincoln as "a magnanimous boy with a larger and kindlier spirit than common."[14] Summarizing the qualities of the future emancipator, they claimed "his generosity, courage, and capability of discerning two sides to a dispute, were remarkable even then, and won him the admiration of those to whom such qualities were unknown."[15] There was no mention of the gangly, physically and socially awkward Lincoln who in his youth was the subject of jests, and, like the young Nicolay, something of an intellectual outcast from his peers.

While there was no mention of his depression at the death of Ann Rutledge, there was mention of his reaction to his breakup with Mary Todd. In discussing his agony of soul upon breaking his engagement with Mary Todd, the authors fashioned a messianic justification for Lincoln's subsequent behavior:

> But it may not be fanciful to suppose that characters like that of Lincoln, elected for great conflicts and trials, are fashioned by different processes from those of ordinary men, and pass their stated ordeals in different ways. . . . That the manner in which he confronted this crisis was strangely different from that of most men in similar circumstances need surely occasion no surprise. Neither in this nor in other matters was he shaped in the average mold of his contemporaries. In many

respects he was doomed to a certain loneliness of excellence. There are few men who have had his stern and tyrannous sense of duty, his womanly tenderness of heart, his wakeful and inflexible conscience, which was so easy towards others and so merciless towards himself.[16]

Described as having been "elected for great conflicts," "fashioned by different processes from those of ordinary men," and not "shaped in the average mold of his contemporaries," Nicolay and Hay's Lincoln is predestined for his role in history—chosen, created, and sent by God. The linkage of Lincoln to the Christ across the sea, so prevalent after his assassination, is woven into the narrative on multiple occasions throughout the work. In speaking of the long transitional period between the election and the inauguration, the authors noted that "It was a *providential blessing* that in such a crisis the President-elect was a man of unfailing common sense and complete control" (authors' italics).[17]

Yet, Lincoln never claimed any special divine favor for himself. In his first inaugural address, he spoke of a "firm reliance on Him who has never yet forsaken this favored land" and referred to God in the abstract as the "Almighty Ruler of Nations." It was only in the second inaugural that Lincoln made multiple and specific references to God. In 1865, he no longer cited divine favor for the country but rather lamented that God may have passed a terrible judgment on the whole nation "until all the wealth piled up by the bondman's two hundred and fifty years of unrequited toil shall be sunk, and every drop of blood drawn with the lash shall be paid by another drawn with the sword."

When the two inaugural speeches are laid side by side, the first inaugural is an appeal to the law and the constitution, while the second is akin to a sermon, reflecting a man who had spent four years as president surrounded by death: of his son, of friends like Edward Baker and Elmer Ellsworth, and of hundreds of thousands of young men from both the North and South. Lincoln was all too aware of his frailties. As one whose religious faith deepened during the war, Lincoln never saw himself as an instrument of God, much less a man "elected for great conflicts." On the contrary, before the outbreak of hostilities he tried to avoid a great conflict.

Throughout his adult life, Lincoln was not an adherent of a particular denomination or creed. Herndon wanted to portray Lincoln as a religious skeptic. It corresponded with Herndon's personal views and probably fit the description of the Lincoln that he had known. Mary Lincoln had been raised in the Presbyterian faith,[18] but in adulthood she had regularly attended Episcopal services with her sister Elizabeth. After the death of her son Eddy in 1850, she returned to the Presbyterian congregation in Springfield. It was at this time that Lincoln began to attend services with her. He rented a family pew for church services while residing both in Springfield and Washington. While he never went to church with the same frequency as his wife, Lincoln would attend with her on a somewhat regular basis. Although he had many spirited philosophical conversations with Dr. James Smith, the pastor of Springfield's Presbyterian flock, Lincoln never became a member of the denomination.[19]

Seeking to define Lincoln's personal approach to religious belief as he said he would when responding to a minister in 1872, Nicolay (in a passage that likely he alone wrote) described the man he had known in the throes of civil war:

Lincoln was a man of profound and intense religious feeling. We have no purpose of attempting to formulate his creed; we question if he himself ever did so.... [W]e have only to look at his authentic public and private utterances to see how deep and strong in all the latter part of his life was the current of his religious thought and emotion. He continually invited and appreciated, at their highest value, the prayers of good people. The pressure of the tremendous problems by which he was surrounded; the awful moral significance of the conflict in which he was the chief combatant; the overwhelming sense of personal responsibility, which never left him for an hour—all contributed to produce, in a temperament naturally serious and predisposed to a spiritual view of life and conduct, a sense of reverent acceptance of the guidance of a Superior Power.... [T]here is not an expression known to have come from his lips or his pen but proves that he held himself answerable in every act of his career [as president] to a more august tribunal than any on earth. The fact that he was not a communicant of any church, and that he was singularly reserved in regard to his personal religious life, gives only the greater force to these striking proofs of his profound reverence and faith.[20]

The last sentence is especially noteworthy. Noting that since Lincoln was not an adherent to any particular creed, Nicolay asserted that this somehow gave Lincoln's beliefs "greater force to these striking proofs of his profound reverence and faith." Nicolay was not a regular churchgoer throughout his life, even though regular church attendance was an expected feature of well-to-do nineteenth-century American society. Consequently, Nicolay's statement begs the question: was Nicolay justifying Lincoln's philosophy or his own? The question will never be resolved, but it suggests that much of Nicolay's own perspective may have been superimposed on Lincoln.

As the life of Lincoln progresses through these pages, the narrative becomes more descriptive. An example can be found in the portrayal of Lincoln the lawyer. This passage was probably written by Nicolay, who had observed Lincoln in the Pike County Courthouse across the street from the offices of the *Free Press*: "He seemed absolutely at home in a court-room; his great stature did not encumber him there; it seemed like a natural symbol of superiority. His bearing and gesticulation had no awkwardness about them; they were simply striking and original. He assumed at the start a frank and friendly relation with the jury which was extremely effective. He usually began, as the phrase ran, by 'giving away his case,' by allowing to the opposite side every possible advantage that they could honestly and justly claim. Then he would present his own side of the case, with a clearness, a candor, an adroitness of statement which at once flattered and convinced the jury, and made even the bystanders his partisans."[21]

Nicolay, a delegate to the 1856 Republican organizing convention in Bloomington, Illinois, was also an eyewitness to Lincoln's famous "Lost Speech." Here again, Lincoln's oratorical skills are described in vivid detail:

> Every one felt the fitness of his making the closing argument and exhortation, and right nobly did he honor their demand. A silence full of emotion filled the assembly as for a moment before beginning his tall form stood in commanding attitude on the rostrum, the impressiveness of his theme and the significance of the occasion reflected in his thoughtful and earnest features. The spell of the hour was visibly upon him; and holding his audience in rapt attention, he closed in a brilliant peroration with an appeal to the people to join the Republican standard. . . . The influence was irresistible; the audience rose and acknowledged the speaker's power with cheer upon cheer. Unfortunately the speech was never reported; but its effect lives vividly in the memory of all who heard it, and it crowned his right to popular leadership in his own State, which thereafter was never disputed.[22]

Lincoln's delivery of the Lost Speech was a critical moment in his political career, and Nicolay's account matches other descriptions of the event; however, as the senatorial election of 1858 would demonstrate, it had not in fact "crowned his [Lincoln's] right to popular leadership in his own State." Also glossed over (or, as in the case of the Know-Nothings, ignored) was Lincoln's public-versus-private views regarding nativism or the nativists' role in securing Lincoln's nomination at the 1860 Republican convention.

Similarly, the account of Lincoln's speech at the Cooper Union in New York in

February 1860, at which neither Nicolay nor Hay was present, was well-crafted and historically accurate, but the authors could not resist concluding with another bit of hyperbole:

> In Lincoln's entire address he neither introduced an anecdote nor essayed a witticism; and the first half of it does not contain even an illustrative figure or a poetical fancy. It was the quiet, searching exposition of the historian, and the terse, compact reasoning of the statesman, about an abstract principle of legislation, in language well-nigh as restrained and colorless as he would have employed in arguing a case before a court. Yet such was the apt choice of words, the easy precision of sentences, the simple strength of propositions, the fairness of every point he assumed, and the force of every conclusion he drew, that his listeners followed him with the interest and delight a child feels in its easy mastery of a plain sum in arithmetic."[23]

It was unlikely that all "his listeners followed him with the interest and delight a child feels" while doing arithmetic. Lincoln's speech dealt with his views on slavery and its extension into the territories. New York City was a stronghold of the Democratic Party, with deep pro-Southern and proslavery views that would be manifested throughout the coming war. While Lincoln's speech at the Cooper Union was an important step on his way to the Republican nomination and election that year, it was not received uncritically by all those in attendance.

Nicolay was at Lincoln's side as his secretary from May 1860 through the interim period between Lincoln's election and inauguration. He, not Hay, was with Lincoln in the private interviews that occurred during the postelection period. Thus, the description of Lincoln acting in the role of the "kind neighbor and genial companion, who had for every one he met the same bearing," who would listen patiently "to counsel from all quarters,"[24] is Nicolay's eyewitness account of what occurred. Knowing what we know of Lincoln from other sources, this was a description of Lincoln the political operative. What the passages do not reflect is that Lincoln then made cold and calculated political decisions that disappointed many of his visitors. As Carl Sandburg noted, Lincoln was always the political animal. However, Nicolay and Hay did recount an important piece of political wisdom in noting that public opinion was the "talisman which wrought the wonders of statesmanship" and "the changes of national destiny."[25] However, the assertion that Lincoln was the "most consummate master of public opinion" is undercut by the results of the 1862 midterm election and Lincoln's despondence over his reelection chances in the summer of 1864. Likewise, the authors' assertion that "no President ever approached his task better informed"[26] would certainly have been contested by the admirers of many of his predecessors or many of Lincoln's less adoring contemporaries.

When accused of an aggressive Northern perspective on most of the events they chronicled, both authors denied the charge, but Nicolay in his 1880 *The Outbreak of Rebellion* had unabashedly pointed the finger at slavery as the root cause of the war. Neither the Southern leadership nor the Fire-eaters were spared when it came to blame. The Lost Cause mythology which claimed that states' rights, not slavery, was the underlying cause of the war, was not accepted by either man. The authors were not interested in the public sentiment, fashionable in the postbellum decades, to whitewash the causes of the war for the sake of national reconciliation. Consequently, the Lincoln history mirrored the approach already taken by Nicolay in his previous book, *The Outbreak of Rebellion*, a decade before: "It is now universally understood, if not conceded, that the Rebellion of 1861 was begun for the sole purpose of defending and preserving to the seceding States the institution of African slavery and making them the nucleus of a great slave empire, which in their ambitious dreams they hoped would include Mexico, Central America, and the West India Islands, and perhaps even the tropical States of South America. Both a real and a pretended fear that slavery was in danger lay at the bottom of this design."[27]

At the same time, the authors accepted some culpability for the North, especially if they could wave the Republican bloody shirt at the Democratic Party. They accused their political opponents in the North of shamelessly keeping the slavery system going by colluding with the Slave Power. They summarized the cardinal sin of the Democratic Party and its adherents by referencing the political events beginning with the introduction of the Wilmot Proviso in 1846. Nicolay and Hay declared: "For fifteen years the Democratic party had stood as sentinel and bulwark to slavery; and yet, despite its alliance and championship, the peculiar institution was being consumed like dry leaves in the fire of war. For a whole decade it had been defeated in every great contest of Congressional debate and legislation. It had withered in popular elections, been paralyzed by confiscation laws, crushed by executive decrees, trampled upon by marching armies."[28] Their analysis was a bit of historical revisionism. It was the Democrats' legislative successes, the passage of the draconic Fugitive Slave Act of 1850, and the repeal of the Missouri Compromise in the Kansas-Nebraska Act of 1854 as much as the abortive attempt to admit Kansas as a slave state that had driven Northern opinion into the arms of the new Republican Party.

Two Democratic leaders who received particular attention were Senator Stephen Douglas of Illinois and President James Buchanan. Stephen A. Douglas, the country's "Little Giant" and Lincoln's political foil throughout the 1850s, is mildly treated in these pages. Until he rejected the attempt to admit Kansas as a slave state under the Lecompton Constitution, Douglas had been a consistent ally of the South, even reversing his earlier position in support of the Missouri Compromise to press for its repeal in the Kansas Nebraska Act. During the secession crisis, Douglas made many proposals in an attempt to assuage Southern concerns. However, at heart Douglas was a Union man, and when compromise failed, he supported the Union and Lincoln until his untimely death on June 3, 1861.

Consequently, as the authors surveyed the pantheon of Democratic politicians, Douglas was viewed as a rare breed, one of the few Democrats who had some virtue. Describing the qualities of the man, they made the following assessment: "Among his many qualities of leadership were strong physical endurance, untiring industry, a persistent boldness, a ready facility in public speaking, unfailing political shrewdness, an unusual power in running debate, with liberal instincts and progressive purposes."[29]

The Nicolay-Hay history lauded Douglas's steadfast stance in support of Lincoln and the Union: "Battling while others feasted, sowing where others reaped, abandoned by his allies and persecuted by his friends, Douglas alone emerged from the fight with loyal faith and unshaken courage, bringing with him through treachery, defeat, and disaster the unflinching allegiance and enthusiastic admiration of nearly three-fifths of the rank and file of the once victorious army of Democratic voters at the North. He had not only proved himself their most gallant chief, but as a final crown of merit he led his still powerful contingent of followers to a patriotic defense of the Constitution and government which some of his compeers put into such mortal jeopardy."[30]

While in their eyes Douglas had redeemed himself during the last six months of his life, he nonetheless bore guilt for what they saw as the shameless reversal of his stand on the Missouri Compromise.[31] But unlike their hero, Douglas was what we would call today a career politician, having held a variety of political offices since the mid-1830s and being a member of Congress since 1843. They ignored the fact that unlike Lincoln, Douglas had a record to defend, and since he desired the Democratic presidential nomination, Douglas had to conform his views to the shifting demands of the Southern wing of the party.

In describing Douglas's debate style, Nicolay and Hay sought to condemn Douglas as having no real principles, painting him as a political chameleon:

"Lacking originality and constructive logic, he [Douglas] had great facility in appropriating by ingenious restatement the thoughts and formulas of others. He was tireless, ubiquitous, unseizable. . . . He delighted in enlarging an opponent's assertion to a forced inference ridiculous in form and monstrous in dimensions."[32]

In contrast, Lincoln was described in these debates as Douglas's superior: "Lincoln's mental equipment was of an entirely different order. His principal weapon was direct, unswerving logic. His fairness of statement and generosity of admission had long been proverbial. . . . Lincoln was his superior in quaint originality, aptness of phrase, and subtlety of definition; and oftentimes Lincoln's philosophic vision and poetical fervor raised him to flights of eloquence which were not possible to the fiber and temper of his opponent."[33] Nevertheless, Douglas, not Lincoln, won the Senate election of 1858.

Yet, if Stephen Douglas had some redeeming features, another Democrat, Lincoln's predecessor in the White House, did not. President James Buchanan was especially targeted for harsh treatment, with just a glimmer of good intent to soften the portrait of the fifteenth president. Historical assessments of Buchanan a century and a half after the beginning of the Civil War are little better than what was outlined in the Nicolay-Hay history. But the authors were using an old rhetorical device to bolster their hero: the bigger the crisis Buchanan appears to have left behind, the greater the achievements of Lincoln by comparison. Lincoln himself never publicly blamed his woes on Buchanan, though Lincoln may have expressed some frustrations to Nicolay privately, especially during the transition period between his election and inauguration.

Unlike Lincoln, Buchanan had come to the presidency with an impressive résumé of public service as congressman, senator, and diplomat to the Court of St. James. His political inclinations throughout his career were pro–state's rights, proslavery and pro-Southern in the Jacksonian tradition. Like Lincoln during the first month of his administration, the lame duck Buchanan was horrified about pushing the nation over the precipice into civil war. Nonetheless, Buchanan was indicted for cowardice: "The sanctity of the Constitution, the majesty of the law, the power of the nation, the patriotism of the people, all faded from his bewildered vision; his irresolute will shrank from his declared purpose to protect the public property and enforce the revenue laws. He saw only the picture of strife and bloodshed which the glib tongues of his persecutors conjured up, and failed to detect the theatric purpose for which it was employed."[34]

The savage treatment of Buchanan was unrelenting. Again referring to the lengthy transition period, "the most serious ignorance was in respect to the character and fidelity of the high officers of the Government. Of the timidity of Mr. Buchanan, of the treachery of three members of the Cabinet, of the exclusion of General Scott from military councils, of the president's refusal to send troops to [Major] Anderson [at Fort Sumter] . . . the people at large knew nothing, or so little that they could put no intelligent construction upon the events."[35] In short, Buchanan had "reasoned the executive power into nothingness,"[36] having "consented to this certain process of national suicide."[37]

Democrats were not the only prominent individuals to receive the rhetorical ire of Nicolay and Hay. Republican politicians and Union generals also failed their hero. The depth of the criticism was dependent on the authors' view of the roadblocks these individuals or groups were perceived to have placed against the implementation of the Lincoln agenda. Consequently, Northerners were more often the targets for censure than Confederates.

Receiving particular condemnation were members of Lincoln's cabinet. Called by historian Doris Kearns Goodwin "a team of rivals," the cabinet was also a team of egos. Four of the original cabinet members had been candidates for the Republican presidential nomination in 1860: Seward, Cameron, Chase, and Edward Bates. Salmon P. Chase, the treasury secretary, harbored ambitions of replacing Lincoln in 1864. Addressing Lincoln's ability to handle conflicting personality types, the authors wrote: "Mr. Lincoln possessed a quick intuition of human nature and of the strength or weakness of individual character. His whole life had been a practical study of the details and rivalries of local partisanship. He was, moreover, endowed in yet unsuspected measure with a comprehensive grasp of great causes and results in national politics."[38]

In the history, Edward Bates as attorney general received the least criticism, but of the four, he had the least to do with the conduct of the war. Seward came to the cabinet thinking that he would be the political power, ruling through Lincoln. Learning of Secretary of State Seward's desire to negotiate privately with Southern sympathizers and to make decisions regarding the reinforcement or surrender of Fort Sumter, Lincoln firmly but tactfully reminded the secretary that he (Lincoln) was in charge.[39] It was a point, the authors noted, that the president made time and again: "With a higher conception of the functions of the Presidential office, Mr. Lincoln treated public clamor and the fretfulness of Cabinet alike, with quiet toleration. Again, as before, and as ever afterward, he listened attentively to such advice as his Cabinet had to give, but reserved the decision for himself."[40]

Over time, Seward came to have great respect for the president, but the feuds among the egos in the cabinet continued throughout the war. Seward and Treasury Secretary Chase both threatened to resign when disagreements between the two men came to a boiling point in 1864. Lincoln was compelled to meet with both men to resolve the dispute: "he [Lincoln] made himself absolute master of the situation; by treating the resignations and the return to the Cabinet of both ministers as one and the same transaction he saved for the nation the invaluable services of both, and preserved his own position of entire impartiality between the two wings of the Union party."[41]

Overall, the portrait of Seward comes out fairly well. However, critical remarks were made about the secretary's positive attitudes at times when the authors believed Seward had no reason to be optimistic. Referring to a cabinet meeting on the day after the ironclad *Merrimack* had roared out into Hampton Roads and began shattering the Union's wooden fleet, "the hasty meeting of the Cabinet [March 9, 1862] and other officials who gathered at the White House was perhaps the most excited and impressive of the whole war. Stanton, unable to control his strong emotion, walked up and down the room like a caged lion. McClellan was dumbfounded and silent. Lincoln was, as usual in trying moments, composed but eagerly inquisitive, critical, critically scanning the dispatches, interrogating the officers, joining scrap to scrap of information, applying his searching analysis and clear logic to read the danger and find the remedy; Chase impatient and ready to utter blame; Seward and [Navy Secretary Gideon] Welles yet without encouraging reasons to justify their hope."[42] In fact, Seward's and Welles's optimism was justified, since the previous evening John Ericson's engineering marvel, the *Monitor*, with its revolving turret, arrived to challenge successfully the *Merrimack* even as the cabinet was meeting.

Lincoln's patience was legendary even in his own time, though it was sometimes interpreted as weakness and vacillation. Nicolay and Hay never interpreted it as such. They always portrayed Lincoln as ever calm, wise, and tolerant of other's foibles. But tolerance had its limits, and those limits were reached with Simon Cameron, Lincoln's first secretary of war. Nicolay and Hay went fairly easy on Cameron's ineptitude in office. Lincoln removed him from the cabinet in early 1862 and sent him to Russia as ambassador to the court of Czar Alexander II. Cameron was the last survivor of the Lincoln cabinet, dying in 1889 at the age of ninety. Consequently, he was alive during the time the chapters on the first year of the Lincoln administration were being composed. Ever mindful of the defamation laws, Nicolay and Hay moved gingerly around the secretary's service.

Adding to his managerial failures, Cameron placed the Lincoln administration in a political crisis when he publicly proposed to arm and prepare African Americans for military service in his December 1861 annual report. Except for Radical Republicans, this proposal shocked the country and put Lincoln into a crisis-control mode, especially with regard to his sensitive relations with the loyal Border States. Like other preemptive moves toward emancipation, Lincoln could not have received this proposal with patient equanimity, but that is exactly how his reaction is described: "Lincoln's uniform good-nature and considerate forbearance, however, enabled him to endure and manage the incident without a quarrel, or even the least manifestation of ill-will on either side. Having corrected his minister's haste and imprudence, the President indulged in no further comment, and Cameron, yielding to superior authority, received the implied rebuke with becoming grace."[43]

While Cameron's incompetence could be brushed aside in the 1880s, the House of Representatives in 1862 was less tolerant. The House, controlled by his own party, voted to censure Cameron for policies "highly injurious to the public service."[44] Lincoln went to Cameron's defense, but the House stood firm in its decision.

One cabinet member who came in for particular evisceration was Treasury Secretary Salmon P. Chase. Throughout Lincoln's first term, Chase continued to nurture presidential ambitions for 1864, hoping to replace Lincoln as the Republican nominee. Philosophically, he was aligned with the more radical wing of the party. His supporters may have been some of the same Radical Republicans who nominated John C. Frémont on a splinter ticket in June 1864 at a convention in Cleveland.

Although the authors recognized Chase's ability at work in the Treasury Department, the secretary was otherwise dealt with mercilessly. Hay once wrote Nicolay that "Chase is going to be a nut to crack."[45] This was not meant to indicate that they did not know what to write; rather, Hay was wrestling with how to convey a hint of impartiality in their portrayal of the treasury secretary. In part, this may have been because Chase's diaries and papers were already available to them, since the secretary had died in 1873. These documents revealed the full extent of his vitriolic animosity towards Lincoln. The former treasury secretary is portrayed as self-seeking, narcissistic, and delusional.

While the authors were still at work on the magazine serial version, Hay wrote Gilder that their treatment of Chase "will give some offense to his special friends." Nonetheless, Hay insisted that the chapter on Chase, entitled "Financial Measures," was in fact laudatory. Yet, the authors did not want that particular chapter to be part of the serialization of the book, unless the editor wanted it. If so, the authors would allow its publication in the magazine. Regarding the overall treatment of Chase, "we shall be hammered black and blue," Hay conceded. A favorable chapter on Chase published in the *Century Magazine* would be "a shade more or less of color," Hay wrote, and "will make no difference."[46]

Lincoln's forbearing and forgiving demeanor, and ultimate act of selfless graciousness in appointing Chase as chief justice of the Supreme Court, was cause for wonder by the former secretaries. Speaking of Chase's flirtation with running for president, Nicolay and Hay wrote:

> in the higher circles of the Administration there was only one man so short-sighted as not to perceive the expediency of the President's renomination and the impossibility of preventing it. Mr. Chase alone had the indiscretion to encourage the overtures of the malcontents, and the folly to imagine that he could lead them to success. Pure and disinterested as he was, and devoted with all his energies and powers to the cause of the country, he was always singularly ignorant of the current public thought and absolutely incapable of judging men in their true relations.... He regarded himself as the friend of Mr. Lincoln; to him and to others he made strong protestations of friendly feeling, which he undoubtedly thought were sincere; but he held so poor an opinion of the President's intellect and character in comparison with his own, that he could not believe the people so blind as deliberately to prefer the President to himself.[47]

"Short-sighted," indiscreet, "singularly ignorant" of public opinion, and "absolutely incapable of judging men" should have been sufficient to smear the character of the now-deceased Chase, but the authors were only warming to the task before them: "There was never a man who found it so easy to delude himself. He believed that he was indifferent to advancement and anxious only for the public good; yet in the midst of his enormous labors he found time to write letters to every part of the country, all protesting his indifference to the Presidency but indicating his willingness to accept it, and painting pictures so dark of the chaotic state of affairs in the Government that the irresistible inference was that only he [Chase] could save the country."[48]

Chase had experienced a successful political career as a U.S. senator and governor. Like many successful politicians before and since, including Lincoln, he needed to have an elevated sense of self to run for high office. Like most men, he wanted to be admired. Yet this natural inclination turned into self-delusion:

"He could not bring himself to feel that the universal demonstrations in favor of the re-election of Mr. Lincoln were genuine. He regarded himself all the while as the serious candidate, and the opposition to him as knavish and insincere."[49]

Yet throughout the ten volumes, Nicolay and Hay frequently describe, mostly without using the precise words, Lincoln's opponents (and by extension theirs) as knaves and hypocrites. It is clear from the pages of the history that they did not perceive themselves as similarly delusional in their opinions of some of their foes. Declaring Chase inept at sizing up other people, they noted: "He was not a good judge of character; he gave his confidence freely to any one who came flattering him and criticizing the President; and after having given it, it was almost impossible to make him believe that the man who talked so judiciously could be a knave."[50]

Chase withdrew his not-so-secret candidacy in early 1864, but Nicolay and Hay were not done with their *bête noire* who dared to challenge their hero. Using the letters he wrote after withdrawing his candidacy, they exposed his character flaws even further: "In numerous letters written during the spring [of 1864] he reiterated his absolute withdrawal from the contest, but indulged in sneers and insinuations against the President which show how deeply he was wounded by his discomfiture."[51]

Chase's disappointment was described as being so deep that he constructed a conspiracy involving the alleged machinations of the conservative postmaster general, Montgomery Blair, and his father and brother: "There was something almost comic in the sudden collapse of his candidacy.... His wounded self-love could find no balm ... except in the preposterous fiction which he constructed for himself that, through 'the systematic operation of the Postmaster-General and those holding office under him a preference for the re-election of Mr. Lincoln was created.' Absurd as this fancy was, he appears firmly to have believed it; and the Blairs, whom he never liked, now appeared to him in the light of powerful enemies."[52]

Lincoln may have been a fountain of magnanimity and forbearance, but the authors demonstrated neither. The attack on Chase continued unabated as he again suffered in comparison to the president: "Although his [Lincoln's] renomination was a matter in regard to which he refused to converse much, even with intimate friends, he was perfectly aware of the drift of things. In capacity of appreciating popular currents and in judgment of individual character Mr. Chase was as a child beside him; and he allowed the opposition to himself in his own

Cabinet to continue, without question or remark, with all the more patience and forbearance because he knew how feeble it was."[53]

When unexpectedly (from Chase's viewpoint) accepting the treasury secretary's resignation on June 30, 1864, Lincoln wrote: "Of all I have said in commendation of your ability and fidelity I have nothing to unsay, and yet you and I have reached a point of mutual embarrassment in our official relation which it seems can not be overcome or longer sustained consistently with the public service."[54] When Supreme Court Chief Justice Roger Taney died on October 12, 1864, after twenty-nine years on the court, Lincoln had a critical appointment to fill. Keeping his choice to himself, he forwarded Chase's name for confirmation to the Senate on December 6, 1864. He was confirmed on the same day. Curiously, Lincoln did not bother to inform Chase of his appointment, who learned about it from his daughter.[55] Lincoln still had not forgiven Chase. Yet, Nicolay and Hay concluded: "Although his appointment had not accomplished all the good which Mr. Lincoln hoped for when he made it, it cannot be called a mistake. Mr. Chase had deserved well of the republic. He was entitled to any reward the republic could grant him; and the President, in giving to his most powerful and most distinguished rival the greatest place which a President ever has it in his power to bestow, gave an exemplary proof of the magnanimity and generosity of his own spirit."[56]

Lincoln's motives for appointing Chase to the court were entirely ignored by Nicolay and Hay. Although holding no office, Chase remained a significant voice among the Radical Republicans. Out of office, he could prove to be as troublesome as he had been in the cabinet. Lincoln's appointment of Chase to the court was intended to achieve two things: remove Chase from any future meddling in politics and placate the Radical Republicans whose votes Lincoln would need in Congress for his reconstruction program. This was not the only time Lincoln had used his appointment power to sideline someone. Two earlier examples had involved the good Dr. Canisius and Simon Cameron. Throughout his whole life, Nicolay could never grasp, much less acknowledge, this political strategy.

Nicolay and Hay tried to soften their brutal portraiture of Chase, but it was too little, too late. At one point, they did refer to Chase as "this able, honest, pure, and otherwise sagacious man."[57] But no one reading the history would be fooled into thinking that Nicolay or Hay had any positive views toward the treasury secretary. They considered the man a traitor to Lincoln's cause.

There were also some choice words for another Republican presidential candidate, John C. Frémont, popularly known as the "Pathfinder." The erratic Frémont was the nominee of a group of Radical Republicans who had met at Cleveland in June 1864. A greater threat to Lincoln's reelection than Chase's abortive campaign within the party, this rump group had the potential of siphoning off critical votes from Lincoln in the general election. However, by 1864, the public was wary of Frémont. Appointed by Lincoln as military commander of Missouri, he issued a proclamation in August 1861 freeing the slaves of that state. When Lincoln, the commander-in-chief, ordered him to rescind the proclamation, Frémont refused. Lincoln removed him for his insubordination. Frémont's wife, Jessie Benton Frémont, wrote a book entitled *The Story of the Guard* in defense of her husband. But the public was no longer infatuated with the Frémonts, having seen this play before when Frémont had been convicted for insubordination relating to his activities in California. Finding little public enthusiasm for him, Frémont's supporters asked him to step aside in hopes of finding a stronger candidate. True to form, he initially refused. Nicolay and Hay wrote:

> Later in the summer some of the partisans of Frémont, seeing that there was pos-itively no response in the country to his candidacy, wrote to him suggesting that the candidates nominated at Cleveland and Baltimore should both withdraw, and leave the field entirely free for a united effort for 'a new convention which should represent the patriotism of all parties.' . . . General Frémont with unbroken dignity refused to accede to this proposition. . . . But a month later [September 17, 1864] . . . he then wrote to his committee, withdrawing his name from the list of candidates. He could not, however, withhold a parting demonstration against the President. . . . "I continue to hold exactly the same sentiments contained in my letter of acceptance. I consider that his [Lincoln's] Administration has been politically, militarily, and financially a failure, and that its necessary continuance is a cause of regret for the country." . . . General Frémont at last subsided into silence.[58]

Nicolay and Hay also had critical remarks about the 1864 Democratic nominee for president, General George B. McClellan. Ironically, the Democrats nomi-nated a general to run on a peace platform. Upon accepting the nomination, the general repudiated the platform he was nominated to carry through.[59] But his candidacy was doomed within days of his nomination when Atlanta finally fell to the Union Army. In fact, Nicolay and Hay spent an inordinate amount of time on the 1864 election, in which Lincoln carried all but three states and won 55 percent of the popular vote.

George B. McClellan received extensive notice. He was castigated for his slowness to action and his disrespect for the president. He was a conservative Democrat who, although he wanted to preserve the Union, at the same time tried to do as little damage to his army and the South while conquering it. "Little Mac," as McClellan was known by his troops, could organize and motivate an army but did not, or could not, use it effectively. He was such a particular target of criticism that Hay openly questioned whether they had gone too far. In a letter to Nicolay, Hay discussed his treatment of Little Mac. Hay hoped that he had achieved his furtive literary objective. "I have toiled and labored through ten chapters of him (McC.)," wrote Hay. "I think I have left the impression of his mutinous imbecility," he continued, "and I have done it in a perfectly courteous manner. . . . It is of the utmost moment that we should *seem* to be fair to him, while we are destroying him."[60] This last sentence sums up the authors' attitude to Little Mac. It was important to have the appearance, if not the substance, of editorial balance. This passage offers an important insight into the composition of the history. Neither man acted as an effective restraint on the other's emotions; they tempered their narrative only to "*seem* fair" to those they viewed as opponents to their hero.

Nonetheless, Nicolay and Hay wrote a description of the general that still resonates with many modern historians:

> Struggling with a command and a responsibility too heavy for him, he [McClellan] had fallen into a state of mind in which prompt and energetic action was impossible. His double illusion of an overpowering force of the enemy in his front, and of a Government at Washington that desired the destruction of his army, was always present with him, paralyzing all his plans and actions. In his private correspondence he speaks of Washington as that "sink of iniquity"; of the people in authority as "those treacherous hounds"; of the predicament he is in, "the rebels on one side and the Abolitionists and other scoundrels on the other." "I feel," he says, "that the fate of a nation depends upon me, and I feel that I have not one single friend at the seat of Government"—this at a moment when the Government was straining every nerve to support him.[61]

McClellan was not entirely responsible for the "illusion of an overpowering force of the enemy in his front." The source for much of the general's exaggerated estimate of enemy strength came from the noted detective Allan Pinkerton, who used an untested mathematical model to estimate the size of the enemy forces that inflated the enemy's numbers. Consequently, the always cautious McClellan was confronted with inaccurate data from a supposedly authoritative source.

McClellan's greatest achievement was the tactical draw with Lee at the Battle of Antietam on September 17, 1862, in western Maryland. Since Lee had re-crossed the Potomac and returned to Virginia after the battle, it was viewed as a great Northern victory. As a result, Lincoln felt empowered to issue the Preliminary Emancipation Proclamation on September 22. However, McClellan's failure to pursue Lee and destroy the Army of Northern Virginia and end the war was a source of deep frustration for Lincoln, as recorded in the history:

> If McClellan, after Antietam, had destroyed the army of Lee his official position would have been impregnable. If, after Lee had recrossed the Potomac, McClellan had followed and delivered a successful battle in Virginia, nothing could afterwards have prevented his standing as the foremost man of his time. The President, in his intense anxiety for the success of the national arms, would have welcomed McClellan as his own presumptive successor if he could have won that position by successful battle. But the general's inexplicable slowness had at last excited the President's distrust. He began to think, before the end of October, that McClellan had no real desire to defeat the enemy. He set in his own mind the limit of his forbearance. . . . If he [McClellan] should permit Lee to cross the Blue Ridge and place himself between Richmond and the Army of the Potomac he would remove him from command.[62]

Lincoln replaced McClellan following the 1862 midterm elections. His failure to pursue Lee after Antietam, was, in Lincoln's mind, later matched by Meade's failure to pursue a battered Lee after Gettysburg. When Lincoln, the authors wrote,

> heard of Lee's escape [back into Virginia] he suffered one of the deepest and bitterest disappointments of the war. "We had them within our grasp," he said; "we had only to stretch forth our hand and they were ours, and nothing I could say or do could make the army move." He had been most unfavorably impressed by a phrase in Meade's general order after the victory in which he spoke of "driving the invader from our soil." He said upon reading it, "This is a dreadful reminiscence of McClellan; it is the same spirit that moved him to claim a great victory because Pennsylvania and Maryland were safe. Will our generals never get that idea out of their heads? The whole country is our soil." He regretted that he had not gone to the army and personally issued the order to attack.[63]

Fortunately, Lincoln did not risk going to the battle. Instead, he wrote a letter to himself: "While the President's disappointment and irritation were at their keenest, he wrote a letter to General Meade which he never signed or sent. It was not an unusual proceeding with him to put upon paper in this way his expressions of dissatisfaction and then to lay them away, rather than wound a deserving public servant by even merited censure."[64] It is debatable whether Meade "merited censure." Military historians and biographers of Meade have long argued about whether Meade's decision not to follow up his victory with a hot pursuit of Lee was the right one. Though Lee had been decisively beaten, the Union army had also been severely battered, and the Army of the Potomac, in Meade's opinion, may not have been ready to fight another battle immediately.

The depiction of Little Mac also recalled his personal disrespect of the president. A very uncharacteristic hint of criticism of Lincoln crept into the narrative but was made into a virtue when discussing Lincoln's personal relationship with the general: "Mr. Lincoln certainly had the defects of his great qualities. His unbounded magnanimity made him sometimes incapable even of just resentments. General McClellan's worst offenses had been committed against the president in person. The insulting dispatch from Savage's Station and the letter from Harrison's Landing, in which he took the president to task for the whole course of his civil and military administration, would probably have been pardoned by no other ruler that ever lived; yet Mr. Lincoln never appeared to bear the slightest ill-will to the general on account of these affronts."[65] By making Lincoln's one defect the result of his "unbounded magnanimity," the authors bolstered their view of Lincoln, with his limitless forbearance, as the greatest ruler that ever lived.

The controversies that swirled around McClellan's leadership died down during the postwar years. He died while the history was being composed. It was perhaps in the national glow that follows an important figure's passing that he was transformed from the traitor some perceived him to be (including, most likely, the authors) into a person of large ego and limited capacity thrust beyond the limits of his abilities. But as with the faint praise they gave Chase for his service to the nation, Nicolay and Hay nonetheless wielded the rhetorical knife while writing a kind word about McClellan:

Now that the fierce passions of the war, its suspicions and animosities, have passed away, we are able to judge him [McClellan] more accurately and more justly than was possible amid that moral and material tumult and confusion. He was as far from being the traitor and craven that many thought him as from being the martyr and hero that others would like to have him appear. It would be unfair to deny that he rendered, to the full measure of his capacity, sincere and honest service to the republic. . . . It was in this native inability to use great means to great ends that his failure as a general lay. It was in his temperament to exaggerate the obstacles in front of him, and this, added to his constitutional aversion to prompt decisions, caused those endless delays which wasted the army, exasperated the country, and gave the enemy unbroken leisure for maturing his plans, and constant opportunity for executing them.[66]

McClellan and Meade were not the only Union generals to receive criticism. Several other important military leaders came under critical scrutiny. Halleck and Hooker are criticized for not getting along, Burnside for his failure to support Rosecrans in Tennessee in the early fall of 1863. Lincoln, the man who went off to the Black Hawk War as a captain and returned as a private, did develop into a very competent military strategist but standing in a war room and pointing fingers at a map is not the same as being on the ground before the enemy. Lincoln's assertion after Gettysburg that "we had had them within our grasp, we had only to stretch forth our hand and they were ours," underscores his frustration and not the military reality with which the seasoned Meade may have been dealing on the ground.

Three Union generals who waged war in the pages of the history managed to emerge with few blemishes. Although the authors were quick to find fault, apparently General Philip Sheridan could do no wrong. The fact that Sheridan was commander of the army through much of the 1880s until his death in 1888 may have influenced their assessment. This praise, in the next-to-last chapter of the history, may have been written around the time of Sheridan's death: "unpretending in manner, but quick to exert all proper authority; absolutely at home in the saddle and seemingly incapable of fatigue; an eye for topography as keen and far-reaching as an eagle's; and that gift for inspiring immediate confidence in all around him which is the most inestimable of all possessions for a soldier. . . . he was as cool as he was courageous, as wise in planning as he was energetic in executing. . . . There was no luck in the splendid series of victories that attended his career in the [Shenandoah] Valley; they were all made in advance and honestly earned."[67]

Nicolay and Hay discussed General William Tecumseh Sherman in numerous passages. Much of their reporting of Sherman's activities is matter-of-fact, with praise served up in ample portions, while criticism is absent. The authors defended

Sherman against charges by "unfriendly newspapers" that Sherman was insane, leading to his removal from command in Kentucky, as "altogether incorrect." Rather, Sherman had asked to be relieved due to his perceived inability to carry out his duties at that time with the very inadequate resources given him.[68] At Chattanooga, Sherman "obeyed his orders with the utmost gallantry and no lack of skill . . . .[69] When moving against Johnston's army in Georgia in April, 1864 in a prelude to the Atlanta campaign, "Sherman, with his usual restless energy, lost not a moment's time . . . ."[70] The authors pointed out that the orders given by Sherman in the Atlanta campaign demonstrated "how minute was the attention he gave to all the details of operations under his charge . . . ."[71] And, when he and his troops captured Atlanta, "Ungrudging honors were paid by the Government to Sherman and his troops for this magnificent achievement . . . ."[72] As Sherman marched through Georgia to the sea, "His army consisted . . . of sixty thousand men, the most perfect in strength, health, and intelligence that ever went to war." Along the way, Sherman's "special field orders are a model of clearness and conciseness."[73] After taking Savannah and heading north to capture Columbia, South Carolina, "Sherman did everything in his power to relieve the houseless and destitute people; he provided shelter for many, gave five hundred beef cattle to the mayor, and took measures to maintain public order after the army should be gone."[74]

In addition to his military prowess, Sherman provided Nicolay and Hay with validation of their praise for Lincoln's top general, Ulysses S. Grant. Sherman lost no time in acknowledging that the plan for the Vicksburg campaign was Grant's, and Grant's alone.[75] Grant was praised regarding his plans to take Chattanooga, where Sherman observed that "all things had been prearranged with a foresight that elicited my admiration."[76] When Grant was promoted to general-in-chief, he wrote to Sherman expressing his indebtedness to Sherman "for whatever I have had of success." Sherman responded that Grant did himself an "injustice" and gave Sherman and others "too much honor in assigning to us so large a share of the merits which have led to your high advancement."[77] Sherman reached the zenith of his praise for Grant as he wrote, "I believe you are as brave, patriotic, and just as the great prototype Washington; as unselfish, kindhearted, and honest as a man should be; but the chief characteristic in your nature is the simple faith in success you have always manifested, which I can liken to nothing else than the faith a Christian has in his Saviour."[78]

As lavish as Sherman's praise was for Grant, Nicolay and Hay then concluded their comments about Sherman by quoting his praise of Lincoln, given shortly after the commander-in-chief's assassination: "Of all the men I ever met, he [Lincoln] seemed to possess more of the elements of greatness, combined with goodness, than any other."[79] The authors also noted that Sherman "repeatedly expressed his admiration and surprise with which he has read Mr. Lincoln's correspondence with his generals and his [Sherman's] opinion of the remarkable correctness of his [Lincoln's] military views."[80]

The other great commander in Nicolay and Hay's estimation was Ulysses S. Grant. Lincoln and Grant were very likeminded in their approach to the war. In particular, Lincoln appreciated Grant because, unlike some of his other generals, "he fights." Grant received complimentary notice since the president and his field commander both saw Lee and the destruction of the Army of Northern Virginia as the real target leading to final victory: "the President, although refraining from any suggestion to General Grant, felt that beginning a siege of Richmond with Lee's army wholly intact and free to move in any direction was thoroughly undesirable. . . . The main consideration in the mind of Grant, and in this he was sustained by the best minds in the Army of the Potomac, was that the war could not be brought to a close until the power of Lee's army was broken; that without this even the capture of Richmond would not avail."[81]

Lincoln had expressed similar sentiments about Lee's army to General Halleck in September 1863, which makes it unlikely that the president refrained "from any suggestions to General Grant" regarding his thoughts on the conduct of the forthcoming campaign: "I have constantly desired the Army of the Potomac to make Lee's army, and not Richmond, its objective point. If our army cannot fall upon the enemy and hurt him where he is, it is plain to me it can gain nothing by attempting to follow him over a succession of intrenched lines into a fortified city."[82]

On April 30, 1864, days before the bloody Overland campaign opened with the Battle of the Wilderness, Lincoln wrote to Grant expressing his full confidence: "Not expecting to see you again before the spring campaign opens, I wish to express in this way my entire satisfaction with what you have done up to this time, so far as I understand it. The particulars of your plan I neither know nor seek to know. You are vigilant and self-reliant; and, pleased with this, I wish not to obtrude any constraints or restraints upon you. While I am very anxious that any great disaster or capture of our men in great numbers shall be avoided, I know these points are less likely to escape your attention than they would be mine. If there is anything wanting which is in my power to give, do not fail to let me know."[83]

Lincoln's confidence in Grant was reflected in the positive treatment of the general throughout the history. In sharp contrast to the work's treatment of McClellan, Grant is praised for his effective command: "in command of all was Grant . . . the most extraordinary military temperament this country has ever seen. . . . [I]n this tremendous war he accomplished more with the means given him than any other two on either side. . . . The popular instinct which hails him as our greatest general is correct."[84] Unlike McClellan, who Lincoln once famously said had the "slows" and whose Army of the Potomac he wished to borrow so that he could use it to fight the war, Grant posed no such difficulties for Lincoln. Grant was always on the move: "through him something was always accomplished. There was absence of excuse, complaint, or delay; always the report of a task performed. If his means or supplies were imperfect, he found or improvised the best substitute; if he could not execute the full requirement, he performed so much of it as was possible. He always had an opinion, and that opinion was positive, intelligible, practical."[85]

But Nicolay and Hay were not reticent about mentioning an ugly incident in Grant's career that brought the censure of Lincoln, making the president appear magnanimous in the process: "Lincoln had a profound respect for every form of sincere religious belief. He steadily refused to show favor to any particular denomination of Christians; and when General Grant issued an unjust and injurious order against the Jews expelling them from his department, the president ordered it to be revoked the moment it was brought to his notice."[86] Yet Grant no doubt greatly endeared himself to Nicolay and Hay for the general's praise of Lincoln. Grant wrote that "Lincoln impressed him as the greatest intellectual force with which he had ever come in contact."[87]

Regarding Confederate leaders, political and military, it is almost as though the authors tried to limit their remarks to a reporting of the facts, with few positive or negative comments. However, they did have some criticism of Robert E. Lee and Jefferson Davis. They compared Lee to another Virginian, General Winfield Scott, who remained loyal to the Union. They criticized Lee for accepting command of the Virginia military forces while still an officer of the United States Army "with all his military obligations to the United States intact and uncanceled." In their opinion, Lee was "thus rendering himself guilty of desertion and treason."[88] Nicolay and Hay continued:

In instructive contrast with the weakness and defects of [Robert E.] Lee, we have the honorable conduct and example of General [Winfield] Scott. He, too, was a Virginian who loved his native State. He, too, was opposed to secession and deprecated war. He, too, as officer, commander, diplomatist, and statesman, had learned from books and from men the principles and practice of loyalty, and perhaps better than any American exemplar was competent to interpret a soldier's oath, a soldier's duty, a soldier's honor. . . . . But underneath pride of home, affection of kindred, and horror of war, on the solid substratum of consistency and character, lay his recognition of the principle of government, his real, not simulated, veneration for the Constitution, his acceptance of the binding force of law, his unswerving fidelity to his oath, his undying devotion to his flag.[89]

While they said some positive things about Lee, those comments were overwhelmed by the authors' view of Lee's fundamental hypocrisy. "Gilder was evidently horrified at your saying that Lee ought to be shot," Hay wrote Nicolay in an August 10, 1885, letter. While Nicolay had addressed the issue with his usual frankness, the more diplomatic Hay agreed that Lee's execution would be "a simple truth of law and equity."[90] The venom poured on Lee may very well have reflected Nicolay and Hay's disgust that as part of the Lost Cause myth and the desire for national reconciliation, Lee was not only becoming an established figure in Southern mythology but also a member of the pantheon of national military heroes, where he remains today.

Jefferson Davis was treated with even less respect. The longest passage in which he is the central character has to do with his flight from Richmond and his capture by Union forces in Georgia the following month.[91] Refusing to recognize the Confederate government as a legitimate entity, the authors never referred to Jefferson Davis as "President Davis" but usually as "Mr. Davis." In assessing Davis's ability as commander-in-chief, Nicolay and Hay concluded: "Mr. Davis had always great confidence in his own military ability and viewed his own plans with a complacency which was not disturbed by their continual failure."[92] Placing the blame for the ruination of the South on Davis, the authors mocked his dedication to the Confederate cause: "With the ruin and defeat of the Confederate cause staring him full in the face Davis could bring himself neither to a dignified refusal nor to a resigned acceptance of the form of negotiation as Mr. Lincoln had tendered it. Even in the gulf of war and destitution into which he had led his people he could not forego the vanity of masquerading as a champion."[93]

It is some of the things that Nicolay and Hay did not reveal that frustrate historians the most. For instance, they might have revealed, however selectively, the content of some of those nocturnal conversations with Lincoln in their bedroom or the subjects of those Sunday afternoon discussions in the White House.

Perhaps they could have given history greater insights into some of the political calculations that formed the core of Lincoln's decisions. These two men had a ringside seat to history but chose not to use their vantage point fully.

In retrospect, one may wish that Nicolay and Hay had been more balanced in their assessments. Unfortunately, their intent was not to write a balanced portrayal of Lincoln and the men around him. Instead, *Abraham Lincoln: A History* is what Robert Lincoln, John George Nicolay, and John Hay wanted: the apotheosis of Abraham Lincoln. Yet, with all its faults, it is recognized as a masterpiece of research and writing, utilizing many original sources, verified by diligent documentation, done as a labor of filial love, which successive generations of historians and Lincoln admirers have read and cited with appreciation.

With the few exceptions of biographies like that produced by William Herndon, Lincoln had been mythologized as the martyred president for a quarter century before the publication of the history. Nicolay and Hay gave a scholarly imprimatur to this image of Lincoln as martyr and demigod. Anticipating opposition to their writing, they responded in a rare, jointly signed letter written to R. W. Gilder in late 1888. "We expect to be contradicted by every dead beat," they asserted, "with a bad memory between the two oceans."[94]

Abraham Lincoln: A History has withstood the test of time. Every true Lincoln scholar consults its pages and absorbs its message of the greatness of the sixteenth president. It is difficult, even today, to find scholarship that is a truly balanced, truly critical study of Lincoln because we have never put aside the image of Lincoln as demigod, nor in our heart of hearts do we really want to. That is the legacy Nicolay and Hay, but especially Nicolay, bequeathed to us, etched on those pages.

CHAPTER TWELVE

Assessing the Man in Lincoln's Shadow
Full Measure of Devotion

John George Nicolay, like all of us, was a complicated and sometimes contradictory human being. He was also a man of his time, and to some degree, our time as well. Although he never sought the spotlight, he played a vital role in the Lincoln administration and in the telling of the Lincoln story after the president's death.

On June 24, 1925, a monument was unveiled in front of the Pike County Courthouse in Pittsfield, Illinois, remaining there to this day. It reads: "Commemorating Abraham Lincoln and Stephen A. Douglas, who practiced at the Pike County Bar in early days and who spoke in this park in the senatorial campaign of 1858; John Hay, author of the Pike County Ballads, Diplomat, and Secretary of State 1898–1905, who received his academic education here; and John G. Nicolay, Private Secretary to President Lincoln, who edited the Whig Free Press published here prior to the Civil War."

This monument is the first of only two known memorials to recognize Nicolay. Both monuments are in the Courthouse Park in Pittsfield, Illinois. Of the four men mentioned in the 1925 monument, two of them, Lincoln and Douglas, never lived in Pike County, much less Pittsfield, although both frequently stopped there while making their judicial and political circuits. Hay stayed in Pittsfield for a short time before moving to another preparatory school in Springfield and then on to Brown University. He did not have any lasting ties to the town on the prairie except perhaps with regard to the characters in his *Pike County Ballads*, drawn from the local population.

That cannot be said of the boy who arrived in Pike County with his family around 1842 and spent approximately sixteen years in the area before moving on to Springfield and then Washington. Unlike Lincoln, Douglas, or Hay, he had lifelong ties to the town. First and foremost, his beloved Therena remained behind in Pittsfield until their marriage in 1865. After their wedding, he then had ties to her parents and her brothers, Dorus and Daniel, who remained in the town. There were also Nicolay relatives: Frederick Lewis, the brother who had dismissed John George from the family business, died in Pike County in 1872, and is buried in nearby Green Pond Cemetery with a millstone from the family mill as his grave marker.[1] Another Nicolay relative, a great-great-nephew named Kenneth Sowers, helped unveil the 1925 monument, though it is uncertain what his connection to Pittsfield and Pike County might have been.[2]

Pittsfield had a profound impact on Nicolay's life. It was here that he found stability in his life and a career in journalism. Whatever official or unofficial role Nicolay was to play throughout the rest of his life, he was, at heart, a reporter. As a successful journalist, and he was always that, he developed indispensable qualities that would serve him throughout his life and make him a valued asset to the president he served so well. He knew how to observe, size up individuals, listen, be unobtrusive (almost invisible when necessary), and report in concise detail what he had seen, heard, and evaluated.

Nicolay's strengths are reflected on the pages of *Abraham Lincoln: A History*. While there are flourishes of literary talent, each chapter is basically an extended, freestanding newspaper article: here are the facts as I see them. Yet, there are times when his journalistic obsession with detail not only gets in the way of the story but also makes for tedious reading. The one-volume condensation of the history, *A Short Life of Abraham Lincoln*, did not improve matters stylistically, although the pages are far fewer in number. Throughout his life, he was fixated on details but often could not grasp how these details fit into a larger picture. As the president's private secretary, his task was to gather detailed information and report back to Lincoln. Then Lincoln, using his keen insights into human nature and his analytic ability, would fit these discrete pieces of information together to construct a broader mosaic of events. This is but one example of how these two men, very different in many ways, complemented each other.

Nicolay's ability to focus on details, organize, manage time, and prioritize work were talents Lincoln did not possess but were essential for a smooth-running administration. Imagine what it must have been like for Abraham Lincoln to function with a support staff of three compared to the myriad who support White House operations in our day. Then consider that any citizen was permitted to walk into the White House, present his or her card, and be granted access to the president if he were available, because that was the way it had always been. And then, in the case of Lincoln, he was expected to be a fully functional commander-in-chief in a brutal civil war, overseeing its military and political aspects in a theater of military engagement spanning an area greater than the size of Western Europe. Finally, there was the emotionally erratic First Lady, who from time to time injected herself into the daily routines of the office or fomented a crisis that either the staff, in the case of her dinner invitation lists, or the president himself, in the matter of her egregious spending habits, were required to resolve, thus diverting their attention from the urgent business at hand. Neither Lincoln nor anyone else could have managed this workload alone.

Nicolay and his staff performed extremely well under these conditions. With only two others to assist him, he performed the modern-day functions of White House chief of staff, legal counsel, appointments secretary, social secretary, messenger, and companion to the president. As the chief of staff, he deserves particular credit. His achievement in providing Lincoln with the necessary administrative support to prosecute the war successfully was in reality a more significant contribution to the nation and the president's legacy than even his later work promoting the Lincoln image. Nicolay, like any modern chief of staff, recognized that access to the president had to be limited if anything was to get done.

Noah Brooks, who hoped at some point to replace Nicolay in the Lincoln White House, described the private secretary as the "Cerberus from hell," the three-headed beast from Greek mythology guarding the gates of the underworld. Brooks characterized his rival as possessing an abrupt and sometimes rude manner towards petitioners in the Executive Mansion. There were times when this was an accurate perception, and it was a necessary trait to protect the interests of his president. William Stoddard noted how difficult it was to stand in Nicolay's stead even for a few days and how glad he was when he could return to his daily routines. But to portray Nicolay, as some critics have done, as always having a disagreeable personality based on the performance of his official duties is an inaccurate characterization. He had a very appealing personality as evidenced by the many party and reception invitations he received in Springfield, in Washington, and on his trips. Well-read and with a quick wit, he would be up on the latest news and gossip without ever revealing any secrets from work. Extremely intelligent and at home in multiple languages—his native German, English, and French—he could easily move among the capital's party goers, foreign and domestic. All of this is clear evidence that he could be charming, and at times a bit of a ladies' man, leaving his acerbic temperament if not always his tongue, back at the Executive Mansion.

In his letters to Therena, he had few emotive moments except when writing something regarding Lincoln or Hay. His expressions of affection for Therena, when they appear at all, seem forced at times, as if he was either afraid to commit himself or fearful that Therena was about to abandon him. He loved Therena as his spouse, but after leaving Pittsfield, his only truly intimate friend beyond her was John Hay. Everyone else was an acquaintance.

It is difficult to describe the precise nature of Nicolay's relationship with Lincoln. What began as a friendship in the Illinois Secretary of State's Office evolved into an employer/employee and mentor/mentee relationship. Clearly, both men liked each other, and though in many ways they had very dissimilar personalities, they were a good fit. Some historians openly wonder what Lincoln saw in Nicolay, but opposites can and do attract each other. Lincoln married Mary Todd, who had a very different and difficult personality and came from a very different background than his. Nonetheless, he loved her deeply through twenty-three years of what was clearly a difficult and often emotionally taxing marriage. And there were, as noted in earlier chapters, some similar experiences in Lincoln's and Nicolay's pasts that would have bound them together. Yet, when addressing his friend in public or private, Helen recorded, her father would call him "Mr. Lincoln." In return, Lincoln would refer to his friend as "Nicolay," since Lincoln addressed most of his friends in this formal manner, "even those he had known since his boyhood." According to her son Robert, Mary Lincoln "habitually addressed the President as 'Mr. Lincoln.'"[3] In Springfield, Lincoln would use the many hours of playing chess and talking with Nicolay about the Bible or Shakespeare as a safe refuge from the stresses of his work and marriage. Nicolay enjoyed such times with Lincoln and proved himself discreet enough never to reveal anything they discussed. Likewise, when Lincoln walked down the hall in the White House for a nocturnal visit with his secretaries to share something he was reading or to relate a comical story, it was to find relief from the stresses that bore upon him. The Sunday afternoon conversations with Nicolay and Hay served the same function.

Lincoln could not share these moments with Mary, as she could be indifferent and preoccupied, or turn hostile at a moment's notice. Tad was too young to understand the context of his father's need to unwind. He could only share these moments with his trusted young secretaries. However we define the Lincoln-Nicolay relationship, it was built on mutual respect and closeness. Nicolay admired and practically worshipped Lincoln from early on and dedicated his life to the man and his image. Lincoln undoubtedly saw in Nicolay glimpses of himself as a young man and came to rely on his secretary's administrative talents and absolute loyalty.

John Sellers, in his biographical sketch of Nicolay, summarized many of the criticisms that have been made against Nicolay by both his contemporaries and later historians.[4] Nicolay's annual government-paid junkets, whether to Minnesota or Colorado, were a source of contention. The Minnesota trip was extended because of the exigencies of the Sioux War. The extended trip to Colorado, which lasted from mid-July to early November 1863, would seem particularly egregious. While Nicolay took full advantage of the delays in the treaty council in Colorado, he was not responsible for the delays in the negotiations with the Utes. Paid vacations were unheard of in the nineteenth century, and all expenses were paid courtesy of the government. Abraham Lincoln arranged for his secretaries, both Nicolay and Hay, to have some sort of official responsibility that would bring them to the desired destination justifying charging the costs of the trip to the federal treasury. From Lincoln's standpoint, both men needed and deserved occasional relief from the pressures of their White House routines while providing Lincoln with eyes and ears wherever he sent them.

Nicolay's criticisms of cabinet members and generals in his contemporary letters to Therena and later on in the history have also come under scrutiny. Historians generally agree that his assessments regarding Secretary of War Simon Cameron's competency and Secretary of the Treasury Salmon Chase's political machinations were justified. But some historians have been less willing to agree with Nicolay's assessment of Union generals and members of Congress.

One of the problems in dealing with Nicolay's criticisms is determining to what extent any particular viewpoint on any civilian or military matter was really his or simply a reflection of Lincoln's thinking.[5] Yet, it is important to remember that the criticisms contained in the Lincoln history reflected not only Nicolay's viewpoints but also those of Hay. Whether then or now, it is difficult for a thoroughly loyal member of the White House staff not to see any position contrary to the official policy of the administration as ill advised, treasonous, anathema to the best interests of the country, and undermining their boss's legitimate goals. The job of the staff is to make the president look good and deflect all the arrows of criticism. In Nicolay's lifelong absolutist view when it came to Lincoln, anyone who he perceived had failed or crossed Lincoln in any way deserved to be labeled incompetent, ignorant, untrustworthy, and just plain wrong. To summarize *Abraham Lincoln: A History*, it is the perfect Lincoln struggling against an imperfect world.

Yet, this storyline is certainly not new as a literary device. In Anglo-American literature, the story of the epic hero starts with Beowulf, who must overcome impossible odds before he achieves the ultimate triumph over the monster Grendel. The bigger, the more terrible the monster, the greater the odds against our hero; then, greater still is the hero's ultimate achievement. Nicolay's Lincoln is posited in this heroic tradition. In the Nicolay-Hay renderings, Lincoln is represented as overcoming multiple dragons by means of his unerring judgment.

The first and greatest of these monsters to be slain by Lincoln was the Slave Power, which, according to Nicolay, planned and executed a vast conspiracy against the peace and survival of the Union. Like a tailor-turned-politician from Tennessee named Andrew Johnson, Nicolay hated not so much the South as he did the slaveholding planter class that he believed dictated the region's politics and social order. Nicolay's distaste for slavery certainly played a significant part in this construction. Like Johnson, he had grown up in poverty and despised the ostentatious display of wealth and political power the planter elite practiced. Consequently, as Sellers correctly stated, Nicolay "completely misjudged the secession movement."[6]

Nicolay's letters to Therena at the beginning of the war verify this assertion. Nor was he alone in his predictions that war would not come about. After all, many Northerners rationalized, since as early as the Constitutional Convention of 1787, Southern leaders had been threatening secession as a means to protect slavery. Yet, war had never come. Lincoln, like many other Northern leaders, believed the conservative element in the South would bring the secessionists to their senses. Nonetheless, twenty years later with the publication of *The Outbreak of Rebellion*, all doubts regarding the inevitability of secession and war were gone not only in Nicolay's writings but in Northern histories of the war as well. Recalling Lincoln's hard line against the extension of slavery into the territories, Nicolay and Hay treated the attempts by John Crittenden and others to reach some compromise between the sections with barely disguised contempt.

The second dragon that Lincoln needed to slay was the inefficiency of the United States military. Prior to 1861, no one could have imagined the size and complexities of a civil war that involved millions of men in the field and what it would take to be victorious in such a struggle. In addition, the Civil War was the first industrial war of the modern era. The coordinated use of steamboats, railroads, ironclads, and the telegraph on a massive scale was a new experience for everyone. Beyond that, if armies are anything, they are moving bureaucracies that engage in warfare. Bureaucracies are by nature inefficient, and they become more inefficient in direct proportion to their increasing size and complexity. Battle plans frequently go awry, and once battles commence, generals often lose control of events.

Yet, Nicolay seems to have thought of armies more as pieces on his chessboard that could be moved easily, not as living behemoths that moved slowly over the landscape in the 1860s. Seeking to absolve Lincoln of any blame for missteps made in the military sphere, Nicolay concluded that these were entirely the fault of the generals. Yet, it was Lincoln who placed these men in positions of authority in the first place, notwithstanding Nicolay's portrayal of Lincoln as an impeccable, if not infallible, judge of men. General Irwin McDowell told Lincoln that the army was not ready for battle, but Lincoln, succumbing to the mounting political pressures in Congress and the press, sent an ill-prepared army off to First Bull Run anyway. When Bull Run turned into a disaster, Lincoln shifted the blame from himself by sacking McDowell, noting that the general had not properly prepared the Union army for battle. Ambrose Burnside begged Lincoln not to appoint him commander of the Army of the Potomac as he felt himself unfit. Burnside proved that assessment correct at Fredericksburg and in the Mud March of January 1863. But unlike any of the other commanders of the Army of the Potomac, Burnside had the courage to admit to his inadequacies and re-signed his position barely a month after the disaster at Fredericksburg. Lincoln could reasonably share the blame for the defeat at Bull Run and the bloodletting at Fredericksburg, but Nicolay and many subsequent historians have seen fit to exonerate the president of any culpability.

Likewise, Lincoln should have foreseen the problems that the abolitionist commander Frémont, whose erratic behaviors and previous insubordination were well documented, would create while in charge of slaveholding Missouri, but Lincoln appointed him anyway. A desk job in Washington with a high-sounding but empty title would have been a wiser course in dealing with the unpredictable Frémont. As regards McClellan, Lincoln uncharacteristically let his frustrations with the general go public with such infamous quips that McClellan had the "slows" or that he (Lincoln) would like to borrow the army so that it could engage the enemy.

The third demon facing Lincoln was the Congress. Here a glaring gap in Nicolay's self-education comes to the fore. Nicolay never developed a solid understanding of either the dynamics of American history or politics. During the nineteenth century, Congress, not the presidency, was the dominant branch of government. Normally, there was very little dispute about this. Andrew Jackson and James Polk stand out as strong presidents vis-à-vis the Congress. Consequently, Congress was jealous of its privileged status being usurped by the major crisis of civil war. Congress, like its Confederate counterpart, fought the centralization of power in the Executive Branch as a necessary result of the war. The demonizing of congressional opponents by the White House staff was not unique to Nicolay. It is part of the ongoing struggle over which branch controls the government. Undoubtedly, Nicolay looked upon the Peace Democrats as a continuation of the antebellum Slave Power, the political alliance between Southern planters and Northern Democrats. Worse yet for the White House staff was the continued harassment by the Congressional Joint Committee on the Conduct of the War, which sought to run the military conflict by second-guessing every move made by Lincoln or the Union army. And unless Lincoln was truly made of marble and not flesh and blood, he must have expressed sentiments behind closed doors about these legislators that did not reflect a generous and forgiving spirit. It is evident that Nicolay never quite understood the perpetual and legitimate struggle for power between the branches of government, nor cared to, since it seemed to work against his hero.

Another criticism of Nicolay, then and now, involved his open admission that he used his political and military connections to assist his relations. He would point out that appointments and promotions were going to other equally unqualified individuals throughout the Union army. It appears that Nicolay assisted his nephew John Nicolay to avoid military service and secured a promotion for his brother-in-law, Dorus Bates. Dorus did not have any apparent qualifications for his new position, but three months later he earned a field promotion to first lieutenant[7] and fought with distinction in the siege of Vicksburg, where he lost an arm. In the same year Dorus Bates was made a lieutenant, a professor from Bowdoin College in Brunswick, Maine, was made a lieutenant colonel of the 20th Maine Infantry. Aside from some time at a military academy in his youth, the only qualification he had for military leadership was that he had read Thucydides and Xenophon in the original Greek. Professor Joshua Lawrence Chamberlain would later save the Union left flank at Gettysburg on July 2, 1863, on a hill called Little Round Top.

One need look no further than Nicolay's boss, Abraham Lincoln, for another example of a well-connected individual using his position to promote a family member. In 1865, Lincoln finally acceded to his son Robert's persistent requests to enlist in the Union Army (over Mary Lincoln's strong objections). Robert entered the Union army on February 11, 1865, with a college degree but, like Dorus Bates and Joshua Chamberlain, with no prior military experience. He was commissioned as a captain and made an assistant adjutant general.[8] To assure that nothing happened to the president's son, he was then imbedded in the safety of Grant's headquarters staff. Lincoln did pay for Robert's "necessary means,"[9] but many a Northern family would have gladly paid for the same privilege for their sons. It was all done quietly, Lincoln being far more circumspect than his secretary. Four months later on June 10, Robert Lincoln resigned his military position. This is not an attempt to draw a moral equivalency. What Nicolay and Lincoln did was, in absolute terms, wrong. In theory, in a republic, everyone is equal. But in fact, whether it be a president or a secretary, if someone can use their influence to protect their flesh and blood from harm's way or help give their kin and friends a boost to their careers, they likely will do it. It is how the world worked in the 1860s and how the world works now. Nicolay's sin, in the eyes of his critics, was that he was not hypocritical but, in fact, rather open about doing it.

Noah Brooks, other contemporaries, and modern-day historians have accused Nicolay the private secretary of having been, in one combination or another, "arrogant, conceited and elitist, neither seeking nor welcoming the company of common people."[10] These attributions are particularly harsh. Nicolay was not interested in the "common people"; such is generally the case with individuals who are climbing the social ladder. Moreover, particularly in his youth, he had few associations with the hardier youth from lower-income families. When his brother dismissed him from the family mill in 1846 at the age of fourteen, he had already been working fulltime. When he went to Pittsfield, he became connected with the more well-to-do elements of the town's social order. His work in the Office of the Illinois Secretary of State brought him into contact with the elites of Springfield. When he went to Washington, by virtue of his position he became a part of the social elite of the capital.

Self-educated, Nicolay was a true savant. He was fluent in at least three languages. He was conversant in the arts, literature, and music and was well-traveled. What would have been his point of reference with common people or they to him? Like many individuals on the make, he wanted to put aside, if not erase, his humble past. Abraham Lincoln never forgot his humble roots, but he was also very glad to have left them behind and preferred not to talk about them. He was a politician who profited from the images of a log cabin and rail splitting.

He had a common touch, and people could relate to him. But after he settled in Springfield, there is little evidence that Lincoln sought out the company of common people except at election time.

It is inaccurate to describe Nicolay as "conceited." Thomas H. Shastid recalled how his father described the way Nicolay avoided bringing attention to himself in both Pittsfield and Washington, an attribute of a good journalist and a valued secretary. There is no evidence that Nicolay was boastful. Of course, Nicolay took justifiable pride in his position and relationship with the president. The striking fact regarding Nicolay's lack of "conceit" is that nowhere in the Lincoln history does he interject himself, first person, into the narrative. Neither did Hay. On the contrary, unless it was unavoidable, there is no mention of the secretary or his assistant in their writings about Lincoln, even though they were at the epicenter of many of the events and daily eyewitnesses to the unfolding story of Lincoln and his management of the Civil War. In their ten-volume work, Nicolay is mentioned by name eight times, Hay nine times.

In many ways, Nicolay tried to erase himself from the historical record altogether. Unlike Hay, he did not keep a diary during the Civil War. Nor did he write a personal memoir about his close association with Abraham Lincoln, a certain best seller. His notes about the personal traits of Lincoln were compiled, edited, and published by his daughter after his death. It is likely that both Nicolay and Hay took more than a few secrets about Lincoln and life in the White House to the grave, a discretion that many modern presidents would appreciate. The fact that Helen's biography of her father was not written or published until nearly a half century after his death suggests that the biography was conceived by Helen as a final tribute to her father. It is likely that Nicolay himself would have discouraged his daughter from writing such a biography. In his mind, the only person who deserved being written about was Abraham Lincoln.

Nicolay's legacy is twofold. First, the efficient and professional performance of his multiple duties as private secretary gave Lincoln the critical precious time that any leader needs to consult, to think, and to decide. It was a stressful time and a very demanding assignment. No doubt the secretary, who did not suffer fools well, acted out the role of the Cerberus from hell or at least a crabby German when necessity called for it. Somebody had to say "no" to the more insistent visitors to the White House. Every task ever asked of him by Lincoln was accomplished to the complete satisfaction of the president. There is no record of Nicolay ever violating a confidence, failing in an assignment, or otherwise disappointing the expectations and trust Lincoln placed in him. Nor did Nicolay ever betray Lincoln's confidence in him even after the president's death. In her summation of her father's life, Helen noted that "every change in his environment and duties came about quietly and naturally, and through every change he was an efficient, constructive force."[11] That may be a proud daughter speaking, but it is also a statement that can withstand scrutiny.

Second, as the primary developer of the Lincoln image, John George Nicolay gave posterity a history of Lincoln and his time that is an invaluable source on the work and contributions of the sixteenth president. Whatever its shortcomings, *Abraham Lincoln: A History* remains the most comprehensive, thorough, and authoritative rendering of the life of Lincoln by men who not only knew him but had lived and worked at his side.

John Sellers noted that "All too often the secretary [Nicolay] has been looked upon almost if he were a shadow image of Abraham Lincoln."[12] Nicolay would have been horrified at any suggestion that he might have somehow existed as a shadow or mirror image of Lincoln. Nicolay would have been proud to say that he stood in the shadow of Lincoln, there to support his hero, not as a spectral image but as a man hidden unobtrusively from the eye of history. John George Nicolay was a man on a life's mission, to which he gave his full measure of devotion. He worked generally behind the scenes to enable Lincoln to do things that made him great, and he interpreted for posterity the nature of Lincoln's life and greatness. It was done, as Carl Schurz pointed out in his review article of the Lincoln history, as "an act of filial love."

Nicolay's sketch of the house and outbuildings on a farm he purchased near Scranton, Kansas. Nicolay never lived here, but his brother John Jacob farmed here for a time and his descendants still live in the area. (Library of Congress)

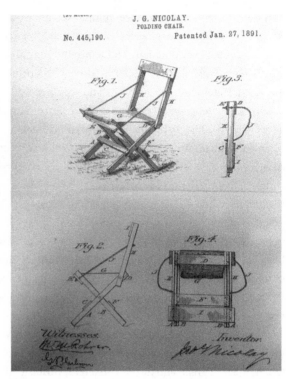

Sketch of a folding chair for which Nicolay received a patent in 1891. Of his five patents, this was perhaps the most practical, although he never received a financial benefit from any of them. (Library of Congress)

Throughout his life, Nicolay had been devoted to Lincoln, as one of his "boys." Following the example of her father's devotion to Lincoln, Helen showered her father with love and fidelity. In summarizing and assessing the life of John George Nicolay, it is important to note his role as a family man—as a loving husband and father. As devastating as the loss of Therena was in 1885, Nicolay and his daughter, Helen, carried on in a mutually devoted relationship that enabled Nicolay to complete the Lincoln history, despite serious eyesight problems. It was his financial success from the serialized and book forms of the Lincoln history that made it possible to fund art lessons with a master artist for Helen. He wanted to share with his daughter his love of nature developed in his boyhood days as well as his own considerable artistic talent. Nicolay frequently made sketches, such as the one he made of his Kansas farm buildings and the folding chair he designed and patented in 1891. He loved watercolors and would spend time on vacations replicating nature scenes on canvas, revealing the deeply sensitive side of his multifaceted personality. Yet, there is no evidence that he ever painted a human form, as his daughter did. He also traveled with Helen to Europe and Egypt.

All evidence points to a remarkable level of devotion and support between Helen and her father that lasted throughout the remainder of his life. Within two years of her mother's death, Helen was supported by her father in furthering her considerable artistic skills by studying under the famous New England painter Benjamin Champney at his summer art classes in Deerfield, Massachusetts. New England had long held a fascination for George as an escape from the heat and humidity of summertime Washington, and he was able to purchase land and have a cottage built within walking distance of the town of Holderness, New Hampshire. The Nicolays, father and daughter, moved into their summer home, designed by the elder Nicolay, called "Tannenruh" (i.e., Peace in the Pines), in the summer of 1895.[13] Helen would take vacations there until her death more than a half century later.

In the summer of 1899, Nicolay took Helen to Europe to visit his ancestral home in Germany, as well as to other cities in Germany and the Netherlands. They returned home in late summer and spent time at Tannenruh. Despite deteriorating health, Nicolay wanted to take Helen on one more overseas adventure and fulfill a dream he had maintained for years: to see Egypt. In October 1899, Helen and her father left New York on the new German luxury liner *Grosser Kurfurst*, reaching Cherbourg, France, ten days later. They spent several days in Paris, where they attended the 1900 World Exposition. Nicolay never cared much for the Parisian weather and likely was reminded of unpleasant memories surrounding his dismissal as U.S. consul years before. But being a devoted father, he wanted Helen to experience the art and culture of Paris, at least briefly, before they headed to the south of France, Italy, and on to Egypt. En route, Helen, soon to be recognized as a talented artist, made several paintings of places they visited.

On board the ship crossing the Mediterranean, the Nicolays met the McClure family. Samuel S. McClure had cofounded and was managing *McClure's Magazine*, and the two families hit it off and decided to do some sightseeing together, including travels up the Nile River. After nearly two months in Egypt, Nicolay and Helen returned to Europe, then journeyed back to their home in Washington after a six-month absence.[14] Nicolay's health was clearly in decline, nothing seemed to help, and soon he was bedridden under Helen's tender care.

As John George Nicolay lay dying, at the age of sixty-nine, his old friend John Hay came for a final visit. It was September 18, 1901, four days after the death of President McKinley from an assassin's bullet. Hay still wore the mourning crepe on his arm when he entered the house. Helen informed him that she had not told her father about the president's death. Hay removed the crepe and, as Helen described it, "mounted the stairs slowly." Helen reported that when Hay descended the stairs, he did so "more slowly still, his face stricken with grief."[15] The next day, Hay wrote a friend, "N—— is dying, I went to see him yesterday and he did not know me."[16] Indeed, as he walked down those stairs, Hay must have known that he would never see his friend again.

It had been a relationship that had lasted for fifty years that summer, begun when Hay came to live with his uncle Milton and attend the Thomson Academy in Pittsfield in 1851. What had been a friendship grew into a partnership when Lincoln agreed to Nicolay's entreaties to take Hay with them to Washington. Those four years together in the White House bonded them together as lifelong companions. They alone could share their private moments and deeply held emotions about the Tycoon. Not only did they cooperate in the reseach, writing, and publication of *Abraham Lincoln: A History* and the subsequent *Collected Papers*, over the years they and their families had spent summer vacations together, first at the Hay cabin in Crystal Park in the Rockies above Colorado Springs, Colorado, later in Newport, Rhode Island, and finally at Nicolay's Tannenruh. Only death could break the cords of a busy lifetime of shared memories that bound these two men together.

Nicolay slipped quietly away in the late afternoon on Thursday, September 26, 1901.[17] The official cause of death listed on his burial certificate was "general dibility [*sic*]."[18] Hay was not in Washington when Nicolay died and was unable to attend the funeral. Official notice was taken in the press, but the notices were perfunctory summaries of his life, with very little said about the private man. Flowers came from Teddy Roosevelt's White House,[19] but the new president had been only seven years old when he viewed the Lincoln funeral cortege from the window of the family's upscale Manhattan home. He only knew Lincoln as a historical figure and did not personally know Nicolay at all. The Century Company also sent flowers to pay tribute to their distinguished author. Not only had he written and compiled a number of successful and still historically significant titles under that company's banner but also a long list of articles in the company's *Century Magazine*. The funeral was held on Saturday, September 28, 1901, at the Nicolay home, and a funeral procession of about fifty people laid him to rest next to his beloved Therena in Georgetown's Oak Hill Cemetery. Among the mourners accompanying Nicolay to his final resting place was the Century Company's Richard Gilder, who was in Washington on business at the time of Nicolay's death. Gilder, a published poet, presented Helen with a tribute to her father's memory, which she appreciated.[20] The poem, though by no means a classic of literary composition, summarized Nicolay's life mission.

This man loved Lincoln, him did Lincoln love,
Through the long storm, right there, by Lincoln's side
He stood, his shield and servitor, when died
The great, sweet sorrowful soul—still high above
All other passions, that for the spirit fled!
To this one task his pure life was assigned:
He strove to make the world know Lincoln's mind:
He served him living, and he served him dead.
So shall the light from that immortal fame
Keep bright forever this most faithful name.[21]

To the day of his death, John George Nicolay had proven himself a Lincoln man all through. Indeed, as his daughter commented nearly a half century later, "The President's [Lincoln's] attitude toward my father is summed up in the latter's statement: 'There was never any red tape between us.'"[22]

Even the timing of Nicolay's passing was meaningful. William McKinley was the last president to have fought in the Civil War. It had been three and a half decades since the death of Lincoln and the end of the war. Americans were moving on to a new century. The automobile was already appearing on the streets of the capital. The airplane was but two years away. Technology was transforming society and leaving behind the world Nicolay had known. John Hay, the last of the triumvirate of Lincoln and his secretaries, died nearly four years later on July 1, 1905. Writing to Robert Lincoln shortly before his death in 1909, Richard Gilder reflected on "how greatly I have missed, during the last few years, being able to turn to Mr. Nicolay or Col. Hay, to ask them questions about their great chief, or simply to talk about him with them."[23] Yet the mystic chords to the sixteenth president that Nicolay and Hay had represented were not entirely severed by their passing. The editor and posterity had the words of Nicolay and Hay, especially Nicolay, enshrined in the Lincoln history and the first major compilation of Lincoln's papers.

Gilder noted one irony with regard to Nicolay's passing. "To think," the editor wrote, "of his [Nicolay's] living just to the death of the third martyred President, —and they did not tell him McKinley had died."[24] But there was another, stranger coincidence that occurred on the very day of Nicolay's death. While the secretary

An unpretentious grave marker
for a self-effacing man in Oak Hill
Cemetery in the Georgetown section
of Washington, D.C. (Photograph by
Allen Carden)

was drawing his last breath, his hero and mentor, Abraham Lincoln, was buried
for the last time. On that day in Oak Ridge Cemetery in Springfield, Illinois, after
being opened to verify it contained his remains, Lincoln's casket was placed in
a steel cage, lowered into the ground and ten feet of concrete poured over it to
insure the president's body would never again be disturbed by would-be tomb
robbers.[25] Lincoln and his world, and that of Nicolay, were quickly becoming
part of the distant past.

It is noteworthy that even in death, Nicolay sought anonymity. A visitor to
Oak Hill Cemetery will find no sign indicating the final resting place of Lincoln's
private secretary like the one for Hay in front of his gravesite at Lake View Cem-
etery in Cleveland, Ohio, which incorrectly proclaims that Hay was "President
Lincoln's Private Secretary and author of a ten volume Lincoln biography."[26]
Nicolay's gravesite is marked by a large but plain monument simply reading,
"John George Nicolay, February 26, 1832–September 26, 1901."[27] A passerby who
had no knowledge of Nicolay would not know that there lies the man who as
Lincoln's private secretary and image maker had a significant behind-the-scenes
impact on American history. Yet, there is a John Hay Center at Hay's birthplace
in Salem, Indiana, and a historic marker outside the boyhood home of William
Stoddard in Homer, New York, but no known marker for Nicolay in his birthplace
of Essingen. Nor was Nicolay's house on Capitol Hill preserved as a historic site;
instead it was torn down to make room for the Adams Building of the Library
of Congress. But for his daughter's biography of him nearly a half century after

his death, even less would be known about the man who preferred to hide in Lincoln's shadow.

Helen noted with pride the condolences she received from young people "who remembered with gratitude his kindness and understanding." But the letter that meant the most to her came from John Hay, the man who knew Nicolay better than any other: "I shall not try to comfort you by any conventional words. . . . But after a while you will take consolation in reflecting what an inheritance of pleasant memories is yours. You have never seen a man purer in heart and in life, of higher principles."[28]

Curiously, the meticulous and detail-oriented secretary never drew up a will, dying intestate. Helen appeared in court on October 15, 1901, requesting to be named administratrix. After posting a $500 bond to pay any outstanding debts owed by her father, she was duly appointed. The estate was valued at $18,700, a tidy but certainly not a large sum for a man of her father's status. There was $10,000 in real estate, including the family home on B Street and the cottage in New Hampshire; $7,000 in U.S. bonds; $1,000 in furniture and books; and a savings account of $200.[29] Eventually, Helen would sell the house on B Street but retain ownership and use of Tannenruh until her death. In January 1905, a portion of her father's considerable book collection was sold at auction.[30]

Helen's devotion to her father and the work of shaping the Lincoln image continued after her father's death. In 1904, Helen had completed her father's condensation of *Abraham Lincoln: A History* entitled *A Short life of Abraham Lincoln*. It was published by the Century Company under the guidance of Richard Gilder. In 1906, she published *A Boy's Life of Abraham Lincoln*. The book was very popular, and some editions included a picture of her father as a young man. She went on to publish a number of historical portraits for young people. However, she also produced two notable historical works. In 1912, she compiled *The Personal Traits of Abraham Lincoln,* published by the Century Company. However, Richard Gilder did not live to see the publication of the work he had urged Nicolay to write as part of the Lincoln history, having died on November 19, 1909. The contents were originally intended by her father to be part of the larger ten-volume history, but its theme never fit into the chronological treatment of the massive work. So Nicolay had delayed the completion of the work past the time that he had either the physical ability or interest to finish it.

Helen took her father's notes and created a more human, and equally adoring, portrait of the president. In many ways, it can be considered a supplement to the history. Then in 1949, at the age of eighty-three, she completed a biography of

Helen Nicolay (undated photograph) at her father's desk
which he had used as Lincoln's
secretary. Years after leaving the
White House, Nicolay was able to
purchase the desk at a government
sale of surplus furniture. Note the
picture of Lincoln, Nicolay, and
Hay above the bookcase. This is
the painted version of the studio
photograph in which a White
House interior background was
added. (From the Lincoln Financial
Foundation Collection, courtesy
of the Allen County Public Library
and Indiana State Museum)

her father, which also contains much about Lincoln. In her papers at the Allen County Public Library in Fort Wayne, Indiana, Helen complained about the material relevant to her father's life that was left on the cutting-room floor. Also, in the Lincoln Collection at the Allen County Public Library are two portraits of her father that Helen painted.

Robert Lincoln survived his father's biographers by another two decades. He died in his sleep on July 26, 1926, several days short of his eighty-third birthday. He bequeathed his father's papers to the Library of Congress. In a strange twist of historical events, he had been present at the scene of three presidential assassinations, that of his father, James Garfield, and William McKinley. After 1901, he became increasingly reclusive, refusing any invitation that would place him in proximity to a sitting president. The only exception he made to this prohibition was his presence on May 30, 1922, at the dedication of the Lincoln Memorial. Chief Justice William Howard Taft ceremonially presented the monument to President Warren G. Harding. As Nicolay and Hay had done with words under his sponsorship, the nation immortalized his father in stone. The apotheosis of Abraham Lincoln that John George Nicolay had so long envisioned was now complete.

Helen Nicolay died in Washington, D.C., on September 12, 1954, at the age of eighty-eight. Her ashes were scattered at Tannenruh. She had been imbued with all things Lincoln. It was not until Helen's death that her father's life work to perpetuate an adoring image of Abraham Lincoln finally came to a close. Her obituary in the *New York Times* not only noted her accomplishments as a writer and an artist but also, following in her father's footsteps, as an accomplished linguist who volunteered her talents to the State Department during the Second World War.[31] With Helen's passing, the last player in the life of John George Nicolay exited the stage.

Helen Nicolay summarized her father's achievements with the final words of the biography she lovingly wrote: "To the world, he left a great book about the greatest man of his age."[32] But John George Nicolay had accomplished so much more. The immigrant boy from Essingen had stood by and for his hero and his adopted country during the nation's darkest and bloodiest hour. He gave his full measure of devotion to Abraham Lincoln and in doing so had not only diligently served a president but also the nation. He did not win victories on the battlefield, write landmark pieces of legislation, or deliver stirring speeches. Nicolay's most important contribution during Lincoln's lifetime was in the quiet, efficient way that he lifted innumerable burdens, large and small, from the president's shoulders. Later, after Lincoln's death, he gave to the nation and then to the world the first scholarly validation of Lincoln's greatness. As the driving force behind the written history, however flawed, of Lincoln's life and times, and the preservation, organization, and first publication of Lincoln's papers, John George Nicolay deserves the gratitude not only of historians but of the nation. Nicolay's labors should earn him the honor of being called the Father of Lincoln Scholars. The contributions of the man who preferred to hide in Lincoln's shadow should be recognized in the full light of day.

Serialization of *Abraham Lincoln:*
A History in *Century Magazine*
November 1886–February 1890

Abraham Lincoln: A History was first serialized in the *Century Illustrated Monthly Magazine* to promote interest and future sales in the book. For the October 1886 issue, Clarence King wrote an article entitled "The Biographers of Lincoln" to assure the reading public of Nicolay and Hay's qualifications to author such an important work. Serialization began with volume 39, no. 1, November 1886. The initial article was preceded by a brief editorial by the *Century Magazine* editors and a short preface by Nicolay and Hay.[1]

Below is a listing of all the articles published between November 1886 and February 1890 in the sequence in which they appeared in the magazine. It should be noted that the index, which served as a table of contents, sometimes listed items that were, in fact, combined into a larger article. There is no consistency in the way the *Century Magazine* handled the titles on the pages where the articles appeared. All articles have the header "Abraham Lincoln: A History." But to use that would not provide the reader with the contents of the article. Sometimes an article title appears immediately below the header but other times not. To assist the reader, articles are listed with the titles that appear in the table of contents. However, sometimes the magazine would list three articles in a row, which in fact read as a single seamless article. Those have been combined into a single title.

"Lincoln as Pioneer." Vol. 33, no. 1 (November 1886): 6–37.
"Lincoln as Soldier, Surveyor and Politician." Vol. 33, no. 2 (December 1886): 250–78.

"Lincoln in Springfield, Collapse of the System, Law in Springfield, Lincoln's Marriage, the Shields Duel, the Campaign of 1844." Vol. 33, no. 3 (January 1887): 366–96.

"Lincoln in Congress and at the Bar." Vol. 33, no. 4 (February 1887): 515–43.

"Movement of Slavery Extension." Vol. 33, no. 5 (March 1887): 685–706.

"The Territorial Experiment." Vol. 33, no. 6 (April 1887): 857–84.

"Border Conflict." Vol. 34, no. 1 (May 1887): 82–110.

"Attack on Sumner and the Dred Scott Decision." Vol. 34, no. 2 (June 1887): 203–19.

"The Lincoln-Douglas Debates." Vol. 34, no. 3 (July 1887): 369–96.

"Lincoln's Cooper Institute Speech." Vol. 34, no. 4 (August 1887): 509–34.

"Lincoln's Nomination and Election." Vol. 34, no. 5 (September 1887): 658–84

"The Secession Movement." Vol. 34, no. 6 (October 1887): 819–50.

"The President-Elect at Springfield." Vol. 35, no. 1 (November 1887): 64–87.

"Lincoln's Inauguration." Vol. 35, no. 2 (December 1887): 265–84.

"Formation of the Cabinet." Vol. 35, no. 3 (January 1888): 419–36.

"Premier or President?" Vol. 35, no. 4 (February 1888): 599–616.

"The Call to Arms." Vol. 35, no. 5 (March 1888): 707–23.

"The National Uprising." Vol. 35, no. 6 (April 1888): 898–922.

"The Border States." Vol. 36, no. 1 (May 1888): 56–77.

"The Advance—Bull Run, Frémont—Military Emancipation." Vol. 36, no. 2 (June 1888): 281–305.

"Lincoln and McClellan." Vol. 36, no. 3 (July 1888): 393–416.

"Tennessee and Kentucky." Vol. 36, no. 4 (August 1888): 562–83.

"The Mississippi and Shiloh." Vol. 36, no. 5 (September 1888): 658–78.

"Plans of Campaigns." Vol. 36, no. 6 (October 1888): 912–33.

"Jackson's Valley Campaign—the Seven Days Battles—Harrison's Landing." Vol. 37, no. 1 (November 1888): 130–48

"First Plans for Emancipation" Vol. 37, no. 2 (December 1888): 276–94.

"Pope's Virginia Campaign—Antietam—Emancipation Announced" Vol. 37, no. 3 (January 1889): 427–47.

"Removal of McClellan – Financial Measures—Seward and Chase." Vol. 37, no. 4 (February 1889): 546–65.

"The Edict of Freedom." Vol. 37, no. 5 (March 1889): 689–704.

"Retaliation and Enrollment." Vol. 37, no. 6 (April 1889): 917–32.

"President and the Draft—Vallandigham—The Defeat of the Peace Party at the Polls." Vol. 38, no. 1 (May 1889): 123–148.

"Pomeroy Circular—The Cleveland Convention—The Resignation of Chase." Vol. 38, no. 2 (June 1889): 278–98.

"Lincoln Renominated—The Wade-Davis Manifesto—Horace Greeley's Peace Mission." Vol. 38, no. 3 (July 1889): 406–26.

"The Chicago Surrender—Conspiracies in the North—Lincoln and the Churches." Vol. 38, no. 4, (August 1889): 546–68.

"Cabinet Changes—Lincoln Re-elected—Chase as Chief Justice." Vol. 38, no. 5, (September 1889): 687–707

"Blair's Mexican Project—The Hampton Roads Conference—XIIIth Amendment." Vol. 38, no. 6, (October, 1889): 838–56.

"Second Inaugural—Five Forks—Appomattox." Vol. 39, no. 1, (November 1889): 132–51.

"Fall of the Rebel Capital—Lincoln in Richmond." Vol. 39, no. 2, (December 1889): 305–13.

"Fourteenth of (April—The Fate of the Assassins—The Mourning Pageant." Vol. 39, no. 3 (January 1890): 428–43.[2]

"Capture of Jefferson Davis—The End of the Rebellion—Lincoln's Fame." Vol. 39, no. 4, (February 1890): 561–76.

Notes

CHAPTER ONE. FROM ESSINGEN TO PITTSFIELD

1. Helen Nicolay, *Lincoln's Secretary: A Biography of John G. Nicolay* (New York: Longmans, Green, 1949), 3.

2. Ibid., 6.

3. Ibid., 4.

4. Ibid.

5. New Orleans passenger lists, 1813–1963, M259, Ancestry.com.

6. Nicolay, *Lincoln's Secretary,* 5.

7. United States Census Office, *1840 Compendium of the Enumeration of the Inhabitants and Statistics of the United States, as Obtained at Department of State, from the Returns of the Sixth Census, by Counties and Principal Towns . . . to Which Is Added an Abstract of Each Preceding Census,* prepared at the Department of State (Washington, D.C.: T. Allen, 1841).

8. 1 US 50, chapter 8, in *The Public Statutes at Large of the United States of America from the Organization of the Government in 1789 to March 3, 1845,* ed. Richard Peters et al. (Boston: Charles C. Little and James Brown, 1845), 1:50.

9. 1 US 123, chapter 14, in Peters, *Public Statutes at Large* (1845), 1:123.

10. Nicolay, *Lincoln's Secretary,* 5.

11. David Henry Shaffer, *Shaffer's Advertising Directory for 1839–40* (Cincinnati: J. B. & R. P. Donogh, 1839), 303.

12. Nicolay, *Lincoln's Secretary,* 5.

13. Ibid., 6.

14. Ibid., 9.

15. Ibid., 5.

16. It should be noted that Helen Nicolay's biography does not have a single reference in the text to the date of text from which she is quoting. There are no footnotes.

17. Nicolay, *Lincoln's Secretary,* 7.

18. Ibid., 7.

19. Ibid., 6.

20. Ibid.

21. J. D. B. Debow, *The Seventh Census of the United States, 1850: Embracing a Statistical View of Each of the States and Territories, Arranged by Counties, Towns, etc.* (Washington, D.C.: Robert Armstrong, Public Printer, 1853), 714.

22. *History of Pike County, Illinois: Together with Sketches of Its Cities, Villages and Townships, Educational, Religious, Civil, Military, and Political History; Portraits of Prominent Persons and Biographies of Representative Citizens* (Chicago: Chas. C. Chapman, 1880), 541–42.

23. Nicolay, *Lincoln's Secretary*, 6.

24. Ibid., 7.

25. Frederick Lewis died in Montezuma Township in 1872. His tombstone in Green Pond Cemetery is a millstone with the legend "This stone from the Nicolay Mill."

26. Nicolay, *Lincoln's Secretary*, 7.

27. *History of Greene and Jersey Counties, Illinois, Together with Sketches of the Towns, Villages and Township, Educational, Civil, Military, and Political History* (Springfield, IL: Continental Historical Co., 1885), 1086.

28. Nicolay, *Lincoln's Secretary*, 7–8.

29. Ibid., 8.

30. Ibid.

31. Ibid.

32. From the address of Jesse M. Thompson, quoted in Lorade Taft, Thomas Rees, and Hieryonmus Speak, "Tablet Erected in Court House Park, Pittsfield, Pike County, Illinois, in Commemoration of Lincoln and Douglas, and Nicolay and Hay," *Journal of the Illinois Historical Society* 18, no. 3 (October 1929): 734–35.

33. Thomas H. Shastid, *My Second Life* (Ann Arbor, MI: G. Wahr, 1944), 63n2.

34. Ibid., 63.

35. Capt. M. D. Massie, *Past and Present of Pike County, Illinois, Together with Biographical Sketches of Many of Its Prominent and Leading Citizens and Illustrious Dead, Illustrated* (Chicago: S. J. Clarke, 1906), 351.

36. *History of Pike County, Illinois*, 397–98.

37. Nicolay, *Lincoln's Secretary*, 12.

38. Seventh Census of the United States, 1850, Records of the Bureau of the Census Record Group 29, National Archives Microfilm Publication M432, 1009 rolls, National Archives, Washington, D.C.

39. Nicolay, *Lincoln's Secretary*, 9–10.

40. Seventh Census of the United States, 1850.

41. Nicolay, *Lincoln's Secretary*, 11.

42. Therena Bates was born in Massachusetts in 1835, the only daughter of Dorus E. (1805–1882) and Emma Lucy Norton Bates (ca. 1808–1873). Therena had two older brothers, Norton (born ca. 1831) and Daniel C. Bates (1832–1895), and two younger brothers, Dorus E. Jr. (ca. 1843–1880) and Milton Bates (born ca. 1844). Daniel and Dorus Jr. are buried in Pittsfield.

43. *History of Pike County, Illinois*, 668.

44. William A. Grimshaw, *History of Pike County: A Centennial Address Delivered by Hon. William A. Grimshaw, at Pittsfield, Pike County, Illinois, July 4, 1876* (Pittsfield, IL: Democrat Job Rooms, 1877), 25.

45. Ibid., 28. Illinois was known at this time as the "Sucker State." Although the

origins of this nickname are uncertain, it has nothing to do with the more modern definition of "one easily duped."

46. Ibid., 34.

47. Nicolay, *Lincoln's Secretary*, 18.

48. Shastid, *My Second Life*, 60.

49. Grimshaw, *History of Pike County*, 26.

50. Helen Nicolay, "The Writing of *Abraham Lincoln: A History*," *Journal of the Illinois State Historical Society* 42, no. 3 (September 1949): 258.

51. Shastid, *My Second Life*, 65n4.

52. John Taliaferro, *All the Great Prizes: The Life of John Hay, from Lincoln to Roosevelt* (New York: Simon & Schuster, 2013), 22–23.

53. Nicolay, "Writing of *Abraham Lincoln: A History*," 268.

54. Ibid.

55. Ibid.

56. Nicolay, *Lincoln's Secretary*, 11.

57. Originally, what we now call the Kansas-Nebraska Act was enacted as the Nebraska-Kansas Act. Because the result of the act was a state of war in Kansas for the following decade and a half, the act became more associated with the violence in Kansas, and over time it has become popularly known as the Kansas-Nebraska Act. In the 1850s, it was still referred to as the Nebraska Act, and opponents to the expansion of slavery in the territories called themselves anti-Nebraska.

58. Nicolay, *Lincoln's Secretary*, 20.

59. Paul Selby, "The Editorial Convention, February 22, 1856," in *Meeting of May 29, 1900 Commemorative of the Convention of May 29, 1856 That Organized the Republican Party in the State of Illinois*, vol. 3 of *Transactions of the McLean County Historical Society, Bloomington, Illinois*, ed. Ezra M. Prince, Secretary of the Historical Society (Bloomington, IL: Pantagraph Printing and Stationery, 1900), 35.

60. Charles A. Church, *The History of the Republican Party in Illinois, 1854–1912, with a Review of the Aggressions of the Slave Power* (Rockford, IL: Wilson Brothers, 1912), 29.

61. Paul Selby, "Editorial Convention of 1856," *Journal of the Illinois State Historical Society* 5, no. 3 (October 1912): 344.

62. John G. Nicolay and John Hay, *Abraham Lincoln: A History* (New York: Century Company, 1890), 2:23.

63. Church, *History of the Republican Party in Illinois*, 31–32.

64. John G. Nicolay, "Abraham Lincoln," in Prince, *Meeting of May 29, 1900*, 95–101.

65. Selby, "Editorial Convention, February 22, 1856," 37.

66. Ibid., 37.

67. Ibid., 38.

68. "Official Record of the Convention," in Prince, *Meeting of May 29, 1900*, 148–58.

69. Ibid., 160–61.

70. Nicolay, "Abraham Lincoln," in *Meeting of May 29, 1900*, 95–102.

71. Nicolay, *Lincoln's Secretary*, 20.

CHAPTER TWO. SPRINGFIELD

1. Scrapbook 1856–1870, Box 1, John G. Nicolay Papers, Library of Congress (hereafter cited as JGN Papers).

2. Thomas Shastid, in *My Second Life*, 71–72, recounted the story about his father, Thomas Shastid, introducing Nicolay and Lincoln. Helen Nicolay, in *Lincoln's Secretary*, 19, got the Shastid family members confused, claiming it was John Shastid, the elder Thomas's father (and Thomas Hall Shastid's grandfather), who claimed to make the introduction.

3. Scrapbook 1856–1870, Box 1, JGN Papers.

4. Robert T. Lincoln, *A Portrait of Abraham Lincoln in Letters by His Son*, ed. Paul M. Angle (Chicago: Chicago Historical Society, 1968), 46–47.

5. *Pike County Free Press*, February 16, 1855.

6. Nicolay and Hay, *Abraham Lincoln*, 2:28.

7. William Herndon and Jesse W. Weik, *Herndon's Life of Lincoln* (1889; repr., New York: Fawcett World Library, 1961), 312.

8. Ronald C. White, *A. Lincoln: A Biography* (New York: Random House, 2009), 224–25.

9. Nicolay and Hay, *Abraham Lincoln*, 2:35–36.

10. A patent for Nicolay's rotary cone printing press is contained in Scrapbook 1856–1870, Box 1, JGN Papers. The document noted that, at that time, Nicolay "has made oath that he is a citizen of the United States."

11. Scrapbook 1856–1870, Box 1, JGN Papers.

12. Ibid., n.p.

13. Ibid.

14. Notebook 1856–1858, 8, Box 1, JGN Papers.

15. Ibid., 9 (page not numbered).

16. Nicolay and Hay, *Abraham Lincoln*, 2:58–80.

17. Ibid., 2:64.

18. Ibid., 2:67.

19. Ibid., 2:71.

20. Ibid., 2:73.

21. Ibid., 2:72–73.

22. Allen C. Guelzo, *Lincoln and Douglas: The Debates That Defined America* (New York: Simon & Schuster, 2008, 94–95.

23. *Chicago Press and Tribune*, August 13, 1858, qtd. in Joshua Zeitz, *Lincoln's Boys: John Hay, John Nicolay, and the War for Lincoln's Image* (New York: Viking Press, 2014), 50–51.

24. Louis Fischer, "Lincoln's 1858 Visit to Pittsfield, Illinois," *Journal of the Illinois State Historical Society* 61, no. 3 (Autumn 1968): 350–64.

25. Ibid.

26. *History of Pike County, Illinois*, 882.

27. Qtd. in David Herbert Donald, *Lincoln*. (1995; repr., New York: Touchstone/Simon & Schuster, 1996), 214.

28. Qtd. in Zeitz, *Lincoln's Boys*, 49.

29. *New York Tribune*, December 21, 29, 1857, May 11, 17, 1858, June 24, 1858, as noted in *The Lincoln-Douglas Debates*, ed. Rodney O. Davis and Douglas L. Wilson (Urbana: University of Illinois Press, 2008), xvii.

30. Direct election of U.S. senators was not nationally mandated until the 1913 adoption of the Seventeenth Amendment to the U.S. Constitution.

31. Nicolay, *Lincoln's Secretary*, 28.

32. Collected Works of Abraham Lincoln ed. Basler, 3:410.

33. Scrapbook 1856–1870, Box 1, JGN Papers.

34. Nicolay, *Lincoln's Secretary*, 26.

35. Scrapbook 1856–1870, Box 1, JGN Papers.

36. Qtd. in John Taliaferro, *All the Great Prizes: The Life of John Hay, from Lincoln to Roosevelt* (New York: Simon & Schuster, 2013), 33.

37. Nicolay and Hay, *Abraham Lincoln*, 2:258.

38. Ibid., 2:188–89.

39. Qtd. in David H. Leroy, *Mr. Lincoln's Book: Publishing the Lincoln-Douglas Debates* (New Castle, DE.: Oak Knoll Press, 2009), 49–50; letter qtd. from Abraham Lincoln, *The Collected Works of Abraham Lincoln*, vol. 10, *First Supplement, 1832–1865*, ed. Ray P. Basler (New Brunswick, NJ: Rutgers University Press, 1974), 47.

40. Nicolay, *Lincoln's Secretary*, 28–29.

41. Ibid., 29–30.

42. St. Paul's Epistle to the Romans, 10:2.

43. Qtd. in Bruce Chadwick, *Lincoln for President: An Unlikely Candidate, an Audacious Strategy, and the Victory No One Saw Coming* (Naperville, IL; Sourcebooks, 2009), 4.

44. Qtd. in Harold Holzer, *Lincoln at Cooper Union: The Speech That Made Abraham Lincoln President* (New York: Simon & Schuster, 2004), 5.

45. Nicolay, *Lincoln's Secretary*, 31.

46. Nicolay and Hay, *Abraham Lincoln*, 2:269–77.

47. Michael F. Holt, *The Election of 1860: "A Campaign Fraught with Consequences,"* (Lawrence, KS: University Press of Kansas, 2017), 101.

48. Donald, *Lincoln*, 250–51.

49. Helen Nicolay, "The Writing of *Abraham Lincoln: A History*," *Journal of the Illinois State Historical Society* 42, no. 3 (September 1949): 264.

50. Nicolay, *Lincoln's Secretary*, 34.

51. John G. Nicolay (hereafter JGN) to Therena Bates, June 7, 1860, Box 1, JGN Papers.

52. Nicolay, *Lincoln's Secretary*, 34.

53. Susan Goodman, *William Dean Howells: A Writer's Life* (Berkeley: University of California Press, 2005), 48.

54. William Dean Howells and John L. Hayes, *Lives and Speeches of Abraham Lincoln and Hannibal Hamlin* (Columbus, OH: Follett, Foster, 1860).

55. Ibid., xi–xii.

56. Goodman, *William Dean Howells*, 48–49.

57. Ibid., 36.

58. Nicolay, *Lincoln's Secretary*, 42.

59. [June 1?], 1860, Box 2, JGN Papers.

60. Henry Villard, *Lincoln on the Eve of '61*, ed. Harold G. and Oswald Garrison Villard (New York: Alfred A. Knopf, 1941), 14–15.

61. Nicolay, *Lincoln's Secretary*, 38.

62. Republican Party, Illinois State Central Committee, *Political Record of Stephen A. Douglas on the Slavery Question: A Tract Issued by the Illinois State Central Committee* (n.p., 1860).

63. Qtd. in Zeitz, *Lincoln's Boys*, 65.

64. JGN to Therena Bates, July 16, 1860, and August 9, 1860, Box 2, JGN Papers.

65. JGN to Therena Bates, October 16, 1860, Box 2, JGN Papers.

66. JGN to Therena Bates, November 8, 1860, Box 2, JGN Papers.

67. JGN to Therena Bates, November 18, 1860, Box 2, JGN Papers.

68. White, *A. Lincoln*, 352.

69. JGN to Therena Bates, December 2, 1860, Box 2, JGN Papers.

70. Chief Justice Taney died on October 12, 1864.

71. JGN to Therena Bates, December 13, 1860, Box 2, JGN Papers.

72. Note dated December 13, 1860, Box 2, JGN Papers.

73. Note dated December 15, 1860, Box 2, JGN Papers.

74. Note dated December 22, 1860, Box 2, JGN Papers.

75. JGN to Therena Bates, December 30, 1860, Box 2, JGN Papers.

76. JGN to Therena Bates, January 6, 1861, Box 2, JGN Papers.

77. JGN to Therena Bates, January 20, 1861, Box 2, JGN Papers.

78. JGN to Therena Bates, January 27, 1861, Box 2, JGN Papers.

CHAPTER THREE. A SLOW, STRATEGIC TRAIN TO WASHINGTON

1. JGN to Therena Bates, October 16, 1860, Box 2, JGN Papers.

2. Nicolay, *Lincoln's Secretary*, 60.

3. Daniel C. Toomey, *The War Came by Train: The Baltimore & Ohio Railroad in the Civil War* (Baltimore: Baltimore and Ohio Railroad Museum 2013), 14.

4. Nicolay and Hay, *Abraham Lincoln*, 3:289.

5. Toomey, *War Came by Train*, 14.

6. John G. Nicolay, *The Outbreak of Rebellion* (1881; repr., Woodbury, NY: Longmeadow Press, 1996), 7.

7. William T. Coggeshall, *Lincoln Memorial: The Journeys of Abraham Lincoln from Springfield to Washington as President-Elect and from Washington to Springfield, 1865 as President Martyred Comprising an Account of Pubic Ceremonies on the Entire Route, and Full Details of Both Journeys* (Columbus, OH: Published for the Benefit of the Ohio Soldier's Monument by the Ohio State Journal, 1865), 25.

8. William Roscoe Thayer, *The Life and Letters of John Hay* (Boston: Houghton Mifflin, 1908), 1:87.

9. Taliaferro, *All the Great Prizes*, 36.

10. Coggeshall, *Lincoln Memorial*, 25.

11. Nicolay, *Lincoln's Secretary*, 63.

12. Henry Villard, *Memoirs of Henry Villard, Journalist and Financier, in Two Volumes* (Boston: Houghton Mifflin, 1904), 1:150.

13. Ruth Painter Randall, *Colonel Elmer Ellsworth: A Biography of Lincoln's Friend and First Hero of the Civil War* (Boston: Little, Brown, 1960), 243–44.

14. Ibid., 149.

15. Villard, *Lincoln on the Eve of '61*, 73.

16. Nicolay and Hay, *Abraham Lincoln*, 3:291n.

17. Nicolay, *Lincoln's Secretary*, 63.

18. Nicolay and Hay, *Abraham Lincoln*, 3:291–92.

19. Ibid., 292.

20. JGN to Therena Bates, February 11, 1861, Box 2, JGN Papers.

21. John G. Nicolay, "Some Incidents in Lincoln's Journey, from Springfield to Washington," in *An Oral History of Abraham Lincoln: John G. Nicolay's Interviews and Essays*, ed. Michael Burlingame, 108–10 (Carbondale: Southern Illinois University Press, 1995).

22. Harold Holzer, *Lincoln President-Elect: Abraham Lincoln and the Great Secession Winter, 1860–1861* (New York: Simon & Schuster, 2008), 292.

23. Nicolay, "Some Incidents in Lincoln's Journey," 108.

24. Holzer, *Lincoln President-Elect*, 308.

25. Coggeshall, *Lincoln Memorial*, 32–33.

26. Nicolay, "Some Incidents in Lincoln's Journey," 110–11.

27. Ibid., 112.

28. JGN to Therena Bates, February 15, 1861, Box 2, JGN Papers.

29. Ibid.

30. Nicolay, "Some Incidents in Lincoln's Journey," 113–14.

31. JGN to Therena Bates, February 15, 1861, Box 2, JGN Papers.

32. JGN to Therena Bates, February 17, 1861, Box 2, JGN Papers.

33. Victor Searcher, *Lincoln's Journey to Greatness: A Factual Account of the Twelve-Day Inaugural Trip* (Philadelphia: John C. Winston, 1960), 130.

34. Terry Alford, *Fortune's Fool: The Life of John Wilkes Booth* (New York: Oxford University Press, 2015), 105.

35. Ibid., 388.

36. Ward Hill Lamon, *Recollections of Abraham Lincoln*, ed. Dorothy Lamon Teillard (Lincoln: University of Nebraska Press, 1994), 34.

37. Garnett Laidlaw Eskew, *Willard's of Washington: The Epic of a Capital Caravansary* (New York: Coward-McCann, 1954), 52.

38. John G. Nicolay, *With Lincoln in the White House: Letters, Memoranda, and Other Writings of John G. Nicolay, 1860–1865*, ed. Michael Burlingame (Carbondale, IL: Southern Illinois University Press, 2000), 28.

39. Robert G. Gunderson, "Lincoln's Mail," *Indiana Magazine of History* 55, no. 4 (1959): 380.

40. JGN to Therena Bates, February 24, 1861, Box 2, JGN Papers.

41. *New York Times*, February 27, 1861.

CHAPTER FOUR. LINCOLN'S CHOICE OF NICOLAY

1. Scrapbook, 1856–1870, Box 1, JGN Papers.

2. Henry C. Whitney to William Herndon, July 18, 1887, in *Herndon's Informants: Letters, Interviews, and Statements about Abraham Lincoln,* ed. Douglas L. Wilson and Rodney O. Davis, with the assistance of Terry Wilson (Urbana: University of Illinois Press, 1998), 621–22.

3. John R. Sellers, "Serving President Lincoln: The Public Career of John G. Nicolay," in *Lincoln Reshapes the Presidency,* ed. Charles M. Hubbard (Macon, GA: Mercer University Press, 2003), 52.

4. Carl Sandburg, *Abraham Lincoln: The Prairie Years,* Sangamon Edition (New York: Charles Scribner's Sons, 1940), 2:83.

5. Ward Hill Lamon, *The Life of Abraham Lincoln: From His Birth to His Inauguration as President* (Boston: James R. Good, 1872), 482.

6. Nicolay, *Lincoln's Secretary,* 34.

7. Lamon, *Recollections of Abraham Lincoln,* 28.

8. Michael Medved, *The Shadow Presidents: The Secret History of the Chief Executives and Their Top Aides* (New York: Times Books, 1979), 12.

9. *Statutes at Large and Treaties of the United States of America from December 3, 1855 to March 3, 1859 and Proclamations since 1791* (Boston: Little, Brown, 1859), 11:221.

10. Ibid., 228. In today's money, the 1860 sum of $2,500 is worth approximately $71,500.

11. George Schneider, "Lincoln and the Anti-Know-Nothing Resolutions," in Prince, *Meeting of May 29, 1900,* 87n.

12. Karl J. R. Arndt and May E. Olson, *German-American Newspapers and Periodicals, 1732–1955: History and Bibliography* (New York: Johnson Reprint Corp., 1965), 105–8.

13. Ibid., 106–7.

14. Sandburg, *Abraham Lincoln: The Prairie Years,* 2:183–84.

15. A. E. Zucker, "Dr. Theodore Canisius, Friend of Lincoln," *American German Review* 16, no. 3 (February 1950): 14.

16. Ibid., 15.

17. F. I. Herriott, *The Premises and Significance of Abraham Lincoln's Letter to Theodore Canisius* (Chicago: n.p., 1915), 15. (Available online at Internet Archive, https://archive.org/details/premisessignificooherriott).

18. Carl Wittke, *The German Language Press in America* (Lexington: University of Kentucky Press, 1957), 143.

19. Herriott, *Premises and Significance,* 26.

20. Ibid., 35.

21. Ibid. 30.

22. Ibid., 31–32.

23. Nicolay and Hay, *Abraham Lincoln,* 2:181.

24. Herriot, "Premises and Significance," 39.

25. Abraham Lincoln to Owen Lovejoy, August 11, 1855, in Lincoln, *Collected Works of Abraham Lincoln*, 2:316–17.

26. Abraham Lincoln to Joshua Speed, August 24, 1855, in Lincoln, *Collected Works of Abraham Lincoln*, 2:323.

27. William Henry Seward, *The Works of William Henry Seward*, ed. George E. Baker (New York: AMS Press, 1972), 282–84.

28. Wittke, *German Language Press in America*, 144.

29. Republican National Convention, *Proceedings of the Republican National Convention held at Chicago, May 16, 17, and 18, 1860* (Albany, NY: Weed, Parsons, 1860), 82.

30. Ibid., 83.

31. Ibid., 84–86.

32. Ibid., 89–90.

33. Ibid., 90.

34. Ibid., 91–92.

35. Ibid., 92–93.

36. Ibid., 93–95.

37. Murat Halstead, *Three Against Lincoln: Murat Halstead Reports the Caucuses of 1860*, ed. William B. Hesseltine (Baton Rouge: Louisiana State University Press, 1960), 149.

38. Ray Orman, *The Convention That Nominated Lincoln: An Address Delivered Before the Chicago Historical Society on May 18, 1916, the Fifty-Sixth Anniversary of Lincoln's Nomination to the Presidency* (Chicago: University of Chicago Press, 1916), 26–27.

39. Thomas H. Dudley, "The Inside Facts of the Lincoln Nomination," *Century Illustrated Monthly Magazine* 40 (July 1890): 477–78.

40. Ibid., 478.

41. Halstead, *Three Against Lincoln*, 160.

42. Dudley, "Inside Facts of the Lincoln Nomination," 478.

43. Ibid.

44. Halstead, *Three Against Lincoln*, 161–62.

45. Wittke, *German Language Press in America*, 146.

46. Nicolay, *Lincoln's Secretary*, 26.

CHAPTER FIVE. PRIVATE SECRETARY

1. Nicolay and Hay, *Abraham Lincoln*, 3:324–25.

2. Nicolay, *Lincoln's Secretary*, 84.

3. Shastid, *My Second Life*, 71.

4. Nicolay, *Lincoln's Secretary*, 84–85.

5. Ibid., 85.

6. James B. Conroy, *Lincoln's White House: The People's House in Wartime* (Lanham, MD: Rowan and Littlefield, 2017), 77.

7. Entry for July 9, 1861, Scrapbook 1855–1870, Box 1, JGN Papers.

8. Shastid, *My Second Life*, 105–6.

9. Nicolay, *Lincoln's Secretary*, 252–53.

10. JGN to Therena Bates, March 5–7, 1861, Box 2, JGN Papers.

11. Nicolay and Hay, *Abraham Lincoln*, 4:68–69.

12. JGN to O. M. Hatch, March 7, 1861, Box 2, JGN Papers.

13. William D'Arcy Haley, *Philp's Washington Described: A Complete View of the American Capital, and the District of Columbia; with Many Notices, Historical, Topographical and Scientific, of the Seat of Government* (Washington, D.C.: Philp & Solomons, [1860?]), 73–74.

14. Ibid., 199.

15. *Etiquette at Washington: Together with the Customs Adopted by Polite Society in the Other Cities of the United States*, 7th ed. (Baltimore: Murphy & Company, 1860), 13–14.

16. Gunderson, "Lincoln's Mail," 380.

17. Donald, *Lincoln*, 102–3.

18. Gunderson, "Lincoln's Mail," 380.

19. John M. Hay, *Inside Lincoln's White House: The Complete Civil War Diary of John Hay*, ed. Michael Burlingame and John R. Turner Ettlinger (Carbondale: Southern Illinois University Press, 1997), 15.

20. John Hay to William Herndon, September 5, 1866, in John Hay, *At Lincoln's Side: John Hay's Civil War Correspondence with Selected Writings*, ed. Michael Burlingame (Carbondale: Southern Illinois University Press, 2000), 111–12.

21. William O. Stoddard, *Inside the White House during War Times: Memoirs and Reports of Lincoln's Secretary*, ed. Michael Burlingame (Lincoln: University of Nebraska Press 1999), 5–6. This is a modern edition of Stoddard's White House memoir, originally published in 1890 by Charles L. Webster & Co. of New York.

22. William O. Stoddard, *Lincoln's White House Secretary: The Adventurous Life of William O. Stoddard*, ed. Harold Holzer (Carbondale: Southern Illinois University Press, 2006), 264.

23. Ibid., 234.

24. Ishbel Ross, *The President's Wife, Mary Todd Lincoln: A Biography* (New York: Putnam, 1973), 111.

25. Stoddard, *Inside the White House* 150–51.

26. Noah Brooks, *Lincoln Observed: Civil War Dispatches of Noah Brooks*, ed. Michael Burlingame (Baltimore: John Hopkins University Press 1998), 83.

27. Stoddard, *Lincoln's White House Secretary*, 57.

28. Ibid., 256.

29. Ibid., 236.

30. Helen Nicolay incorrectly identifies him as Edward Neale.

31. Edward D. Neill, *Reminiscences of the Last Year of President Lincoln's Life: Read at a Meeting of the Minnesota Commandery of the Military Order of the Loyal Legion, St. Paul, Minn., Nov. 4, 1885* (St. Paul, MN: Pioneer Press, 1885), 2.

32. John Hay to John G. Nicolay, October 28, 1862, in Hay, *Inside Lincoln's White House*, 27.

33. John Hay to John G. Nicolay, September 22, 1864, in ibid., 95.

34. Wayne Temple, "Charles Henry Philbrick: Private Secretary to President Lincoln," *Illinois College Alumni Magazine,* Summer 1997, i–viii.

35. Nicolay, *Lincoln's Secretary,* 87–88.

36. JGN to Therena Bates, March 10, 1861, Box 2, JGN Papers.

37. Catherine Clinton, *Mrs. Lincoln: A Life* (2009; repr., New York: Harper Perennial, 2010), 124, 130.

38. Justin G. Turner and Linda Levitt Turner, *Mary Todd Lincoln: Her Life and Letters* (New York: Harper & Row, 1972), 376.

39. Ross, *President's Wife, Mary Todd Lincoln,* 255.

40. Turner and Turner, *Mary Todd Lincoln: Her Life and Letters,* 376n.

41. Ross, *President's Wife, Mary Todd Lincoln,* 111.

42. JGN to Therena Bates, March 10, 1861, Box 2, JGN Papers.

43. JGN to Therena Bates, March 24, 1861, Box 2, JGN Papers.

44. JGN to Therena Bates, March 17, 1861, Box 2, JGN Papers.

45. JGN to Therena Bates, March 20. 1861, Box 2, JGN Papers.

46. JGN to Therena Bates, March 31, 1861, Box 2, JGN Papers.

47. JGN to Therena Bates, April 7, 1861 Box 2, JGN Papers.

48. JGN to Therena Bates, April, 11, 1861, Box 2, JGN Papers.

49. JGN to Therena Bates, April 19, 1861, Box 2, JGN Papers.

50. Nicolay and Hay, *Abraham Lincoln,* 4:61.

51. Ibid., 4:156.

52. JGN to Therena Bates, April 27, 1861, Box 2, JGN Papers.

53. JGN to Therena Bates, May 12, 1861, Box 2, JGN Papers.

54. Zeitz, *Lincoln's Boys,* 329.

55. JGN to Therena Bates, May 25, 1861, Box 2, JGN Papers.

56. JGN to Therena Bates, May 31, 1861, Box 2, JGN Papers.

57. JGN to Therena Bates, June 2, 1861, Box 2, JGN Papers.

58. JGN to Therena Bates, June 7, 1861, Box 2, JGN Papers.

59. JGN to Therena Bates, June 18, 1861, Box 2, JGN Papers.

60. JGN to Therena Bates, July 21, 1861, Box 2, JGN Papers.

61. JGN to Therena Bates, July 23, 1861, Box 2, JGN Papers.

62. JGN to Therena Bates, July 26, 1861, Box 2, JGN Papers.

63. JGN to Therena Bates, July 28, 1861, Box 2, JGN Papers.

64. JGN to Therena Bates, August 2, 1861, Box 2, JGN Papers.

65. Nicolay, *Lincoln's Secretary,* 88.

66. Conroy, *Lincoln's White House,* 86.

67. JGN to Therena Bates, August 11, 1861, Box 2, JGN Papers.

68. JGN to John Hay, August 11, 1861, Box 2, JGN Papers.

69. JGN to Therena Bates, August 14, 1861, Box 2, JGN Papers.

70. JGN to Therena Bates, August 22, 1861, Box 2, JGN Papers.

71. JGN to Therena Bates, September 8, 1861, Box 2, JGN Papers.

72. Abraham Lincoln, Second Inaugural Address, March 4, 1865.

73. JGN to Therena Bates, September 8, 1861, Box 2, JGN Papers.

74. JGN to Therena Bates, September 15, 1861, Box 2, JGN Papers.

75. Journal entry, September 17, 1861, Box 2, JGN Papers.

76. JGN to Therena Bates, October 15, 1861, Box 2, JGN Papers.

77. JGN to John Hay, October 21, 1861, Box 2, JGN Papers.

78. JGN to Therena Bates, October 21, 1861, Box 2, JGN Papers.

79. Daniel M. Epstein, *Lincoln's Men: The President and His Private Secretaries* (Garden City, NY: Doubleday, 1968), 69–71.

80. JGN to Therena Bates, October 2, 1861, Box 2, JGN Papers.

81. Notes on a private conversation with Lincoln, October 2, 1861, Box 2, JGN Papers.

82. Qtd. in Donald, *Lincoln,* 326.

83. Nicolay, *Lincoln's Secretary,* 84.

84. JGN to Therena Bates, November 21, 1861, Box 2, JGN Papers.

85. JGN to Therena Bates, November 28, 1861, Box 2, JGN Papers.

86. JGN to Therena Bates, December 25, 1861, Box 2, JGN Papers.

CHAPTER SIX. WAR ON MANY FRONTS, 1862

1. *Etiquette at Washington,* 52.

2. Noah Brooks, qtd. in Allen C. Guelzo, *Lincoln's Emancipation Proclamation* (New York: Simon & Schuster, 2004), 206.

3. JGN to Therena Bates, January 14, 1862, Box 2, JGN Papers.

4. JGN to Therena Bates January 15, 1862, Box 2, JGN Papers.

5. Ross, *President's Wife: Mary Todd Lincoln,* 97–98.

6. JGN to Therena Bates, February 2, 1862, Box 2, JGN Papers.

7. JGN to Therena Bates, February 6, 1862, Box 2, JGN Papers.

8. JGN to Therena Bates, January 30, 1862, Box 2, JGN Papers.

9. JGN to Therena Bates, February 11, 1862, Box 2, JGN Papers.

10. Nicolay, *Lincoln's Secretary,* 132–33.

11. JGN to Therena Bates, February 21, 1862, Box 2, JGN Papers.

12. Ibid.

13. JGN to Therena Bates, February26, 1862, Box 2, JGN Papers.

14. JGN to Therena Bates, March 23, 1862, Box 2, JGN Papers.

15. Donald, *Lincoln,* 340.

16. JGN to Therena Bates, April 2, 1862, Box 2, JGN Papers.

17. JGN to Therena Bates, April 24, 1862, Box 2, JGN Papers.

18. JGN to Therena Bates, May 4 and 9, 1862 Box 2, JGN Papers.

19. JGN to Therena Bates, May 21, 1862, Box 2, JGN Papers.

20. JGN to Therena Bates, June 5, 1862, Box 2, JGN Papers.

21. JGN to Therena Bates, June 27, 1862, Box 2, JGN Papers.

22. JGN to Therena Bates, June 29, 1862, Box 2, JGN Papers.

23. JGN to Therena Bates, June 15, 1862 Box 2, JGN Papers. See also Matthew Pinsker, *Lincoln's Sanctuary: Abraham Lincoln and the Soldiers' Home* (New York: Oxford University Press, 2003), 22.

24. JGN to Therena Bates, July 4, 1862, Box 2, JGN Papers.

25. JGN to Therena Bates, July 13 1862 Box 2, JGN Papers.

26. JGN to Therena Bates, July 13, 1862, Box 2, JGN Papers.

27. John G. Nicolay, *Lincoln's Secretary Goes West: Two Reports by John G. Nicolay on Frontier Indian Troubles, 1862*, ed. Theodore C. Blegen (La Crosse, WI: Sumac Press, 1965), 10. For a complete list of materials checked out from the Library of Congress under Lincoln's name, see Emanuel Hertz, *Abraham Lincoln: A New Portrait* (New York: Horace Liveright, 1931), 1:269–71. The list, which contains many foreign-language titles, indicates that Nicolay and Hay often used the president's library privileges for their own reading interests. Therefore, it cannot be used to decipher Lincoln's reading interests during his time as president.

28. Nicolay, *Lincoln's Secretary*, 151.

29. U.S. Office of Indian Affairs, *Annual Report of the Commissioner of Indian Affairs for the Year, 1862* (Washington, D.C.: GPO), 1862.

30. Gustav Niebuhr, *Lincoln's Bishop: A President, a Priest, and the Fate of 300 Dakota Sioux Warriors* (New York: HarperOne, 2014), 93–94.

31. Abraham Lincoln, Annual Address to Congress, December 1, 1862, in *Collected Works of Abraham Lincoln*, 5:525.

32. Niebuhr, *Lincoln's Bishop*, 94.

33. Lincoln, Annual Address to Congress, December 1, 1862, 5:525.

34. Niebuhr, *Lincoln's Bishop*, 90.

35. United States War Department, *War of the Rebellion: A Compilation of the Official Records of the Union and Confederate Armies*, ser. 1, vol. 13 (Washington, D.C.: GPO, 1885), 599.

36. Ibid., 599–600.

37. United States Bureau of Indian Affairs, *Annual Report of the Commissioner for Indian Affairs for the Year 1862* (Washington, D.C.: GPO, 1862), 57.

38. John G. Nicolay, "Hole-in-the-Day," *Harper's New Monthly Magazine* 26 (January 1863): 186–91, repr. in Nicolay, *Lincoln's Secretary Goes West*, 21–42.

39. Nicolay, *Lincoln's Secretary*, 155.

40. Nicolay, "Hole-in-the-Day," 30.

41. Ibid., 31.

42. John G. Nicolay, "The Sioux War," *Continental Monthly* 3 (February 1863): 195–204, repr. in Nicolay, *Lincoln's Secretary Goes West*, 68–69.

43. Ibid., 68.

44. "Lincoln's Sioux War Order," *Minnesota History* 33, no. 2 (Summer 1952): 77–99. The article replicates the first page of the list of names that Lincoln thought deserved death. The manuscript was found in the papers of Edward Neill.

45. Jane S. Davis, "Two Sioux War Orders: A Mystery Unraveled," *Minnesota History* 41, no. 3 (Fall 1968): 120.

46. Nicolay, *Lincoln's Secretary*, 155.

47. JGN to John Hay, September 8, 1862, Box 2, JGN Papers.

48. JGN to Therena Bates, October 13, 1862, Box 2, JGN Papers.

49. A. H. Guernsey to JGN, October 24, 1862, Box 2, JGN Papers.
50. JGN to Therena Bates, October 26, 1862, Box 2, JGN Papers.
51. JGN to John Hay, October 26, 1862, Box 2, JGN Papers.
52. Donald, *Lincoln,* 380–81.
53. JGN to John Hay, October 26, 1862, Box 2, JGN Papers.
54. JGN to Therena Bates, November 9, 1862, Box 2, JGN Papers.
55. JGN to Therena Bates, November 13, 1862, Box 2, JGN Papers.
56. JGN to Therena Bates, November 27, 1862, Box 2, JGN Papers.
57. American Civil War Research Database, http:www.civilwardata.com.
58. Ibid.
59. JGN from O.M. Hatch, March 11, 1862, Box 2, JGN Papers.
60. JGN to Therena Bates, December 7, 1862, Box 2, JGN Papers.
61. JGN to Therena Bates, December 11, 1862, Box 2, JGN Papers.
62. JGN to Therena Bates, December 17, 1862, Box 2, JGN Papers.
63. Donald, *Lincoln,* 400.
64. Ibid., 400, 404.
65. JGN to Therena Bates, December 23, 1862, Box 2, JGN Papers.
66. JGN to Therena Bates, December 25, 1862, Box 2, JGN Papers

CHAPTER SEVEN. EMANCIPATION, EUPHORIA, AND FRUSTRATION, 1863

1. Nicolay, *Lincoln's Secretary,* 163–64.
2. Nicolay and Hay, *Abraham Lincoln,* 7:429–30.
3. Qtd. in Nicolay, *With Lincoln in the White House,* 101–2.
4. Horace Greeley to JGN, January 10, 1863, Box 2, JGN Papers.
5. JGN to Therena Bates, January 11, 1863, Box 2, JGN Papers.
6. JGN to Therena Bates, January 25, 1863, Box 2, JGN Papers.
7. JGN to Therena Bates, February, 15 1863, Box 2, JGN Papers.
8. JGN to Therena Bates, March 8, 1863, Box 2, JGN Papers.
9. JGN to Therena Bates, March 19, 1863, Box 2, JGN Papers.
10. JGN to Therena Bates, March 22, 1863, Box 2, JGN Papers.
11. JGN to Therena Bates, April 12, 1863, Box 2, JGN Papers.
12. JGN to Therena Bates, April 16, 1863, Box 2, JGN Papers; Donald, *Lincoln,* 434.
13. JGN to Therena Bates, April 29, 1863, Box 2, JGN Papers.
14. JGN to Therena Bates, May 3, 1863, Box 2, JGN Papers.
15. JGN to Therena Bates, May 4–6, 1863, Box 2, JGN Papers.
16. JGN to Therena Bates, May 25, 1863, Box 2, JGN Papers.
17. Nicolay, *Lincoln's Secretary,* 170.
18. JGN to *Chicago Tribune,* June 19, 1863, in Nicolay, *With Lincoln in the White House,* 115–16.
19. Qtd. in Donald, *Lincoln,* 248, 342, 399, 401.
20. Hertz, *Abraham Lincoln,* 370.
21. Treasury Department Requisition No. 6306, July 14, 1863, Box 3, JGN Papers.
22. Stephen J. Leonard, "John Nicolay in Colorado," in *Essays and Monographs in Colorado History,* no. 11 (Denver: Colorado Historical Society, 1990), 30.

23. Nicolay, *Lincoln's Secretary,* 170.

24. Robert L. Cole, *John Hay* (Boston: Twayne, 1978), 57.

25. JGN to Therena Bates, June 21, 1863, Box 2, JGN Papers.

26. JGN to Therena Bates, June 30, 1863, Box 2, JGN Papers.

27. JGN to Therena Bates, July 5, 1863, Box 3, JGN Papers.

28. JGN to Therena Bates, July 12, 1863, Box 3, JGN Papers.

29. Qtd. in Noah Andre Trudeau, *Gettysburg: A Testing of Courage* (New York: HarperCollins, 2008), 539.

30. Qtd. in Michael Burlingame, *Abraham Lincoln: A Life* (Baltimore: Johns Hopkins University Press, 2008), 511.

31. Order of the Secretary of War, War Department, Washington, July 9, 1863, Box 3, JGN Papers.

32. United States Bureau of Indian Affairs, *Annual Report of the Commissioner of Indian Affairs for the Year 1863* (Washington, D.C.: GPO, 1863), 143.

33. Ibid., 144.

34. The fort in Nebraska was named for the military explorer, Stephen Kearney. The fort should not be confused with Fort Philip Kearny in the Powder River country of Wyoming, which was the site of the Fetterman battle of December 21, 1866.

35. JGN to John Hay, August 9, 1863, Box 3, JGN Papers.

36. JGN to Therena Bates, August 9, 1863, Box 3, JGN Papers.

37. JGN to Therena Bates, August 17, 1863, Box 3, JGN Papers.

38. U.S. Bureau of Indian Affairs, *Annual Report . . . 1863,* 148.

39. JGN to Therena Bates, August 25, 1863, Box 3, JGN Papers.

40. JGN to John Hay, August 30, 1863, Box 3, JGN Papers.

41. JGN to Therena Bates, September 25, 1863, Box 3, JGN Papers.

42. U.S. Bureau of Indian Affairs, *Annual Report . . . 1863,* 148.

43. Ibid., 126.

44. For a discussion of peace medals in general and the history of the Lincoln Peace Medal in particular, see Francis P. Prucha, *Indian Peace Medals in American History* (Madison: State Historical Society of Wisconsin, 1971).

45. U.S. Bureau of Indian Affairs, *Annual Report . . . 1863,* 149.

46. Ibid., 151.

47. Ibid., 145.

48. Ibid., 146.

49. John Pierce to JGN, November 29, 1863, Box 3, JGN Papers.

50. Virginia McConnell Simmons, *The Ute Indians of Utah, Colorado, and New Mexico* (Boulder: University Press of Colorado 2000), 116.

51. Hay, *Inside Lincoln's White House,* 87.

52. Ibid., 102.

53. Hay, *Inside Lincoln's White House,* 109.

54. Charles Hamilton, *Lincoln in Photographs: An Album of Every Known Pose* (Norman: University of Oklahoma Press, 1963), 163.

55. Hay, *Inside Lincoln's White House,* 110.

56. Ibid., 325–26n271.

57. Nicolay and Hay, *Abraham Lincoln,* 8:192.

58. Nicolay, *Lincoln's Secretary,* 176.

59. Hay, *Inside Lincoln's White House,* 112–13.

60. Nicolay and Hay, *Abraham Lincoln,* 8:199–202.

61. Nicolay, *Lincoln's Secretary,* 178.

62. Nicolay and Hay, *Abraham Lincoln,* 8:203.

63. John George Nicolay, "Lincoln's Gettysburg Address," *Century Magazine* 47, no. 4 (February 1894): 596–608.

64. Note dated December 19, 1863, Box 3, JGN Papers.

65. Nicolay and Hay, *Abraham Lincoln,* 8:310–12.

66. Ibid.

67. Stoddard, *Inside the White House during War Times,* 108–9.

68. U.S. Bureau of Indian Affairs, *Annual Report . . . 1863,* 125.

69. Nicolay, *Lincoln's Secretary,* 180.

70. Ibid., 182–84.

CHAPTER EIGHT. VICTORY AND TRAGEDY, 1864–1865

1. JGN to Therena Bates, January 2, 1864, Box 3, JGN Papers.

2. Nicolay, *Lincoln's Secretary,* 78.

3. Stoddard, *Inside the White House during War Times,* 49.

4. Nicolay, *Lincoln's Secretary,* 83.

5. Ibid., 79.

6. JGN to John Hay, January 2, 1864, Box 3, JGN Papers.

7. JGN to John Hay, January 18, 1864, Box 3, JGN Papers.

8. Ruth Painter Randall, *Mary Lincoln: Biography of a Marriage* (Boston: Little, Brown, 1953), 369.

9. Mary Todd Lincoln to Abram Wakeman, February 18, 1865, in Turner, *Mary Todd Lincoln,* 201.

10. Nicolay, *Lincoln's Secretary,* 121.

11. JGN to John Hay, January 29, 1864, Box 3, JGN Papers.

12. Nicolay, *Lincoln's Secretary,* 192.

13. JGN to Therena Bates February 12, 17, 21, 1864, Box 3, JGN Papers.

14. JGN to John Hay, February 17, 1864, Box 3, JGN Papers.

15. JGN to Therena Bates, February 28, 1864, Box 3, JGN Papers.

16. Stoddard, *Inside the White House during War Times,* 77–78.

17. Ibid, 79.

18. JGN to John Hay, February 10, 1864, Box 3, JGN Papers.

19. An act of February 13, 1864, Chapter 9, 13 Stat. at Large 3.

20. JGN to Thaddeus Stevens, February 15, 1864, Box 3, JGN Papers.

21. A check of both the *Congressional Globe* and the *Statutes at Large* does not reveal any private bill on Nicolay's behalf.

22. Shastid, *A Second Life,* 72n.

23. Memorandum, March 8, 1864, Box 3, JGN Papers.

24. Memorandum, March 9, 1864, Box 3, JGN Papers.

25. Hay, *Inside Lincoln's White House*, 183.

26. JGN to Therena Bates, March 25, 1864, Box 3, JGN Papers.

27. JGN to Therena Bates, April 1, 1864, Box 3, JGN Papers.

28. John Evans to JGN, March 29, 1864, Box 3, JGN Papers.

29. JGN to Therena Bates, April 10, 1864, Box 3, JGN Papers.

30. JGN to Therena Bates, April 17, 1864, Box 3, JGN Papers.

31. JGN to Therena Bates, April 24, May 1, 1864, Box 3, JGN Papers.

32. JGN to Therena Bates, May 15, 1864, Box 3, JGN Papers.

33. JGN to Therena Bates, May 22, 1864, Box 3, JGN Papers.

34. JGN to John Hay, June 5, 1864, Box 3, JGN Papers.

35. Qtd. in Donald, *Lincoln*, 505.

36. JGN to John Hay, June 6, 1864, Box 3, JGN Papers.

37. Nicolay, *Lincoln's Secretary*, 209–10.

38. JGN to John Hay, July 17, 1864, Box 3, JGN Papers.

39. Memorandum, August 23, 1864, in Lincoln, *Collected Works*, 7:514.

40. JGN to Therena Bates, August 21, 1864, Box 3, JGN Papers.

41. JGN John Hay, August 25, 1864, Box 3, JGN Papers.

42. Nicolay and Hay, *Abraham Lincoln*, 9:244, 250, 252, 261–62.

43. Ibid., 253.

44. JGN to Therena Bates, September 4, 1864, Box 3, JGN Papers.

45. JGN to Therena Bates, September 11, 1864, Box 3, JGN Papers.

46. Provost Marshal's Office, District of Columbia, to JGN, September 20, 1864, Box 1, JGN Papers.

47. JGN to Therena Bates, September 29, 1864, Box 3, JGN Papers.

48. *New York Times*, September 29, 1864, 4.

49. Nicolay, *Lincoln's Secretary*, 219.

50. American Civil War Research Database, http://www.civilwardata.com.

51. JGN to Therena Bates, September 29, 1864, Box 3, JGN Papers.

52. JGN to Therena Bates, October 2, 1864, Box 3, JGN Papers.

53. JGN to Therena Bates, October 4, 1864, Box 3, JGN Papers.

54. JGN to Abraham Lincoln, October 10, 1864, in Nicolay, *With Lincoln in the White House*, 162.

55. JGN to John Hay, November 10, 1864, Box 3, JGN Papers.

56. JGN to Therena Bates, November 30, 1864, Box 3, JGN Papers.

57. JGN to Therena Bates, December 4, 1864, Box 3, JGN Papers.

58. JGN to Therena Bates, December 8, 1864, Box 3, JGN Papers; White, *A. Lincoln*, 649–50.

59. JGN to Therena Bates, December 11, 1864, Box 3, JGN Papers.

60. JGN to Therena Bates, December 16, 1864, Box 3, JGN Papers.

61. JGN to Therena Bates, December 18, 1864, Box 3, JGN Papers.

62. JGN to Simon Cameron, December 23, 1864, qtd. in Nicolay, *With Lincoln in the White House*, 168.

63. JGN to Therena Bates, December 24, 1864, Box 3, JGN Papers.
64. JGN to Therena Bates, December 25, 1864, Box 3, JGN Papers.
65. JGN to Therena Bates, December 30, 1864, Box 3, JGN Papers.
66. JGN to Therena Bates, January 6, 1865, Box 3, JGN Papers.
67. JGN to Therena Bates, January 13, 1865, Box 3, JGN Papers.
68. JGN to Therena Bates, February 4, 1865, Box 3, JGN Papers.
69. Ibid.
70. JGN to Therena Bates, February 10, 1865, Box 3, JGN Papers.
71. JGN to Therena Bates, February 14, 1865, Box 3, JGN Papers.
72. JGN to Therena Bates, February 26, 1865, Box 3, JGN Papers.
73. JGN to Therena Bates, March 5, 1865, Box 3, JGN Papers.
74. JGN to Therena Bates, March 12, 1865, Box 3, JGN Papers.
75. Hertz, *Abraham Lincoln,* 1:371.
76. JGN to Therena Bates, April 17, 1865, Box 3, JGN Papers.
77. JGN to Therena Bates, April 18, 1865, Box 3, JGN Papers.
78. John G. Nicolay, *A Short Life of Abraham Lincoln* (1902; repr., London: Forgotten Books, 2015), 545.
79. Ibid., 544.
80. Ibid., 544–45.
81. General John Blair Smith Todd, Delegate for Dakota Territory in the House of Representatives and a cousin of Mary Todd Lincoln.
82. Coggeshall, *Lincoln Memorial.*
83. Gideon Welles, *The Civil War Diary of Gideon Welles,* ed. William E. Gienapp and Erica L. Gienapp (Urbana: University of Illinois Press, 2014), 631–32.
84. Nicolay, *Short Life of Abraham Lincoln,* 546.
85. Zeitz, *Lincoln's Boys,* 168.

CHAPTER NINE. TO PARIS AND BACK

1. JGN to Andrew Johnson, April 20, 1865 in Nicolay, *With Lincoln in the White House,* 178.
2. Clinton, *Mrs. Lincoln,* 252–54.
3. JGN to Therena Bates, April 24, 1865, Box 3, JGN Papers.
4. JGN Papers, Letter from James C. Derby, April 28, 1865, Box 3, JGN Papers.
5. JGN to Therena Bates, May 5, 1865, Box 3, JGN Papers.
6. Shastid, *My Second Life,* 72n.
7. JGN to Therena Bates, May 30, 1865, Box 3, JGN Papers.
8. Nicolay, *Lincoln's Secretary,* 241.
9. Ibid., 241.
10. JGN Papers, Box 1, Scrapbook 1856–1870, JGN Papers.
11. Shastid, *My Second Life,* 1.
12. John Bigelow to JGN, May 31, 1865, Box 3, JGN Papers.
13. See misc. correspondence, March 1865, Box 3, JGN Papers.
14. Peter J. Hugill, *World Trade since 1431: Geography, Trade, and Capitalism* (Baltimore: Johns Hopkins University Press, 1993), 128.

15. Scrapbook 1856–1870, Box 1, JGN Papers.

16. Qtd. in Zeitz, *Lincoln's Boys,* 164.

17. Nicolay, *Lincoln's Secretary,* 241–42.

18. Zeitz, *Lincoln's Boys,* 175.

19. JGN to Therena Nicolay, September 11, 1866, Box 3, JGN Papers.

20. Nicolay, *Lincoln's Secretary,* 243.

21. Taliaferro, *All The Great Prizes,* 110.

22. JGN to Charles Walker, December 14, 1865, Box 3, JGN Papers.

23. Nicolay, *Lincoln's Secretary,* 245–46.

24. JGN to Charles Walker, December 14, 1865, Box 3, JGN Papers.

25. Valentine Haefner to JGN, September 28, 1865, Box 3, JGN Papers.

26. Albert Bierstadt to JGN, May 24, 1867, Box 3, JGN Papers.

27. Roscoe Conkling to JGN, March 21, 1868, Box 4, JGN Papers.

28. Nicolay, *Lincoln's Secretary,* 247.

29. Suez Canal Company to JGN, April 12, 1867, Box 3, JGN Papers.

30. Allan Pinkerton to JGN, June 12, 1867, Box 3, JGN Papers.

31. Various notes between January and July 1866, Box 3, JGN Papers.

32. John Jay and E. E. Brier, *The American Thanksgiving Celebration in Paris Thursday Evening, December 7, 1865* (Paris: E. Brière Rue Saint-Honoré, 1865), 257.

33. Nicolay, *Lincoln's Secretary,* 246.

34. Various notes and letters, September 1865, Box 3, JGN Papers.

35. Act of March 26, 1790, Chapter 3 1 Stat 103.

36. Paris Consular Records, 1866, 233, National Archives, College Park, MD.

37. JGN to Therena Nicolay, August 18, 1866, Box 3, JGN Papers.

38. JGN to Therena Nicolay, September 1, 1866, Box 3, JGN Papers.

39. "Letters of Application and Recommendation During the Administrations of Lincoln and Johnson, 1861–69," in "John G. Nicolay," Cabinet 20, Drawer 6, Reel 18, National Archives, College Park, MD.

40. Frederick W. Seward to JGN, October13, 1866, Box 3, JGN Papers.

41. Therena Nicolay to Emma Bates, August 14, 1867, Box 3, JGN Papers.

42. Montgomery Gibbs was an agent of the U.S. Treasury Department in Europe charged with monitoring the prices of goods sent from Europe to the United States. His diligence was questioned, but he had friends in the Senate. Nicolay apparently had no use for him.

43. JGN to Therena Nicolay, October 30, 1866, Box 3, JGN Papers.

44. JGN to Frederick W. Seward, November 2, 1866, Box 3, JGN Papers.

45. Frederick W. Seward to JGN, November 19, 1866, Box 3, JGN Papers.

46. Letters of Application and Recommendation During the Administrations of Lincoln and Johnson, 1861–69," in "Jacob R. Freese," Cabinet 20, Drawer 6, Reel 18, National Archives, College Park, MD.

47. Therena Nicolay to Mrs. Dorus Bates, August 14, 1867, Box 3, JGN Papers.

48. JGN to Therena Nicolay, September 20, 21, 1867, Box 3, JGN Papers.

49. JGN to Therena Nicolay, September 23, 1867, Box 3, JGN Papers.

50. Dispatch No. 73, Paris Consular Records, 1868, National Archives, College Park, MD.

51. J. R. Biggs Jr. to JGN, February 9, 1869, Box 4, JGN Papers.

52. James Harlan to JGN, April 29, 1869, Box 4, JGN Papers.

53. Dispatch No. 95, Paris Consular Records, 1869, National Archives, College Park, MD.

54. Zeitz, *Lincoln's Boys,* 186–87.

55. In Nicolay's papers at the Library of Congress, there is a sketch, presumably drawn by Nicolay, of the farm buildings, as well as property maps of the Kansas farm.

56. [Illegible] Dubois, Jacob Bunn, and O.M. Hatch to JGN, July 9, 1870, Box 4, JGN Papers.

57. John Hay to "My Dear Household Circle," August 10, 1870, qtd. in Taliaferro, *All the Great Prizes,* 125.

58. JGN to *Chicago Republican* Directors, August 1870, Box 4, JGN Papers.

59. Nicolay, *Lincoln's Secretary,* 262–63.

60. Ibid., 264.

61. Ibid, 267; JGN to Schuyler Colfax, June? 1872, and Schuyler Colfax to JGN, July 2, 1872, Box 4, JGN Papers.

62. *Philadelphia Public Ledger and Daily Transcript,* December 16, 1872, in Box 4, JGN Papers.

63. Justice Samuel Nelson had retired from the court on November 28, 1872.

64. *New York Times,* December 15, 1872, 1. The article incorrectly refers to him as Frederick Schlev.

65. Ibid.

66. Charles Lewis Wagandt, *The Mighty Revolution: Negro Emancipation in Maryland, 1862–1864* (Baltimore: Johns Hopkins University Press, 1964), 62–63.

67. Ibid., 141.

68. *New York Times,* December 15, 1872, 1.

69. *New York Times,* April 14, 1889, 1.

CHAPTER TEN. CRAFTING THE LINCOLN LEGACY

1. Scrapbook 1856–1858, Box 1, JGN Papers.

2. Qtd. in William C. Harris, *Lincoln and Congress* (Carbondale: Southern Illinois University Press, 2017), 132.

3. David C. Mearns, *The Lincoln Papers: The Story of the Collection with Selections to July 4, 1861* (Garden City, N.Y.: Doubleday, 1948), 1:48.

4. David Herbert Donald, *Lincoln's Herndon: A Biography* (1948; repr., New York: Da Capo Press, 1989), 177.

5. Mearns, *Lincoln Papers,* 1:18, 22, 139; Zeitz, *Lincoln's Boys,* 232.

6. Robert Lincoln to Francis James Child, April 27, 1865, qtd. in Mearns, *Lincoln Papers,* 1:45.

7. Mearns, *Lincoln Papers,* 1:48.

8. Qtd. in Donald, *Lincoln's Herndon,* 231.

9. Robert Lincoln to JGN, December 16, 1872, Box 4, JGN Papers.

10. JGN to Rev. J. A. Reed, December, 24, 1872, Box 4, JGN Papers.

11. JGN to Robert Lincoln, May 31, 1873, Box 4, JGN Papers.

12. Adams, Charles Francis, *The Address of Charles Francis Adams, of Massachusetts on the Life, Character and Services of William H. Seward: Delivered by Invitation of the Legislature of the State of New York, in Albany, April 18, 1873* (New York: D. Appleton, 1873), 31–32.

13. JGN to Robert Lincoln, May 31, 1873, Box 4, JGN Papers.

14. Zeitz, *Lincoln's Boys*, 248.

15. Mearns, *Lincoln Papers*, 1:51.

16. JGN to Robert Lincoln, March 3, 1873, Box 4, JGN Papers.

17. Ibid.; Zeitz, *Lincoln's Boys*, 250–51.

18. JGN to Robert Lincoln, n.d., 1874, Box 4, JGN Papers.

19. JGN to Robert Lincoln, July 17, 1874, Box 4, JGN Papers.

20. John Hay to Richard W. Gilder, December 29, 1886, John M. Hay Papers, Huntington Library, San Marino, CA (hereafter cited as JMH Papers).

21. Mearns, *Lincoln Papers*, 1:69.

22. JGN to Robert Lincoln, February 17, 1875, Box 4, JGN Papers.

23. JGN to John Hay, November 16, 1875, Box 4, JGN Papers.

24. Nicolay, *Lincoln's Secretary*, 280

25. Nicolay, "Writing of *Abraham Lincoln: A History*," 269.

26. Ibid., 267.

27. Taliaferro, *All the Great Prizes*, 169.

28. Ibid.

29. George McCrary to JGN, March 19, 1877, Box 4, JGN Papers.

30. JGN to John Hay, June 25, 1877, Box 4, JGN Papers.

31. Edward L. Burlingame to JGN, March 4, 1881, Box 4, JGN Papers.

32. JGN to Charles Scribner's Sons, March 15, 1881, Box 4, JGN Papers.

33. JGN to Mrs. Lucretia R. Garfield, November 1, 1881, Box 4, JGN Papers.

34. JGN to Therena Bates Nicolay, February 26, 1882, Box 4, JGN Papers.

35. Century Company Editorial Department to JGN, March 7, 1882, JGN Papers.

36. JGN to the Editor, *Century Magazine*, March 21, 1882, Box 4, JGN Papers.

37. JGN to the Editor, *Century Magazine*, July 3, 1882, Box 4, JGN Papers.

38. JGN to Frank Bates, December 16, 1882, Box 4, JGN Papers.

39. Nicolay, "Writing of *Abraham Lincoln: A History*," 271.

40. Zeitz, *Lincoln's Boys*, 270.

41. JGN to John Hay, March 19, 1885, Box 4, JGN Papers.

42. JGN to John Hay, March 26, 1885, Box 4, JGN Papers.

43. Arthur John, *The Best Years of the Century: Richard Watson Gilder,* Scribner's Monthly, *and* Century Magazine, *1870–1909* (Urbana: University of Illinois Press, 1981), 120.

44. Ibid, 130.

45. Richard W. Gilder, *Letters of Richard Watson Gilder*, ed. Rosamund Gilder (Boston: Houghton Mifflin, 1916), 172

46. Roswell Smith to John Hay, June 13, 1885, Box 4, JGN Papers.

47. John, *Best Years of the Century*, 130.

48. Taliaferro, *All the Great Prizes*, 224–25.

49. JGN to John Hay, July 19, 1885, Box 4, JGN Papers.

50. JGN to R. W. Gilder, August 5, 1886, Box 4, JGN Papers.

51. Gilder, *Letters of Richard Watson Gilder,* 175.

52. Nicolay Collection, Box 3 of Lincoln Financial Foundation Collection, Allen County Public Library, Fort Wayne, IN.

53. Nicolay, *Lincoln's Secretary,* 286–88.

54. R. W. Gilder to JGN, November 2, 1885, Box 4, JGN Papers.

55. JGN to R. W. Gilder, November 13, 1885, Box 4, JGN Papers.

56. The interment record of Oak Hill Cemetery, Washington, D.C., dated November 27, 1885, lists dysentery as the cause of Therena's death. Therena was buried in plot 273E.

57. Undated obituaries in unnamed Washington newspapers, Box 4, JGN Papers.

58. Nicolay, Helen *Lincoln's Secretary,* 291.

59. JGN to John Hay, December 9, 1885, JGN Papers.

60. Nicolay, *Lincoln's Secretary,* 291.

61. Ibid., 292.

62. JGN to Roswell Smith, December 5, 1885, Box 4, JGN Papers.

63. Roswell Smith to JGN, December 29, 1885, Box 4, JGN Papers.

64. Herbert B. Adams, secretary, American Historical Association, to JGN, March 25, 1886, Box 4, JGN Papers; JGN to Herbert Adams, April 2, 1886, Box 4, JGN Papers. In comparison to Nicolay's $25 fee, lifetime membership in the AHA as of 2016 requires a $3,500 one-time contribution.

65. JGN to R.W. Gilder, June 26, 1887, Box 4, JGN Papers.

66. John Hay to Richard W. Gilder, November 20, 1888, JMH Papers.

67. JGN to R. W. Gilder, October 15, 1886, Box 4, JGN Papers.

68. R. W. Gilder to JGN, December 29, 1886, Box 4, JGN Papers.

69. JGN to Roswell Smith, December 31, 1886, Box 4, JGN Papers.

70. JGN to R. W. Gilder, February 3, 1887, Box 4, JGN Papers.

71. JGN to R. W. Gilder, February 16, 1887, Box 4, JGN Papers.

72. JGN to Roswell Smith, March 4, 1887, Box 4, JGN Papers.

73. John Hay to R. W. Gilder, November 30, 1886(?), JMH Papers.

74. R. W. Gilder to JGN, March 30, 1887, Box 4, JGN Papers.

75. John Hay to R. W. Gilder, November 12, 1890, JMH Papers.

76. JGN to J. C. Derby, December 11, 1886, Abraham Lincoln Presidential Library, Springfield, IL.

77. JGN to R. W. Gilder, June 7, 1887, Box 4, JGN Papers.

78. JGN to William Carey, April 2, 1888, Box 4, JGN Papers.

79. JGN to Robert T. Lincoln, January 1, 1888, Box 5, JGN Papers.

80. Undated typed sheet headed, "Not to be used before December 23rd [1887]," JGN Papers, Box 5, JGN Papers.

81. JGN to Frank H. Scott, May 8, 1888, Box 5, JGN Papers.

82. E. H. Simons to JGN, May (?) 1888, Box 5, JGN Papers.

83. R. W. Gilder to JGN, June 16, 1888, Box 5, JGN Papers.

84. R. W. Gilder to JGN, July 12, 13, 1888, Box 5, JGN Papers.

85. Payment statement and check from the Century Company, December 31, 1888, Box 5, JGN Papers.

86. Typed copy of memorandum with notation in pencil [1888], Box 5, JGN Papers. Letters between Nicolay and the Century Company in March 1889 refer to the memorandum as having been sent in May 1888.

87. JGN to Roswell Smith, January 19, 1889, Box 5, JGN Papers.

88. John Hay to Richard W. Gilder, August 13, 1885, JMH Papers.

89. Frank H. Scott to JGN, March 2, 1889, Box 5, JGN Papers.

90. JGN to Frank H. Scott, March 5, 1889, Box 5, JGN Papers.

91. Frank H. Scott to JGN, March 6, 1889, Box 5, JGN Papers.

92. Frank H. Scott to JGN, December 28, 1889, Box 5, JGN Papers.

93. R. W. Gilder to JGN, January 2, 1890, Box 5, JGN Papers.

94. John, *Best Years of the Century,* 130.

95. JGN to R. W. Gilder, January 24, 1890, Box 5, JGN Papers.

96. JGN to C. C. Buel, June 13, 1890, Box 5, JGN Papers.

97. JGN to R. W. Gilder, July 18, 1890, Box 5, JGN Papers.

98. Mss. entitled "Newspaper notices of the Book," beginning November 16, 1890, Box 5, JGN Papers.

99. Printed testimonial, "What Hannibal Hamlin says of Nicolay & Hay Lincoln History," n.d., Box 5, Box 5, JGN Papers.

100. Nicolay and Hay, *Abraham Lincoln,* 9:73.

101. JGN to R. W. Gilder, July 18, 1890, Box 5, JGN Papers.

102. JGN to Frank H. Scott, November 16, 1892, Box 5, JGN Papers.

103. Frank H. Scott to JGN, June 13, 1895, Box 5, JGN Papers.

104. John G. Nicolay, *A Short Life of Abraham Lincoln: Condensed from Nicolay and Hay's* Abraham Lincoln: A History (New York: Century Co., 1902). This "short" life came to 578 pages as originally published.

CHAPTER ELEVEN. THE APOTHEOSIS OF ABRAHAM LINCOLN

1. See Hans L. Trefousse, *Carl Schurz: A Biography* (Knoxville: University of Tennessee Press, 1982) for a summary of Schurz's life and work.

2. *New York Times,* May 25, 1891, 3.

3. Carl Schurz, "Abraham Lincoln," *Atlantic Monthly* 67, no. 304 (June 1891): 721–22.

4. William Dean Howells, *New York Tribune,* February 9, 1891, qtd. in Taliaferro, *All the Great Prizes,* 262.

5. Taliaferro, *All the Great Prizes,* 263.

6. Qtd. in Benjamin Thomas, *Portrait for Posterity: Lincoln and His Biographers* (New Brunswick, NJ: Rutgers University Press, 1947), 123–24.

7. Nicolay, *Lincoln's Secretary,* 285.

8. Nicolay and Hay, *Abraham Lincoln,* 1:38.

9. The photograph was discovered by Ronald Rietveld in the Nicolay-Hay papers located at the Illinois State Library in 1952, when Rietveld was a fourteen-year-old

Lincoln researcher. Dr. Rietveld supervised coauthor Allen Carden's master's thesis in history in 1972.

10. In the ten volumes or 4,800 pages of the history, Nicolay is only mentioned by name eight times and Hay nine times.

11. Thayer, *Life and Letters of John Hay,* 2:32–33.

12. Ibid., 33.

13. Nicolay and Hay, *Abraham Lincoln,* 1:37.

14. Ibid., 1:42.

15. Ibid.

16. Ibid., 1:201.

17. Ibid., 3:256.

18. Jean H. Baker, *Mary Todd Lincoln: A Biography* (New York: W. W. Norton, 1987), 62.

19. Turner, *Mary Todd Lincoln,* 40–41.

20. Nicolay and Hay, *Abraham Lincoln,* 6:39–40. According to Nicolay's letter to a clergyman in 1872, when it came to "President Lincoln's religious belief, he (Nicolay) would in writing the biography of Lincoln "endeavor therein clearly to state what I know and think on this subject . . . as fully and carefully as possible" (JGN to Rev. J. A. Reed, December, 24, 1872, Box 4, JGN Papers). It seems reasonable to assume that Nicolay, rather than Hay, authored this passage.

21. Nicolay and Hay, *Abraham Lincoln,* 1:307.

22. Ibid., 2:29–30.

23. Ibid., 2:220.

24. Ibid., 3: 247, 257.

25. Ibid., 6:120.

26. Ibid., 3:318.

27. Ibid., 3:312.

28. Ibid., 10:82.

29. Ibid., 1:330–31.

30. Ibid., 1:377.

31. Ibid., 1:351.

32. Ibid., 2:147.

33. Ibid.

34. Ibid., 2:384.

35. Ibid., 2:429.

36. Ibid., 3:10.

37. Ibid., 2:381.

38. Ibid., 3:373.

39. Ibid., 3:447–48.

40. Ibid., 4:167.

41. Ibid., 6:271.

42. Ibid., 5:226.

43. Ibid., 6:127–28.

44. Ibid., 5:130.
45. Thayer, *Life and Letters of John Hay,* 2:33.
46. John Hay to R. W. Gilder, November 17, 1888, JMH Papers.
47. Nicolay and Hay, *Abraham Lincoln,* 8:310–11.
48. Ibid., 8:312.
49. Ibid., 8:313.
50. Ibid., 9:85.
51. Ibid., 8:325.
52. Ibid., 9:79.
53. Ibid., 8:317–18.
54. Ibid., 9:95.
55. Ibid., 9:394–95.
56. Ibid., 9:401–2.
57. Ibid., 9:403.
58. Ibid., 9:43–44.
59. Ibid., 9:261.
60. Qtd. in *Abraham Lincoln: The Observations of John G. Nicolay and John Hay,* ed. Michael Burlingame (Carbondale: Southern Illinois University Press, 2007), 2–3.
61. Nicolay and Hay, *Abraham Lincoln,* 5:370.
62. Ibid., 6:188.
63. Ibid., 7:278.
64. Ibid., 7:279.
65. Ibid., 6:22–23.
66. Ibid., 6:189–90.
67. Ibid., 9:291.
68. Ibid., 5:64.
69. Ibid., 8:144.
70. Ibid.,9:17.
71. Ibid., 9:285.
72. Ibid., 9:289.
73. Ibid., 9:481.
74. Ibid., 10:232.
75. Ibid., 7:326.
76. Ibid., 8:132–33
77. Ibid., 8:337.
78. Ibid., 8:338.
79. Ibid., 10:350.
80. Ibid., 10:353.
81. Ibid., 8:350.
82. Ibid., 8:236.
83. Ibid., 8:354–55.
84. Ibid., 10:166.
85. Ibid., 5:111–12.

86. Ibid., 6:339.
87. Ibid., 10:350.
88. Ibid., 4:101.
89. Ibid., 4:102–3.
90. Thayer, *Life and Letters of John Hay,* 2:32.
91. Nicolay and Hay, *Abraham Lincoln,* 10:270–74.
92. Ibid., 7:128.
93. Ibid., 10:111.
94. Letter signed by Hay and Nicolay to R. W. Gilder, November 13, 1888, JMH Papers.

CHAPTER TWELVE. ASSESSING THE MAN IN LINCOLN'S SHADOW

1. Find a Grave, www.findagrave.com.
2. Taft, Rees, and Speak, "Tablet Erected in Court House Park," 728.
3. Nicolay, *Lincoln's Secretary,* 85–86.
4. Sellers, "Serving the President," 52–64.
5. Ibid., 60.
6. Ibid., 63.
7. American Civil War Research Database, www.civilwardata.com.
8. Ibid.
9. *New York Times,* July 27, 1926, 1.
10. Sellers, "Serving the President," 63.
11. Nicolay, *Lincoln's Secretary,* 346.
12. Sellers, "Serving the President," 63.
13. Ann Marie Maguire and John Maguire, *Lincoln's Secretary's Secretary: Helen Nicolay Artist and Author* (Swan Island, ME: Atlantic Road Books, 2017), 36.
14. Ibid., 58, 85, 96.
15. Nicolay, *Lincoln's Secretary,* 342.
16. Letter of John Hay to Adams, Washington, D.C., September 19, 1901, in John Hay, *Letters of John Hay and Extracts from the Diary* (New York: Gordian Press, 1969), 231.
17. "Death of John G. Nicolay," *Washington Times,* September 27, 1901, 2.
18. Oak Hill Cemetery, Washington D.C., Interment Fee Record, September 26, 1901, D.C. Permit # 139461, Lot 273E.
19. Nicolay, *Lincoln's Secretary,* 343.
20. Richard W. Gilder to a Friend, September 30, 1901, in *Letters of Richard Watson Gilder,* 342.
21. Richard Watson Gilder, *The Poems of Richard Watson Gilder,* illustrated by Helena de Kay Gilder (Boston: Houghton Mifflin, 1908), 310.
22. Nicolay, *Lincoln's Secretary,* 85.
23. Richard Watson Gilder to Robert Lincoln, August 28, 1909 in *Letters of Richard Watson Gilder,* 488–89.
24. Richard Watson Gilder to a Friend, September 30, 1901, in *Letters of Richard Watson Gilder,* 342.

25. Thomas Craugwell, *Stealing Lincoln's Body* (Cambridge, MA: Belknap Press of Harvard University Press, 2007), 195.

26. Find a Grave, www.findagrave.com.

27. Find a Grave, www.findagrave.com.

28. Nicolay, *Lincoln's Secretary*, 343.

29. "John Nicolay Dies Intestate," *Washington Post*, October 16, 1901, 10.

30. John G. Nicolay, *A Rich Collection of Books and Pamphlets Mainly of the Civil War Period; Being a Portion of the Private Library of the Late Col. John G. Nicolay (Washington, D.C.) for Sale at Auction . . . January 6, 1905*, George D. Morse, auctioneer (New York: Anderson Auction Company, 1905).

31. *New York Times*, September 14, 1954, 27.

32. Nicolay, *Lincoln's Secretary*, 346.

APPENDIX

1. Clarence King, "The Biographers of Lincoln," *Century Illustrated Monthly Magazine* 32 no. 6 (October 1886): 861–69.

2. In the April 1890 issue, on p. 797, the *Century Magazine* published the following statement regarding this article: "Surgeon C. S. Taft and Alex. Williamson (tutor at the White House) write to say that their names were omitted from the list in the January *Century* of persons present at the deathbed of President Lincoln."

Bibliography

PUBLISHED WRITINGS OF JOHN G. NICOLAY

The following list includes titles for which the Library of Congress recognizes John G. Nicolay as an author or editor. Many of these works have been reprinted a number of times and are still in print today. Only the original printing is listed here; information on other editions used by the authors is cited in the notes. For a bibliographical listing of the *Century Magazine* serialization of *Abraham Lincoln: A History,* see the appendix.

Books

Abraham Lincoln: A History. Coauthored with John Hay. 10 volumes. New York: Century Company, 1890.

Abraham Lincoln: The Observations of John G. Nicolay and John Hay. Edited by Michael Burlingame. Carbondale: Southern Illinois University Press, 2007.

Lincoln, Abraham. *Complete Works: Comprising His Speeches, Letters, State Papers, and Miscellaneous Writing.* Coedited with John Hay. 2 volumes. New York: Century Company, 1894.

Hole-in-the-Day. Roseville, MN: Prairie Echoes, 2005.

Lincoln's Secretary Goes West: Two Reports by John Nicolay on Frontier Indian Troubles, 1862. Edited by Theodore C. Blegen. La Crosse, WI: Sumac Press, 1965.

An Oral History of Abraham Lincoln: John G. Nicolay's Interviews and Essays. Edited by Michael Burlingame. Carbondale: Southern Illinois University Press, 1996.

The Outbreak of Rebellion. New York: Charles Scribner's Sons, 1881.

A Rich Collection of Books and Pamphlets Mainly of the Civil War Period; Being a Portion of the Private Library of the Late Col. John G. Nicolay (Washington, D.C.) for Sale at Auction . . . January 6, 1905. George D. Morse, auctioneer. New York: Anderson Auction Company, 1905.

A Short Life of Abraham Lincoln: Condensed from Nicolay and Hay's Abraham Lincoln: A History. New York: Century Company, 1902.

With Lincoln in the White House: Letters, Memoranda, and Other Writings of John G. Nicolay, 1861–1865. Edited by Michael Burlingame. Carbondale: Southern Illinois University Press, 2000.

Pamphlets

Abraham Lincoln. Boston: Little, Brown, 1882.
Lincoln's Gettysburg Address. New York: Century Company, 1894.

Articles

"Abraham Lincoln." In *Encyclopaedia Britannica,* 14:658–63. Edinburgh, 1875–1889.
"Abraham Lincoln." In *Meeting of May 29, 1900 Commemorative of the Convention of May 29, 1856 That Organized the Republican Party in the State of Illinois.* Vol. 3 of *Transactions of the McLean County Historical Society, Bloomington, Illinois.* Edited by Ezra M. Prince, Secretary of the Historical Society. Bloomington, IL: Pantagraph Printing and Stationery, 1900.
"Hole-in-the-Day." *Harper's New Monthly Magazine* 26, no. 42 (January 1863): 186–91.
"The Hole-in-the-Day Encounter." *Minnesota Archaeologist* 36, no. 2 (July 1977): 76–96.
"Lincoln's Gettysburg Address." *Century Illustrated Monthly Magazine* 47, no. 4 (February 1894): 596–608. Available online at https://archive.org/details/lincolnsgettys buoonico.
"Lincoln's Literary Experiments with Lectures and Verses Hereto Unpublished." *Century Illustrated Monthly Magazine* 47, no. 6 (April 1894): 823–32.
"Lincoln's Personal Appearance." *Century Illustrated Monthly Magazine* 42, no. 6 (October 1891): 932–38.
"Sioux War." *Continental Monthly* 3, no. 2 (February 1863): 194–204.
"Sioux War." *Minnesota Archaeologist* 38, no. 4 (1979): 179–89.
"Thomas Jefferson's Home." *Century Illustrated Monthly Magazine* 34, no. 5 (September 1887): 643–58.

OTHER SOURCES

Archival Sources

Abraham Lincoln Presidential Library, Springfield, IL.
Hay, John M. Papers. Huntington Library, San Marino, CA.
Nicolay Collection. Box 3 of Lincoln Financial Foundation Collection. Allen County Public Library, Fort Wayne, IN.
Nicolay, John G. Papers. Library of Congress, Washington, D.C.
Paris Consular Records. National Archives, College Park, MD.

Articles

Davis, Jane S. "Two Sioux War Orders: A Mystery Unraveled." *Minnesota History* 41, no. 3 (Fall 1968): 117–25.
Dudley, Thomas H. "The Inside Facts of the Lincoln Nomination." *Century Illustrated Monthly Magazine* 40 (July 1890): 477–79.
Fischer, Louis. "Lincoln's 1858 Visit to Pittsfield, Illinois." *Journal of the Illinois State Historical Society* 61, no. 3 (Autumn 1968): 350–64.

Gunderson, Robert G. "Lincoln's Mail." *Indiana Magazine of History* 55, no. 4 (1959): 379–92.

Leonard, Stephen J. "John Nicolay in Colorado." In *Essays and Monographs in Colorado History,* no. 11, 25–54. Denver: Colorado Historical Society, 1990.

"Lincoln's Sioux War Order." *Minnesota History* 33, no. 2 (Summer 1952): 77–99.

Nicolay, Helen. "The Writing of *Abraham Lincoln: A History.*" *Journal of the Illinois State Historical Society* 42, no. 3 (September 1949): 259–71.

"Official Record of the Convention." In *Meeting of May 29, 1900 Commemorative of the Convention of May 29, 1856 That Organized the Republican Party in the State of Illinois.* Vol. 3 of *Transactions of the McLean County Historical Society, Bloomington, Illinois.* Edited by Ezra M. Prince, Secretary of the Historical Society. Bloomington, IL: Pantagraph Printing and Stationery, 1900.

Schneider, George. "Lincoln and the Anti-Know-Nothing Resolutions." In *Meeting of May 29, 1900 Commemorative of the Convention of May 29, 1856 That Organized the Republican Party in the State of Illinois.* Vol. 3 of *Transactions of the McLean County Historical Society, Bloomington, Illinois.* Edited by Ezra M. Prince, Secretary of the Historical Society. Bloomington, IL: Pantagraph Printing and Stationery, 1900.

Schurz, Carl, "Abraham Lincoln." *Atlantic Monthly* 67, no. 304 (June 1891): 721–51.

Selby, Paul. "The Editorial Convention, February 22, 1856." In *Meeting of May 29, 1900 Commemorative of the Convention of May 29, 1856 That Organized the Republican Party in the State of Illinois.* Vol. 3 of *Transactions of the McLean County Historical Society, Bloomington, Illinois.* Edited by Ezra M. Prince, Secretary of the Historical Society. Bloomington, IL: Pantagraph Printing and Stationery, 1900.

———. "Editorial Convention of 1856." *Journal of the Illinois State Historical Society* 5, no. 3 (October 1912): 343–49.

Sellers, John R. "Serving President Lincoln: The Public Career of John G. Nicolay." In *Lincoln Reshapes the Presidency,* edited by Charles M. Hubbard, 52–65. Macon, GA: Mercer University Press, 2003.

Taft, Lorade, Thomas Rees, and Hieryonmus Speak. "Tablet Erected in Court House Park, Pittsfield, Pike County, Illinois, in Commemoration of Lincoln, Douglas, and Nicolay and Hay." *Journal of the Illinois Historical Society* 18, no. 3 (October 1929): 726–42.

Temple, Wayne, "Charles Henry Philbrick: Private Secretary to President Lincoln." *Illinois College Alumni Magazine,* Summer 1997, i–viii.

Zucker, A. E. "Dr .Theodore Canisius, Friend of Lincoln." *American German Review* 16, no. 3 (February 1950): 13–15, 38.

Books

Adams, Charles Francis. *The Address of Charles Francis Adams, of Massachusetts, on the Life, Character, and Services of William H. Seward: Delivered by Invitation of the Legislature of the State of New York, in Albany, April 18, 1873.* New York: D. Appleton, 1873.

Alford, Terry. *Fortune's Fool: The Life of John Wilkes Booth.* New York: Oxford University Press, 2015.

Arndt, Karl J. R., and May E. Olson. *German-American Newspapers and Periodicals, 1732–1955: History and Bibliography.* New York: Johnson Reprint Corporation, 1965.

Baker, Jean H. *Mary Todd Lincoln: A Biography.* New York: W. W. Norton, 1987.

Brooks, Noah. *Lincoln Observed: Civil War Dispatches of Noah Brooks.* Edited by Michael Burlingame. Baltimore: Johns Hopkins University Press, 1998.

Burlingame, Michael. *Abraham Lincoln: A Life.* Baltimore: Johns Hopkins University Press, 2008.

Carden, Allen. *Freedom's Delay: America's Struggle for Emancipation. 1776–1865.* Knoxville: University of Tennessee Press, 2014.

Chadwick, Bruce. *Lincoln for President: An Unlikely Candidate, an Audacious Strategy, and the Victory No One Saw Coming.* Naperville, IL: Sourcebooks, 2009.

Church, Charles A. *The History of the Republican Party in Illinois, 1854–1912, with a Review of the Aggressions of the Slave Power.* Rockford, IL: Wilson Brothers, 1912.

Clinton, Catherine. *Mrs. Lincoln: A Life.* 2009. Reprint, New York: Harper Perennial, 2010.

Coggeshall, William T. *Lincoln Memorial: The Journeys of Abraham Lincoln from Springfield to Washington as President-Elect and from Washington to Springfield, 1865 as President Martyred Comprising an Account Of Pubic Ceremonies on the Entire Route, and Full Details of Both Journeys.* Columbus, OH: Published for the Benefit of the Ohio Soldier's Monument by the Ohio State Journal, 1865. Reprint, BiblioLife, 2010.

Cole, Robert L. *John Hay.* Boston: Twayne, 1978.

Conroy, James B. *Lincoln's White House: The People's House in Wartime.* Lanham, MD: Rowan and Littlefield, 2017.

Craugwell, Thomas. *Stealing Lincoln's Body.* Cambridge, MA: Belknap Press of Harvard University Press, 2007.

Davis, Rodney O., and Douglas L. Wilson, eds. *The Lincoln-Douglas Debates.* Knox College Lincoln Studies Center Edition. Urbana: University of Illinois Press, 2008.

Debow, J. D. B. *Seventh Census of the United States 1850 Embracing a Statistical View of Each of the States and Territories, Arranged by Counties, Towns, etc.* Washington, D.C.: Robert Armstrong, Public Printer, 1853.

Donald, David Herbert. *Lincoln.* 1995. Reprint, New York: Touchstone/Simon & Schuster, 1996.

———. *Lincoln's Herndon: A Biography.* 1948. Reprint, New York: Da Capo Press, 1989.

Epstein, Daniel M. *Lincoln's Men: The President and His Private Secretaries.* Garden City, NY: Doubleday, 1968.

Eskew, Garnett Laidlaw. *Willard's of Washington: The Epic of a Capital Caravansary.* New York: Coward-McCann, 1954.

Etiquette at Washington: Together with the Customs Adopted by Polite Society in the Other Cities of the United States. 7th ed. Baltimore: Murphy & Company, 1860.

Gilder, Richard W. *Letters of Richard Watson Gilder.* Edited by Rosamund Gilder. Boston: Houghton Mifflin, 1916.

———. *The Poems of Richard Watson Gilder.* Illustrated by Helena de Kay Gilder. Boston: Houghton Mifflin, 1908.

Goodman, Susan. *William Dean Howells: A Writer's Life.* Berkeley: University of California, Press, 2005.

Grimshaw, William, A. *History of Pike County: A Centennial Address Delivered by Hon. William A. Grimshaw, at Pittsfield, Pike County, Illinois, July 4, 1876.* Pittsfield, IL: Democrat Job Rooms, 1877.

Guelzo, Allen C. *Lincoln's Emancipation Proclamation: The End of Slavery in America.* New York: Simon and Schuster, 2004.

——. *Lincoln and Douglas: The Debates That Defined America.* New York: Simon & Schuster, 2008.

Haley, William D'Arcy. *Philp's Washington Described: A Complete View of the American Capital, and the District of Columbia; with Many Notices, Historical, Topographical and Scientific, of the Seat of Government.* Washington, D.C. Philp & Solomons [1860?].

Halstead, Murat. *Three Against Lincoln: Murat Halstead Reports the Caucuses of 1860.* Edited, with an introduction, by William B. Hesseltine. Baton Rouge: Louisiana State University Press, 1960.

Hamilton, Charles. *Lincoln in Photographs: An Album of Every Known Pose.* Norman: University of Oklahoma Press, 1963.

Harris, William C. *Lincoln and Congress.* Carbondale: Southern Illinois University Press, 2017.

Hay, John M. *At Lincoln's Side: John Hay's Civil War Correspondence with Selected Writings.* Edited by Michael Burlingame. Carbondale: Southern Illinois University Press, 2000.

——. *Inside Lincoln's White House: The Complete Civil War Diary of John Hay.* Edited by Michael Burlingame, and John R. Ettlinger. Carbondale: Southern Illinois University Press, 1997.

——. *Letters of John Hay and Extracts from the Diary.* New York: Gordian Press, 1969.

Herndon. William, and Jesse W. Weik. *Herndon's Life of Lincoln.* 1889. Reprint, New York: Fawcett World Library, 1961.

Herriott, F. I. *The Premises and Significance of Abraham Lincoln's Letter to Theodore Canisius.* Chicago: n.p,, 1915. Reprinted from *Deutsch-Amerikanische Geshichtsblätter* [*German-American Historical Review*], vol. 15, and available online at Internet Archive, https://archive.org/details/premisessignificooherriott.

Hertz, Emanuel. *Abraham Lincoln: A New Portrait.* Foreword by Nicholas Murray Butler. New York: Horace Liveright, 1931.

History of Greene and Jersey Counties, Illinois, Together with Sketches of the Towns, Villages and Township, Educational, Civil, Military, and Political History. Springfield, IL: Continental Historical Co., 1885.

History of Pike County, Illinois; Together with Sketches of Its Cities, Villages and Townships, Educational, Religious, Civil, Military, and Political History; Portraits of Prominent Persons and Biographies of Representative Citizens. Chicago: Chas. C. Chapman, 1880.

Holzer, Harold. *Lincoln at Cooper Union: The Speech That Made Abraham Lincoln President.* New York: Simon & Schuster, 2004.

———. *Lincoln President-Elect: Abraham Lincoln and the Great Secession Winter, 1860–1861.* New York: Simon & Schuster, 2008.

Howells, William Dean, and John L. Hayes, *Lives and Speeches of Abraham Lincoln and Hannibal Hamlin.* Columbus, OH: Follett, Foster, 1860.

Hubbard, Charles M., ed. *Lincoln Reshapes the Presidency.* Macon, GA: Mercer University Press, 2003.

Hugill, Peter J. *World Trade Since 1431: Geography, Trade, and Capitalism.* Baltimore: Johns Hopkins University Press, 1993.

Jay, John, and E. E. Brier. *The American Thanksgiving Celebration in Paris Thursday Evening, December 7, 1865.* Paris: E. Brière Rue Saint-Honoré, 1865.

John, Arthur. *The Best Years of the Century: Richard Watson Gilder, Scribner's Monthly, and* Century Magazine, *1870–1909.* Urbana: University of Illinois Press, 1981.

Lamon, Ward Hill. *The Life of Abraham Lincoln: From His Birth to His Inauguration as President.* Boston: James R. Good, 1872.

———. *Recollections of Abraham Lincoln.* Edited by Dorothy Lamon Teillard. Introduction to the Bison Books edition by James A. Rawley. Lincoln: University of Nebraska Press, 1994.

Leroy, David H. *Mr. Lincoln's Book: Publishing the Lincoln-Douglas Debates.* New Castle, DE: Oak Knoll Press, 2009.

Lincoln, Abraham. *The Collected Works of Abraham Lincoln.* Edited by Ray P. Basler et al. 11 volumes (including Supplements). New Brunswick, NJ: Rutgers University Press, 1953–1955, 1974, 1990.

Lincoln, Robert T. *A Portrait of Abraham Lincoln in Letters by His Son.* Edited by Paul M. Angle. Chicago: Chicago Historical Society, 1968.

Maguire, Ann Marie, and John Maguire. *Lincoln's Secretary's Secretary: Helen Nicolay, Artist and Author.* Swan Island, ME: Atlantic Road Books, 2017.

Massie, Capt. M. D. *Past and Present of Pike County, Illinois, Together with Biographical Sketches of Many of Its Prominent and Leading Citizens and Illustrious Dead, Illustrated.* Chicago: S. J. Clarke, 1906.

Mearns, David C. *The Lincoln Papers: The Story of the Collection with Selections to July 4, 1861.* Introduction by Carl Sandburg. 2 volumes. Garden City, NY: Doubleday, 1948.

Medved, Michael. *The Shadow Presidents: The Secret History of the Chief Executives and Their Top Aides.* New York: Times Books, 1979.

Neill, Edward D. *Reminiscences of the Last Year of President Lincoln's Life: Read at a Meeting of the Minnesota Commandery of the Military Order of the Loyal Legion, St. Paul, Minn., Nov. 4, 1885.* St. Paul, MN: Pioneer Press, 1885.

Nicolay, Helen. *Lincoln's Secretary: A Biography of John G. Nicolay.* New York: Longmans, Green, 1949.

Niebuhr, Gustav. *Lincoln's Bishop: A President, a Priest, and the Fate of 300 Dakota Sioux Warriors.* New York: HarperOne, 2014.

Orman, Ray P. *The Convention That Nominated Lincoln: An Address Delivered before the Chicago Historical Society on May 18, 1916, the Fifty-Sixth Anniversary of Lincoln's Nomination to the Presidency.* Chicago: University of Chicago Press, 1916.

Peters, Richard, et al., eds. *The Public Statutes at Large of the United States of America from the Organization of the Government in 1789 to March 3, 1845.* Boston: Charles C. Little and James Brown, 1845.

Pinsker, Matthew. *Lincoln's Sanctuary: Abraham Lincoln and the Soldiers' Home.* New York: Oxford University Press, 2003.

Prince, Ezra M., ed. *Meeting of May 29, 1900 Commemorative of the Convention of May 29, 1856 That Organized the Republican Party of Illinois.* Vol. 3 of Transactions of the McLean County Historical Society, Bloomington, Illinois. Bloomington, IL: Pantagraph Printing and Stationery, 1900.

Prucha, Francis P. *Indian Peace Medals in American History.* Madison: State Historical Society of Wisconsin, 1971.

Randall, Ruth Painter. *Colonel Elmer Ellsworth: A Biography of Lincoln's Friend and First Hero of the Civil War.* Boston: Little, Brown, 1960.

Randall, Ruth Painter. *Mary Lincoln: Biography of a Marriage.* Boston: Little, Brown, 1953.

Republican National Convention. *Proceedings of the Republican National Convention Held at Chicago, May 16, 17, and 18, 1860.* Albany, NY: Weed, Parsons, 1860.

Republican Party, Illinois State Central Committee. *Political Record of Stephen A. Douglas on the Slavery Question: A Tract Issued by the Illinois State Central Committee.* N.p., 1860.

Ross, Ishbel. *The President's Wife, Mary Todd Lincoln: A Biography.* New York: Putnam, 1973.

Sandburg, Carl. *Abraham Lincoln: The Prairie Years.* Vol. 2. Sangamon Edition. New York: Charles Scribner's Sons, 1940.

Searcher, Victor. *Lincoln's Journey to Greatness: A Factual Account of the Twelve-Day Inaugural Trip.* Philadelphia: John C. Winston, 1960.

Seward, William Henry. *The Works of William Henry Seward.* Edited by George E. Baker. New York: AMS Press, 1972.

Shaffer, David Henry. *Shaffer's Advertising Directory for 1839–40.* Cincinnati: J. B. & R. P. Donogh, 1839.

Shastid, Thomas Hall. *My Second Life.* Ann Arbor, MI: G. Wahr, 1944.

Simmons, Virginia McConnell. *The Ute Indians of Utah, Colorado, and New Mexico.* Boulder: University Press of Colorado, 2000.

Statutes at Large and Treaties of the United States of America from December 3, 1855 to March 3, 1859 and Proclamations since 1791. Vol. 11. Boston: Little, Brown, 1859.

Stoddard, William O. *Inside the White House during War Times: Memoirs And Reports Of Lincoln's Secretary.* Edited by Michael Burlingame. Lincoln: University of Nebraska Press, 1999.

———. *Lincoln's White House Secretary: The Adventurous Life of William O. Stoddard.* Edited by Harold Holzer. Carbondale: Southern Illinois University Press, 2006.

Swimm, Katherine. "In Lincoln's Shadow: John George Nicolay, Private Secretary." Ph.D. diss., University of Mississippi, 2002.

Taliaferro, John. *All the Great Prizes: The Life of John Hay, from Lincoln to Roosevelt.* New York: Simon & Schuster, 2013.

Thayer, William Roscoe. *The Life and Letters of John Hay.* Boston: Houghton Mifflin, 1929.

Thomas, Benjamin P. *Portrait for Posterity: Lincoln and His Biographers.* New Brunswick, NJ: Rutgers University Press, 1947.

Toomey, Daniel C. *The War Came by Train: The Baltimore & Ohio Railroad in the Civil War.* Baltimore: Baltimore and Ohio Railroad Museum, 2013.

Trefousse, Hans L. *Carl Schurz: A Biography.* Knoxville: University of Tennessee Press, 1982.

Trudeau, Noah Andre. *Gettysburg: A Testing of Courage.* New York: HarperCollins, 2002.

Turner, Justin G., and Linda Levitt Turner. *Mary Todd Lincoln: Her Life and Letters.* With an introduction by Fawn M. Brodie. New York: Harper & Row, 1972.

United States Bureau of Indian Affairs. *Annual Report of the Commissioner for Indian Affairs for the Year 1862.* Washington, D.C.: GPO, 1862.

——. *Annual Report of the Commissioner of Indian Affairs for the Year 1863.* Washington, D.C.: GPO, 1863.

United States Census Office. *1840 Compendium of the Enumeration of the Inhabitants and Statistics of the United States, as Obtained at Department of State, from the Returns of the Sixth Census, by Counties and Principal Towns . . . to Which Is Added an Abstract of Each Preceding Census.* Prepared at the Department of State. Washington, D.C.: T. Allen, 1941.

United States War Department. *War of the Rebellion: A Compilation of the Official Records of the Union and Confederate Armies.* Series 1, volume 13. Washington, D.C.: Government Printing Office, 1885.

Villard, Henry. *Lincoln on the Eve of '61.* Edited by Harold G. and Oswald Garrison Villard. New York: Alfred A. Knopf, 1941.

——. *Memoirs of Henry Villard, Journalist and Financier, in Two Volumes.* Boston: Houghton Mifflin, 1904.

Wagandt, Charles Lewis. *The Mighty Revolution: Negro Emancipation in Maryland, 1862–1864.* Baltimore: Johns Hopkins University Press, 1964.

Welles, Gideon. *The Civil War Diary of Gideon Welles, Lincoln's Secretary of the Navy.* Edited by William E. Gienapp and Erica L. Gienapp. Urbana: University of Illinois Press, 2014.

White, Ronald C. *A. Lincoln: A Biography.* New York: Random House, 2009.

Wilson, Douglas L., and Rodney O. Davis, eds., with the assistance of Terry Wilson. *Herndon's Informants: Letters, Interviews, and Statements about Abraham Lincoln.* Urbana: University of Illinois Press, 1998.

Wittke, Carl. *The German Language Press in America.* Lexington: University of Kentucky Press, 1957.

Zeitz, Joshua. *Lincoln's Boys: John Hay, John Nicolay, and the War for Lincoln's Image.* New York: Viking Press, 2014.

Websites

American Civil War Research Database. http://civilwardata.com/.

Ancestry. https://www.ancestry.com/.

Find a Grave. https://www.findagrave.com/.

Index

Fredericksburg, 139, 144, 149, 151, 295

Free Press. See Pike County Free Press

Frémont, John C., 22, 115, 182, 275, 279, 295

Galloway, Samuel, 37–38

Garbutt, Philimelia, 11, 206–8

Garbutt, Zachariah N., 11–15, 19, 22–23, 30, 90

Gardner, Alexander, 161–62

Garfield, Lucretia, 237–38

German American immigrants: abandon Democratic party, 19, 28–29; compared to the Irish immigrants, 76; Dutch plank, 80–82; George Schneider spokesman for, 20; German language campaign biography of Douglas, 85; German language newspapers, 74; JGN fails to identify with, 82; Lincoln's need to pacify, 85; nativism and, 20; in Republican Convention, 1860, 80–85; political influence of, 76, 86; support for Seward, 37; Two Year Amendment, 76–78; Yagers, 62

Gettysburg, Battle of, 153–55

Gettysburg Address, 163–66

"Gibbs coalition," 217, 331n42

Giddings, Joshua, 80–82, 85

Gilder, Richard Watson: authors poem honoring Nicolay, 303; as *Century Magazine* editor, 232, 241–43; death of, 305; editorial concerns with Lincoln history, 232–33, 248–49, 252; as Lincoln devotee, 232; present at JGN's funeral, 302; presses JGN on *Personal Traits of Abraham Lincoln*, 252; and serialization of Lincoln history, 240, 246–47, 254; trip to New Hampshire, 241–42. See also *Abraham Lincoln—A History*; Century Company and Magazine

Goodrich, Aaron, 81

Grant, Ulysses S.: acceptance speech as Lt. General, 178; anti-Semitic

order issued by, 286; called to the eastern front, 176; commissioned as Lt. General, 177; contrasted with McClellan, 286; in Lincoln history, 284–86; JGN applauds fighting style of, 181; JGN assured by, 220; meets Lincoln, 176; receives votes of Missouri delegation, 1864, 183; siege of Petersburg ends, 197

Greeley, Horace, 84, 97, 145, 210

Grimes, James W., 77, 225–26

guidebooks to Washington, D.C., 94–95

Halleck, Henry, 148, 283, 285

Halstead, Murat, 83

Hamlin, Hannibal, 44, 183, 255–56

Hampton Roads peace conference, 194

Hanks, Dennis, 227

Harlan, James, 220, 223

Harper's Weekly, 132, 136, 260

Hatch, Ozias M.: asks favor of JGN, 138; assumed JGN a citizen, 91; director for *Chicago Republican*, 221; hires Philbrick, 103; as Illinois Secretary of State, 18, 22; informs JGN of appointment as campaign secretary, 43; informs Lincoln about JGN, 38; JGN describes work with, 26; as mentor and sponsor of JGN, 21, 25, 35, 90, 94

Hay, John Milton: access to Congress, 174–75; acquaintance with JGN, 16; anonymity in Lincoln biography, 298; appointed JGN's assistant, 56–57; appointment to Interior Department, 106; approach to Lincoln history, 235, 238, 253; army major, 169; arrival in Pittsfield, 16; assists JGN with expenses of writing history, 235; assignment to Vienna, 210; attends Lincoln burial, 201; attends Thomson Academy, 16; best man for JGN, 206; *The Bread Winners*, 241; cabin in Crystal Springs, Colorado, 302; death of, 303; declines job

Lamon, Ward Hill, 58, 64, 66–67, 70–71, 73, 86
Latham, George C., 58
Lear, Tobias, 72
Lee, Robert E., 127, 136, 153, 177, 197, 251–52, 282, 286–87
Lincoln, Abraham: agrees with Henry Clay on slavery, 32; annual messages, 117, 131, 170, 188; anti-slavery voice of reason, 35; arranges vacations for JGN and Hay, 114; assassination of, 198; avoids abolitionist label, 146; and Black Hawk War, 135, 283; at Bloomington Anti-Nebraska Convention, 29; and bombardment of Fort Sumter, 109; breakup with Mary Todd, 265–66; chooses JGN as private secretary, 86–87, 93; commemorative medal of, 105–6; concerns for defenses of Washington, 108; contracts smallpox, 167; Cooper Union speech in Lincoln history, 268–69; correspondence with Dr. Canisius, 75–80; crisis left by Buchanan, 272; criticism of Simon Cameron, 116–17; and death of Ellsworth, 110; and death of Willie Lincoln, 124; death threats on inaugural trip, 66; debates with Stephen A. Douglas, 33–34; description in Lincoln history, 262–65; disappointment with General Meade, 154–55; final burial, 304; frantic search for inaugural address, 61–62; funeral of, 200–201; and *Illinois Staats-Anzeiger*, 75–76; inaugural addresses of, 21, 61–62, 89, 266; inaugurations, 57, 89, 195; Independence Hall speech, 54; intimacy with secretaries, 112–14, 161–63, 287, 292; JGN as gendarme for, 45, 94–97; and John Wilkes Booth, 163; loses Senate race to Douglas, 35; Lost Speech, 22, 268; marriage of, 292; moves to Springfield, 25; names Simon

Cameron minister to Russia, 117; New Year's receptions, 121, 143–44, 169, 192; nomination strategy of, 36; opposes Frémont, 279; photographed, 40, 162, 264, 335n9; political operative, 269; presidential correspondence, approach to, 98; relations with Congress, 105, 117, 168 , 174, 180–81; relations with his father, 233; relations with Shastid family, 15; relationship with Chief Justice Chase, 149, 166–67, 274, 278; relationship with Grant, 176–79, 181, 286; relationship with JGN, 292; relationship with Seward, 149, 274; reliance on JGN's organizational skills, 97–98; religious views of, 266–67; removes John Evans, 160; removes McClellan, 281; re-nomination of, 182; at Republican conventions, 29, 42–43, 84; secession, opposition to, 49; Senate campaign stop in Pittsfield, 34; sends JGN and Hay on sensitive missions, 99; similarities to JGN, 71; and Sioux uprising, 131, 135; Springfield farewell address, 59–60; trapped in office with Quakers, 136; on Two Year Amendment, 78; viewed as Christ figure, 226; viewed as Moses, 226; views on nativism, 79; writes letter of reference for JGN, 35
Lincoln, Mary Todd: accused of Southern sympathies, 105; bad temper of, 172; carriage accident, 155; church affiliation, 267; early breakup with Lincoln, 265–66; erratic behavior in White House, 291; fires coachman, 175; fires McManus, 173; fond of William Stoddard, 101; as "Her Satanic Majesty," 123; holds large White House reception, 122–23; ignored in Lincoln history, 106; inaugural train, 57; invites secretaries to dinner, 139; moves to Soldier Home, 128; overspending of,

Parsons, Richard C. 224, 251
peace medals, 158
Pennington, Joel, 7, 10, 12–13, 59, 90
Personal Traits of Abraham Lincoln, 248,
  252, 255, 305
Philbrick, Charles, 103–5
Pierce, Franklin, 18, 65, 70, 72, 73, 133
Pierce, John, 160
Pike County, Ill., 9–10, 18, 22, 180, 208–9
Pike County Ballads, 152
Pike County Courthouse monument,
  289–90
Pike County Free Press, 11–14, 18–19, 22,
  33, 38, 268
Pike County Journal, 38
Pinkerton, Allen, 60, 213, 280,
Pittsburgh Evening Chronicle, 225, 245
Pittsfield, Ill.: impact on JGN, 15,17, 22–23,
  30, 290; JGN arrives in, 11–13; JGN
  avoids local elites, 176; JGN first sees
  Lincoln in, 26; JGN wedding in, 208–
  9; Lincoln speech in, 34; monument
  in, 11, 289–90; named for Pittsfield,
  MA, 9; as New England town, 13;
  newspapers of, 14; *Pike County Ballads*
  and, 152; political and judicial center,
  15; population in 1850, 9; Thomson
  Academy, 16, 302
Pope, John, 58
Preliminary Emancipation Proclamation,
  136, 281
"Prince of Rails," 61
Private Secretary to the President, Office
  of, 72–74

Radical Republicans, 176, 182–83, 188, 275,
  278–79
Ramsey, Alexander, 131
Reid, John Meredith, 220
Reno, Aaron, 10, 22, 90
Republican National Convention, 1856, 29
Republican National Convention, 1860,
  42, 76, 80–85, 151

Republican National Convention, 1864,
  180, 182–83, 256
Richmond Enquirer, 34
Ridgely, Nicholas, 35
Roosevelt, Theodore, 302
Rosey, 152
Ross, William, 13–14, 18, 21–22, 135

Sandburg, Carl, 70, 75, 279
Sanford, E. S., 210
Schley, Frederick A., 223–24
Schneider, George, 19–20, 23–25,
Schurz, Carl, 61, 80–82, 85–86, 260–62,
  299
Scott, Frank N., 251, 253–54, 256
Scott, Winfield, 51, 64, 89, 127, 192, 273,
  286
Selby, Paul, 19–20
Seward, Frederick W., 66, 214, 217–18, 220
Seward, William H.: anti-nativist
  position, 79–80; behind-the-scenes
  negotiations with Confederates, 237;
  conflict with Salmon Chase, 139–40;
  distrusted by Mary Lincoln, 106;
  elegized by Charles Francis Adams,
  229–30, 232; German American
  support, 37, 75; at Grant reception,
  177; at Hampton Roads Conference,
  194; irresistible conflict speech, 31;
  in Lincoln history, 273–74; Medill
  calls for resignation, 152; opposed
  at Republican convention, 82–85;
  opposes nativism, 37, 39; perceived
  radicalism, 37; praises Douglas'
  opposition to Lecompton, 34;
  presumptive Republican nominee,
  1860, 37; Thurlow Weed a close
  friend, 56
Shastid, John, 13, 22, 316n2
Shastid, Thomas H., 11, 27, 90, 176, 205,
  208, 298, 316n2
Shastid, Thomas W., 11, 13, 38, 316n2
Sheridan, Philip, 181, 283